THE CIVIL COURT IN ACTION
DAVID BARNARD

THE CIVIL COURT
IN ACTION

by

DAVID BARNARD, B.A.

of Gray's Inn and of the South-Eastern Circuit, Barrister; Lecturer in Civil and Criminal Procedure at the
Council of Legal Education

LONDON
BUTTERWORTHS
1977

ENGLAND   BUTTERWORTH & CO (PUBLISHERS) LTD
             LONDON 88 KINGSWAY WC2B 6AB
AUSTRALIA   BUTTERWORTHS PTY LTD
             SYDNEY 586 PACIFIC HIGHWAY, CHATSWOOD, NSW 2067
             Also at MELBOURNE, BRISBANE, ADELAIDE and PERTH
CANADA   BUTTERWORTH & CO (CANADA) LTD
             TORONTO 2265 MIDLAND AVENUE, SCARBOROUGH M1P
             4S1
NEW ZEALAND BUTTERWORTHS OF NEW ZEALAND LTD
             WELLINGTON 26/28 WARING TAYLOR STREET 1
SOUTH AFRICA BUTTERWORTH & CO (SOUTH AFRICA) (PTY) LTD
             DURBAN 152/154 GALE STREET
USA   BUTTERWORTH (PUBLISHERS) INC
             BOSTON 19 CUMMINGS PARK, WOBURN, MASS 01801

© Butterworth & Co (Publishers) Ltd
1977

ISBN—Casebound 0 406 55620 2
        Limp 0 406 55621 0

Filmset, printed and bound in Great Britain by
Cox & Wyman Ltd, London, Fakenham and Reading

PREFACE

The average student almost invariably finds the study of civil procedure confusing and tedious. This is particularly unfortunate because, when he qualifies, he will find that the every-day problems which take up most of his time are not matters of substantive law but are questions of practice. This book is intended to assist the student barrister, articled clerk and legal executive in understanding civil litigation by showing how the rules are applied in real instances. It is also designed to be used by anybody who is starting out in practice and needs a straightforward explanation of the basic procedure.

Throughout the text, I have followed the method adopted in "The Criminal Court in Action" of using examples which refer to actual localities and courts. All the examples, however, are purely fictional and no reference is intended to any persons living or dead.

I wish to thank the editorial staff of Butterworths for their very great assistance to me in preparing this book. I am most grateful to Mr. R. C. L. Gregory of the Lord Chancellor's Office for permission to reproduce from the County Court Practice the table on pre-trial review which he originally prepared for the Rules Committee. I have received a great deal of help and criticism from members on both sides of the profession in producing the manuscript; in particular, I should like to thank Mr. Harry Herman who read the whole of the introductory part of the book, Mr. Edward Davidson who made valuable suggestions on the section concerning originating summons procedure, Mr. Andrew Pitt who gave me the benefit of his knowledge and experience of enforcing judgments and Mr. Seton Pollock C.B.E. who very kindly advised me on the passages dealing with the Legal Aid Scheme. Needless to say the responsibility for any errors which may remain is entirely mine.

I am very conscious in writing a practical guide to civil litigation of the debt I owe to my pupil-masters, the late Mr. Peter Downe and Mr. Julian Priest (now one of Her Majesty's Counsel), who in a few months taught me more about litigation than I could have learnt from years of studying the White Book.

Finally I would like to express my best thanks to my typist who in more ways than one is responsible for the appearance of this work.

David Barnard

The Temple
July 1977

ACKNOWLEDGMENTS

The Forms on 11–13, 18–23, 55, 60, 93, 117 and 204 are reproduced by kind permission of Oyez Publishing Ltd.

Form IT1, Originating Application to an Industrial Tribunal, and Form IT3, Notice of Appearance by Respondent, are reproduced with the permission of the Controller of Her Majesty's Stationery Office, Crown Copyright Reserved.

The extracts from *Going to Law* are reproduced by kind permission of Justice.

TABLE OF CONTENTS

TABLE OF STATUTES

References in this Table to **"*Statutes*"** are to Halsbury's Statutes of England (Third Edition) showing the volume and page at which the annotated text of the Act will be found. Page references printed in bold type indicate where the Act is set out in part or in full.

LIST OF CASES

PART ONE

OLIVER TWIST *v*. WEST MIDDLESEX SALVAGE CO., LTD.

TWIST *v*. WEST MIDDLESEX SALVAGE CO., LTD.

On 1 April 1975 Oliver Twist (who was just 17) began working at a factory in Southall belonging to the West Middlesex Salvage Company. Oliver had only just left school and this was his very first job. His employers were a company who had a contract with the local council for disposing of bulky salvage. One of the machines Oliver was going to learn to work consisted of a large press. Cardboard boxes, crates, paper, etc. were forced into a special compartment by a hydraulic ram while at the same time a press came down and pressed the salvage into a compact bale. This machine was always operated by a man called Sikes. Oliver used to watch Mr. Sikes working the press and pretty quickly understood how it worked. There was one snag; sometimes odd boxes would spill out of the press compartment. When that happened Sikes would grab the box and pull it away while the ram was working and before the press descended. Of course this should have been done with the machine switched off but since there was always a lot to be done and since Sikes was anxious to earn the biggest bonus possible every week, he used to pull the boxes out quickly before the ram had stopped moving and the press had fully descended. It all looked very easy.

After Oliver had been working at the factory for a couple of weeks, Sikes let Oliver have a go on the press and Oliver showed he knew just how to work it. There was a great deal to be done and it was a help to Mr. Sikes to have a boy available who could take over when he was busy.

One Wednesday when Oliver had been at the factory for about three weeks Sikes left him in charge of the machine whilst he went over to the manager's office. Oliver went on working the press quite happily for about a quarter of an hour until to his annoyance he saw one of the cases was coming out of the compartment. Oliver did not bother to stop the machine—Mr. Sikes never did that. He just went over to the press compartment and started to tug the box. It would not come out and Oliver grasped the top of the box and tried to get it free. Oliver realised the press was coming down but had not appreciated the force of the ram because quite suddenly he realised he could not get his hand free. "Help!" he shouted, "Bill come quickly." Luckily for him Mr. Sikes was just coming out of the manager's office—he ran to the machine and threw the master switch and everything stopped, but by this time Oliver was unconscious because his hand had been crushed by the ram. Sikes put the machine in reverse whilst one of the men telephoned for an ambulance.

Oliver spent a month in hospital. There was very little the doctors could do for his hand. His thumb and a finger were amputated, but they managed to save the remaining three fingers. After he had been in hospital for about a week the shop steward came round to see Oliver. When Oliver started work he had joined the union and had regularly paid his dues. He only had a very hazy idea about the union's activities and one of the things he had not realised was that trade unions keep funds available to assist the members who are injured at work to get compensation. The shop steward explained to Oliver that:

(*a*) Everybody who is injured at work is entitled to benefit under the state-run National Insurance Scheme. The state, the employer and the employee contribute to provide a fund to assist persons injured at work irrespective of questions of fault. Oliver was told to apply at once to the local insurance office for benefit.

(*b*) *In addition* to obtaining compensation through the state scheme, Oliver could sue his employers for damages for the personal injuries he received. Whether Oliver would succeed in such an action would depend on whether his employer was in some way at fault. The shop steward thought the machine should have been guarded so that Oliver could not have put his hand in the way of the moving parts. He strongly advised Oliver to fill in a union claim form which he would forward to the union's solicitors. This form is a questionnaire drawn up by the union to establish sufficient particulars of the accident for their solicitors to decide whether there is a valid claim. In a sense it fulfils the same function as the claim form drivers send in to their insurance company after an accident.

A couple of days later Mr. Nathaniel Wilkins received Oliver's claim form. Mr. Wilkins was employed by a large London firm of solicitors who specialised in trade union work. The very first thing he did was to write to Oliver's employers telling them that he was acting for Oliver and that on the information he had it was clear that his client's injuries had been caused by their negligence or breach of statutory duty under the Factories Act. At the same time he wrote to Oliver asking for:

(*a*) a detailed statement of how the accident occurred;
(*b*) the names and addresses of any witnesses;
(*c*) a plan of the machine;
(*d*) details of Oliver's loss of pay.

He also told Oliver that he would like to arrange for a medical inspection by a specialist on hand injuries when Oliver had been discharged from hospital. In the event Oliver remained in the hospital for a month before he was allowed home. Even then he had to return twice a week for an intensive course of physiotherapy on his hand. In the meantime Mr. Wilkins had received a reply from the insurers who acted for the company denying all liability and saying the accident was entirely Oliver's fault for putting his hand into a moving machine. Mr. Wilkins was not in any sense distressed by this letter; indeed, he would have been very surprised if it had said anything else. He noted that the letter ended: "Without prejudice, we would be grateful for the opportunity of arranging our own medical examination of your client". Mr. Wilkins wrote back agreeing to such an examination on condition that the insurers were responsible for his client's expenses in attending and would provide a copy of their report to Mr. Wilkins. He also asked in this letter for the name and address of the company's solicitors so that he could effect service of a writ upon them. This last remark was not pure belligerence. Although Mr. Wilkins fully expected the action eventually to be settled out of court, he knew that the insurers were more likely to treat Oliver's claim expeditiously if litigation was commenced against the employers. It followed that it was in Oliver's interest for the writ to be issued at the earliest possible moment. As Oliver was under 18, it was technically necessary for the action to be brought in his father's name and so Mr. Wilkins wrote and obtained authority from Mr. Twist to bring the case.

The day after Mr. Wilkins received written authority from Oliver's father he sent his clerk down to the Law Courts to issue a writ. A writ is a formal document issued under the authority of the Lord Chancellor telling a defendant that a claim has been brought against him and that he must "enter an appearance", i.e. place himself on the court record, or judgment will be given against him. Every writ must have written on the back a statement, usually only in general terms, of the nature of the case against the defendant. In the present case it can be seen from the writ contained in counsel's brief (p. 12, *post*) that this "general indorsement" states the nature of the cause of action (i.e. negligence and breach of statutory duty), the date upon which the cause of action arose and the type of relief claimed (i.e. damages). The writ is prepared in the solicitor's office and the clerk takes two copies to the Central Office of the Law Courts. These copies are sealed with the court seal and one of them is stamped to show that a fee has been paid. The copy with the stamp is then retained by the court and the other copy is given back to the solicitors. The writ is then deemed to have been *issued*.

The next step was for Mr. Wilkins to arrange for the writ to be *served*. In theory this could have been done by delivering a copy of the writ at the company's registered office but, since Mr. Wilkins had received a reply from the company's insurers stating the name of the solicitors instructed to accept service, he effected service on those solicitors. This was quite simply done by sending the original writ with the court seal and a photostat copy to the defendants' solicitors who retained the copy and sent the original back indorsed with a note to the effect that they accepted service on behalf of their clients. If you look at the writ (11, *post*) you can see the indorsement in the margin. At the same time the defendants' solicitors completed two "memorandum of appearance" forms (see p. 13) which they sent to the Central Office. The purpose of such an appearance is that the defendant has thereby placed himself on the court record. The court keeps a record of all appearances and sends one of the copies of the forms to the plaintiff's solicitors.

Several months now went by whilst both solicitors collated the evidence and obtained their medical reports. Both sides hoped that the case could be settled out of court. There were really three issues that concerned Mr. Wilkins:

(1) Was there any negligence on the part of the defendant at all? He felt confident there was. Nobody, let alone an inexperienced apprentice, should be allowed to operate a machine with moving parts that are not fenced in.

(2) Was there contributory negligence on the part of Oliver? Where an employee is also to blame for his accident the court has the power to reduce his damages "to such extent as the court thinks just and equitable having regard to the claimant's share in the responsibility for the damage". If Oliver had been an experienced workman, then Mr. Wilkins had little doubt that the judge would have held him substantially to blame for the accident. The position, however, seemed different in the case of a young boy just starting his first job.

(3) Finally Mr. Wilkins was concerned to have an estimate of the damages Oliver would be likely to receive. So far as the actual money lost by Oliver

to the date of trial (called the "special damage") was concerned, this was a simple matter of calculation. The largest item of this special damage would be Oliver's loss of earnings whilst he was recovering. However, much more difficult to determine was the amount the judge would award Oliver as "general damages" for

(a) the pain and suffering attached to the injury;

(b) the irritation and loss of amenity and cosmetic defect in having a maimed hand particularly as Oliver was right handed;

(c) his vulnerability on the labour market as effectively a one-handed man;

(d) future loss of earnings if (as seemed likely) he would not be able to earn as high a salary in future as he would if he had retained the full use of both hands.

Mr. Wilkins knew that an award in the region of £7,000 could be expected for the first three heads of damage. So far as future loss of earnings were concerned this could not even be guessed at until Oliver had made a sufficient recovery to start back to work. In fact, Oliver spent some time at a government rehabilitation centre being trained to work with his left hand. Six months after the accident Oliver started a new job as a messenger boy working on a newspaper in Fleet Street at £20 per week take-home pay. Mr. Wilkins was able to use his contacts with the unions concerned to ascertain that if Oliver had carried on in the engineering firm his wages would have risen from £25 net per week at seventeen to £40 net at twenty-one. In the newspaper job, he would only be earning about £35 at twenty-one. It looked therefore as if there was a continuing loss of earnings in the region of £5 per week.

At this stage Mr. Wilkins decided to send his papers to counsel for an advice both on quantum (i.e. the amount of damages likely to be recovered) and on the question of contributory negligence. Counsel advised that Oliver was likely to receive £11,000 general damages (£7,000 in respect of the injury itself and £4,000 in respect of future loss of earnings) and that the court was unlikely to make any substantial deduction for contributory negligence. Mr. Wilkins then instructed counsel to draft a *statement of claim*.

Before any civil action comes to court, both sides are required to prepare a written statement of the allegation they intend to make. In the present case the statement setting out Oliver's claim would show:

(1) that on the relevant date the accident took place whilst Oliver was working for the defendants:

(2) that it was caused by the negligence of the defendants;

(3) that as a result Oliver sustained injuries and suffered loss and expense (i.e. special damage).

The statement of claim is set out at pp. 14–16 in counsel's brief. When counsel's draft came back, Mr. Wilkins checked one or two details and then had the pleading typed on special paper (known as "judicature") and sent it by post to the defendants' solicitors.

It was then the defendants' turn to file a pleading in reply to the statement of claim. Although they knew that it was likely that the court would hold them to a certain extent to blame for the accident, their pleaded case would be that Oliver was wholly responsible for his own misfortune. Therefore they denied liability and counter-pleaded Oliver's negligence. So far as the injuries and "special damage" were concerned, as a matter of common sense they knew this was likely to be substantially correct but since they wished to put Oliver to strict proof of his claim, they said that "they did not admit" the particulars of injuries and loss. The defence is set out at p. 17 in counsel's brief.

Whilst counsel were drafting the pleadings, negotiations continued between the solicitors. However, it gradually became clear that there was a serious difference of opinion between the two sides as to the extent to which Oliver was the author of his own misfortune. The defendants were prepared to accept that they were 50 per cent to blame. They calculated that on the basis of full liability Oliver would be awarded damages in the region of £9,000 and so were prepared to offer £5,000 as an opening gambit. Mr. Wilkins was not prepared to reduce the claim by more than 10 per cent to cover Oliver's carelessness so that on the basis of the advice he had received from counsel on quantum he was not prepared to accept at this stage less than £9,500. It gradually became more and more likely that the action would be fought and so Mr. Wilkins started making serious preparations for trial.

The first step was for *both* sides to compile and exchange lists of all documents held by them at any time which related to the case. This is the way by which each side in an action can find out in advance what documentary evidence has been in the possession of their opponents. Each side will be entitled to inspect all relevant documents which are not privileged. This process is known as "Discovery and Inspection". It will be appreciated that this is an important step in the preparation of the case for trial. You will see in the defendants' notice (at pp. 18–20 in counsel's brief) that the list of documents is divided into three sections:

(1) documents held by them which they are prepared to reveal;
(2) documents held by the defendants which they refuse to disclose on the ground of privilege (for example, anything prepared with a view to the proceedings such as reports, counsel's advice, etc.);
(3) documents which were formerly in their possession but are no longer with them.

The form concludes with a statement of the date and time when the other party can *inspect* these documents. In practice, the solicitors usually photocopy for each other the documents which are required. In Oliver's case, Mr. Wilkins would have been especially interested in seeing the report of the incident in the company's Accident Book. He might well also have wanted to see any operating instructions provided by the manufacturers of the machine. It will be seen from the defendants' list that no such documents were revealed. In those circumstances Mr. Wilkins wrote to the defendants' solicitors asking whether such instructions did exist and also whether the defendants were prepared to disclose them. In the event they replied sending copies. If they had not been prepared to do this Mr. Wilkins would have applied to the court for an order for *specific discovery*.

After discovery had taken place Mr. Wilkins sent all his papers to counsel to "advise on evidence". This enabled the barrister who was eventually going to conduct the case in court to make a résumé of:

(*a*) the issues;
(*b*) the evidence at present available on each issue; and
(*c*) any extra evidence required.

Thus, for example, on the question of Oliver's own negligence the only evidence Mr. Wilkins had was Oliver's own statement. Counsel asked for statements to be taken from Sikes and other employees as to the system of operating the machine and for a letter to be obtained from the Inspector of Factories who would have investigated the case. Again counsel asked for a plan of the machine to be prepared and for a consulting engineer to be asked to report on the operation of the machine. He requested that the correspondence (except letters marked "without prejudice") should be copied and placed in an agreed bundle for the judge. He also asked the solicitors to endeavour to agree with the other side the items of special damage. This meant in effect agreeing Oliver's average pre-accident earnings, the amount he received from the Department of Social Security, the amount he would have been likely to receive if he had continued with the defendants and the amount he had in fact received from his new employers. If the defendants were not prepared to agree these figures it would be necessary to serve the documents on them with notice under the Civil Evidence Act 1968 that they would be put in at the trial without the makers attending court (see p. 26 *post*).

Once Mr. Wilkins had received counsel's advice, he issued a *summons for directions*. This summons requires the defendant to appear before a senior officer of the court known as a *Queen's Bench Master* who (amongst many other things) is responsible for supervising the proceedings from the issue of a writ until the case is set down for trial and for resolving at any time any procedural disputes between the parties. For example, he would have had to decide whether an order for specific discovery should have been made if the defendants had not produced the operating instructions for the machine. You can see from the standard form of summons for direction (set out at pp. 21–23) the sort of matters dealt with. Basically it is a final chance to decide disputes about procedure and also for seeing the action is ready for trial (e.g. plans have been prepared, reports are agreed, etc.) In this case there was substantial agreement on procedural matters between the parties so that the defendants merely agreed to the plaintiff's proposals and the summons was dealt with by consent. If, however, there had been an objection they would have served a counter-notice setting out the orders they wanted made and would then have attended and argued these points before the master.

At the formal hearing of the summons for directions the master gave directions as to the mode and place of trial (in our case by a judge sitting without a jury in London) and fixed a period of one month within which the plaintiff was to *set the action down for trial*. This was done quite simply by sending to the head clerk at the Crown Office in the Law Courts a request that the action should be entered in the list of cases for trial in the Queen's Bench Division and delivering to him copies of the pleadings. At the same time the parties exchanged their medical reports.

Now at this stage it was fairly obvious to the defendants that the action was not going to be settled. It was also obvious, and they had been so advised by counsel, that Oliver would recover *some* damages from them. In other words he would be able to establish some negligence by them even though his damages might be cut because of his own carelessness. If the defendants did nothing at this stage then, even though Oliver only recovered a fairly small award at the trial, they would still have to pay his costs (which after a two day trial might well amount to over a thousand pounds). In a sense this would not be fair because, as we have seen, the defendants had already made a substantial offer to Oliver. The fair course would be to place this offer formerly on record and say that if Oliver did not get more than the offer he should pay the legal fees incurred by defendants thereafter. This is the system known as *payment into court*. The defendants are entitled to estimate what they consider a claim is worth and deposit this sum with the court together with a notice to the plaintiff's solicitors of this formal offer. Mr. Wilkins was not therefore very surprised when he received a letter from the defendants' solicitors notifying him that they had paid £7,000 into court. This figure is a great deal more than the £5,000 already offered in negotiation. It is in fact mid-way between the figure the defendants expected the plaintiff would get if he succeeded entirely and the figure they thought would be awarded to him if they succeeded in showing that he was equally responsible for the accident. For Oliver the action now became a gamble. He could take the money paid into court *and* recover all his costs to date or he could continue the case. If he won and was awarded more than £7,000 he would also obtain an order for costs. If he got £7,000 or less he would obtain an order for the costs to date of payment-in but he would have to pay not only his own solicitors' costs but the defendants' costs as well from that date to the trial. The result was that he might lose well over a thousand pounds. This was the dilemma that faced Mr. Wilkins as the case waited its turn for trial.

We now set out part of the brief Mr. Wilkins delivered to counsel shortly before the case was due to be heard. Study the documents, especially the pleadings, carefully before reading the transcript which follows. For reasons of space we have omitted some of the documents which would have been included in counsel's brief, in particular the bundle of correspondence. A full list of the documents which would normally be contained in the brief is however set out in counsel's instructions.

<u>In the High Court of Justice</u>   <u>1975-T-No. 3102</u>

<u>Queen's Bench Division</u>

    Between:

Oliver Twist

(an infant, by his father and

next friend, Arthur Albert Twist)   <u>Plaintiff</u>

and

West Middlesex Salvage Company   <u>Defendants</u>

Limited

Brief to Counsel for the Plaintiff

Counsel has herewith:

(1) Writ
(2) Appearance
(3) Statement of Claim
(4) Defence
(5) List of Documents
(6) Summons for Directions and Order thereon
(7) Plaintiff's proof of Evidence
(8) Plan of machine and Consultant Engineer's Report
(9) Statement of H.M. Inspector of Factories
(10) Bundle of correspondence
(11) Notice under Civil Evidence Act
(12) Documents relating to loss of earnings claim
(13) Bundle of agreed medical reports
(14) Notice of Payment into Court
(15) Previous Papers before Counsel and his Advice thereon.

Counsel is instructed on behalf of Oliver Twist (who is now 18 years of age) and who is claiming damages for serious injuries to his right hand sustained in an accident at the defendants' premises in Southall in April 1975. Instructing solicitors have endeavoured to obtain a proof of evidence from Mr. Sikes but have learnt that he is to be called as a witness by the defendants. It had been intended that the Inspector of Factories should be called as a witness but the defendants have agreed that the statement from him (document 9) can be read at the trial. We anticipate that there they will not dispute our contention that the machine was dangerous in that it was inadequately fenced. It appears therefore that the real issue will be whether our client's damages should be reduced because of contributory negligence on his part. Counsel will note that the defendants have paid into court the sum of £7,000. Counsel is accordingly instructed to attend on behalf of the plaintiff and endeavour to secure an award of damages and costs.

In the High Court of Justice

QUEEN'S BENCH DIVISION

1975.— T .—No. 3102

A. 1

Ordinary Writ
(Unliquidated
Demand)

Oyez Publishing
Limited
Oyez House
237 Long Lane
London SE1 4PU
a subsidiary of
The Solicitors' Law
Stationery Society
Limited

F3367 12-9-74 BW17722

Between OLIVER TWIST

(an infant, by his father and next friend,

ARTHUR ALBERT TWIST)

Plaintiff

and

WEST MIDDLESEX SALVAGE COMPANY LIMITED

Defendants

Elizabeth the Second, by the Grace of God, of the United Kingdom of Great Britain and Northern Ireland and of Our other Realms and Territories Queen, Head of the Commonwealth, Defender of the Faith:
To WEST MIDDLESEX SALVAGE COMPANY LIMITED

~~of~~

whose registered office is at 201 Uxbridge Road, Southall
in the area of Greater London
WE COMMAND YOU that within 14 days after the service of this Writ on you, inclusive of the day of service, you do cause an appearance to be entered for you in an action at the suit of
OLIVER TWIST

and take notice that in default of you so doing the Plaintiff may proceed therein, and judgment may be given in your absence.

Witness, Frederick Baron Elwyn-Jones
, Lord High Chancellor of Great Britain, the
26th day of July 1975.

Note.—This Writ may not be served later than 12 calandar months beginning with the above date unless renewed by order of the Court.

DIRECTIONS FOR ENTERING APPEARANCE

The Defendant may enter an appearance in person or by a Solicitor either (1) by handing in the appropriate forms, duly completed, at the Central Office. Royal Courts of Justice, Strand, London, WC2A 2LL or (2) by sending them to that office by post. The appropriate forms may be obtained by sending a postal order for 14p with an addressed envelope, foolscap size, to the Clerk of Accounts. Account Office Royal Courts of Justice, Strand, London, WC2A 2LL.

[over

THE PLAINTIFFS CLAIM is for personal injuries loss and expense arising out of an accident at the Defendants' premises at Southall in the area of Greater London on the 23rd day of April 1975 caused by the Defendants' negligence and breach of statutory duty under the Factories Act 1961.

This Writ was issued by Evans and Bartlam of 5 South Square, Gray's Inn, WC1

Solicitor for the said Plaintiff, whose address is 25 Acacia Gardens, Ealing, London W5

Indorsement as to service.

This Writ was served by me at

on the Defendant
on   , the   day of   19 .
            Indorsed the   day of   19 .

(Signed) ....

(Address) ....

E.21   ORDER 12, RULE 3 (2)

This form should be used only
where the writ was issued in London.
There is a special form for use in
District Registry actions.

MEMORANDUM OF APPEARANCE

To be completed in duplicate and delivered or sent to the Action Department, Central Office,
Royal Courts of Justice, Strand, London WC2A 2LL, or (Family Division proceedings) to the
Principal Registry of the Family Division, Somerset House, Strand, London WC2R 1LP, or
(Admiralty action) to the Admiralty Registry, Royal Courts of Justice, Strand, London WC2A 2LL.

(¹) Copy year, letter and number
from writ.

1975₁– **T** .–No.(¹) 3102

(²) Enter name of Division as
shown in writ.

IN THE HIGH COURT OF JUSTICE

QUEEN'S BENCH   (²) DIVISION

Between   OLIVER TWIST
           (an infant, by his father and next friend,
           ARTHUR ALBERT TWIST)

(³) Copy name(s) of plaintiff(s)
from writ.

(³)Plaintiff(s)

and WEST MIDDLESEX SALVAGE COMPANY LIMITED

(⁴)Defendant(s)

(⁴) Copy name(s) of defendant(s)
from writ.

PLEASE ENTER AN APPEARANCE FOR

(⁵) Give full name of defendant
wishing to appear (see Note 1 on
back).

(⁵) WEST MIDDLESEX SALVAGE COMPANY LIMITED

(⁶) Give name by which defendant
is described in writ if this differs
from defendant's full name, otherwise delete words in square brackets.

[sued as(⁶)

                                                                                    ]

in this Action.

Dated the 1st   day of   August   , 19 75

(⁷) To be signed by the defendant
or solicitor entering the appearance.

Signed(⁷)   Dodson and Fogg

(⁸) A defendant appearing in
person must give his residence and,
if he does reside in England or
Wales, some other place in England
or Wales to which communications
for him should be sent. Where the
defendant appears by solicitor, the
solicitor's place of business in
England of Wales should be given
and, if he is the agent of another
solicitor, the name or firm of
business of the solicitor for whom
he is acting.

Whose address for service is(⁸)

            Freeman's Court, Cornhill, London EC3

[and who is agent for

                                                                                    ]

N.B.–Additional notes for the guidance of defendants seeking to enter an appearance are given on the
back. Please read them carefully. <u>The form may have to be returned if any of the information required</u>
<u>is omitted or given incorrectly.</u> The delay may result in judgment being entered against the defendant.
If judgment is entered, the defendant or his solicitor may have to pay the costs of applying to set it
aside.

In the High Court of Justice
Queen's Bench Division   1975.-T.-No. 3102

(Writ issued the 26th day of July, 1975)

        Between:

                            Oliver Twist
                    (an infant, by his father and next
                        friend, Arthur Albert Twist)

                                                            Plaintiff

                                and

                    West Middlesex Salvage Company
                        Limited

                                                            Defendants

                    _____

                        Statement of Claim

                    _____

1. The Plaintiff was at all material times employed by the Defendants
    as a trainee machine operator at their premises at Southall in the
    area of Greater London being premises to which the provisions of
    the Factories Act 1961 applied.

2. On the 23rd day of April, 1975 the Plaintiff whilst so employed by
    the Defendants was injured at work when his right hand was trapped
    in a hydraulic ram and press.

3. The Plaintiff's said injuries were caused by the Defendants'
    negligence and/or breach of statutory duty under the said Factories
    Act.

<u>Particulars of Negligence</u>
<u>and Breach of Statutory Duty</u>

The Defendants their servants or agents:-

(a) Permitted the Plaintiff to operate the said ram and press when
the moving parts thereof were unfenced.

(b) Failed to give the Plaintiff any or any adequate instruction or
supervision in the operation of the said machine.

(c) Failed to warn the Plaintiff of the danger of placing his hand
into the press compartment when the machine was operating.

(d) Failed to provide any emergency switch or other mechanism by
which the Plaintiff could switch off the machine upon his hand
being caught in the said compartment.

(e) Failed in the matters set out in paragraphs (a) - (d) herein to
provide the Plaintiff with a safe system of work or safe plant.

(f) Failed to fence the said machinery contrary to section 14 of
the Factories Act.

4.   By reason of the matters aforesaid the Plaintiff has sustained
personal injury loss and expense.

<u>Particulars of Injuries</u>

The Plaintiff was aged 17 at the date of the accident.

Traumatic amputation of the thumb and index finger of the right hand.
Fractures of ring and little fingers. The Plaintiff was detained in
hospital for 5 weeks and thereafter received physiotherapy and underwent a course of rehabilitation. He was off work for 6 months.

The Plaintiff was right handed.

He has effectively lost the complete use of the right hand. The stumps
are unsightly and constitute a substantial cosmetic defect.

There is a loss of earnings at the rate of £5 per week which is
continuing.

<u>Particulars of Special</u>
<u>Damage</u>

Loss of net earnings from 23rd April to 25th October, 1975	£650
Less one half National Insurance Benefits received	£130
	£520
Shirt ruined in accident	£ 5
Fares to hospital and physiotherapy centre	£ 25
	£550

And the Plaintiff claims DAMAGES

JONATHAN PHUNKY

Served this 1st day of November 1975 by
Evans and Bartlam of 5 South Square,
Gray's Inn, London WC1. Solicitors for
the Plaintiff.

In the High Court of Justice,   1975.-T.-No. 3102
Queen's Bench Division

    Between:

Oliver Twist

(an infant, by his father and next
friend, Arthur Albert Twist)

                                               Plaintiff

and

West Middlesex Salvage Company
Limited

                                               Defendants

—————————

Defence

—————————

1.   Paragraphs 1 and 2 of the Statement of Claim are admitted.

2.   Paragraph 3 of the Statement of Claim is denied.

3.   It is not admitted that the Plaintiff sustained injury loss or expense
as alleged in paragraph 4 of the Statement of Claim or at all.

4.   If the Plaintiff sustained such injury loss or expense it was wholly
caused by or alternatively contributed to by his own negligence.

**Particulars of Contributory
Negligence**

The Plaintiff:

(a) placed his hand in the said machine when it was unsafe so to do,

(b) failed to stop the said machine before inserting his hand therein,

(c) failed to summon the assistance of a more experienced employee
before attempting to remove the obstruction,

(d) failed to notice and/or heed the lateral motion of the ram
mechanism and withdraw his hand from the said machine.

SEBASTIAN SNUBBINS

Served this 1st day of December 1975
by Dodson and Fogg of Freeman's Court,
Cornhill, London EC3. Solicitors for
the Defendants.

In the High Court of Justice

QUEEN'S BENCH   DIVISION

1975.—T.—No. 3102

B.9

—

List of
Documents
(0.24, r.5)

Oyez Publishing
Limited
Oyez House
237 Long Lane
London SE1 4PU
a subsidiary of
The Solicitors' Law
Stationery Society
Limited

F2917 8-5-74 BW17372

Between .... OLIVER TWIST (an infant, by his father

.... and next friend, ARTHUR ALBERT TWIST)

....

Plaintiff

and

....

WEST MIDDLESEX SALVAGE COMPANY LIMITED
....

....

Defendants

LIST OF DOCUMENTS

The following is a list of the documents relating to the matters in question in this action which are or have been in the possession, custody or power of the above-named (¹) DEFENDANTS

(1) Plaintiff(s) (or Defendant(s)) A.B.

and which is served in compliance with Order 24, rule 2 [or the order herein dated the   day of   , 19].

(2) Plaintiff(s) or Defendant(s).

1. The (²) DEFENDANTS   have in their possession, custody or power the documents relating to the matters in question in this action enumerated in Schedule 1 hereto.

2. The (²) DEFENDANTS   object to produce the documents enumerated in Part 2 of the said Schedule 1 on the ground that (³)

(3) State ground of objection.

the said documents are by their very nature privileged

3. The (²) DEFENDANTS   have had, but have not now, in their possession, custody or power the documents relating to the matters in question in this action enumerated in Schedule 2 hereto.

(4) Plaintiff's or Defendant's.
(5) State when.

4. Of the documents in the said Schedule 2, those numbered **1 and 2**   in that Schedule were last in the (⁴) DEFENDANTS'   possession, custody or power on (⁵) **1st May 1975**

(6) Here state what has become of the said documents and in whose possession they now are.

(⁶) **when they were sent to H.M. Inspector of Factories,**

Ealing District Office. Uxbridge Road, Ealing W5

(2) Plaintiff(s) or Defendant(s).

5. Neither the (^{2}) **Defendants** nor their Solicitors nor any other person on their behalf, have now, or ever had, in their possession, custody or power any document of any description whatever relating to any matter in question in this action, other than the documents enumerated in Schedules 1 and 2 hereto.

SCHEDULE 1.—Part 1.

(Here enumerate in a convenient order the documents (or bundles of documents, if of the same nature, such as invoices) in the possession, custody or power of the party in question which he does not object to produce, with a short description of each document or bundle sufficient to identify it.)

Description of Document	Date
1. Accident Book.	
2. Correspondence between the Defendants and their insurers and solicitors and Plaintiff's solicitors.	1.6.75 to date

SCHEDULE 1.—Part 2.

(Here enumerate as aforesaid the documents in the possession, custody or power of the party in question which he objects to produce.)

Description of Document	Date
Correspondence and communications between the Defendants' Solicitors and the Defendants' Insurance Co. with the Defendants and their agents. Instructions to and Opinion of Counsel; drafts of pleadings and other documents settled by Counsel; statements and proofs of witnesses and other correspondence and documents prepared and obtained for the purpose of this action.	

SCHEDULE 2.

(Here enumerate as aforesaid the documents which have been, but at the date of service of the list are not, in the possession, custody or power of the party in question.)

1. Copy of entry in Accident Book	23.4.75
2. Letter to H.M. Inspector of Factories	29.4.75

Dated the **17th** day of   **December**   , 19**75**.

NOTICE TO INSPECT

Take notice that the documents in the above list, other than those listed in Part 2 of Schedule 1 [and Schedule 2], may be inspected at [the office of the

(7) Plaintiff(s) *or* Defendant(s) *(inser‹ address) or as may be.*

Solicitor of the above-named (⁷) **Defendants**

.

on the   **21st**   day of   **December**   , 1975, between the hours of **10.30 am.** and **4.30 pm.**

(8) Defendant(s) (or Plaintiff(s)) C.D.

To the (⁸)

. **Plaintiff**

.

and his Solicitor .

Served the   **17th**   day of **Dec.** , 1975, by **Dodson and Fogg** of **Freemans Court, London EC3** Solicitor**s** for the **Defendants**

In the High Court of Justice

QUEEN'S BENCH DIVISION

[Group........................] 1975.— T.—No. 3102

S.30

—

Summons for
Directions,
pursuant to
Order 25

Oyez Publishing
Limited
Oyez House
237 Long Lane
London SE1 4PU
a subsidiary of
The Solicitors' Law
Stationery Society
Limited

F3188 8-7-74 BW17558

N.B.—Applicants to
complete the text of
any matter required
and to strike out
the number opposite
any matter not
required but *not to
strike out the text,*
which must be left
for the Master.

Master..................**Cowper**...Master in Chambers.

Between OLIVER TWIST

(a infant, by his father and next friend,
ARTHUR ALBERT TWIST) Plaintiff
and

WEST MIDDLESEX SALVAGE COMPANY LIMITED Defendant

Let all parties concerned attend the Master in Chambers, in Room No. 95 ,
Royal Courts of Justice, Strand, London, on **Thursday** day the
11th day of **March** 19 76 , at 10.30 o'clock in the
fore noon on the hearing of an application for directions in this action, that

1. This action be consolidated with action(s) 19 , , No.
and 19 , , No.

2. The action be referred to an Official Referee [a Master] and that the costs of
this application be costs in the cause.

3. The action be [by consent] transferred to
County Court, and that the costs of this application be in the discretion of the
County Court.

4. Unless the Plaintiff within days gives security for the Defendant's
costs in the sum of £ to the satisfaction of the Master, the
action be transferred to the County Court
with stay meanwhile, and that the costs of this application be in the discretion
of the County Court, [and that if the security be so paid the directions be as
follows:—]

5. The Plaintiff have leave to amend the Writ by
and that
the service of the Writ and the Defendant's appearance stand, and that the costs
incurred and thrown away by the amendment by the Defendant's in any event.

6. The Plaintiff have leave to amend the Statement of Claim as shown in the
document served herewith and to re-serve the amended Statement of Claim in
days, with leave to the Defendant to re-serve an amended
Defence (if so advised) in days thereafter, [and with leave to the
Plaintiff to re-serve an amended Reply (if so advised) in
days thereafter] and that the costs incurred and thrown away by the amendments
be the Defendant's in any event.

7. The Defendant have leave to amend the Defence as shown in [the document
served with] the Defendant's notice under this Summons and to re-serve the
amended Defence in days [with leave to the Plaintiff to
re-serve an amended Reply (if so advised) in days thereafter]
and that the costs of and the costs thrown away as the result of the amendments
be the Plaintiff's in any event.

2

8. The Plaintiff serve on the Defendant within   days the further and better particulars of the Statement of Claim specified in [the document served with] the Defendant's notice under this Summons.

9. The Defendant serve on the Plaintiff within   days the further and better particulars of the Defence specified in the document served herewith.

10. The Plaintiff serve on the Defendant within   days the further and better particulars of the Reply specified in [the document served with] the Defendant's notice under this Summons.

11. The Plaintiff give security for the Defendant's costs to the satisfaction of the Master in the sum of   on the ground

       and that in the meantime all further proceedings be stayed.

12. The Plaintiff within   days serve on the Defendant a list of documents [and file an affidavit verifying such list] [limited to the documents relating to the—
     [special damage claimed]
     [Plaintiff's industrial injury, industrial disablement, or sickness benefit rights]
     [period from   to   ]
     [issues raised in paras.   of the Statement of Claim
         and paras.   of the Defence]
     [issues of   ]]

13. The Defendant within   days serve the Plaintiff with a list of documents [and file an affidavit verifying such list] [limited to documents relating to the—
     [period from   to   ]
     [issues raised in paras.   of the Statement of Claim
         and paras.   of the Defence]
     [issues of   ]]

14. There be inspection of documents within   days of the service of the lists [filing of the affidavits]

15. The Plaintiff have leave to serve on the Defendant the Interrogatories shown in the document served herewith, and that the Defendant answer the Interrogatories on affidavit within   days.

16. The Defendant have leave to serve on the Plaintiff the Interrogatories shown in the document served with the Defendant's notice under this Summons, and that the Plaintiff answer the Interrogatories on affidavit within   days.

17. The Plaintiff [Defendant] [retain and preserve pending the trial of the action] [upon   days notice to give inspection of] [the subject-matter of the action, to the Defendant [Plaintiff] and to his legal advisers [and experts]]

18. The statements in
be admissable in evidence at the trial without calling as a witness the maker of the statements [and, if a copy of that document certified by
     to be a true copy is produced, without production of the original document.]

19. An affidavit of
[in the form of the draft affidavit [served herewith] [with the Defendant's notice under this Summons]] [to be served within   days] be admissable in evidence at the trial.

3

20. Evidence of the following fact(s), namely,

be received at the trial by statement on oath of information and belief [by the production of the following documents or entries in books or copy documents or copy entries in books, namely,

]

21. It be recorded that the parties [[Plaintiff] [Defendant] refuses to] admit for the purposes of this action that[

[the truth of the statements in the document served [herewith] [with the Defendant's notice under this Summons]]

22.   , a witness on behalf of the Plaintiff [Defendant] may, upon   days notice, be examined before one of the Examiners of the Court [a Master] [a Special Examiner to be agreed upon by the parties or appointed by the Master] and that the said witness need not attend at the trial.

23. A medical report be agreed, if possible, and that, if not, the medical evidence be limited to   **two**   witnesses for each party.

24. A report by Engineers [~~Surveyors~~] [~~expert~~   ]
be agreed if possible, and that, if not, the expert evidence be limited to
       two   witnesses for each party.

25. A plan of the *locus in quo* other than a sketch plan be receivable in evidence at the trial.

26. Photographs and a plan of the *locus in quo* be agreed, if possible.

27. By consent, [the right of appeal be excluded] [any appeal be limited to the Court of Appeal] [any appeal be limited to questions of law only].

28.

29. Trial. Place:— **London**   Mode:—   **Judge alone**
Listing Category:—
[Estimated length:— **1 day**   .   To be set down within   28   days
[and to be tried immediately after the action 19   ,   , No.   ].]

30. The costs of this application be costs in the cause.

       Dated the   **8th**   day of   **February**   1976 .

To the Defendant and to **Messrs Dodson and Fogg, Freemans Court, Cornhill, EC3**	This Summons was taken out by . Evans and Bartlam of 5 South Square, Grays Inn, WC1 Agent for of
~~his~~ their Solicitor or Agent	Solicitor for the Plaintiff

PROOF OF EVIDENCE

Oliver Twist, 25 Acacia Gardens, Ealing W5

will say:

I left school at Easter 1975 and started work at West
Middlesex Salvage Co.'s factory at Southall. My foreman was
Mr. Sikes. One of our jobs was to operate the ram press for
compressing salvage into bales. I had watched Mr. Sikes do this
many times and I understood how it worked and was allowed to operate
it myself. On 23 April 1975 I was operating the machine when
some boxes began to spill out of the ram compartment. I tried to pull
them out and that was how my hand was caught in the machine. I had
seen Mr. Sikes do this on many occasions and nobody had told me not
to do it.

I was kept at Ealing General Hospital for one month and lost
my right thumb and index finger. I was off work for 6 months
attending physiotherapy and rehabilitation courses. I now have a
job in Fleet Street as a messenger and have a take-home pay of
£27 net per week.

FACTUAL STATEMENT OF MR. C. J. BARKER
H.M. INSPECTOR OF FACTORIES, HOUNSLOW

On 1 May 1975, I visited the salvage pressing plant of W. Middlesex Salvage
Company at Southall. It had been reported to H.M. District Inspector of
Factories that Mr. Oliver Twist had been injured in an accident on 23 April
whilst operating a ram/press at the above works.

I was shown a ram/press which consisted of (i) a compartment in which
material for compression had been placed (ii) a ram/press mechanism operated
on a hydraulic principle with the hydraulic pump driven by an electric motor.
A control panel consisting of an on/off switch was situated beside the motor
unit some 6' from the nearest point of the press compartment. Marked on the
motor control panel were the following words 'Murdstone Manufacturing Company,
Blackfriars, England. BHP 75; Speed 1440; Volts 400/440; Phase 3; Cycles 50;
Amps 98; Motor no. 17849'.

The press compartment comprised a box of fabricated steel some 3' in height.
On the control side of the machine a wire screen 18" in height enclosed the
area above the compartment. This screen appeared to be a temporary structure
since there were location points for the insertion of a solid guard which
would have extended to a height of 7' from the ground and corresponded to
the guard on the opposite side of the compartment.

I have no first hand knowledge as to how the accident occurred.

                                        C. J. Barker

<u>In the High Court of Justice</u>   <u>1975.-T.-No. 3102</u>

<u>Queen's Bench Division</u>

        Between:

           Oliver Twist

        (an infant, by his father and

        next friend, Arthur Albert Twist)   <u>Plaintiff</u>

            and

    West Middlesex Salvage Company

        Limited   <u>Defendants</u>

———————————————

Take notice that at the trial of this action the Plaintiff
desires to give in evidence the statements made in the following
documents pursuant to the provisions of the Civil Evidence Act 1968:-

    1. Letters dated the 21st day of March 1976 and 1st day of
        April 1976 from the Department of Health and Social
        Security (Ealing Branch Office).

    2. Letters dated the 17th day of March 1976 and 10th day of
        April 1976 from A. R. Lansbury, Research Department,
        Transport and General Workers' Union.

Copies of the said documents are annexed hereto. And further
take notice that the Plaintiff does not propose to call the makers
of the said documents listed under paragraph 1. The makers thereof
cannot reasonably be expected to have any recollection of matters
relevant to the accuracy or otherwise of the statement.

To the Defendants and to their Solicitors
Dated the 3rd day of May 1976.

01—242—1873   **MR LANCELOT SPRATT**   267 Wimpole Street
London W1

REPORT ON

Name.... Oliver Twist

Address.. 25 Acacia Gardens, Ealing W5

Occupation. Messenger .... Age.. 17 .... Date.. 1st June 1976

<u>Previous Trouble</u>: Nil

<u>Present Injury</u>: Mr. Twist states that he was injured on 23rd April 1975 when
his right hand was caught in a hydraulic ram he was in the process of operating.
From the records made available I note that he was taken to Southall General
Hospital where the stumps of his right thumb and index finger were cleansed
and sutured under general anaesthetic. X-rays were taken of the right hand
and revealed displaced fractures of the terminal phalanges of the 3rd and 4th
digits: these were reduced under anaesthetic and splints applied. He was
discharged home on 26th May and thereafter underwent an intensive course of
physiotherapy for 2 months commencing 1st July 1975. He returned to work in
November 1975 as a messenger.

<u>On Examination</u>
The right thumb and index finger have been amputated at the metacarpo-phalangeal
joint. The stumps are well-healed and pain-free.
The fractures of the right ring and little fingers have united well and there
is full range of movement in these fingers although Mr Twist complains that
they become swollen and ache on occasions.

<u>Conclusion</u>
This young man sustained injuries involving the thumb and index finger of his
right hand. In as much as it is generally accepted that one-half of the manual
capacity of the hand is attributable to the thumb, the injuries sustained by
Mr Twist mean that for most practical purposes he should be treated as a
one-handed man.

                                    Lancelot Spratt, F.R.C.S.
                                    Hon. Consultant, St. Swithins'
                                    Hospital, N1

<u>In the High Court of Justice</u>   <u>1975.-T.-No.3102</u>

<u>Queen's Bench Division</u>

        Between:

Oliver Twist
(an infant, by his father and
next friend, Arthur Albert Twist)   <u>Plaintiff</u>

and

West Middlesex Salvage Company
Limited   <u>Defendants</u>

TAKE NOTICE that the Defendants have paid £7000 into court.
The said £7000 is in satisfaction of all the causes of action
in respect of which the Plaintiff claims

Dated the 21st day of May 1976
To the Plaintiff and
to Messrs Evans and Bartlam
5 South Square, Grays Inn, WC1
his Solicitors.

OLIVER TWIST v. WEST MIDDLESEX SALVAGE CO. LIMITED
BEFORE MR. JUSTICE STARELEIGH

Transcript

(The Law Courts, Strand, London. It is just before half past ten o'clock and the parties are waiting in Court for the judge to arrive. Behind counsel sit their respective solicitors and behind them Oliver and the other witnesses. Since these are civil proceedings the witnesses are permitted to remain in court and hear the evidence unless an application is made to the judge to exclude them. As the clock strikes the hour the usher calls for silence and the judge enters, bows to counsel and sits down. The associate, who is wigged and gowned and sits immediately below the judge, then rises and calls the action on.)

Associate: Twist against West Middlesex Salvage Company.

Judge: Yes, Mr. Phunky.

Counsel for the plaintiff: May it please you, my lord, I appear in this matter for the plaintiff and my learned friend Mr. Snubbins appears for the defendant. Milord, this is a claim for damages for personal injuries sustained in an accident at the defendants' factory at Southall in April 1975. The defendants, milord, are concerned in the collection and processing of paper and cardboard as salvage and to that end have a machine which compresses the salvage into bales which can be marketed. Milord there is an agreed plan which perhaps I could put in at this stage.

Judge: Yes, let that be marked exhibit P1.

Counsel: Your lordship will see from the plan that the machine consists of a ram which moves horizontally and compresses material contained in the compartment marked A—does your lordship see that?—whilst at the same time, milord, a press descends from above. Your lordship will also note that the wire screen which encloses the sides of the compression compartment only extends some 18 inches above the edge of the compartment.

Judge: Are there any photographs of this machine?

Counsel: Milord, no; I regret not.

Judge: Well, why on earth not? I would have thought it was quite obvious if I am expected to try this action I would need a set of photographs of the machine in question.

Counsel: Milord it was thought that the plan would be adequate.

Judge: I find that quite amazing. Well, we are certainly not going to waste any time by adjourning this matter. If the parties don't choose to prepare the case properly they must take the consequences.

(Counsel confer.)

Counsel: Milord, those instructing me will endeavour to obtain a set of photographs this afternoon but I understand from my learned friend that the machine has been considerably modified since the accident.

Judge: I have no doubt it has. What I am complaining about is the failure of your solicitors to take the elementary step of photographing the machine before it was modified. We had better get on as best we can.

Counsel: Well, Milord, the plaintiff began work with the defendants at the beginning of April 1975, he had just left school . . . *(counsel then proceeded to outline the facts of the case to the judge).* Milord, may I now ask your lordship to look at the pleadings?

Judge: I have had an opportunity of glancing through the pleadings before we started.

Counsel: I'm very much obliged: then your lordship will have seen that the basis of the plaintiff's case is set out in the allegations in paragraph 3 of the statement of claim—in effect that this young man should have been given proper instructions as to the operation of the machine and that the machine itself was dangerous in that the emergency switch was not readily accessible.

Judge: And of course the defendants say that the plaintiff was the author of his own misfortune in putting his hand into the compartment.

Counsel: Milord, yes, but we say that the important factor in this case is that this was not an experienced operator but in effect a lad who had just left school and had no experience whatsoever in handling dangerous machinery.

Judge: How old is your client now?

Counsel: Milord, I'll take instructions *(he confers with Oliver).* Milord, I am instructed he is now 18 years of age.

Judge: Has notice been filed that he is adopting this action? The papers before me show him to be suing as an infant by his next friend.

Counsel: (counsel again confers with his solicitors) Milord, it appears that those instructing me have overlooked this point.

Judge: The practice is quite clear. It's here in the White Book, paragraph 80/2/6. Your solicitors had better undertake to file a notice forthwith.

Counsel: Milord, yes, I'm very much obliged.

Judge: This isn't just pedantry you know—it could have an effect on any order as to who pays the costs.

Counsel: Milord, yes.

Judge: Very well. Now I've read the particulars of injuries in the statement of claim. Is there an agreed medical report?

Counsel: Milord, there is a bundle containing the reports on both sides and these are agreed.

Judge: If there is agreement on the medical evidence, wouldn't it have been more sensible to put one report before me? I suppose I am now going to have to wade through pages of repetition.

Counsel: Milord, there is no discrepancy between the doctors' findings or conclusions.

Judge: Well, then I wholly fail to see why I have to read through *two* reports. What is the position with regard to the special damage?

Counsel: Milord, I am afraid that is not as yet agreed.

Judge: Not *as yet* agreed? When is it going to be agreed? What is the point Mr. Snubbins?

Counsel for the defendants: Well, milord, there is some area of difference concerning the calculation of the plaintiff's loss of earnings.

Judge: You know it's going to be very regrettable if we have to spend hours on this sort of detail at goodness knows what cost to the parties. I expect you gentlemen over the short adjournment to put your heads together and see if something can be agreed. Yes, very well then, Mr. Phunky, I take it that concludes your opening? You had better call the plaintiff.

(Oliver now goes into the witness box and is sworn and gives his account of the matter which is taken down by the judge in his note. We rejoin the hearing at the crucial point, where Oliver deals with the suggestion of contributory negligence.)

Counsel for the plaintiff: Had you ever seen Mr. Sikes put his hand in the compartment?

Oliver: Yes.

Counsel: How often?

Oliver: Not often.

Counsel: How many times do you think?

Oliver: Two or three times I should think.

(This of course contradicts Oliver's proof of evidence where he says that Sikes had put his hand in the compartment "on many occasions"; counsel, however, is not permitted to refer his own witness to any earlier statement inconsistent with the evidence now given nor, as we shall see, to cross-examine his own witness.)

Counsel: Only two or three times!

Oliver: Yes.

Counsel: That is all you remember?

Counsel for the defendants: Milord, my learned friend has already received his answer to that question.

Judge: Yes, I think you had better move on to something else, Mr. Phunky.

You wouldn't want to embarrass Mr. Twist by cross-examining him, would you?

Counsel for the plaintiff: If your lordship pleases. (*To Oliver*) Do you remember the last time you had seen him trying to pull salvage out of the compartment.

Oliver: Yes. He had to do it on the morning of the accident . . .

Counsel: Had he ever told you not to put your hand into the machine?

Oliver: No.

Counsel: And of course there were no notices in the factory warning you?

Counsel for the defendants: Milord, that is a grossly leading question.

Judge: Well, it is leading, but are you suggesting that there were notices?

Counsel for the defendants: No, we don't suggest that.

Judge: Then I cannot see there is anything improper in the question. There is no reason why counsel shouldn't ask leading questions on matters not in dispute . . .

(Oliver then goes on to deal with his efforts to get a job and the extent of his present disability. After his examination-in-chief by his own counsel is concluded, counsel for the defendants is entitled to cross-examine.)

Counsel for the defendants: Did you do metal work at school?

Oliver: Yes.

Counsel: I think you were quite proficient at it.

Oliver: Yes.

Counsel: Did that involve operating lathes.

Oliver: Yes.

Counsel: Other machinery?

Oliver: Yes.

Counsel: And you were always aware of the need to take care with moving machinery?

Oliver: Of course.

Counsel: This machine you operated at the factory, it's quite simple, isn't it?

Oliver: Yes, it's easy.

Counsel: It's simply two presses: one coming from above and one from the side.

Oliver: Yes.

Counsel: And it is obviously dangerous to put your hand into the pressing compartment.

Oliver: Yes, it is.

Counsel: You don't need to be a mechanic to see that, do you?

Oliver: I suppose not.

Counsel: If you'd thought for a moment, you'd have realised the stupidity of what you were doing?

Oliver: I suppose so, but Mr. Sikes did it.

Counsel: You didn't need Mr. Sikes to tell you it was dangerous?

Oliver: No . . .

(After Oliver's cross-examination is concluded, his own counsel is entitled to re-examine on any points that had arisen during the cross-examination.)

Counsel for the plaintiff: Who showed you how to operate the machine?

Oliver: Mr. Sikes.

Counsel: Did he ever tell you about safety precautions?

Oliver: No.

Counsel: Did he ever tell you not to pull boxes out of the way like he did?

Oliver: No.

Counsel: Milord, that's all the questions I have.

Judge: Very well, thank you Mr. Twist.

(The witness withdraws.)

Counsel: Milord I wonder if your Lordship would be kind enough to look at the statement from H.M. Inspector of Factories—at page 5 in your Lordship's Bundle—and milord it's an agreed document.

Judge: Just give me a moment *(he reads the statement)*. It seems fairly clear from this that there was a breach of duty in not fencing the machine. What do you say about this Mr. Snubbins?

Counsel for the defendants: Milord I have obviously considered this very carefully with those instructing me—we do not propose to dispute the contention that the machine was not adequately guarded.

Judge: Then the real issue will be as to contributory negligence.

Counsel: Milord, yes.

Judge: Very well.

Counsel for the plaintiff: Milord, I would now put before your lordship two letters, and milord notice has been given under the Civil Evidence Act. Your lordship sees the first letter is from the Transport and General Workers Union and sets out details of the present average earnings of machine operators according to their age and position. The second letter milord is from the same union and gives details, milord, of earnings which the plaintiff could expect in the sort of unskilled work it appears he will now be following.

Judge: Yes, it seems that at the moment he has continuing loss of earnings of about £5 per week.

Counsel: Milord, yes. Milord, that then is the case for the plaintiff.

(Counsel for the defendant then calls his evidence. The factory manager deposes that there had never been any previous incident at the machine and he had never noticed anybody putting their hand into the press compartment. Sikes then gives evidence . . .)

Counsel for the defendants: Have you ever put your hand in the press compartment while the machine was operating?

Sikes: I have pulled boxes and bits of cardboard clear when they have spilt over the top of the compartment.

Counsel: Did that involve putting your hand into the compartment?

Sikes: Once or twice I've had to pull something clear which has been stuck.

Counsel: Have you ever done that in front of the plaintiff?

Sikes: I can remember doing so that morning, but I warned young Oliver not to try it himself.

(This answer catches counsel for the defendants by surprise since there was no suggestion in Sikes's proof of evidence that he had given any warning to Oliver. It also surprises counsel for the plaintiffs.)

Judge: Are you saying you had told this boy not to do it?

Sikes: I said to him "we shouldn't really do this".

Counsel for the plaintiff: Milord, I must protest. This is a very serious allegation and it's nowhere suggested in the defence that the plaintiff had been warned.

Judge: Let me just see the defence . . . yes, that's quite correct. Mr. Snubbins, why isn't this matter pleaded?

Counsel for the defendants: Milord, it takes me as much by surprise as it does my learned friend.

Judge: Well, assuming Mr. Sikes hasn't made this up, it suggests that those instructing you have been very seriously at fault. It was quite clear at an early stage what the issues were in this case and it should have been obvious what questions ought to have been asked of the witnesses. Where does this leave us now?

Counsel for the defendants: Milord, I think I must formally ask for leave to amend the defence to raise the allegation that the plaintiff disregarded a warning from his foreman.

Judge: What do you say, Mr. Phunky?

Counsel for the plaintiff: Milord, I take the strongest possible objection to the course proposed by my learned friend. In my submission, it's far too late in the day now for the defendants to amend to plead, in effect, a totally different case, a case which of course hasn't been put to my client in cross-examination.

Judge: Well, I have a great deal of sympathy with what you say Mr. Phunky; as I've already indicated, it is disgraceful that the plaintiff should be confronted with such an allegation at the trial in this way. It makes a mockery of the whole concept of pleadings. However, it seems to me I cannot now prevent the defendants raising this point, but I shall certainly grant you an adjournment and the costs thrown away if you desire it. Perhaps it would be convenient if I rose for a few moments so that you can take instructions.

(The learned judge rises. Counsel for the plaintiffs has now to decide whether to continue with the case that day or have the matter adjourned to see if he can produce any evidence concerning the alleged conversation. Having discussed the matter with Oliver who cannot remember anything at all except that there had been an incident earlier that morning when Sikes pulled out some boxes which were coming out of the press, counsel decides not to ask for an adjournment. Sikes's evidence is then continued and finally Oliver is recalled to say he has no recollection of any warning being given by Sikes. Counsel for the defendants then addresses the judge on the question of contributory negligence and also upon Oliver's potential loss of future earnings. After he has finished his address, counsel for the plaintiff rises to address the judge . . .)

Judge: I needn't trouble you on the question of liability and contributory negligence, Mr. Phunky.

Counsel: I'm very much obliged, milord.

Judge: Are there any particular matters you wish to refer to on the issue of quantum?

(This exchange which might have appeared confusing to a spectator tells counsel that the judge has decided to find for Oliver on the issue of liability without any deduction for contributory negligence. Where a judge decides that the plaintiff should succeed there is no point in his counsel addressing the judge further; where, however, counsel for the plaintiff is called on, it does not necessarily mean that he has lost the case for it may be that the judge is still uncertain.)

Judge: In this case, the plaintiff, Oliver Twist, who was an infant when these proceedings were commenced but has since attained his majority and adopted this action, sues his former employer for damages for personal injuries sustained whilst he was operating a mechanical press at their premises in Southall. *(The learned judge goes on to recite the facts of the case.)* The plaintiff contends and (this is not now disputed) that the defendants were in breach of their duty at common law and by statute in permitting him to work at machinery which was not securely fenced. I find the absence of fencing clear evidence of such breach of duty. If it was necessary to consider further I would also hold that the relative inaccessibility of the emergency switch rendered it dangerous to permit the machine to be operated by one man. The real issue in this case, however, has been as to the extent which, if at all, the plaintiff's damages fall to be reduced by reason of his own negligence. The defendants' case as pleaded and put to him in cross-examination was that he should himself have realised the danger inherent in what he was doing and was therefore the author of his own misfortune. I reject that contention. The plaintiff had left school but three weeks at the date of the accident; he had seen his foreman removing boxes in exactly the manner which led to the accident; he had received no formal instruction concerning the safe operation of the machine. I am not prepared in the circumstances to make any finding of contributory negligence. At a late stage in the proceedings counsel for the defendants applied for leave to amend the defence so as to include an allegation that the plaintiff had disregarded a warning given to him that morning by his foreman. This amendment was necessary because the foreman, one Sikes, had raised the matter in his evidence-in-chief although, apparently, he had never disclosed it to the defendants' solicitors. I permitted the amendment to be made. The plaintiff was in due course recalled and gave evidence that he had no recollection of such a warning. I was impressed by the plaintiff as a witness—I found him truthful and accurate and where his evidence conflicts with that of Mr. Sikes, I prefer his account. Therefore I reject Mr. Sikes' evidence on this point. He may now believe that he gave such a warning but, if it had been given in the explicit terms suggested, he would have been bound to have mentioned the matter to his employers after the incident. *(The learned judge then dealt with the medical evidence and the*

question of loss of future earnings.) I have decided that the appropriate sum for general damages in the circumstance is £10,000. In addition there is the figure of £700 which has been agreed as the special damage to include loss of earnings to date and interest.
Counsel for the plaintiff: Milord, I ask for judgment for £10,700 and costs.
Judge: So be it. Is there any payment into court?

(The Associate hands the judge a copy of the notice of payment in.)

Judge: I will order that the sum of £7,000 paid into court by the defendants be paid out to the plaintiff's solicitors in part satisfaction.
Counsel for the plaintiff: I am very much obliged.

PART TWO
THE RULES OF CIVIL PROCEDURE

CHAPTER ONE

STARTING PROCEEDINGS

WHICH COURT?

Civil proceedings in England and Wales are brought either in the High Court or in the county court. High Court cases are begun by the issue of process out of the Central Office at the Royal Courts of Justice in London or out of one of the district registries in the provinces. County courts exist in almost every major town and are the appropriate tribunal for most small or medium-sized claims. We set out below a summary of the county court jurisdiction.

Type of Action	Limit	Statute
debts, contract, tort rent	sum claimed not over £2,000	County Courts Act 1959, s. 39
recovery of chattels	value not over £2,000	Ibid.
hire purchase cases	no limit if Acts apply	Hire-Purchase Act 1965, ss. 35 and 49 (1) Consumer Credit Act 1974, s. 141
possession of land	rateable value not over £1,000	County Courts Act 1959, s. 48
possession of protected dwelling house	no limit	Rent Act 1977, s. 141
applications for new tenancy of business premises	rateable value not over £5,000	Landlord and Tenant Act 1954, s. 63
claim for possession by mortgagees	rateable value not over £1,000	County Courts Act 1959, s. 48
equity proceedings	value of fund or property in question does not exceed £15,000	County Courts Act 1959, s. 52

It should be noted that (a) a defendant may bring a counter-claim for any relief notwithstanding it falls outside the county court limit but the plaintiff has the right in such a case to apply to a High Court judge for an order transferring the action to the High Court,[1] (b) where an action is begun in a county court which involves considering the title to land which has a rateable

---

[1] County Courts Act 1959, s. 65.

value over £1,000 (e.g. an action for damages for trespass) the defendant may apply to the High Court for transfer. It should also be noted that the county court has no jurisdiction to grant an injunction (or make a declaration) if that is the *only* relief sought; it can, however, grant such relief as ancillary to a remedy within its jurisdiction.[1]

The sensible plaintiff will normally wish to bring his claim in the county court because he will thereby achieve a relatively speedy trial and the costs he will have to pay to his solicitor will be comparatively low. There is also, however, a substantial sanction against bringing proceedings in the High Court when the county court is the appropriate forum, in that the successful plaintiff may only recover costs on the county court scale.

> *Example*—Alan sues in the High Court for £900 being the cost of repairs of his motor car damaged in a road accident. He succeeds but only obtains county court costs. These tax out at £150. His solicitors' bill is £400. If the case had been brought in the county court, his solicitors' bill would only have been £200. The result is he loses £200 because he brought his case in the wrong court.

The relevant provisions are set out in section 47 of the County Courts Act 1959 which in effect provides that in any action brought in the High Court in *contract* or *tort* where the damages recovered are less than:

£350 — the plaintiff is to receive *no costs*
£1,200—the plaintiff is only to receive costs on the appropriate *county court scale.*[2]

It should be noted that in personal injury cases any deduction for contributory negligence is ignored for the purposes of section 47. In other words the relevant figure is the sum the plaintiff would have received but for the deduction. It should also be noted that the court may award High Court costs if there was reasonable ground for supposing the amount recoverable would be in excess of the county court limit (i.e. over £2,000) or if there was some other good reason for bringing the case in the High Court (e.g. an important test case although involving a small sum).

> *Example*—Benjamin sues for personal injuries consisting of a broken arm. He is found to have been 50 per cent to blame for the accident. The judge awards him £500. The award before deduction would have been £1,000 and so below the limit set by section 47. In order to obtain High Court costs he would have to satisfy the court by reference to awards for similar injuries or special factors in his case that there were reasonable grounds for expecting an award in excess of £2,000.

We will see later that sometimes actions are commenced in the High Court where the claim is far below the county court limit because the plaintiff wishes to obtain summary judgment on the basis there can be no defence to his claim. If he does not obtain such an order the action will be transferred for trial at a county court.

QUEEN'S BENCH OR CHANCERY DIVISION?

If the case is to be brought in the High Court the plaintiff must decide which is the appropriate division. Actions comprised in the list set out below must be brought in the Chancery Division:

---

[1] Ibid., s. 75.
[2] If the action is for conversion or detinue one adds the value of the chattel concerned and any damages in calculating the amount awarded for the purpose of s. 47.

(i) actions for the administration of the *estate of a deceased person*, claims by dependants against the estate under the Inheritance (Provision for Family and Dependants) Act 1975, and contested probate actions;
(ii) actions concerned with the administration or construction of a *trust*.
(iii) *land*—claims for specific performance of contracts for sale of land and agreements for leases and for rectifying or cancelling deeds;
(iv) *foreclosure actions* and claims for orders for sale where land is subject to a charge;
(v) *bankruptcy, winding up companies, dissolving partnerships*;
(vi) *revenue matters*—income tax and estate duty disputes;
(vii) *patent actions* and claims for infringing registered designs.

WHICH COUNTY COURT?

If the case is to be brought in the county court the plaintiff must decide which is the appropriate court in which to bring the action. The basic rules[1] are that an action may be commenced:

(i) in the court for the district in which the *defendant* or one of the defendants *resides* or *carries on business*;
(ii) in the court for the district in which the *cause of action wholly or in part arose*.

This second limb can materially assist the plaintiff:

Example 1—Clive's car is damaged in a road accident in Brentford by a lorry owned by D. E. Contractors of Newcastle. Clive lives in West London near Brentford. He can bring his action at the Brentford County Court.
Example 2—Eric, who lives at Brentford, orders certain gramophone records by post from a firm in Manchester. They are delivered in a damaged condition. Eric can bring his action in the Brentford County Court.

THE PARTIES

(a) Joinder of parties

The basic rule is that two or more persons must sue or be sued in one action where they are jointly entitled to the relief claimed or jointly liable under any contract on which the plaintiff sues. In addition two or more persons may sue or be sued on one action where:

(i) if separate actions were brought, a *common question of law* or *fact* would arise in all the actions, *and*
(ii) the claims arise out of the *same transaction or series of transactions*.

The above is a paraphrase of R.S.C. Order 15, rule 4(1) and C.C.R. Order 5, rules 1 and 2 which are for practical purposes identical.

Example 1—Albert and Mary rent a flat from Bernard. There is no written lease. They fall into arrears of rent and fail to keep the interior of the premises in proper repair. One action for forfeiture will be brought against them both as they are jointly liable under the terms of the lease.
Example 2—Eric is driving a lorry owned by his employer David when he knocks down a pedestrian, Peter. Peter can sue David alone and will normally do so since the employer will be vicariously liable for his servants' negligence. He can also sue Eric alone or he may sue both David and Eric in one action. This would be appropriate where a question arose whether Eric was acting within the course of his employment at the relevant time.

---

[1] C.C.R. Ord. 2, r. 1. Note throughout the text C.C.R. refers to the County Court Rules 1936; R.S.C. refers to the Rules of the Supreme Court 1965.

Where two or more persons *sue* as co-plaintiffs they must employ the same solicitor and counsel, the theory being that as there should be no conflict of interest between them, the employment of separate counsel and solicitors would duplicate work and increase costs.

> *Example*—The Daily Telegraph published an article to the effect that the police were investigating the affairs of a certain company. The chairman of the company and the company itself brought actions alleging libel. These actions were consolidated, i.e. treated as one case. The company went into liquidation but the liquidator carried on the action. Differences arose between the liquidator and the company chairman who then obtained separate representation. The Court of Appeal held this was improper. *Per* Russell, L.J.: "Prima facie, co-plaintiffs, whether in one original action or in an action consisting of consolidated actions must be jointly represented by solicitor and counsel. In a proper case, an order may be made authorising severance in part of representation but this must be, I think, rare and should only be done to avoid injustice" *(Lewis* v. *Daily Telegraph*, [1964], 2 Q.B. 601 at p. 623).

An example of a case where separate representation was permitted on the ground of substantial conflict of interest between co-plaintiffs is *The Bosworth*, [1960] 1 All E.R. 146; [1961], 1 W.L.R. 312:

> *Example*—At Christmas 1957 *The Bosworth* was carrying a cargo of coal from Scotland to Norway when she developed a list in a heavy gale. A trawler called the *Wolverhampton Wanderers* stood by in answer to a distress call and eventually took off the crew. Another trawler, *The Faraday* put four men on to *The Bosworth* and towed her into Aberdeen. Both trawlers sued the owners of the collier for salvage but since there was a substantial dispute between them as to the proper apportionment of the sum recovered, they were allowed separate representation.

(b) Consolidation

What happens if parties who could sue as co-plaintiffs instead bring separate actions? Generally speaking, the defendant will wish to have the matters which each action has in common with the other tried at one time to save costs. There are a number of possibilities open to the court in such cases:

(i) to order that one action be tried as a test case (usually with the defendant undertaking to be bound by the decision in the subsequent actions);[1]

(ii) to order that the actions come on one after the other so that the judge hears the evidence in all the cases before giving judgment:

(iii) to order that the actions be consolidated, i.e. treated as one action;[2]

(iv) to order that the actions be consolidated so far as the common issues are concerned but thereafter tried separately.

An example which illustrates this problem is *Healey* v. *Waddington & Sons*, 1954] 1 All E.R. 861, n.; [1954] 1 W.L.R. 688.

> *Example*—Six miners were killed and two seriously injured in a colliery accident. The injured men and the dependants of the deceased brought separate actions in negligence against the mine owners. The judge ordered that one action should be tried first as a test case on the issue of liability. This is the usual order in a case where the issue of liability is common, e.g. railway or aircraft accidents. However, the defendants felt that somewhat different questions on liability arose in respect of the different claims and so would not have been satisfied with the result of the test case.

---

[1] C.C.R. Ord. 17, r. 2.
[2] R.S.C. Ord. 4, r. 10; C.C.R. Ord. 17, r. 1.

Nevertheless it was obvious that six separate cases would cause great expense: the Court of Appeal therefore ordered that there should be consolidation of the actions on the question of liability, i.e. so that the slightly different issues in respect of each action could be heard together and determined at one time, but that there should then be separate trials with separate representation on the issues of quantum.

(c) Representative Actions

There will be some cases where so many people have an interest in proceedings that it would be impracticable for them all to be joined as co-plaintiffs or co-defendants. To cover this eventuality R.S.C. Order 15, rule 12[1] provides that:

> Where numerous persons have the same interest in proceedings[2] ... the proceedings may be begun and, unless the Court otherwise orders, continued, by or against any one or more of them as representing all or as representing all except one or more of them.

The essence of such a case is that all the persons represented have a common interest which is threatened and that the relief claimed benefits them all.

Example 1—A cleaner employed by the City Livery Club fell at work and sued the secretary and chairman of the club "on their own behalf and on behalf of all other members of the club". The court ordered that the persons sued should represent all the members of the club as at the date of the accident *(Campbell* v. *Thompson,* [1953] 1 Q.B. 445; [1953] 1 All E.R. 831).

Example 2—The Duke of Bedford was granted a charter by statute to run a market at Covent Garden. The market gardeners of Middlesex obtained preferential rights for themselves under the statute as "growers" to sell their produce at lower tolls than the middlemen or merchants. The Duke was alleged to have levied excessive tolls. In a representative action by four growers for a declaration and an account, the Duke took the point that the four could not represent anyone but themselves since the growers had no *proprietary* rights in common. This argument was rejected by the House of Lords. *Per* Lord McNaughton: "Given a common interest and a common grievance, a representative suit is in order if the relief sought is in its nature beneficial to all whom the plaintiffs propose to represent" *(Duke of Bedford* v. *Ellis,* [1901] A.C. 1).

It should be noted that the conditions stated by Lord McNaughton must all apply before a representative action can be brought.

Example 1—A ship carrying various cargoes from New York to Japan was sunk by a Russian cruiser during the Russo–Japanese war because some of the cargo was contraband. An action was brought against the shipowners for breach of contract in permitting contraband on board. The case was brought by a number of cargo-owners "on behalf of themselves and other owners of cargo lately laden on board the steamship *Knight Commander*". The shipowners objected on the basis that the cargo-owners did not have common rights; thus though some were ignorant of the contraband, others knew it was on board and all had separate contracts with the shipowners. The objection was sustained. The cargo-owners could have joined together as co-plaintiffs but a representative action was not in order because the rights of the parties were not identical. *Semble* where the claims by the cargo-owners and any defence of the shipowners are identical a representative action would be appropriate *(Markt & Co.* v. *Knight Steamship Co.,* [1910] 2 K.B. 1021).

Example 2—Cardiff Corporation decided to increase the total rent income from

---

[1] And C.C.R. Ord. 5, r. 8.

[2] Special rules apply to proceedings concerning the administration of a deceased's estate, property subject to a trust, or the construction of an instrument, including a statute, where all the members of the class cannot be ascertained, R.S.C. Ord. 15, r. 13.

council houses by an increase payable by tenants of over a certain income. An action was brought by four tenants acting "on behalf of themselves and all other tenants of houses provided by the defendants under [the Housing Act 1936]" claiming a declaration that the scheme was ultra vires. It was held that since the scheme did not affect *all* the council tenants adversely, the representative action as brought was misconceived.

It should be carefully noted that the essence of a representative action is that the eventual judgment *binds the persons represented although not appearing personally*. Therefore a plaintiff suing representative defendants must obtain an order of the court that the persons he has nominated are to act as representives of the class.[1] If the plaintiff is purporting to represent a class of persons but some of them object, they are entitled to take part in the proceedings by being added as defendants to the action.

(d) Corporate Bodies etc.

Much of the business and public life of the country is carried on by individuals grouped together in associations. Some of these groupings are recognised by the law as having corporate status, thus a district council or a limited company can sue and be sued as if it was an individual. Other groupings do not have corporate status but it is considered convenient that actions should be brought against the groups as a whole, e.g. partnerships and trade unions. It is of vital importance to ascertain at the commencement of proceedings the exact legal identity of the parties. The table on pp. 44–46 sets out the principal entities which the beginner is likely to encounter. The student should note in particular the methods whereby partners and sole traders can be sued.

INFANTS[2]

Persons who have not attained their majority (i.e. who are under 18) can neither bring proceedings nor defend save through the agency of an adult acting on their behalf. In the case of an infant plaintiff, the adult is called his "next friend"; in the case of an infant defendant, he is called the "guardian *ad litem*". We set out below the procedure adopted in the High Court and county court respectively.

High Court

The procedure is regulated by R.S.C. Order 80. The next friend of an infant plaintiff *must* employ a solicitor to act for him. In the Queen's Bench Division the title of an action by an infant plaintiff shows that he is suing by his next friend; in the Chancery Division the title merely records that he is an infant and the details as to his next friend are set out in the body of the writ or originating summons. The next friend is liable to the defendant for costs if they are awarded against the plaintiff but has a right of indemnity against the infant. Where an infant is sued, service should not be effected on him but on his father or guardian or the person with whom he resides or in whose care he is.[3] If that person so chooses he may agree to be the guardian *ad litem*. In that case he must appoint a solicitor to represent the infant and file at court a

---

[1] R.S.C. Ord. 15, r. 12(3), C.C.R. Ord. 5, r. 8.
[2] Strictly speaking these persons should be referred to as "minors" but we have kept throughout this book the traditional term "infant". Similar provisions apply to mental patients. See R.S.C. Ord. 80; C.C.R. Ord. 5.
[3] R.S.C. Ord. 80. r. 16.

written consent to act and a certificate by the solicitor to the effect that the guardian has no interest in the action.[1] He will then enter an appearance in the usual way. Where no appearance is entered, the plaintiff cannot enter judgment in default but must apply to the court for the appointment of a guardian *ad litem*; if no one is prepared to act, then the court will appoint the Official Solicitor to act as guardian *ad litem*. The guardian *ad litem* is liable to an order for costs subject to a remedy over against the infant.

County court

In the county court an infant may bring proceedings in his own right to recover wages up to £2,000.[2] An infant may be sued to judgment in respect of a liquidated sum[3] without the intervention of a guardian *ad litem*.[4] In all other cases a next friend or guardian must act for him. Where an infant sues by his next friend, the next friend must sign an undertaking at the court office to be liable for any costs awarded to the defendant, before process will issue;[5] he is, of course, entitled to be indemnified by the infant. Where proceedings are brought against an infant service is to be effected upon his father, guardian etc.[6] If that person or any other responsible adult is prepared to act as guardian he will apply to the registrar to be appointed as such.[7] If no such application is made then (*a*) if it appears from the face of the proceedings that the defendant is an infant, the plaintiff must apply to the registrar for the appointment of a guardian,[8] and (*b*) if it only becomes apparent at the trial that the action is against an infant then, if the infant appears a guardian may be appointed at once but, if he does not appear, the case may be adjourned for the plaintiff to make application for the appointment of a guardian.[9] If judgment is entered against a defendant who does not appear and it subsequently transpires that he was an infant, the judgment may be set aside.[10] In county court proceedings, the guardian is not personally liable for any costs unless the same were occasioned by his personal negligence or misconduct.[11]

In both the High Court and county court where the infant attains majority during the course of the action, a notice that he adopts the proceedings should be filed at court and served on the other parties.[12] It should be noted that special rules apply as to the settlement of claims on behalf of infants and as to investment of sums awarded to them.[13]

---

[1] Ibid., r. 3.
[2] County Courts Act 1959, s. 80.
[3] E.g. a debt.
[4] Proviso to C.C.R. Ord. 5, rr. 13 and 14.
[5] C.C.R. Ord. 3, r. 2.
[6] C.C.R. Ord. 8, r. 13.
[7] C.C.R. Ord. 5, rr. 12 and 13.
[8] Ibid., r. 13(*c*).
[9] Ibid., r. 14.
[10] Ibid., r. 17.
[11] Ibid., r. 16.
[12] See *Oliver Twist* v. *West Middlesex Salvage Co. Ltd.*, p. 30 *ante*.
[13] See pp. 148–149 *post*.

Entity	Sues or is sued as	Example	Rules	Service (if not on solicitor)	Commentary
Limited company	Company name	"Mammoth Law Book Company Limited"	Companies Act 1948, ss. 18 and 437	Registered office	Leave at, or send writ to, registered office. Foreign company trading in England is required by s. 407 to provide Registrar with name and address of person resident and authorised to accept service. If company in liquidation by order of the court, leave is necessary to issue the writ and it is served on liquidator
Partners	Firm name	Smith and Jones (a firm)	R.S.C. Ord. 81 C.C.R. Ord. 5, r. 21	Either one partner or person in charge at principal place of business. Appearance in the High Court must be entered by the partners individually. Where partners sue or are sued they must on demand serve a notice of the names of all persons who were partners at the date the cause of action occurred	It is also possible to sue partners as individuals, e.g. "John Smith and Peter Jones (trading as Smith and Jones)", but this mode of action has the disadvantage that execution cannot levy against the firm's property except after a special application. This method is employed, however, where the firm does not carry on business within the jurisdiction. It should also be noted that many partnerships carry on business in the style "Smith, Jones and Co." although they are not a limited company. Again persons may trade in a name distinct from the firm name. However the true identity of such a body can be ascertained by consulting the Register of Business Names which also discloses the principal place of business
Individual carrying on business in name other than his own	Can be *sued* in business name	Joseph Soap (trading as Mick's Café)	R.S.C. Ord. 81 C.C.R. Ord. 5, r. 24	Service as partnership	The true identity of the owner can usually be ascertained by consulting the Register of Business Names. If it cannot be found it is permissible to describe the defendant by his trade name thus "Mick's Café (a trade name)"

Category	Description	Party name	Statute / Rule	Service	Notes
Members clubs	(a) Contract: persons authorising contract (b) tort: representative action	(a) Albert Smith and John Higgins (b) Albert Smith and John Higgins on behalf of themselves and all members of the Gray's Inn Rugby Club	R.S.C. O. 15, r. 12 C.C.R. O. 5, r. 8	Service on individuals named	(a) In contract cases, the committee members authorising the contract sue or are sued as individuals (b) In tort cases, the appropriate procedure is by way of representative action—see *Campbell v. Thompson* (1953) 1 Q.B. 445 supra (c) Property disputes are usually brought by or defended by trustees
Government departments	Name of department	Home Office, Department of Employment	Crown Proceedings Act 1947, s. 17	Solicitor of Department or Treasury Solicitor	A list is periodically published setting out (a) departments which have their own solicitor, e.g. Commissioners of Inland Revenue, Department of Employment, and (b) those for whom the Treasury Solicitor acts, e.g. Home Office, Department of Environment, H.M. Stationery Office. The list should be checked in the current S.C. or C.C. Practice. If no department appears to be the appropriate defendant, proceedings are brought against the Attorney-General and served on the Treasury Solicitor
Local authorities	Name of county, district or parish council	Hampshire County Council, Rushmoor District Council, Hook Parish Council	Local Government Act 1972, ss. 2(3) and 14(1)	Solicitor to authority, chairman, clerk to the council	Or chairman, town clerk or similar officer—see O. 65, r. 3
State schools	Name of education authority	Hampshire County Council		Solicitor to authority, chairman, clerk to the council	Education Act 1944 provides for county councils to be responsible for education. In the case of private schools, it is necessary to investigate their constitution in order to determine the proper plaintiffs or defendants

Entity	Sues or is sued as	Example	Rules	Service (if not on solicitor)	Commentary
Hospitals	Hospital Bd, Regional H. Bd, H. Management Committee or Bd of Governors	Manchester Regional H. Board, West Herts Group H. Mgt Comtee, Bd of Governors of University College Hospital	National Health Service Act 1946, s. 13(1) and 1964 Act, s. 1	Solicitor appointed chairman or secretary of board	The National Health Service Acts provide for delegation of the Minister's functions to "Regional Hospital Boards" (also called "Hospital Boards") who may sub-delegate to "Hospital Management Committees". Teaching hospitals are run by "Boards of Government". Actions are brought by or against the appropriate authority and *not* against the Minister of Health
Trade union	Name of union	Transport and General Workers' Union	Trade Union and Labour Relations Act 1974, s. 2(1)(c)	At Head or Main Office	Unions even though not registered are entitled to sue and be sued in their own names
Police	In London, Metropolitan Police Receiver; elsewhere Chief Constable	Sir A B (Chief Constable of the Rutland Police Authority)	Police Act 1964	Solicitor to Authority	
Trusts	Trustees	A B and C D (as trustees of the Estate of E F deceased)	R.S.C. Ord. 15, r. 14 C.C.R. Ord. 5, r. 7	Trustees personally	Trustees, executors and administrators may sue and be sued on behalf of the fund or estate without joining the persons beneficially entitled. The pleading is headed "In the Matter of the Trusts of the Will (Deed) of E F [deceased]" Where an action is brought against trustees, executors or administrators for the administration of a fund or estate it will normally be proper to add the beneficiaries interested as defendants
Infants	In own name but as plaintiffs by "next friend" and as defendants by "guardian ad litem"	A B (by his father and next friend C B) or A B (by his guardian *ad litem* C B)	R.S.C. Ord. 80 C.C.R. Ord. 5 r. 11 et seq	On father, guardian, person with whom he resides or in whose care he is	In Chancery Division the next friend's name is *not* referred to in the title

LEGAL AID

The State provides assistance out of public funds for persons who wish to bring or defend civil proceedings under a statutory scheme administered by the Law Society.[1] The scheme distinguishes between (a) preliminary advice and assistance and (b) court proceedings.

Advice and assistance
A client is entitled to obtain assistance from a solicitor belonging to the scheme provided his means fall within certain limits. The solicitor fills in a questionnaire (the "green form") designed to show:
(a) His client's disposable income, i.e. his net income after deduction is made for tax, national insurance contributions, etc. and due allowance given for his dependants.
(b) His client's disposable capital, i.e. the value of capital such as savings, car, etc. but generally ignoring the value of the house he lives in.
Provided his disposable income and capital do not exceed the statutory limit the client will be entitled to assistance either free of charge or subject to a contribution.[2]
The work which can be done at this stage includes drafting letters, negotiating with the other side and obtaining an opinion from counsel.[3] The maximum costs which can be returned however must not exceed £25 unless he obtains prior authority from the Area Secretary.

Legal aid for civil proceedings
.If the client wishes to bring or defend proceedings then his solicitor prepares an application to the secretary of the local area committee for a *legal aid certificate*. The decision whether a certificate should be granted depends on
(a) the merits of his case: these are usually obvious or he may have a preliminary advice from counsel given under the "green form scheme". In rare cases, the certificate issued will be limited to obtaining counsel's advice in the first instance;
(b) his means, as determined by the Supplementary Benefits Commission.[4] Frequently the certificate will be subject to the condition that the assisted person pays a contribution by monthly instalments based on his disposable income. He may also be required to make a capital contribution from his savings before a certificate is issued.
The certificate issued, unless specially limited, will cover the ordinary steps in the litigation but a further application should be made for express authority to take any unusual steps, e.g. obtaining expert reports. Where a certificate is issued, notice of issue (but *not* the certificate itself) *must* be served on all other parties to the proceedings and a copy filed with the court. This is very important because a party who is sued by or sues a legally aided litigant will only be able to obtain a limited order for costs against him.[5] This may have a

---

[1] See Legal Aid Act 1974, and the Regulations made therein.
[2] The limits are changed from time to time. As at 1st April 1977, if the client's disposable capital is not more than £300 and his income not more than £42 p.w. he will be entitled to advice under the scheme. If his disposable income is £20 or less he will not have to make any contribution.
[3] In fact there is nothing that a solicitor would normally do for a paying client that cannot be done under the "green form" except taking a step in proceedings.
[4] The limits since 15 November 1976 are: disposable capital not more than £1,400; disposable income £2,085; where disposable capital is below £300 and income is below £665 the applicant will not have to make any contribution.
[5] See p. 170, *post.* Note a person sued by a legally aided litigant can apply for costs against the fund if he can show severe financial hardship.

very important bearing on his future conduct of the litigation. It should be noted that the Legal Aid Fund has a *first charge* on any property recovered or preserved for an assisted litigant in order to cover the costs incurred by the Fund to the extent these are not paid by the other party.

IS THE ACTION STATUTE–BARRED?

(a) The general rules
The law requires that proceedings should be brought within a limited time from the date upon which the matters of complaint occurred (*a*) because of the destruction of evidence as time elapses and (*b*) because of the unfairness to a defendant if matters could be litigated many years after they had occurred. The principal periods of limitation are set out in tabular form below.

Type of case	Period in years	Statute	Notes
Contract	6	Limitation Act 1939, s. 2(1)(*a*)	Time runs from the breach complained of
Contract under seal	12	Ibid., s. 2(3)	Called an action "upon a specialty"
Action for an account	6	Ibid., s. 2(2)	
Tort	6	Ibid., s. 2(1)	If the tort is actionable *per se*, time runs from date of commission of tort (e.g. conversion); if actionable only on proof of damage, from date damage occurred (e.g. nuisance, *Rylands* v. *Fletcher* situation)
Personal injury cases	3 (in exceptional cases can be overridden)	Limitation Act 1975	Applied to "actions for damages for negligence, nuisance or breach of duty (whether the duty exists by virtue of a contract or of provision made by or under a statute or independently of any contract or any such provision)". When the damages claimed by the plaintiff consist of or include damages in respect of personal injuries, time runs from date of cause of action or knowledge, see p. 51 post

Type of case	Period in years	Statute	Notes
Fatal accident cases	3 (in exceptional cases can be overridden)	Fatal Accidents Act 1976 Limitation Act 1975	1975 Act prescribes special rule where plaintiff unaware of cause of action
Other cases by or against deceased persons		Proceedings Against Estates Act 1970	The appropriate period now depends only on the type of case involved— there are now no special rules
Recovery of land	12		Action arises as at date of dispossession; where plaintiffs interest not then vested, it runs from date he became entitled to possession
Rent	6	Limitation Act 1939, s. 17	
Mortgagee's claim for foreclosure and sale	12	Ibid., s. 18(1)	As from date when right to sue occurred
Mortgage interest	6	Ibid., s. 18(5)	
Recovery of trust property from trustee	no period	Ibid., s. 19(1)	
Fraudulent breach of trust	no period	Ibid., s. 19(1)	
Other breaches of trust	6	Ibid., s. 19(2)	E.g. claims against trustee for unauthorised investment

(b) Extension of period
In some cases the limitation periods prescribed would work injustice if the law did not permit exceptions. The three exceptional cases are:

   (i)   where the plaintiff is under a disability;
   (ii) where the right of action arises out of fraud or mistake or has been concealed;
   (iii) where the plaintiff has been unaware that he has sustained personal injuries.

   We shall consider each of these cases in turn.

(i) *Plaintiff under a disability.* The general rule is that where a plaintiff was an infant or mental patient when the cause of action accrued and subsequently attains majority (or recovers), he may bring the action within six years of his majority (or recovery). In personal injury cases, the relevant period is three years from the date upon which the disability ended (Limitation Act 1939, s. 22 as amended by Limitation Act 1975, s. 2).

(ii) *Fraud, concealment and mistake.* Section 26 of the Limitation Act provides that where an action is based on the defendant's fraud (e.g. an action in deceit or to recover damages for fraudulent misrepresentation) or for relief against the consequences of mistake, time does not begin to run until the plaintiff has discovered the fraud or mistake or could with reasonable diligence have discovered it.[1] It should be noted that this section does not apply wherever the plaintiff has made a mistake about his legal position; it only applies where the claim is for equitable relief from the consequences of a mistake.

> *Example*—a solicitor entered into a contract of employment whereby she would receive a share of profits from the practice. She was underpaid by mistake for twelve years. The defendants pleaded the statute of limitations in respect of the first six years. She claimed that her action was "for relief against the consequences of a mistake". *Held:* her action was to recover monies unpaid under a contract and not for relief against mistake. *Per* Pearson, J.: "It seems to me that [the statutory] wording is carefully chosen to indicate a class of actions where a mistake has been made which has had certain consequences and the plaintiff seeks to be relieved from those consequences. Familiar examples are, first, money paid in consequence of a mistake: in such a case the mistake is made, in consequence of the mistake the money is paid, and the action is to recover that money back. Secondly, there may be a contract entered into in consequence of a mistake and the action is to obtain the rescission or, in some cases, the rectification of the contract. Thirdly, there may be an account settled in consequence of mistakes; if the mistakes are sufficiently serious there can be a re-opening of the account ... Probably [this provision] applies only where the mistake is an essential ingredient of the cause of action, so that the statement of claim sets out, or should set out, the mistake and its consequences and prays for relief from those consequences".[2]

Section 26 also provides that where the right of action has been *concealed by the fraud* of the defendant or his agent, time shall not begin to run against the plaintiff until he has discovered the fraud or could have done so with reasonable diligence. What does the expression "concealed by ... fraud" mean? There are logically two possibilities: *either* it could mean "concealed by a deliberate act of deception" *or* it could mean "concealment in circumstances amounting to a reckless disregard of the defendant's duty to tell the plaintiff the true situation". It is this second, more extensive definition which has been adopted by the courts.

> *Example 1*—In 1935 P deposited certain packages containing jewellery with D. In 1940 D's agent who was closing the business because of the war opened the packages, decided the jewellery was of no value and gave it to the Salvation Army. In late 1946 (after six years had elapsed) P discovered her jewellery had been disposed of and sued D who pleaded the limitation period. Denning J. at first instance held that D had not acted with any dishonest motive and consequently could not be said to have "concealed the right of action by fraud". The Court of Appeal reversed this decision and held that the very act of conversion without attempting to give notice to P amounted to "fraudulent concealment". *Per* Lord Greene M.R.: "the conduct of the defendants by the very manner in which they

---

[1] These provisions are not to operate so as to defeat the right of third parties who have acquired property in ignorance of the fraud or mistake in question.
[2] *Phillips-Higgins* v. *Harper*, [1954] 1 Q.B. 411, at p. 418.

converted the plaintiff's chattels in breach of the confidence reposed in them and in circumstances calculated to keep her in ignorance of the wrong they had committed amounted to a fraudulent concealment of the cause of action".[1]

Example 2—F purchased certain shares in the names of his children. Subsequently he sold the shares but placed the proceeds of sale into deposit accounts in the names of his children. Thereafter he drew on those accounts and never replaced the monies therein. These matters came to light many years later on his death. The children sued the executors as creditors of the estate. The executors raised the defence that the claim was statute-barred. The Court of Appeal rejected this argument. *Per* Denning L.J.: "When he drew the money from the bank, either he intended to use the children's money as his own, or he did not. If he did intend to use it as his own and told them nothing about it, then the very nature of his dealing amounted to a fraudulent concealment from them of their right of action; and the period of limitation did not start to run until the children discovered it: see section 2(6) of the Limitation Act 1939.... If the father did not intend to use the money as his own, but on behalf of the children as he ought to have done, then he was a trustee of it and he has since converted it to his own use and the children are not bound by any period of limitation ... see also section 19(1) of the Limitation Act 1939."[2]

(iii) *Personal injury where plaintiff not aware he can sue.* It has already been stated that in tort cases where damage is an essential ingredient of the cause of action time begins to run from the date when the damage occurred. What is the position, however, if that damage remains dormant for many years and is only discovered after the period of limitation has elapsed?

Example 1—A miner contracts pneumoconiosis whilst working in a colliery but the symptoms do not appear for many years.[3]

Example 2—An operation is performed to prevent conception. Four years later the woman conceives a child.

Example 3—A is injured at work but does not realise he could sue his employers. After the limitation period has expired he reads of a similar case in a newspaper and at once consults solicitors.[4]

The Limitation Act 1975 seeks to solve this problem by providing that in claims arising out of personal injuries and death the three-year period of limitation begins to run either from the date the cause of action accrued *or* from the date upon which the plaintiff became aware or should reasonably have become aware of his right to sue the defendant. The relevant provisions are set out in sections 2A(3)–(5) of the Limitation Act 1939:

"(3) Subject to section 2D below, an action to which this section applies shall not be brought after the expiration of the period specified in subsections (4) and (5) below.

(4) Except where subsection (5) applies, the said period is three years from—

(a) the date on which the cause of action accrued, or
(b) the date (if later) of the plaintiff's knowledge.

(5) If the person injured dies before the expiration of the period in subsection (4) above, the period as respects the cause of action surviving for the benefit of the estate of the deceased by virtue of section 1 of the Law Reform (Miscellaneous Provisions) Act 1934 shall be three years from—

---

[1] *Beaman* v. *A.R.T.S.* [1949] 1 K.B. 550, at p. 566.
[2] *Re Shephard, Shephard* v. *Cartwright* [1953] Ch. 728, at p. 756, C.A. See also *Kitchen* v. *Royal Air Force Association* [1958] 2 All E.R. 241.
[3] *Cartledge* v. *E. Jopling & Sons, Ltd.* [1963] A.C. 758; [1963] 1 All E.R. 341.
[4] *Harper* v. *National Coal Board* [1974] Q.B. 614; [1974] 2 All E.R. 441.

(a) the date of death, or
(b) the date of the personal representative's knowledge,
whichever is the later.

(6) In this section, and in section 2B below, references to a person's date of knowledge are references to the date on which he first had knowledge of the following facts—

(a) that the injury in question was significant, and
(b) that that injury was attributable in whole or in part to the act or omission which is alleged to constitute negligence, nuisance or breach of duty, and
(c) the identity of the defendant, and
(d) if it is alleged that the act or omission was that of a person other than the defendant, the identity of that person and the additional facts supporting the bringing of an action against the defendant,

and knowledge that any acts or omissions did or did not, as a matter of law, involve negligence, nuisance or breach of duty is irrelevant.

(7) For the purposes of this section an injury is significant if the plaintiff would reasonably have considered it sufficiently serious to justify his instituting proceedings for damages against a defendant who did not dispute liability and was able to satisfy a judgment.

(8) For the purposes of the said sections a person's knowledge includes knowledge which he might reasonably have been expected to acquire—

(a) from facts observable or ascertainable by him, or
(b) from facts ascertainable by him with the help of medical or other appropriate expert advice which it is reasonable for him to seek,

but a person shall not be fixed under this subsection with knowledge of a fact ascertainable only with the help of expert advice so long as he has taken all reasonable steps to obtain (and, where appropriate, to act on) that advice."

Section 2B makes similar provision in cases brought on behalf of the dependants of a deceased person under the Fatal Accident Act 1976.

The Act of 1975 also provides that in personal and fatal injury cases the court can override the statutory time limits if it would be just so to do:—

"2D.—(1) If it appears to the court that it would be equitable to allow an action to proceed having regard to the degree to which—

(a) the provisions of section 2A or 2B of this Act prejudice the plaintiff or any person whom he represents, and
(b) any decision of the court under this subsection would prejudice the defendant or any person whom he represents.

the court may direct that those provisions shall not apply to the action, or shall not apply to any specificed cause of action to which the action relates."

The relevant factors to be taken into account are set out in section 2D(3):

"(3) In acting under this section the court shall have regard to all the circumstances of the case and in particular to—

(a) the length of, and the reasons for, the delay on the part of the plaintiff;
(b) the extent to which, having regard to the delay, the evidence adduced or likely to be adduced by the plaintiff or the defendant is or is likely to be less cogent than if the action had been brought within the time allowed by section 2A or as the case may be 2B;
(c) the conduct of the defendant after the cause of action arose, including the extent if any to which he responded to requests reasonably made by the plaintiff for information or inspection for the purpose of ascertaining facts

which were or might be relevant to the plaintiff's cause of action against the defendant;

(*d*) the duration of any disability of the plaintiff arising after the date of the accrual of the cause of action;

(*e*) the extent to which the plaintiff acted promptly and reasonably once he knew whether or not the act of omission of the defendant, to which the injury was attributable, might be capable at that time of giving rise to an action for damages;

(*f*) the steps, if any, taken by the plaintiff to obtain medical, legal or other expert advice and the nature of any such advice he may have received.

(4) In a case where the person injured died when, because of section 2A, he could no longer maintain an action and recover damages in respect of the injury, the court shall have regard in particular to the length of, and the reasons for, the delay on the part of the deceased.

(5) In a case under subsection (4) above, or any other case where the time limit, or one of the time limits, depends on the date of knowledge of a person other than the plaintiff, subsection (3) above shall have effect with appropriate modifications, and shall have effect in particular as if references to the plaintiff included references to any person whose date of knowledge is or was relevant in determining a time limit."

In the examples on p. 51, the Act would work as follows:

(1) The miner would be able to bring an action within three years of the date he realised that he was suffering from pneumoconiosis *and* that this was attributable to some action or omission by his employer (see section 2A(4) and (6)).

(2) The lady who conceived after a sterilisation operation could bring an action within three years of the date upon which she received (or should reasonably have received) expert advice indicating that she had a cause of action against the hospital (section 2A(4), (6) and (8)).

(3) So far as the example of the employee who did not realise he had a legal right to sue his employer is concerned, section 2A(6) provides that in fixing the relevant date when the plaintiff first had knowledge of the matters complained of, the fact that he was not aware at that time that he had a legal right to sue is irrelevant. However this might be a case where the court would exercise its power to override the limitation period (section 2D).

PROCESS, SERVICE AND APPEARANCE IN THE HIGH COURT

Note: the reader is referred to the short description of the issue and service of a writ in Part I at p. 5.

(a) The Writ of Summons

High Court proceedings are normally commenced by writ.[1] A writ is a document addressed to the defendant by the Crown giving him notice that an action has been commenced against him and requiring him to place himself on the court record by filing a *memorandum of appearance*. The writ is prepared by the plaintiff's solicitor who must take particular care to see:—

(i) the parties are correctly described in the title (see table pp. 44–46).

(ii) that on the back of the writ he has set out 'a concise statement of the

---

[1] In Chapter 13 we shall consider the principal alternative form of process, namely the *originating summons* which is used extensively in the Chancery Division usually in matters where the issues of fact are not substantially in dispute.

nature of the claim made or the relief or remedy required in the action".[1] This is known as *"the general indorsement"*. In an action for contract the indorsement should state the date of the contract, whether oral or written, the breach complained of and the remedy claimed, thus:

"The Plaintiff's claim is for damages for breach by the Defendant of a written contract dated the 2nd day of February 1975 whereby the Defendant agreed to appear at the Plaintiff's theatre at Drury Lane for six months commencing the 3rd day of May 1975 and for an injunction restraining the Defendant from appearing at any other theatre during the said period in breach of the aforesaid contract."

In an action for tort, the indorsement should state the date, place and nature of the alleged tort, thus:

"The Plaintiff's claim is for damages for personal injuries, loss and expense arising out of a road traffic collision on the 2nd day of August 1975 at Chancery Lane, London WC1 caused by the negligent driving of an omnibus by the Defendants' servant one Watts".

In an action for recovery of possession of land the indorsement must state whether the land is a dwelling house and if so whether its rateable value brings it within the provisions of the Rent Act 1977:

"The Plaintiff's claim is for possession of a dwelling house known as 23 Acacia Gardens in the London Borough of Hammersmith and for mesne profits from [date of expiry of notice to quit] until judgment. The net annual value for rating of the said premises does not exceed £1,000".

The purpose of the general indorsement is to provide a short summary of the nature of the claim and the relief sought. It should not be confused with the *statement of claim* which is the formal and detailed expression of the plaintiff's case generally served after the defendant has entered an appearance.

(iii) if the plaintiff's claim is only for a fixed sum (e.g. a debt, the price of goods, a sum claimed for services by way of *quantum meruit*), then there is set out on the back of the writ a statement telling the defendant that provided he pays the amount claimed and costs within the 14-day period limited for entering an appearance, further proceedings will be stayed.[2] The form of words used is set out in the example on p. 55. This sort of claim, i.e. where the amount due is fixed or can be calculated by simple arithmetic, is known as a liquidated claim.

(iv) if the writ is issued out of a district registry and the cause of action in respect of which relief is claimed wholly or in part arose in that district, an indorsement to that effect is inserted so that appearance is entered at that registry and the matters proceed therein.[3]

Once the writ has been drafted, two copies are taken to the Central Office (or district registry). One copy is signed by the plaintiff or his solicitor, sealed (i.e. given an official court stamp) and stamped (i.e. to show the fee has been paid) and filed at the court. The other copy is sealed and returned to the plaintiff. Before sealing, a reference number is assigned to the action and, in

---

[1] R.S.C. Ord. 6, r. 2.
[2] R.S.C. Ord. 6, r. 2(1)(b). Where the plaintiff is abroad and resides outside the sterling area, the defendant is to pay the monies claimed into court.
[3] R.S.C. Ord. 6, r. 4; Ord. 12, r. 2(2); Ord. 4, r. 6.

EXAMPLE OF A SPECIALLY INDORSED WRIT

(The front of the writ is in the standard form save that a note is added at the foot requiring the defendant to file a defence within 14 days of the last date for entering an appearance.

Note: the paragraph relating to payment of claim would also appear in a generally indorsed writ if the claim was for a fixed sum.)

STATEMENT OF CLAIM

THE PLAINTIFFS CLAIM is **for £1475.25** the price of goods sold and delivered by the Plaintiff to the Defendant.

Particulars

1975 Jan 1st – March 31st	To goods, full particulars of which have been delivered to the Defendant and which exceed three folios	£1675.25p
	Credit: Cheque dated 3 April 1975	£ 200.00p
	Balance due	£1475.25p

(Signed).......*Dodson and Fogg*........

And £ 25.00p (or such sum as may be allowed on taxation) for costs, and also, if the Plaintiff obtain an order for substituted service, the further sum of £15.00p (or such sum as may be allowed on taxation). If the amount claimed and costs be paid to the Plaintiff , his Solicitor or Agent within 14 days after service hereof (inclusive of the day of service), further proceedings will be stayed, but if it appears from the indorsement on the Writ that the Plaintiff is/are resident outside the scheduled territories, as defined by the Exchange Control Act 1947, or is/are acting by order or on behalf of a person so resident, proceedings will only be stayed if the amount claimed and costs is paid into court within the said time and notice of such payment in is given to the Plaintiff , his Solicitor or Agent

---

This Writ was issued by **Dodson and Fogg**
of **Freeman's Court, Cornhill, London EC3**
[ ]

Solicitor for the said Plaintiff , whose address is **89 Castle Street, Easthampton in the County of Sussex.**

Indorsement as to service.

This Writ was served by me at

on the Defendant
on , the day of 19 .
Indorsed the day of 19 .

(Signed)...

(Address)...

the Chancery Division, it is allocated between the two groups of judges. The writ is issued when it is sealed.

(b) Specially indorsed writs

The plaintiff may if he wishes serve his *statement of claim* at the same time that he serves the writ. He would probably only wish to do this if he thought the defendant had no defence to the action and so intended to apply in due course for *summary judgment*[1], i.e. an order giving him judgment on the basis the defendant could not show even a prima facie defence. In such a case, instead of serving the statement of claim as a separate document, the plaintiff may, instead, set out the statement of claim on the back of the writ in place of the general indorsement. Although this can be a fully drafted statement of claim running to several pages, this practice is usually only followed in simple actions in debt or for the balance of an account where it is accepted that an abbreviated form may be used (see p. 55).

(c) Service of writ

Once the writ has been issued it is the plaintiff's task to effect service; service is not effected by the court. In practice this is normally done by sending a copy of the writ and the sealed original to the defendant's solicitors who return the original with a dated indorsement stating that they accept service on behalf of their client.[2] If the defendant has no solicitor authorised to accept service on his behalf, the plaintiff must try to effect *personal* service. This is done as follows:

(i) *On individuals.* The server satisfies himself that the person to be served is the defendant and gives him a copy of the writ.[3] The server must show him the sealed original on request and must within three days of service write on the original writ the day, date, place of service and person upon whom it was served.[4] If the defendant refuses to accept the copy writ, it is sufficient to tell him the nature of the document and leave it as nearly as his possession or control as possible.[5]

(ii) *On companies.* This is effected by leaving the writ or sending it by post to the registered office. In the case of a foreign company trading in England, the Registrar of Companies holds a list of the names and addresses of persons resident in Great Britain and authorised to accept service of process.[6]

(iii) *On firms.* Where a partnership is sued as a *firm*, service is effected either by personal service on one partner or by leaving the writ at the principal place of business of the partnership within the jurisdiction on any person having at the time of service the control or management of the partnership business there.[7]

---

[1] See p. 91.

[2] R.S.C. Ord. 10, r. 1(2). See the case of Oliver Twist, p. 11.

[3] R.S.C. Ord. 65, r. 2. The method of service appears to have changed little over the centuries. Thus *Pickwick Papers*, Chap. xx: "'As you offer no terms, sir,' said Dodson, displaying a slip of parchment in his right hand, and affectionately pressing a paper copy of it on Mr. Pickwick with his left, 'I had better serve you with a copy of this writ, sir. Here is the original, sir,' 'Very well, gentlemen, very well,' said Mr. Pickwick, rising in person and wrath at the same time, 'you shall hear from my solicitor, gentlemen.' 'We shall be very happy to do so,' said Fogg, rubbing his hands. 'Very,' said Dodson."

[4] R.S.C. Ord. 10, r. 1(4): the sanction is that unless this information appears on the writ, the plaintiff will not be entitled to enter judgment in default of appearance or defence.

[5] It is not sufficient, however, to give the writ to the defendant's wife or servant or to hand it to him in a sealed envelope without telling him what the envelope contains (*Heath* v. *White* [1844] 2 Dow. & L 40; *Banque Russe et Française* v. *Clarke* [1894] W.N. 203).

[6] Companies Act 1948, ss. 437 and 407.

[7] R.S.C. Ord. 81, r. 3.

(iv) *On bodies corporate.* Service can validly be effected on the chairman or clerk to the council of a local authority or to similar offices of other public bodies.[1]

(v) *Minors.* Service is to be effected on the child's father, guardian or (if he has no father or guardian) upon the person with whom he resides or in whose care he is.[2].

There will however be some cases where personal service is not possible either because the defendant is evading service or because his present whereabouts are unknown. In these circumstances the plaintiff can apply to the master setting out in an affidavit the efforts made to trace the defendant. The master can order that notice of the writ should be effected by some other method, e.g. by letter to the defendant's address or by advertisement. If this order for *substituted service* is complied with, the court deems valid service to have been effected. It should be noted, however, that substituted service will only be ordered where the plaintiff can persuade the master that it is likely to be effective in bringing to the attention of the defendant the fact that the writ has been issued. Where therefore the plaintiff has no idea of the whereabouts of the defendant, an order for substituted service will not be made unless:

(i) the plaintiff's claim is for personal injury arising out of a road traffic accident—in which case service may be effected on the defendant's insurers or the Motor Insurers' Bureau, *or*

(ii) the plaintiff is claiming possession of land in which case the master may permit service by affixing a copy of the writ to some conspicuous part of the land.[3]

(d) Renewal of writ

The writ must be served not later than 12 calendar months from the date of issue unless the plaintiff obtains its renewal. An application to the master for renewal may be made either before or after the expiry of the writ. The renewed writ dates back to the original. It will not be granted unless the plaintiff can show reasonable grounds for his failure to serve (e.g. the defendant's absence abroad) and, in particular, where the limitation period has expired the writ will only be renewed in the most exceptional cases.

Example 1—The plaintiff was injured in March 1961. In December 1963 his solicitors issued a writ but took no steps to effect service whilst they were negotiating with the defendant's insurers. Those negotiations broke down in September 1964. In January 1965 the plaintiffs obtained a renewal of the writ. The defendants entered a *conditional appearance* and applied to set the writ aside. Megaw J. held that in the absence of exceptional circumstances leave should not be granted to renew a writ where a fresh writ would be met with a defence under the statute of limitations (*Heaven* v. *Road and Rail Wagons, Ltd.*, [1965] 2 Q.B. 355; [1965] 2 All E.R. 409).

Example 2—After the writ had been issued the plaintiff's solicitors did not serve it or renew it because negotiations were proceeding with the insurers. The insurers however never waived service and subsequently objected to the renewal of the writ. *Per* Lord Denning M.R., "Negotiations for a settlement do not afford any excuse for failing to serve a writ in time or to renew it" (*Easy* v. *Universal Anchorage Co.*, [1974] 2 All E.R. 1105 at p. 1107.)

(e) Service outside the jurisdiction

Our courts assume jurisdiction over all persons who are served in England

---

[1] R.S.C. Ord. 65, r. 3.
[2] R.S.C. Ord. 80, r. 16.
[3] R.S.C. Ord. 10, r. 4 and see also Ord. 113, p. 101 *post*.

and Wales notwithstanding that the subject matter of the dispute is entirely foreign.

> *Example*—D was served with a writ whilst in London on business with the plaintiffs. The writ was in respect of monies received by him in the United States of America where he had been the plaintiff's agent. The House of Lords held that the service was valid notwithstanding he was only temporarily within the country, but also approved the judgment of Kekewich J. at first instance who had said that "if it was made out that a person had been induced by fraud of any kind to come within the jurisdiction for the concealed purpose of serving him with a writ in an action, he should have no hesitation in setting aside the service as an abuse of the process of the court".[1]

Conversely where the proposed defendant is abroad, the court will decline to exercise jurisdiction over him. However, this principle is considerably relaxed by the operation of Order 11 which provides that service of notice of the writ[2] may be effected abroad if two conditions are satisfied:

(i) the action falls within the categories set out in Order 11, rule 1 (e.g., actions founded on a tort committed within the jurisdiction, actions relating to the enforcement of contracts[3] made within the jurisdiction, actions for breach of contract occurring within the jurisdiction, actions relating to land within the jurisdiction, actions where one of two defendants is within the jurisdiction); and

(ii) the case is a proper one for service out of the jurisdiction.[4]

The application for leave to serve out of the jurisdiction is made by the plaintiff *ex parte* to the master supported by an affidavit setting out:

(i) the nature of the case in sufficient detail to show it falls within rule 1;
(ii) the deponent's belief that the plaintiff has a good cause of action;
(iii) in what country or place the defendant is or probably may be found.

It is important to note that it is not sufficient to show the case falls within Order 11 rule 1 to obtain leave; the master must also be satisfied that the English court is the *most appropriate forum*.

> *Example 1*—A collision occurred on the Elbe between two British ships and a German vessel. The British vessels were released after agreeing to the mutual provision of sureties for any action between them and the German vessel. The owners of one of the British ships commenced proceedings in London against the other British ship and sought leave to serve on the German ship owners. Meanwhile proceedings were pending in Hamburg. The Court of Appeal held that leave should not be granted in such a case notwithstanding the conditions of Order 11 rule 1 were satisfied since the balance of convenience clearly pointed to Hamburg as the appropriate place of trial (*The Hagen*, [1908] P 189).
>
> *Example 2*—D (a Frenchman) obtained judgment in an action in England and an order that a sum paid into court be paid out to him. P applied by way of injunction to restrain D taking this money on the basis that he had a valid claim to the monies in question. An action between them in respect of these monies was already pending in Paris. The question was whether the English court should determine the question or permit D to take out his money and leave P to proceed in France. The Court held

---

[1] *Watkins v. North American Land and Timber Co. Ltd.* [1904] 20 T.L.R. 534, at pp. 535–536.
[2] In Scotland and Northern Ireland the writ itself may be served.
[3] Unless the defendant is domiciled or ordinarily resident in Scotland or Northern Ireland.
[4] If the application is to serve in Scotland or Northern Ireland the court is to consider whether there is any concurrent remedy there and the comparative cost and convenience of proceedings in England.

leave should not be granted. *Per* Pearson J.: "it becomes a very serious question, and ought always to be considered a very serious question, . . . whether this court ought to put a foreigner, who owes no allegiance here, to the inconvenience and annoyance of being brought to contest his rights in this country, and I for one say, most distinctly, that I think this court ought to be exceedingly careful before it allows a writ to be served out of the jurisdiction". (*Societe Générale de Paris* v. *Dreyfus Brothers* (1885), 29 Ch. D. 239.)

(f) Memorandum of appearance[1]

Once the defendant has been served with a writ he is required to file two copies of a memorandum of appearance at the Central Office[2] in effect placing himself on the court record. One copy is retained by the court and the other is sent to the plaintiff or his solicitors. The relevant form can be seen at p. 13. The rules require that the appearance be entered within 14 days of service. This does not mean that an appearance cannot be entered thereafter, but what it does mean is that once 14 days have elapsed the plaintiff may enter *judgment in default of appearance*. Until such judgment is entered, the defendant is free to enter an appearance notwithstanding the 14-day period has expired.[3]

Judgment is entered in default by the plaintiff obtaining a sealed judgment form at the Central Office.[4] It is a purely administrative act; there is no appearance involved before any judge or master. The plaintiff's solicitor takes to the office the original writ (duly indorsed as to service), and an affidavit verifying service[5] and two completed judgment forms. The officials check the register of appearances and if no entry is found, judgment is entered for the plaintiff. This judgment will either be:

(a) *final judgment*, where the claim is liquidated (for a fixed sum, e.g. £100 debt) or for possession of land, *or*

(b) *interlocutory judgment*, where the amount of damages to be awarded has to be decided by the court (e.g. damages for negligence or nuisance or trespass). In this case the damages will be assessed by the master and the defendant must be notified of the hearing and may attend to argue the question of *quantum* of damages (although he may not dispute his liability).

It frequently happens that a defendant against whom judgment has been entered in default will wish to have the judgment set aside, in other words to be allowed to dispute the claim. He may apply to the master by summons (under R.S.C. Order 13, rule 9)[6] for an order setting the judgment aside and for leave to enter an appearance. It is standard practice to file an affidavit stating why judgment was allowed to be entered (e.g. mistake, delay etc.) and

---

[1] See R.S.C. Ord. 12.

[2] Or district registry if the writ is indorsed with the statement that the cause of action arose in the district or if the defendant is an individual residing in or carrying on business in the district or a company whose registered office is in the district or which carries on business therein. In other cases of writ issued out of district registries, the defendant may appear there or in London (R.S.C. Ord. 12, r. 2).

[3] At first sight it might appear that the appearance stage is a pointless formality inasmuch as all the defendant has to do is to complete a simple form. The Justice Committee in their report *Going to Law* (1974, Stevens) noted that in 1971 and 1972 more than 60 per cent of all cases ended with judgment in default of appearance. It therefore seems that the system effectively provides a method of enabling plaintiffs to obtain the speedy default judgment necessary before execution can take place.

[4] Or district registry.

[5] Unless the original writ has been also indorsed by the *defendant's* solicitor.

[6] The summons must be served on the defendant not less than two clear days before the return day.

SUMMONS FOR ATTENDANCE BEFORE MASTER

In the High Court of Justice
QUEEN'S BENCH DIVISION

1975 .— 5 .—No.206

*If action assigned *Master .... COWPER ....

S.1A

Master's Summons
(General Form)
(O.32)

Oyez Publishing
Limited
Oyez House
237 Long Lane
London SE1 4PU
a subsidiary of
The Solicitors' Law
Stationery Society
Limited

F21551 3-9-73
★ ★ ★

Between

        James Montgomery Snaresbrook   Plaintiff

                    AND

        Imperial Publishing Company Limited   Defendant S

Let all parties concerned attend the Master in Chambers, in Room No. 97   ,
Central Office, Royal Courts of Justice, Strand, London, on   Monday,
the   3rd   day of   November   1975 , at   10.30 o'clock in
the   forenoon, on the hearing of an application on the part of

the Defendants that the judgment herein dated the
10th day of October, 1975 be set aside and that the
Defendants have leave to enter an appearance out of
time.

Dated the   14th   day of   October,   19 75.

To Messrs. Higgins and Co.   This Summons was taken out by
10 Gray's Inn Square,
London WC1   Dodson and Fogg

                              of Freeman's Court, Cornhill, London EC1
Solicitor s for the Plaintiff   Solicitor s for the Defendants

In the High Court of Justice,   1975.-S.-No.206

Queen's Bench Division

Between:

James Montgomery Snaresbrook   Plaintiff

and

Imperial Publishing Company
Limited   Defendants

I, Peter Roger Snow, of 21, Ruislip Avenue, in the London Borough of Hounslow, Legal Executive, make oath and say as follows:-

1. I am a Legal Executive in the employ of Dodson and Fogg, Solicitors for the above-mentioned Defendants and have the conduct of this case under the supervision of my principal.

2. On the 1st day of September, 1975 I received by post from the Plaintiff's solicitors the writ of summons herein together with a copy writ. I returned the writ of summons duly indorsed on the 2nd day of September, 1975.

3. On the 3rd day of September I went on my annual leave. Unfortunately I forgot to mention to my court clerk the necessity of filing a memorandum of appearance by the 14th day of September. On the 21st day of September I returned from my holidays and owing to pressure of work the question of filing an appearance was overlooked.

4. On the 10th day of October, 1975 I received a copy of the judgment in default of appearance herein.

5. I am informed by the Defendants' managing director, Peter Quentin Leavis, that his company have a valid defence to this claim inasmuchas the goods delivered did not accord to specification.

6. In the circumstances I respectfully apply to this Honourable Court that the judgment herein be set aside and that the Defendants have leave to enter an appearance.

Sworn at *Ealing*

this *14th* day of *October 1975*   *Peter Roger Snow*.

Nicholas Nickleby

A Commissioner of Oaths

This affidavit is filed on behalf of the Defendants.

showing that the defendant has a prima facie defence to the action (otherwise it would be a pointless exercise to set the judgment aside). In *Evans* v. *Bartlem* 1937] AC. 473 at p. 480 (where the defendant had allowed judgment to be entered in default of appearance for what was in effect a gaming debt and then applied to set the judgment aside), Lord Atkin explained the true position and at the same time formulated the classic statement of the basic principle of procedural law, namely that a failure to follow the rules of procedure are not to debar a defendant from seeking judgment on the merits:

> The principle obviously is that unless and until the Court has pronounced a judgment upon the merits or by consent, it is to have the power to revoke the expression of its coercive power where that has only been obtained by a failure to follow any of the rules of procedure.

The form of summons and affidavit which would be used in a typical case are set out on pp. 60 and 61.

(g) Conditional Appearance

If the defendant wishes to object that the court should not entertain the claim against him (for example, because he has diplomatic immunity) he may apply ex parte to the master for leave to enter a conditional appearance.[1] This prevents the plaintiff entering judgment in default provided the defendant within the time allowed by the master issues a summons to strike out the writ. The most common example of a conditional appearance is where a writ against a firm is served on a person who denied he was a partner at the material time. He will be allowed to enter a conditional appearance and then either side can effectively apply to the master to give directions as to trial of this specific issue or they can allow the proceedings to continue to trial on a defence specifically raising the issue of the defendant's status.[2]

STAY OF PROCEEDINGS PENDING ARBITRATION

By section 4 of the Arbitration Act 1950 any party to a contract which provides for disputes to be settled by arbitration and against whom legal proceedings have been commenced may before delivery of any pleadings[3] or taking any other steps in the proceedings apply to the court for a stay pending the reference of the matter to an arbitrator. The power to grant a stay is however discretionary and would normally be refused if it would cause injustice (e.g. where the plaintiff could obtain legal aid for court proceedings but not for arbitration) or where issues of honesty are involved.

PROCESS IN THE COUNTY COURT

The County Court Rules distinguish between:

(a) *default actions*, i.e. claims for a debt or other liquidated sum (a liquidated sum is where the amount claimed can be verified by arithmetic calculation, e.g. the price of goods sold); and

(b) *ordinary actions*, i.e. claims for damages which have to be assessed by the court (e.g. damages for non-delivery of goods or for personal injuries) and claims for other relief (e.g. possession of land or for an injunction).

---

[1] R.S.C. Ord. 12, r. 7. As to the special position of a foreign defendant objecting to the issue or service of the writ, see *Henry v Geoprosco International Ltd* [1975] 3 W.L.R. 620.

[2] R.S.C. Ord. 81, r. 4.

[3] For this purpose entering an appearance does *not* count as delivery of pleadings or taking a step in the proceedings.

COUNTY COURT PROCEDURE

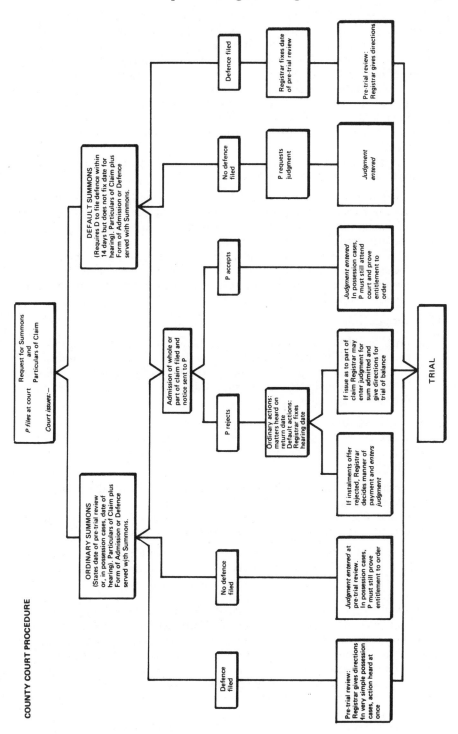

The importance of the distinction is that in a *default action* the defendant is required to file a defence within 14 days of service at the court office; if he does so, the case proceeds to trial but if he fails to do so the plaintiff may *sign judgment* against him. In an *ordinary action*, the summons fixes a date for the hearing of the case (or, more usually, for an initial hearing where the registrar will give directions for trial—the *pre-trial review*). Thus in an ordinary action there is no automatic judgment in default so that, although the rules require the defendant to file a defence in an ordinary action within 14 days, if he does not do so the plaintiff will still have to *attend on the return day* and *prove his case* by evidence.

Actions are commenced in the county court by the plaintiff submitting at the court office:

(a) Two copies of a *praecipe*, that is, a form applying for the issue of a summons and setting out the names and status of the parties and showing how the court has jurisdiction. The form of praecipe varies according to the nature of the case.

(b) Two copies of *particulars of claim*. This document is exactly the same as the *statement of claim* in High Court proceedings, i.e. it is the initial pleading. Accordingly the drafting of such particulars is considered in the section on pleadings, p. 74, *post*.

The court staff then:

(a) prepare a *plaint note* which is given to the plaintiff and is a receipt for the fees paid by him and in the case of an *ordinary summons* sets out the date of hearing or pre-trial review and in the case of a *default summons* sets out in what circumstances he can sign judgment in default of a defence.

(b) prepare a summons to the defendant.

Service of the summons, praecipe and particulars can be effected personally in the manner described under the service of a writ out of the High Court. However, in practice, service in the county court is normally effected by the court[1] either

(a) sending the summons by post to the defendant's residence or, if he owns a business, to his place of business, *or*

(b) by the court bailiff delivering the summons to any person over 16 at the defendant's residence or, if he owns a business, at his place of business.

Where personal service or service by the court is not effective, the registrar may direct that service shall be effected by sending the documents by post to the defendant's last address, by advertisement or by such other means as is likely to give him notice of the action.[2]

It is vitally important to note that whether the plaintiff is signing judgment in a *default action* or proceeding to prove his claim in an *ordinary action*, he must be able to prove service. The novice attending the hearing of an ordinary action at the county court may find (to his relief) that the defendant has not appeared but, though he may be armed with all the evidence needed to prove his case, it will be to no avail if he cannot satisfy the court as to service.[3]

---

[1] C.C.R. Ord. 8, r. 8.

[2] C.C.R. Ord. 8, r. 6.

[3] One can check whether there has been service by seeing from the praecipe whether postal service has been requested; if so, the court staff will know whether the documents have been returned by the post office; in other cases one should ask to see the bailiff's indorsement on the summons.

Many actions in the county courts are brought in circumstances where there is no defence to the claim but, because the defendant is in financial difficulties, he cannot afford to pay the sum due. For this reason, the rules provide that the defendant is to be sent with the summons a document divided into four parts:

(1) A form of admission. If the claim is admitted but the defendant wishes time to pay he sets out his proposals and a statement of his means and expenses. This is then sent to the plaintiff who may accept the proposal If he does not do so the matter is resolved on the return day or, in the case of a default summons, at a *disposal* day notified to both parties by the registrar.

(2) A form of defence. The defendant is invited to set out the nature of his case. If he is acting by solicitor, this form will not be used but he will deliver a formal pleading.

(3) A form of counterclaim.

(4) A note that if he disputes the claim, he may ask that the matter should go to arbitration. If the sum claimed in the case does not exceed £100 the registrar may refer the proceeding to arbitration. Arbitration is intended as a quick and informal method of disposing of a case.[1]

---

[1] The Registrar is empowered under the *Lord Chancellor's Direction*, 21, September 1973 to make any of the following orders as to the conduct of the arbitration:

(i) The rules of evidence shall not apply in relation to the arbitration.

(ii) With the consent of the parties, the arbitrator may decide the case on the basis of the statements and documents submitted by the parties. Otherwise he should fix a date for the hearing.

(iii) The hearing should be informal and held in private.

(iv) That at the hearing the arbitrator may adopt any method of procedure which he may consider to be convenient and to afford a fair and equal opportunity to each party to present his case.

(v) If any party does not appear at the arbitration, the arbitrator may make an award on hearing any other party to the proceedings who may be present.

(vi) With the consent of the parties and at any time before giving his decision and either before or after the hearing, the arbitrator may consult any expert or call for an expert report on any matter in dispute or invite an expert to attend the hearing as an assessor.

(vii) The costs of the action up to and including the entry of judgment shall be in the discretion of the arbitrator to be exercised in the same manner as the discretion of the court under the provisions of the County Court Rules.

APPENDIX

EXAMPLE OF DEFAULT ACTION
IN THE COUNTY COURT

Easyrider Garages carry on business in a mews in Covent Garden. On 21 August 1975 they sell a second-hand Ford Capri to James Smith for £450. James pays by cheque and they allow him to take the car. The cheque is returned to them marked "refer to drawer". Letters to James evoke no response. Now the garage can base their claim either on the basis of non-payment of the price or for dishonour of the cheque or both. In the present case the claim is founded on the basis of dishonour. The plaintiff's local county court will have jurisdiction since the cause of action (i.e. the drawing of the cheque) arose in that district. It follows that it is *not* necessary to bring the action in the defendant's local county court (see C.C.R. Order 2, rule 1). Set out below are:

(1) praecipe and request for postal service;
(2) summons;
(3) particulars of claim;
(4) form of defence and admission.

PRAECIPE FOR DEFAULT SUMMONS

11. *Request for Default Summons against Defendant out of District.* Order 6, Rule 3 (1) (a).	Two copies of the Plaintiff's particulars of Claim are required before a plaint can be entered, and if there are two or more Defendants to be served, an additional copy for each additional Defendant.	In the	Westminster	County Court.
To be served by	Court	Entered	19	No. of Plaint

Statement of Parties	
1. **PLAINTIFF'S** names in full, and residence or place of business. 2. If a female, state whether married, single, or a widow. 3. If suing in a representative capacity, state in what capacity. 4. If an infant required to sue by a next friend, state that fact, and names in full, residence or place of business, and occupation of next friend. 5. If an assignee, state that fact, and name, address and occupation of assignor. 6. If co-partners suing in the name of their firm, add "(Suing as a Firm)". 7. If a company registered under the Companies Act, 1948, state the address of the registered office and describe it as such.	Easyrider Garages (a firm) 25 Garrick Mews, London WC2
8. **DEFENDANT'S** surname, and (where known) his or her initials or names in full; defendant's residence or place of business (if a proprietor of the business). 9. Whether male or female, and if female, whether Mrs. or Miss. 10. Occupation (where known). 11. If sued in a representative capacity, state in what capacity. 12. If co-partners are sued in the name of their firm, or a person carrying on business in a name other than his own name is sued in such name, add "(Sued as a Firm)". 13. If a company registered under the Companies Act, 1948, is sued, the address given must be the registered office of the company, and must be so described.	James Smith 26 Doughty Street, WC1

Such of the following questions as are applicable in the circumstances of the case must be answered by the Plaintiff to show that the Court has jurisdiction to entertain the Action pursuant to Order 2, Rule 1, of the County Court Rules, 1936:—

NOTE.—Where the claim is for the amount of any instalment or instalments due and unpaid under a hire-purchase agreement Question 3 must be answered.

Where the claim is founded on a contract for the sale or hire of goods Question 1 must be answered and if the answer is "No", Question 3 must be answered.

Where neither of the foregoing descriptions applies, such of Questions 2, 4 and 5 as are applicable should be answered, or, if none of these are applicable, Question 6 must be answered. (NOTE.—If the answer to Question 2 is "Yes" no further questions need be answered.)

1.	Was the purchase price or rental payable in one sum?	
2.	Was the contract made in the district of the Court, and, if so, where?	Yes - at Plaintiffs' address
3.	Did the defendant reside or carry on business in the district of the Court at the time when the contract was made and, if so, where?	
4.	Where, and how, was the order for the goods [*or* given by the Defendant to the Plaintiff?]	as above
5.	Where was payment to be made by the Defendant under the contract?	as above

6. What are the facts upon which the Plaintiff relies as showing that the cause of Action arose wholly, or in part, in the district of the Court?

The defendant delivered a cheque to the Plaintiffs at their business address which was subsequently dishonoured.

7. The Defendant is not a person under disability.

Date 18th June 1977. SIGN HERE *Bullen Leake and Co. Solicitors for the* Plaintiff.

NOTE.—If, owing to any misstatement made in the foregoing answers the Action is wrongly entered in this Court the Court may transfer the Action or order it to be struck out, and may order the Plaintiff to pay the Defendant's costs.

WHAT THE CLAIM IS FOR £450 due on unpaid cheque	AMOUNT CLAIMED.................	£450
	FEE ON ENTERING PLAINT	
	SOLICITOR'S COSTS	
	TOTAL	

[*Strike out if inappropriate* – I apply for this action, if defended, to be referred to arbitration.] (See back)

Solicitor's Name and Address for service
Bullen, Leake and Co.
119 Monmouth St., London WC2

The certificate overleaf should be completed if service by post is required

REQUEST FOR POSTAL SERVICE

6.—*Certificate for Postal Service*
   of Ordinary and Default Summons
Order 8, Rule 8 (2) 14 (2)

BETWEEN Easy Rider Garages (a firm) .... *Plaintiff,*

AND .James. Smith .... *Defendant.*

(1) Here insert   I hereby request that the defendant[1]   James Smith
full names where
known, other-   be served with the summons in this action by post and I hereby certify that:—
wise surname(s)
and initial(s).

(a) I have reason to believe that the summons, if sent to the said defendant(s) at the address(es) stated in the praecipe, will come to his (their) knowledge within 12 days after the day on which the summons would be delivered in the ordinary course of post.

(2) Or, where   *(b)* I [2] [The plaintiff] understand(s) that if judgment is obtained as a result of postal service and is afterwards
the certificate   set aside on the ground that the service did not give the said defendant(s) adequate notice of the proceedings,
is given by a   I [2] [the plaintiff] may be ordered to pay the costs of setting aside the judgement.
solicitor

Dated this 18th day of   June   , 1977

Bullen, Leake and Co.

Plaintiff (or Plaintiff's Solicitor)

DEFAULT SUMMONS

22. *Default Summons*
Order 6. Rule 3 (2) (b).

Address all communications for the Court to:—
"The Registrar, County Court.
St. Martin's Lane, London WC2
Westminster County Court

PLAINT No. 77. 01653

Which must be mentioned in any
letter to the Court about this case.

EASYRIDER GARAGES
a firm
25 Garrick Mews,
London WC2
Plaintiff

SEAL

James Smith
26 Doughty Street
London WC1
Defendant

TO THE DEFENDANT

THE PLAINTIFF CLAIMS	£	p
DEBT (Particulars are attached)	450	--
COSTS { Court Fee...	5	–
Solicitor's Charge	8	–
TOTAL	463	--

Judgment may be obtained against you and enforced without further notice unless within 14 days of the service of this summons, inclusive of the day of service, you:

Pay the total amount of the claim and costs into Court

or

Send to the Court an Admission, Defence or Counterclaim for which the attached form should be used.

Issued 20th June 1977

C. J. Street
Registrar.

To the Defendant. ——————————————————— **IMPORTANT—FOR INSTRUCTIONS TURN OVER**

Form 22.

INSTRUCTIONS

(1) If you admit the claim or any part of it, pay the amount admitted and costs into Court within 14 days after service of this summons inclusive of the day of service. If you do this and payment satisfies the claim, you will not be liable for any further costs unless the Court otherwise orders. If you require longer time for payment complete the form of ADMISSION attached.

(2) If you dispute the claim or any part of it, complete the form of DEFENCE attached.

(3) If you have any claim against the plaintiff, complete the form of COUNTERCLAIM attached.

(4) After completing and signing the form, send it by pre-paid post to reach the Court not later than 14 days after service of this summons, inclusive of the day of service. Unless you make an admission and proposal for payment which is accepted, you will receive notice from the Court of a day on which you will have an opportunity of being heard on your proposal for payment, defence or counterclaim.

(5) Delay in payment or in returning the form may add to the costs.

(6) If you have paid the amount of the claim since the date of issue of the summons, you should inform the Court on the attached form, stating the date of payment, and pay the costs into Court within the 14 days mentioned in the foregoing Instructions.

(7) You can obtain help in completing the form at any County Court Office or Citizens' Advice Bureau.

(8) If the Court issuing this summons is not the Court for the district in which you reside or carry on business, you may write to the Registrar of the issuing Court asking for the action to be transferred to the Court for your district. In deciding whether to order the transfer, the Court will take into account the question whether the claim is disputed. Transfer of the action may add to the costs which you may have to pay if you lose.

The plaintiff has asked for these proceedings, if defended to be referred to arbitration. If you complete the Form of Defence or Counterclaim you should state whether or not you agree.

METHOD OF PAYMENT

1. *By calling at the Court Office.* Payment may be made in cash or by BANKER'S DRAFT, GIRO DRAFT or by CHEQUE SUPPORTED BY A CHEQUE CARD SUBJECT TO THE CURRENT CONDITIONS FOR ITS USE. Drafts and Cheques must be made payable to HER MAJESTY'S PAYMASTER GENERAL and crossed.

2. *By Post.* Remittances to the court by post must be by POSTAL ORDER, BANKER'S DRAFT or GIRO DRAFT only, made payable to HER MAJESTY'S PAYMASTER GENERAL and crossed. Cheques, giro cheques and stamps are not accepted. Payment cannot be received by bank or giro credit transfer.

This form should be enclosed and postage must be prepaid. A stamped addressed envelope must be enclosed to enable this form, with a receipt, to be returned to you.

THE COURT { St. Martin's Lane
OFFICE at { London WC2
is open from 10 a.m. till 4 p.m.
on Mondays to Fridays only.

31.
Order 8, Rules 9(1) & (2)

No. of Plaint

The summons of which this is a true copy, was served by me

(a) on the   day of   19

at the *residence*
place of business of the defendant

as stated in the summons, or at

by delivering the summons to the said defendant personally or to said defendant the same day (1)

apparently not less than 16 years old, who promised to give the same to the

(1) *or as the case may be*

or (b) by posting the same to the said defendant

on the   day of   19

at the address stated in the summons in accordance with the certificate of the plaintiff or his solicitor.
or (c) [by posting the same to the said defendant]
[or by inserting the same, enclosed in an envelope addressed to the said defendant in the letter box] at the address stated in the summons because (2)

(2) *State reasons for thinking summons would reach defendant in sufficient time.*

Bailiff/Officer of the
County Court

or The summons of which this is a true copy has not been served for the following reasons:—

Bailiff/Officer of the
County Court

PARTICULARS OF CLAIM

In the Westminster County Court   Plaint No. _____

Between

Easyrider Garages

(a firm)   **Plaintiffs**

and

James Smith   **Defendant**

Particulars of Claim

---

1. The Plaintiffs are the payees of a cheque for £450 dated the 21st day of August 1976 and drawn by the Defendant on the Midland Bank Limited, Mile End Road, London E9.
2. On the 22nd day of August 1976 the Plaintiffs duly presented the said cheque for payment but it was dishonoured.
3. On the 25th day of August 1976 the Plaintiffs sent notice of the aforesaid dishonour to the Defendant but he has not paid the said cheque.

       And the Plaintiffs claim the sum of £450 and costs.

Dated this 18th day of June 1977

       Bullen Leake & Co., 119 Monmouth Street,
       London WC2. Solicitors to the
       Plaintiffs who will accept service
       of all proceedings on behalf of the
       Plaintiffs at such address.

To the Registrar of the Court

and to the Defendant

FORM OF DEFENCE

18A.—*Form of Admission, Defence and
   Counterclaim to accompany Forms 18, 19 and 22*
Order 6, Rule 3(2) (c)

WESTMINSTER County Court.

No. of Plaint. . . . . 77. 01653 . . . .

Easyrider Garages (a firm) . . . . v . . . . James Smith . . . .

DEFENCE

1. Do you dispute the plaintiff's claim?   YES/NO

2. If so, what are your reasons for disputing the plaintiff's claim?

> I bought a Ford Capri
> 1967 from Mr. Fagin of
> Easyrider Garages for £450 but it
> broke down on the way home so I stopped
> the cheque. It cost me £100 to put it right
> and I can produce bills to prove it.

COUNTERCLAIM

1. Do you wish to make a claim against the plaintiff?   YES/NO

2. If so, for how much?   £. 100

3. What is the nature of the claim?

> As above

NOTE: If your claim against the plaintiff is bigger than his claim against you, you may have to pay a fee before it can be dealt
with. You can find out whether a fee is payable by inquiring at any County Court Office.

If you dispute the plaintiff's claim or wish to make a claim against him do you want the proceedings referred to
arbitration?   YES/NO

SIGN HERE:. . . *James Smith* . . . .

DATE. . . . . 1 . . . . day of. . . . July .19 77.

Where should notices
about this case be
sent to you   { . . . . . Clerkenwell Road Law Centre,
                       . . . . 26 Farringdon Road, EC1 . . . .

If you have any difficulty in filling in this form, ask for help at your local Citizen's Advice Bureau or at any County Court Office.
Immediately after you have filled in this form, send it by post or take it to the Court Office as stated in the summons.

FORM OF ADMISSION

18A.—*Form of Admission, Defence and*
Counterclaim to accompany Forms 18, 19 and 22
Order 6, Rule 3(2) (c)

WESTMINSTER County Court.

No. of Plaint. 77. 01653

Easyrider Garages (a firm) . . . . v . . . . James Smith . . . .

ADMISSION

If you do not admit this claim in full or in part or if you wish to make a claim against the plaintiff please complete the form overleaf.

If you have any difficulty in filling in this form, ask for help at your local Citizen's Advice Bureau or at any County Court office. Immediately after you have filled in this form, send it by post or take it to the Court office as stated on the summons.

1. Do you admit the plaintiff's claim in full? — **YES**/NO
2. Do you admit part of the plaintiff's claim? — YES/**NO**
   If so, how much do you admit? — . . . . £ 350 . . . . . .
   What are your reasons for disputing the balance?

   See over-page

   Continue overleaf
   if necessary

3. Do you want time to pay the amount admitted? — YES/**NO**
4. If you want time to pay, answer these questions:—
   PAYS AND MEANS
   (a) What is your occupation? . . . . . . *Student Teacher* . . . . .
   (b) What is your basic pay before deductions? . . . . £ *40* . . . per week/~~month~~
   (c) What overtime, bonuses, fees, allowances or commission
       do you receive? . . . . £ *None* . . . .
   (d) What deductions are normally made from your pay? . . . . £ *2.50* . . . .per week/~~month~~
   (e) What is your usual take-home pay? . . . . £ *37.50* . .per week/~~month~~
   (f) Do you receive a pension or any other income? — ~~YES~~/NO
       Please give details:—

   (g) What contributions, if any, are made by any member of your household? — *None*
   LIABILITIES
   (a) What persons, if any are financially dependent on you? Please give details — *Wife*
       including the ages of any dependent children — *2 Children, 6 and 4*

   (b) What rent or mortgage instalments do you have to pay? — £ . . . *10* . . .per week/~~month~~
   (c) What rates, if any, do you have to pay? — £ . . . *2* . . . .per week/~~month~~
   (d) Do you have to pay under any Court Orders? Please give details:—
       No

   (e) What other regular payments do you have to make?
   (f) Have you any other liabilities which you would like the Court to take into account?
       Please give details:—
       I owe £60 to London Electricity Board
       and £54 to the Gas Board

WHAT OFFER OF PAYMENT DO YOU MAKE?

Payment on the   day of   19

OR   by instalments of   £ . . . *4* . . . . . .per month

SIGN HERE . . . . . . *James Smith* . . . . DATE . . . . *1* . . . .day of . . *July* 19 7 7

Where should notices
about this case be
sent to you   {   . . . . *Clerkenwell Road Law Centre* . . . .
                  . . . . *26 Farringdon Road EC1* . . . .

CHAPTER TWO

PLEADINGS

In both High Court and county court actions, the parties are required to set out in writing the factual bases of their respective cases in formal pleadings. The principal purposes of such pleadings are:

(*a*) to clarify the matters in dispute between the parties so that the court can readily understand what are the real issues in the case;

(*b*) to enable both sides to know in advance the allegations being made against them so that they will not be taken by surprise at the trial.

The basic pleadings which the rules require to be exchanged are:

(1) A *statement of claim* by the plaintiff setting out the basis of his claim. In the High Court, the rules require that this document should be served within 14 days of the defendant entering an appearance, although in practice the time is frequently extended by agreement between the parties. In the county court, the pleading is called the *particulars of claim*. The rules require that it be delivered to the court office with the praecipe and served with the summons.

(2) A *defence* in which the defendant is required to state in terms the grounds upon which he resists the plaintiff's claim. In the High Court, the defence should be served within 14 days of service of the statement of claim; in the county court, the rules require a defence to be filed at the court within 14 days of service of the summons.

The drafting of pleadings is one of the most important functions of common law counsel. Although under the modern system the aim is for pleadings to be simple and clear, there is still a considerable art in drafting and the discussion below can only be a very rough guide.

DRAFTING THE STATEMENT OF CLAIM

The *statement* (or *particulars*) *of claim* should set out every fact which must be proved by the evidence at the trial if the plaintiff is to succeed in his claim. Before we consider the rules to be applied, it would be helpful to look at three very simple examples:

Contract
　　You are instructed by Albert and Eliza Doolittle who run a business known as Covent Garden Florists. On 1 September 1975 they bought a second-hand Ford lorry from Easyrider Garages Ltd. of Ealing for £3000. Three weeks later the lorry seized up on the motorway. Repairs to make it serviceable cost £800. Whilst it was under repair Albert was forced to hire another lorry for £500.

In the High Court of Justice   1976—C—No. 1234

Queen's Bench Division

(Writ issued the 10th day of October 1976)
        Between:

Covent Garden Florists
(a firm)   Plaintiffs
and
Easyrider Garages Limited   Defendants

Statement of Claim

1. By an agreement in writing dated the 1st day of September 1975 the Defendants sold and delivered to the Plaintiffs a Ford motor lorry registration number MAA 831 L for the sum of £3,000.
2. The following were inter alia implied terms of the said contract of sale:
   (a) that the said lorry should be of merchantable quality;
   (b) that the said lorry should be fit for its purpose.
3. In breach of the aforesaid terms the said lorry was not of merchantable quality nor fit for purpose at the date of delivery in that there was a serious oil leak from the sump and the cylinders were glazed and worn so that the engine seized up after 500 miles.
4. By reason of the matters aforesaid the plaintiff has incurred loss and expense and suffered damage.

Particulars of Loss and Expense

Cost of repairs	£800
Hire of alternative transport from 21st September to 30th November 1976	£500

And the Plaintiffs claim damages

(Signature)

Served, etc.

It can be seen in this very simple example that most statements of claim in contract will set out:

1. the date of the contract, whether it was written or oral and the gist of the contract (e.g. employment, sale of goods, carriage, etc.);
2. any term which it is alleged has been broken by the defendants;
3. the relevant breach;
4. an allegation of damage together with detailed particulars.

Tort

On 21 August 1975 John Smith, an accountant is driving out of Chancery Lane when he collides with a lorry being driven west along Holborn. The accident was seen by a number of eyewitnesses who confirm the lights in Holborn were red. The driver apologised profusely to John and said "I can't think why I missed the lights. I must have been asleep". John sustained rather serious fractures of the femur of his left leg. He was detained in hospital for six weeks and was unable to go back to work for four months. During the period off work he received £300 national insurance payments.

In the High Court of Justice   1976—S—No. 2067

Queen's Bench Division

(Writ issued the 2nd day of May 1976)
    Between:

John Smith   Plaintiff
and
Mammoth Law Book Publishing
Company Limited   Defendants

Statement of Claim

1. On the 21st day of August 1975 at the junction of Chancery Lane and High Holborn, London WC1 a collision occurred between a Sunbeam Alpine sports car owned and driven by the Plaintiff and a Ford lorry owned by the Defendants and driven by their servant one Smee.
2. The said collision was caused by the negligent driving and/or management of the said lorry by the Defendants' said servant.

Particulars of Negligence

The Defendants' said servant:

(a) Failed to stop at the traffic lights in Holborn which were red against him.
(b) Drove across Chancery Lane when by reason of traffic emerging therefrom it was unsafe so to do.
(c) Failed to notice and/or heed the presence and proximity of the Plaintiff's motor car emerging from Chancery Lane.

On the 3rd day of October 1975 the said Smee was convicted at the Bow Street Magistrates' Court of driving the said lorry on the occasion above referred to without due care and attention contrary to section 3 of the Road Traffic Act 1972. The said conviction is pleaded as relevant to the issue of the negligence of the Defendants' servant.

3. By reason of the Defendants' said negligence the Plaintiff sustained personal injuries and has been put to loss and expense.

Particulars of Injuries

The Plaintiff who is 28 years of age sustained a crack fracture of the left femur. He was detained in hospital for 3 weeks and immobilised in plaster for 6 weeks. Thereafter he underwent physiotherapy. He was off work for 4 months. The Plaintiff's left leg has been shortened by ¼" and he has a permanent limp. He experiences aching and discomfort in the ankle.

Particulars of Loss and Expense

Cost of repairs to motor car		£206 20 p
Loss of earnings to 1st January 1976	£950	
Less ½ National Insurance Benefits received	£150	£800

And the Plaintiff claims damages

(Signature)

Served, etc.

It will be noted that in this typical personal injury statement of claim, the structure of the pleading is very simple:

(1) A neutral statement that a collision has occurred setting out the date and place and persons involved.

(2) An allegation of negligence by the defendants followed by detailed particulars of what it is alleged they have done wrong. Where one intends to rely at the trial on a conviction as evidence in the case under Section 12 of the Civil Evidence Act 1969 it must be pleaded in the statement or particulars of claim.

(3) An allegation of damage caused by that negligence resulting in
   (a) personal injuries, set out as particulars, showing the plaintiff's age, the injury sustained, the treatment he received and finally the extent of disability at the date of the pleading.
   (b) Special damage—the particulars are set out in note form.

(4) A prayer for damages. In the High Court one does not need to claim interest or costs specially in the pleading.

<u>Possession</u>

Mr. Peter Grimes has let two rooms on the first floor of his house at 23 Jubilee Road, Kennington to a student called Jonah Stevenson. Peter lives on the premises so Jonah is not a protected tenant under the Rent Acts. Peter now wants to sell the house and has given Jonah notice to quit. Jonah has promised to go but he still has not left.

In the Lambeth County Court	Plaint No. 7600365

Between:

Peter Grimes   Plaintiff

and

Jonah Stevenson   Defendant

Particulars of Claim

1. The Plaintiff is the freehold owner of certain premises known as 23 Jubilee Road, Kennington, London SE1 and resides therein.

2. On or about the 1st day of October 1974 the Plaintiff let two rooms on the 1st floor of the said premises to the Defendant as a weekly tenant at a rent of £6 per week.

3. By notice in writing served the 7th day of January 1976 the Plaintiff required the Defendant to quit the said premises on the 7th day of February 1976 (or at the end of the period of his tenancy which should expire next after 4 weeks from the date of service of the said notice).

4. Since the expiry of the said notice, the Defendant has remained in possession of the said rooms as a trespasser therein.

5. The net annual value for rating of the premises of which the said rooms form part is £250.

And the Plaintiff claims:
   1. Possession of the said premises.
   2. Mesne profits at the rate of £6 per week from the 7th day of January 1976 to judgment.
   3. Costs.

(Signature)

Dated etc.

In this basic example of a claim by a landlord for possession it can be seen that the pleading is built up out of the following allegations:

(1) The plaintiff's status—i.e. his ownership of the house and the fact that he is a resident landlord so the tenant is not protected by the Rent Acts.

(2) The letting—date, period and rent.
(3) The termination of the letting.
(4) The defendant is still in occupation.
(5) The value of the premises—this is necessary to establish the jurisdiction of the county court.

From these illustrations it is hoped that the reader will have gathered the basic idea behind pleadings. The draft must set out in numbered paragraphs the matters of fact which have to be proved before the plaintiff can ask the court for the relief claimed in his prayer. Nothing more than those statements of fact should be pleaded so, for example, in the possession case, it is not relevant that Peter wants to sell the house or that Jonah had promised to leave. Again the plaintiff must not plead the evidence by which he intends to prove the facts alleged so, in the road accident case, the reports of eyewitnesses and the admissions of the defendants' driver although they will be crucial evidence at the trial are not pleaded. It should, however, be noted that it is not generally enough to make a bare allegation of misconduct or damage against the defendant. The defendant is entitled to know precisely the case he has to answer: therefore, wherever the pleading contains an allegation of negligence, breach of duty, fraud, breach of trust, justification of a libel, personal injuries or special damage, the draftsman must set out detailed particulars of the allegation.

In addition to these rules, a certain style has developed which has become standard practice. The most important stylistic rules are:

(1) Plead chronologically.
(2) The parties are always referred to as "the Plaintiff" or "the Defendant".
(3) Figures and sums must be set out in arabic numerals.
(4) Dates are usually set out as "the ———— day of (month), 197–".

The important and overriding stylistic principle is of course that the pleading should be simple.

DRAFTING THE DEFENCE

The defence should set out clearly the answers made by the defendant to every material allegation in the statement of claim. It is sensible to begin by considering each paragraph of the statement of claim. The defendant may then take one of three possible steps in respect to each allegation:

(1) He may *admit* the allegation, i.e. he may concede that the particular point is not in dispute. This relieves the plaintiff from the necessity of producing any evidence to prove the particular point at the trial.
(2) He may *deny* the allegation. This not only means the plaintiff will be required to prove the allegation at the hearing but puts him on notice that the defendant intends to put forward a contrary case. The defendant must go on to set out the nature of that case; it is not sufficient for him merely to deny the allegation without stating what he says the true position is.
(3) He may require the other side to prove an allegation without specifically denying it; this is effected by employing the phrase "the Defendant does not admit...." This formula is used to deal with matters which are essential elements in the plaintiff's case but upon

which the defendant has insufficient information to make any affirmative response.

We set out below the form of defence which might be anticipated in the road traffic case discussed above; notice that the neutral facts of the collision are *admitted*, the allegation of negligence is *denied* (and the defendants' contrary case is set out and *particularised*), while the allegations of injury and loss are *not admitted* so that the plaintiff will have to prove these matters strictly.

In the High Court of Justice　　　　　　　　　　1976—S—No. 2067

Queen's Bench Division

Between:

John Smith　　　　　　Plaintiff

and

Mammoth Law Book Publishing
Company Limited　　　　　Defendants

Defence

1. Paragraph 1 of the Statement of Claim is admitted.
2. Save that it is admitted that the Defendants' said servant Smee was convicted as alleged in paragraph 2, it is denied that the Defendants their servants or agents were negligent as alleged therein or at all.
3. The said collision was caused wholly by or contributed to by the Plaintiff.

Particulars of Negligence

The Plaintiff:

　(a) Emerged from Chancery Lane into Holborn when the traffic signal was showing amber against him.
　(b) Failed to look right before entering Holborn and/or notice the presence and proximity of the Defendants' vehicle in Holborn.
　(c) Drove at too fast a speed.

4. It is not admitted that the Plaintiff sustained injuries or was put to loss as alleged in paragraph 3 of the Statement of Claim or at all.
5. Save as is herebefore expressly admitted, the Defendants deny each and every allegation contained in the Statement of Claim as if the same were here set out and specifically traversed.

(Signature of Counsel)

Served, etc.

The reader will notice that paragraph 5 contains a "blanket" denial of the allegations in the Statement of Claim—strictly in a good pleading this should not be necessary since every point should have been covered. However the formula is commonly used since it protects the draftsman to a certain extent if he has omitted to plead to some point.[1] In complex cases involving many points of complaint (e.g. a building dispute) the defendant may annex to his pleadings a schedule[2] setting out in columns the items involved and his complaints and then require the plaintiff to complete a third column showing his answer to the complaints. Generally a fourth column is left blank for the use of the trial judge.

---

[1] Note R.S.C. Ord. 18, r. 13(1): "any allegation of fact made by a party in his pleading is deemed to be admitted by the opposite party unless it is traversed by that party in his pleading". Note also r. 13(3) prohibits the use of a general traverse without more.
[2] Called a Scott Schedule.

COUNTERCLAIM

It very often happens that the defendant not only wishes to defend the claim made by the plaintiff but also desires to bring a cross-action against him. Thus, for example, in our road traffic case, the defendants would almost certainly wish to bring a claim against the plaintiff for the cost of repairs to their lorry. It would in theory be possible for them to bring a completely separate action and apply for the cases to be heard together but in practice, in order to save expense and time, the defendant raises his cross-action by adding a *counterclaim* to his defence as follows:

Counterclaim

6. The Defendants repeat paragraphs 1–3 of the Defence.
7. By reason of the Plaintiff's negligence as aforesaid the Defendants have incurred loss and expense.

Particulars

Cost of repairs to lorry	£506. 74 p
Hire of alternative vehicle	
for 2 weeks	£100. 00
Total	£606. 74 p

And the Defendants counterclaim
against the Plaintiff damages.

(Signature)

Served, etc.   _____

Where the counterclaim arises directly out of the facts constituting the claim it may also be a *defence* to the claim: for example, if P sues for the price of goods sold and delivered, D may be able to set up a counterclaim for damages for breach of condition as to merchantable quality which will reduce or extinguish P's claim. Such a counterclaim is termed a *set-off*. Where a counterclaim may amount to a defence and so be set-off, it is important to plead it as such since this has an important effect on the costs. The basic rule is that if P wins his claim and D wins the counterclaim each is awarded costs, so, for example, P gets £600 costs on the claim and D gets £300 on the counterclaim—net result D pays £300 costs. If however the counterclaim also acts as a set-off and so is a *defence* to the action, P's claim will be *dismissed* and P will be ordered to pay *all* D's costs. When the defendant wishes to make it clear that his counterclaim is to be treated as a set-off he will normally add a paragraph as follows at the conclusion of the defence and before the counterclaim:

"Further or in the alternative, the Defendant claims to set-off against the Plaintiff's claim herein such damages as he may be awarded upon his counterclaim as set out hereafter extinction or diminution thereof."

REPLY AND DEFENCE TO COUNTERCLAIM

Where a counterclaim is served on the plaintiff he must within 14 days serve a defence to the counterclaim (unless the action is proceeding in the county court and the counterclaim is in effect nothing more than the converse case to the plaintiff's claim, e.g. an allegation of contributory negligence and damage).

Where the defence raises an issue which is a good answer to the plaintiff's claim as it stands so that the plaintiff cannot succeed unless he raises another matter in answer it will be necessary for him to file a *reply*.

Example 1—D provides a reference for P which is highly damaging. P issues a writ for defamation and serves a statement of claim setting out the circumstances of the case and the libel. D serves a defence claiming privilege—on the grounds he was furnishing a reference. In order to answer the claim of privilege P will have to serve a reply alleging malice.

Example 2—D's salesman, A, regularly calls on P and takes orders from him. Unbeknown to P, A leaves D's employ and sets up in business on his own account. P places an order with A and pays him but the goods are not delivered. P sues D for non-delivery; D's defence shows that D was not employed at the date of the order and had no authority to contract on D's behalf. In order to succeed, P will have to file a reply alleging that D held out A as having authority to act as their agent.

We set out below the form of pleading which would be used in the second example:

Reply

1. The Plaintiffs do not admit the matters set out in paragraph 2 of the Defence herein and join issue with the Defendants upon their Defence.
2. If (which is not admitted) the said Antrobus was not employed by the Defendants as their agent at the time of the agreement referred to in paragraph 1 of the Statement of Claim herein, the Plaintiffs say that the Defendants should be estopped from denying the said agency by reason of the fact that they had prior to the said agreement frequently held out the said Antrobus to be their agent and had not at the time of the said agreement notified the Plaintiffs that they had withdrawn from the said Antrobus his authority to act as their agent so that the Plaintiffs were induced to contract with him in the belief that he was acting for the Defendants.

AMENDMENT OF WRIT AND PLEADINGS

At almost any stage in an action one side or other may realise that they need to alter the writ or the pleadings so as to enable them to deal with a new point which has emerged or to correct a mistake. The most common examples of amendment are:

(1) where the plaintiff wishes to add another person as defendant; for instance, in the example of the reply discussed above the plaintiff would certainly wish to add the agent as a second defendant (if he is worth suing) and plead breach of warranty of authority by him;
(2) where the plaintiff wishes to plead his case in an alternative manner, e.g. if he wishes to add an allegation of breach of statutory duty to a claim based on negligence;
(3) where either side wish to alter or add to detailed statements in the pleadings, e.g. the calculations of special damage.

The basic rule is that the party wishing to amend requires leave so to do and must issue a summons returnable before a master[1] for such leave and annex to the summons a copy of the proposed amended pleading. Leave will normally

---

[1] See R.S.C. Ord. 20. Application can be made to the registrar in the county court or reserved to the trial judge after amended pleadings have been informally exchanged: C.C.R. Ord. 15, rr. 3–4.

be granted to make the proposed amendment on terms that the party wishing to amend pays the costs of and occasioned by the amendment. An amendment will only be refused if the other side can show prejudice, e.g. it raises an issue upon which they can no longer hope to obtain evidence although such evidence would have been available if the issue had been pleaded at the correct time. The basic principle was expressed thus by Brett M.R.:

> "however negligent or careless may have been the first omission, and, however late the proposed amendment, the amendment should be allowed if it can be made without injustice to the other side. There is no injustice if the other side can be compensated by costs".[1]

Where an amendment is made it takes effect *not* from the date of amendment but from the date of the original document. This has created a problem where it is proposed to make an amendment by, for example, adding a party or a new cause of action *after* the limitation period has expired.

> *Example*—P sues D on the basis of conversion of his chattels in September 1969. A writ is issued in 1975. D serves a defence in 1976 blaming T. In October 1976 D serves an amended writ adding T as a second defendant. T applies to set the amended writ aside on the basis that the amendment would enable P to proceed notwithstanding the expiry of the limitation period.

This problem can sometimes be solved by reliance on the provisions of section 26 of the Limitation Act 1939 (fraud, concealment or mistake) or, in personal injury cases, upon the court's power to override the limitation period under the 1975 Act.[2] Neither of these solutions will avail in the present case. One therefore has to look at the specific provisions of R.S.C. Order 20 rule 5[3]:

> (1) Subject to Order 15, rules 6, 7 and 8 and the following provisions of this rule, the court may at any stage of the proceedings allow the plaintiff to amend his writ, or any party to amend his pleading, on such terms as to costs or otherwise as may be just and in such manner (if any) as it may direct.
>
> (2) Where an application to the Court for leave to make the amendment mentioned in paragraph (3), (4) or (5) is made after any relevant period of limitation current at the date of issue of the writ has expired, the Court may nevertheless grant such leave in the circumstances mentioned in that paragraph if it thinks it just to do so.
>
> (3) An amendment to correct the name of a party may be allowed under paragraph (2) notwithstanding that it is alleged that the effect of the amendment will be to substitute a new party if the Court is satisfied that the mistake sought to be corrected was a genuine mistake and was not misleading or such as to cause any reasonable doubt as to the identity of the person intending to sue or, as the case may be, intended to be sued.
>
> (4) An amendment to alter the capacity in which a party sues (whether as plaintiff or as defendant by counterclaim) may be allowed under paragraph (2) if the capacity in which, if the amendment is made, the party will sue is one in which at the date of issue of the writ on the making of the counterclaim, as the case may be, he might have sued.
>
> (5) An amendment may be allowed under paragraph (2) notwithstanding that the effect of the amendment will be to add or substitute a new cause of action if the new cause of action arises out of the same facts or substantially the same facts as a cause of action in respect of which relief has already been claimed in the action by the party applying for leave to make the amendment.

---

[1] *Clarapede & Co.* v. *Commercial Union Association* [1883] 32 W.R. 262 and p. 263.
[2] See *ante* pp. 48 *et seq.*
[3] The county court follows the High Court practice, C.C.R. Ord. 15, r. 3(2).

It is clear from the terms of the above order that there are three cases where an amendment will be allowed notwithstanding its effect is to defeat a defence under the Limitation Act, namely

(i) where the amendment is to alter the name of a party where the mistake misled nobody,

(ii) where the amendment is only so as to alter the capacity in which a party sues or is sued, and

(iii) where the amendment adds a new cause of action arising out of the same facts as the original claim (e.g. claim framed in negligence; amendment to add claim of breach of statutory duty).

The question however remains whether this list is merely intended to set out *examples* of where an amendment will be permitted after the expiry of the limitation period or whether these are the *only* instances where such an amendment would be permitted. The prevailing view expressed by Lord Widgery C.J.,[1] and by Lord Edmund Davies and Lord Cross[2] is that these are now the only circumstances where an amendment will be allowed to defeat vested rights under the Statute of Limitations. The opposite view expressed by Lord Denning M.R. is that the court has an overriding discretion under Order 20 rule 5(1) to permit *any* amendment notwithstanding the expiry of the limitation period if it would be just to do so.[3] In the problem we discussed above the amendment would only be permitted if Lord Denning's interpretation of the rule is correct.

Although as stated above a party who desires to amend the writ or pleadings is usually required to issue a summons for leave to amend,[4] the rules permit each party to make *one* set of amendments without obtaining leave:

(a) The *writ*[5] may be amended once at any time up to the close of pleadings by taking the original with the proposed amendments written in red to the Central Office or district registry and getting it re-sealed. The writ should be headed "Amended the—day of—197– pursuant to R.S.C. Order 20 rule 3". Once the writ has been served, however, any amendment which would have the effect of adding a party, changing the capacity in which a party sues or is sued or adding a new cause of action will require leave.

(b) The *pleadings*[6] may be amended once at any time up to the close of pleadings by merely delivering the amended pleading to the other side. The other party is automatically given the right to serve within 14 days pleading in answer thereto.

REQUEST FOR FURTHER AND BETTER PARTICULARS

It may well happen that the party upon whom a pleading has been served will feel that it gives him insufficient information to enable him to answer the case

---

[1] *Braniff* v. *Holland and Hannan and Cubitts (Southern), Ltd.* [1969] 3 All E.R. 959; [1969] 1 W.L.R. 1533.

[2] *Brickfield Properties* v. *Newton* [1971] 3 All E.R. 328; [1971] 1 W.L.R. 862.

[3] *Chatsworth Investments* v. *Cussons* [1969] 1 All E.R. 143; [1969] 1 W.L.R. 1, *Sterman* v. *Moore* [1970] 1 Q.B. 596; [1970] 1 All E.R. 581.

[4] In the county court it is not normally necessary to take out a special appointment for leave to amend, one serves the amended pleadings but the other side can apply to the judge at the trial to disallow the amendment: C.C.R. Ord. 15, r. 4.

[5] R.S.C. Ord. 20, r 1.

[6] R.S.C. Ord. 20, r. 3.

or prepare his own case for trial. Consider, for example, the statement of claim set out below:

Statement of Claim

1. On the 1st day of August 1975 the Defendants agreed to sell and deliver a combine harvester to the Plaintiffs for £2,500
2. It was a term of the said contract that the said harvester should be of excellent quality.
3. In breach of this term the harvester when delivered was defective and is not worth £2,500 so that the Plaintiffs have suffered loss.

And the Plaintiffs claim damages.

Clearly the defendant will want a great deal more information than is set out in this pleading. He will therefore send a letter to the plaintiff's solicitors asking for them to provide further and better particulars[1] of the statement of claim. He will enclose with his letter a request set out in a formal document. This is done because the request and answer become part of the pleadings at the trial. We set out below a request for particulars which would be appropriate in the case above:

In the High Court of Justice   1975—A—No. 206

Queen's Bench Division

Between:

Albert Higgins and Co.
(a firm)   Plaintiffs

and
Mammoth Motor Sales Limited.

                                                         Defendants

Request for Further and Better
Particulars of the Statement
of Claim.

Under Paragraph 1

Of "agreed to sell" state whether the alleged agreement was oral or in writing; if oral, state the date, time and place thereof, between whom made and the words alleged to have constituted the agreement; if in writing, identify every relevant document.

Under Paragraph 2

Of "a term" state whether the alleged term was express or implied and if implied, state all matters which will be relied upon at the trial hereof in support of the Plaintiffs' contention that the said term should be implied into the alleged agreement.

Under Paragraph 3

Of "defective" state each and every item which is alleged to have been defective and the nature of the alleged defect.
Of "loss" state precisely what loss it is alleged the Plaintiffs' have sustained.
(Signature)
Served, etc.

---

[1] He must also serve a defence in outline since it is not normally a sufficient ground for delaying the defence that the defendant has sought further and better particulars of the statement of claim.

Usually the other side will answer such a request without any formal order but if the request is refused or not sufficiently answered the party seeking particulars can apply by a summons to the master for an order that the other party do give the particulars sought within so many days.[1] It should however be pointed out that the scope of particulars is limited: particulars may not be sought in order to discover the evidence which the other side will call at the trial. Indeed since each draftsman is under an obligation to his client to leave as much ground open for manoeuvre at the trial as possible, the pleadings still tell one little more than the very basic issues in dispute. The practice has been well described in the Justice Report "Going to Law":[2]

> "these issues will still resemble an abstract diagram more than a detailed map of the areas of disputes since one of the principal duties which the pleaders on both sides owe their clients is to keep open for them the widest possible area for manoeuvre at the trial, while scattering as many hurdles as possible into the manoeuvring area of the opposition. Pleading therefore resembles nothing so much as naval warfare before the advent of radar, when each side made blind forays into the sea area of the other, while giving away as little as possible about the disposition of his own forces".

STRIKING OUT WRIT OR PLEADINGS

R.S.C. Order 18, rule 19 enables the defendant[3] to apply by summons to the master for an order striking out the indorsement of the writ or the statement of claim (or part thereof) on the grounds that:

(i) on the face of the pleadings it is clear there is no reasonable course of action (e.g. where a claim for defamation specifically pleaded that the words in question had been spoken by a judge in court);

(ii) the claim is scandalous, frivolous or vexatious (e.g. where the plaintiff is seeking to have re-litigated a matter already determined by the court[4]);

(iii) part of the pleading raises a point which would prejudice, embarrass or delay the fair trial of the action;

(iv) the pleading is otherwise an abuse of the process of the court.

If the application falls within the last three categories set out above, the defendant will produce affidavit evidence to support his contention.

---

[1] If the particulars are still not given, one applies for a final order from the master, i.e. that "unless the particulars are delivered by ... the Plaintiff's claim be struck out (*or* the Defendant be disbarred from defending the action)". The rules as to particulars are the same in the county court as in the High Court.

[2] Stevens 1974, para. 50.

[3] Or, in respect of a defence and counterclaim, the plaintiff. The equivalent procedure in the county court is set out at C.C.R. Ord. 13, r. 6.

[4] As in *Asher* v. *Secretary of State* [1974] Ch. 208; [1974] 2 All E.R. 156, where the Clay Cross councillors having failed in an appeal to the High Court against a surcharge by the district auditor commenced fresh proceedings seeking a declaration that the audit had been unlawful.

APPENDIX

This book contains a number of pleadings which can be used as basic precedents. The beginner will be tempted to consult the precedent books such as *Bullen and Leake and Jacobs* and *Atkins Court Forms before* drafting his pleadings. This can lead him into error because he may attempt to distort the facts of his case so as to fit one of the model precedents. The correct way to use a precedent book is to make a rough draft first and then check it against the examples in the precedent books. Used in this way such books are of invaluable assistance.

The most important thing for the student is to learn the *structure* of the basic pleadings: the more complex pleading can almost always be built up from that structure. For that reason throughout this book only the most simple pleadings have been employed: together they should be sufficient for the student to discover the essential framework.

List of precedents

1. Negligence—running down case.
2. Factory accident.
3. Occupiers Liability.
4. Fatal Accident Claim.
5. Nuisance—claim for injunction.
6. Contract—simple breach—claim for damage.
7. Contract—breach—claim for injunction.
8. Contract—misrepresentation—claim for rescission.
9. Claim for account.
10. Landlord and tenant—claim against non-protected tenant.
11. Claim against a protected tenant.
12. Claim on unpaid cheque.

---

1. *Negligence—Road Traffic*
   (1) On or about the   day of   197 at (*state vicinity*) in the County of   a collision occurred between a motor car owned and driven by the Plaintiff and a   driven by the Defendant (*or* by the Defendant's servant X).
   (2) The said collision was caused by the negligent driving and/or management of the said   by the Defendant (*or* by the Defendant's said servant) in that (*set out detailed Particulars of Negligence*).
   (3) By reason of the Defendant's said negligence the Plaintiff sustained injuries and has been put to loss and expense (*set out Particulars of Injuries detailing (a) age plus injuries (b) treatment (c) extent of disability, and the Particulars of Loss and Expense*).
       And the Plaintiff claims damages.

(See text p. 76)

2. *Factory Accident*
   (1) The Plaintiff was at all material times employed by the Defendants as (*job*) at their premises at   in the County of   to which the provisions of the Factories Act 1961 (*or* the Construction (Working Places) Regulations 1966 *or whatever*) applied
   (2) On the   day of   197 the Plaintiff whilst so employed by the Defendants at their said premises was injured when (*set out basic details of accident*).
   (3) The matters aforesaid were caused by the negligence and/ or breach of statutory duty of the Defendants, their servants or agents in that:
       (*Set out in detail particulars of negligence and particulars of every statutory provision or regulation alleged to have been broken identifying the same specifically.*)
   (4) By reason of the Defendants' said negligence and/or breach of statutory duty the Plaintiff sustained injuries and has been put to loss and expense.
       (*Set out particulars of injuries and loss and expense.*)
       And the Plaintiff claims damages.

(see text p. 14)

3. *Occupier's liability case*
   (1) The Defendants at all material times were the occupiers of premises at (*address*).
   (2) On the (*date*) the Plaintiff whilst a visitor at the said premises within the meaning of the Occupiers' Liability Act 1957 was injured when he (*state what occurred*).
   (3) The matters aforesaid were caused by the negligence and/or breach of statutory duty under the said Act by the Defendants their servants or agents in that (*set out particulars*).
   (4) By reason of the matters aforesaid the Plaintiff has sustained injuries and been put to loss and expense.
       (Set out particulars of injuries and particulars of loss and expense.)
       And the Plaintiff claims damages.

4. *Fatal accident claims*
   (1) The Plaintiff is the widow and administratrix (*or* the Plaintiffs are the executors) of the estate of A.B. deceased and brings this action on behalf of the dependants of the deceased under the Fatal Accidents Act 1976 and on behalf of the estate under the Law Reform (Miscellaneous Provisions) Act 1934. Letters of Administration (*or* Probate) were granted to the Plaintiff(s) out of the Principal Registry on (*date*).
   (2) *(Set out neutral facts of accident.)*
   (3) *(Allege negligence and/or breach of duty as appropriate and particulars.)*
   (4) By reason of the matters aforesaid the deceased sustained injuries from which he died on (*date*).
   (5) Particulars pursuant to the Fatal Accidents Act are as follows:
       (*a*) The names and dates of birth of the persons for whose benefit this action is brought are

       (*b*) The nature of the claim is that:
       The deceased was aged   at the time of his death and was earning £   per week net. The plaintiff received from him the sum of £   for housekeeping and for her own benefit. In addition the deceased discharged the rent of £   per week on the family house at (*address*) and the rates thereon which average £   per year and clothed and supported the said children.
   (6) Further, by reason of the matters aforesaid, the expectation of life of the deceased was shortened and his estate has thereby suffered loss and damage. In addition, funeral expenses have been incurred amounting to £
       And the Plaintiff claims
       (1) Under the Fatal Accidents Act, damages for the aforesaid dependants.
       (2) Under the Land Reform Act, damages for the benefit of the estate.

5. *Claim for Nuisance*
   (1) The Plaintiff is and at all material times has been the owner and occupier of a dwellinghouse and premises known as (*address*).
   (2) Since about the month of June 1976 the Defendant who is the tenant of premises adjoining the Plaintiff's garden has caused offensive and noxious smells to emanate from his premises into the Plaintiff's said garden and house by reason of pigs and goats which he has kept in his said premises. *(Where appropriate set out detailed particulars.)*
   (3) By reason of the matters aforesaid, the Plaintiff has suffered in the enjoyment of his house and garden and thereby suffered damage.
   (4) The Defendant intends, unless restrained from so doing by order of this Honourable Court, to continue the said nuisance.
       And the Plaintiff claims:
       (1) An injunction restraining the Defendant by himself, his servants or agents or otherwise howsoever from continuing or repeating the said nuisance.
       (2) Damages (*limited to £   *).

6. *Contract—breach*
   (1) On the   day of   197 (*or by a contract in writing dated or whatever*) the Defen-
       dants agreed to (*nature of obligation*) for the Plaintiff at a price of £   (*or whatever
       consideration was given*).
   (2) It was an express (implied) term of the said agreement that (*set out term*).
   (3) On (*date*), in breach of the said term the Defendants (*set out specific breach*).
   (4) By reason of the matters aforesaid the Plaintiff has suffered damage (*set out particulars*).
       And the Plaintiff claims damages and interest pursuant to statute (*or at the rate pre-
       scribed in the contract*).

7. *Contract—Claim for Injunction*
   Set out paragraphs 1–4 as above and then add:
   (5) The Defendant intends, unless restrained from so doing by this Honourable Court, to
       repeat (*or continue*) to (*detail*) in breach of his obligations under the said agreement.
       And the Plaintiff claims:
       (1) Damages
       (2) An injunction to restrain the Defendant by himself, his servants or agents or otherwise
           howsoever from (*detail precisely the conduct complained of*). (See text on p. 118, *post.*)

8. *Contract—Misrepresentation*
   (1) On the   day of   197   the Defendants by their servant or agent one
                     orally represented to the Plaintiff that (*set out gist of representation*).
   (2) The Plaintiff was induced by the said representation to purchase the said   from the
       Defendants (*or whatever*) and paid to the Defendants the sum of £   being the price
       thereof.
   (3) The said representation was false in that (*set out why it is alleged the statement was untrue*).
   (4) By reason of the matters aforesaid the Plaintiff has suffered loss and damage.
       And the Plaintiff claims:
       (1) The rescission of the said agreement, the return to him of all sums paid thereunder, an
           indemnity in the sum of £   , interest on such sum(s) pursuant to statute, and all
           proper consequential directions.
       (2) Further or alternatively, damages.

9. *Claim for an account*
Where it is not certain what sum is due from the Defendant (e.g. between partners in a business or
where a salesman is suing for commission or an author for royalties) the court will order an
account to be taken which involves the Defendant delivering a draft account upon which the
Plaintiff, having obtained discovery, can examine him. (See R.S.C. Order 43; C.C.R. Order 7,
rule 2.)
   (1) By an agreement in writing dated the   day of   197 the Plaintiff undertook to
       promote the Defendants' products at shops and other business establishments within 10
       miles of   (*or whatever*).
   (2) The following were inter alia express terms of the said agreement:
       (*a*) That the Plaintiff should be entitled to receive commission at the rate of   per cent on
           the value of all orders placed by customers introduced by him.
       (*b*) That on the 31st day of December in each year the Defendants should prepare a
           statement of account showing the value of each and every order placed by such
           customers and the amount due to the Plaintiff thereon.
   (3) In breach of the aforesaid terms the Defendants have failed to prepare such accounts for the
       year ending the 31st day of December 197 or pay to the Plaintiff the commission due
       thereon.
       And the Plaintiff claims:
       (1) That an account may be taken of all orders placed by such customers with the
           Defendants during the year ending the 31st day of December 197 .
       (2) That the Defendants may be ordered to pay to him the sum found due to him on the
           taking of such account together with interest at such rate and for such period as this
           Honourable Court may think fit.

10. *Landlord and Tenant—tenant not protected—residential landlord*
   (1) The Plaintiff is the owner and entitled to possession of the premises known as and situated at (*address*) at which the Plaintiff resides.
   (2) On or about the   day of   197 the Plaintiff let (*details of rooms occupied*) at the said premises to the Defendant on a weekly tenancy at a rent of £   per week.
   (3) By notice in writing served the (*date*) the Plaintiff required the Defendant to render up possession of the said premises on (*date*) or at the expiry of the week of his tenancy which should end next after four weeks from the service of the said notice upon him.
   (4) Since (*date of expiry*) the Defendant has remained in possession of the said rooms (*or whatever*) as a trespasser thereon.
   (5) At (*date of expiry of notice*) the Defendant was in arrears of rent to the extent of £
   (6) The net annual value for rating of the said premises is £
      And the Plaintiff claims:
      (1) Possession of the said premises.
      (2) £   arrears of rent.
      (3) Mesne profits from (*date of expiry of notice*) at the rate of £   until possession is delivered up.
      (4) Costs.

(See text on p. 78 *ante*)

11. *Landlord and Tenant—protected tenant—arrears of rent and nuisance and premises required by landlord for his own use*
   (1) The Plaintiff is the owner of and entitled to possession of the premises known as and situated at (*address*).
   (2) On or about the   day of   197 the Plaintiff let (*details or* "the whole of") the said premises to the Defendant on a weekly tenancy at a rate of £   per week.
   (3) The provisions of the Rent Act 1977 apply to the said premises.
   (4) By notice in writing served the (*date*) the Plaintiff required the Defendant to render up possession of the said premises on (*date, then complete as in paragraph 3 of precedent No. 10*).
   (5) Since the expiry of the said notice the Defendant has remained in occupation of the said premises as a statutory tenant therein.
   (6) The said rent is £   in arrear at the date hereof.
   (7) The Defendant has been guilty of conduct which is a nuisance or annoyance to adjoining occupiers in that:
   (*set out Particulars of each matter complained of*).
   (8) The said premises are reasonably required by the Plaintiff as a residence for himself.
   (9) The net annual value for rating of the said premises is £
      And the Plaintiff claims:
      (1) Possession of the said premises pursuant to Cases 1, 2 and 9 of Schedule 15 to the Rent Act 1977.
      (2) £   arrears of rent.
      (3) Mesne profits at the rate of £   from the date hereof until possession is delivered up.
      (4) Costs.

12. *Claim on an unpaid cheque* (see p. 68 and text p. 96)
   (1) The Plaintiff is the payee of a cheque for £   dated the   day of   197 drawn by the Defendant on (*bank*).
   (2) The said cheque was duly presented for payment on the   day of   197 but payment was refused on the orders of the Defendant (*or the said cheque was dishonoured*).
   (3) *In cases of dishonour*. Notice of dishonour was given to the Defendant by letter dated the   day of   but the Defendant has failed to pay the said sum.
      And the Plaintiff claims:
      (1) The sum of £
      (2) Interest at the rate of   from the date of dishonour to the date hereof.
      (3) Such further interest thereafter as this Honourable Court shall think fit.

STAGES IN QUEEN'S BENCH ACTIONS

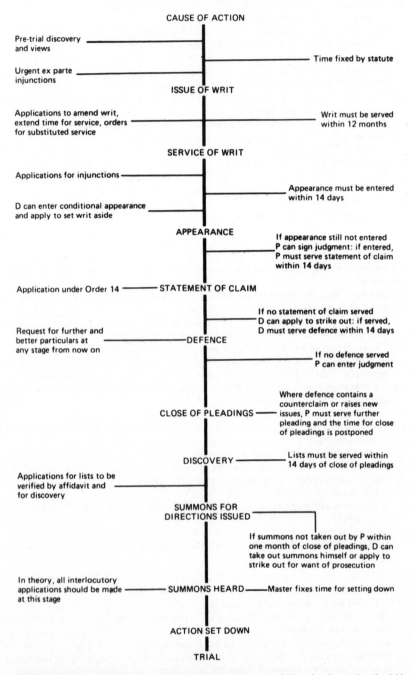

Pre-trial discovery and views

Time fixed by statute

Urgent ex parte injunctions

ISSUE OF WRIT

Applications to amend writ, extend time for service, orders for substituted service

Writ must be served within 12 months

SERVICE OF WRIT

Applications for injunctions

Appearance must be entered within 14 days

D can enter conditional appearance and apply to set writ aside

APPEARANCE

If appearance still not entered P can sign judgment: if entered, P must serve statement of claim within 14 days

Application under Order 14 ——— **STATEMENT OF CLAIM**

If no statement of claim served D can apply to strike out: if served, D must serve defence within 14 days

Request for further and better particulars at any stage from now on ——— **DEFENCE**

If no defence served P can enter judgment

Where defence contains a counterclaim or raises new issues, P must serve further pleading and the time for close of pleadings is postponed

CLOSE OF PLEADINGS ———

Lists must be served within 14 days of close of pleadings

DISCOVERY ———

Applications for lists to be verified by affidavit and for discovery

SUMMONS FOR DIRECTIONS ISSUED

If summons not taken out by P within one month of close of pleadings, D can take out summons himself or apply to strike out for want of prosecution

In theory, all interlocutory applications should be made at this stage ——— **SUMMONS HEARD** ——— Master fixes time for setting down

ACTION SET DOWN

TRIAL

Note: This basic table is intended to be a reminder of the overall stages of the action. In practice, the rigid time periods prescribed by the rules are invariably waived by the parties once an appearance has been entered. Notice that the left hand column gives only a very general idea as to when certain ancillary proceedings occur.

CHAPTER THREE

SUMMARY PROCEEDINGS, INTERIM PAYMENTS AND SECURITY

SUMMARY JUDGMENT

The minimum period which can elapse between the issue of a High Court writ and setting an action down for trial is in the order of six months. In practice the process of exchanging pleadings and lists of documents almost always takes much longer. Even after an action is set down there may well be considerable delay before it is heard. The reality of the situation is that an ordinary Queen's Bench action takes about two years to come to trial so that a successful plaintiff may well be kept out of his money for a substantial time and, although he may eventually be awarded interest on his judgment, that is often inadequate compensation particularly, for example, to a small business with cash flow problems. It is of course right that a real dispute should be adjudicated upon after careful discovery and examination of oral evidence. It would however be outrageous if an unscrupulous defendant could exploit the procedure of the court by filing a defence and thereby automatically obtaining a year or more of grace before judgment. Order 14 provides a means of preventing a defendant taking advantage of the delay inherent in the procedure before a case comes for trial by providing that, if the plaintiff can prove to the master that there can be no defence to his action, he shall have judgment forthwith. This *summary* judgment effectively denies the defendant the chance of testing the plaintiff's case by discovery and oral evidence and therefore will only be granted where the plaintiff is able to show an *unanswerable* case; it is not enough for a plaintiff to show that he has a strong case or that he is likely to succeed, he will only obtain judgment if he can show that he is bound to succeed.

PRACTICE ON ORDER 14 APPLICATION

The plaintiff may apply for summary judgment at any stage after the defendant has entered an appearance and he has served his statement of claim. If, of course, no appearance has been entered he will sign a default judgment (see p. 59). The plaintiff who is considering applying under Order 14 will probably indorse the statement of claim on the back of the writ of summons (see p. 56 *ante*). This may be a full pleading or, as frequently happens where the action is for a liquidated sum, merely a statement of the amount due by reference to an invoice (see example p. 55 *post*). Provided these two conditions are satisfied, i.e. an appearance has been entered by the defendant and the plaintiff has served his statement of claim he can apply in the Action Department at the Law Courts for a summons requiring the defendant to attend before the master and show that there is a triable defence to the plaintiff's claim.[1] The summons must be served on the defendant 10 clear days before the return date.[2] Service can be effected by post on the defendant's solicitors or, if he has no solicitors, at his usual or last known address. The plaintiff must serve with the summons an affidavit (*a*) verifying his claim (this is often done by simply deposing that the matters set out in the statement of claim are true) and (*b*) asserting that there is no defence to the claim. Although as a general rule hearsay evidence is not permitted when an application is made for judgment, there is an exception in the case of an Order 14 affidavit: the master has the power to act on statements of information in the affidavit provided the deponent sets out clearly the source of his information (see p. 94 *post*). If the defendant appears on the return day he can oppose the application either by pointing to a procedural irregularity (e.g. short service) or on the merits or, indeed, on both grounds. If in fact he does wish to defend on the merits, he should serve the plaintiff with an affidavit setting out his case 3 clear days before the return day. Formerly it was a common practice for the defendant to hand in an affidavit at the hearing which frequently forced the plaintiff to ask for an adjournment to consider the evidence; nowadays the summons served on the defendant expressly directs him to serve his affidavit 3 clear days in advance so that if he fails to do so and the plaintiff requires an adjournment, the defendant will be ordered to pay the costs incurred. The plaintiff on receipt of the defendant's affidavit may serve an affidavit in reply; this is not very frequently done because, if it simply contests the evidence of the defendant, it usually only serves to prove that there is indeed an issue to be tried between the parties so that summary judgment is inappropriate. It is however worth serving an affidavit in reply where the plaintiff has evidence (usually correspondence) which effectively destroys the defendant's case or goes so near revealing it to be a sham that the master will impose conditions on granting leave to defend (see below). If the defendant fails to appear at the hearing, the master may give judgment forthwith provided the plaintiff's own pleading is in order, the affidavit proves his case and he can prove service of the summons and the affidavit on the defendant. It should be noted that if the plaintiff thinks the defendant may not appear he must attend with an affidavit or some other evidence of service.[3] If the defendant appears at the hearing (or exceptionally writes to the court) the master will have to consider on the arguments addressed to him whether to grant judgment. Before discussing this matter it may be convenient to summarise in tabular form the practice up to the hearing.

PRELIMINARY STEPS IN ORDER 14 PROCEDURE

(1) P issues and serves writ (usually indorsed with statement of claim).
(2) D enters an appearance.
(3) P serves statement of claim (if not already indorsed on writ).

---

[1] In London, if the matter is unlikely to be contested, the summons is assigned to the "Solicitors' List" which is heard by the master between 10.30 a.m. and noon. Where a contest is likely, the summons will be assigned either to "Counsels' List" at noon (if it is not expected to take more than 20 minutes), or else a special appointment for counsel is taken out.

[2] In this case one counts intervening weekends and holidays in calculating the period but discounts the day of service and the day on the summons is due to be heard (i.e. the "return day").

[3] Under s. 26 Interpretation Act 1889 service by post is deemed to have been effected by properly addressing, prepaying and posting a letter containing the document and, unless the contrary is proved, to have been effected at the time at which the letter would be delivered in the ordinary course of post. The court today normally reckons that a first-class letter will be delivered on the day following posting.

S.3

Summons
under Order 14

Oyez Publishing
Limited
Oyez House
237 Long Lane
London SE1 4PU
a subsidiary of
The Solicitors' Law
Stationery Society
Limited

F3994 24-3-75 BW18200
✱✱✱✱

Counsel

In the High Court of Justice.

QUEEN'S BENCH DIVISION

1975.— G.—No. 2634

Master . Cowper . . . . Master in Chambers

Between

Grand Oriental Carpet Company Limited   Plaintiff

and

Ali Baba (Male) (trading as "Magic Floors Inc.")   Defendant

Let all parties concerned attend the Master in Chambers, in Room No. 97
Central Office, Royal Courts of Justice, Strand, London, on   day

†The Defendant (or if against one or some of several Defendants insert names).

the   *15th*   day of   *Janry*   1976 , at   *12.30*   o'clock in
the   *after*   noon on the hearing of an application on the part of the Plaintiff
for final judgment in this action against† **the Defendant**

‡Or as the case may be, setting out the nature of the claim.

for the‡ amount claimed in the statement of claim with interest, if any, and costs.

Take Notice that a party intending to oppose this application or to apply for a stay of execution should send to the opposite party or his solicitor, to reach him not less than three days before the date above-mentioned, a copy of any affidavit intended to be used.

Dated the   **7th**   day of   **December**   1975 .

This Summons was taken out by **Snell, Son and Hanbury**

10 **New Square, Gray's Inn, WC1**

Agent for
of
Solicitor**s** for **the Plaintiffs**

To Messrs **Street, Winfield and Salmond**

1 **Crown Office Row, Temple, EC4**

Solicitor**s** or Agent for the Defendant

```
IN THE HIGH COURT OF JUSTICE
QUEEN'S BENCH DIVISION                          1975.-G.-No. 2634


B E T W E E N:-

            Grand Oriental Carpet Company         Plaintiffs
                     Limited

                    - and -

                    Ali Baba                        Defendant
                    (Male)
            (trading as ''Magic Floors Inc.'')
```

I, Percival Archibald Fotheringay, of Pinewood House, Haslemere in the County of Surrey, Company Director make oath and say as follows:-

1. I am a Director of the Plaintiff Company and duly authorised to make this affidavit on their behalf.
2. The Defendant is, and was at the commencement of this action, justly and truly indebted to the Company in the sum of £2,500 being the price of goods sold and delivered by the Company to the Defendant.
3. The Particulars of the said claim appear by the Statement of Claim in this action.
4. I am informed by one Joseph Smith, the Manager of our sales department and verily believe to be true that the said debt was incurred and is still due and owing as aforesaid.
5. I verily believe that there is no defence to this action.

Sworn at *Fleet Street EC4*
this *7th* day of *December 1975*   *Percival Archibald Fotheringay*
Before me
Nathaniel Wilkins
A Commissioner of Oaths

(4) P issues summons at Action Department.

(5) P serves summons and affidavit of merits on D. Service can be by post. 10 clear days (weekends and holidays count) must elapse before return date.

(6) D may serve affidavit in reply. If it is not served 3 clear days (weekends and holidays do *not* count) before the hearing, P can apply for adjournment and costs.

(7) P may prepare affidavit in reply.

(8) If no affidavit is received by P from D, P should prepare an affidavit of service to put in at hearing in case D does not appear.

Note: (a) D may use Order 14 proceedings to obtain summary judgement on a *counter-claim.*

(b) P may employ Order 14 proceedings in respect of *part only* of his claim.

(c) P may obtain judgment against *one* or more defendants: if he does so and executes it will *not* prevent him pursuing his claim against the co-defendants even if they are jointly liable.

THE HEARING OF THE SUMMONS

(a) Technical objections. As indicated above the defendant may oppose summary judgment either on the grounds that the case does not fall within the scope of the order or because of a procedural irregularity committed by the plaintiff in making his application. The following cases do *not* fall within the provisions of Order 14:

(i) Claims for libel, slander, malicious prosecution on false imprisonment.

(ii) Claims framed in deceit (i.e. actions alleging fraud as a cause of action): but note that the master may order the allegation of fraud to be struck out and proceed to give judgment on some other part of the claim, e.g. innocent or negligent misrepresentation.

(iii) Actions for the specific performance or rescission of a contract for the sale of land or grant or assignment of a lease or for the forfeiture or return of a deposit in connection with such matters. But note there is an equivalent procedure in the Chancery Division under Order 86 which deals with these matters (see below).

(iv) Actions not begun by *writ*.

Where the defendant takes a technical objection on the basis of some irregularity to procedure (for example, that there has been short service or the affidavit does not verify the claim) the master may adjourn the hearing or give the plaintiff leave to amend or file a further affidavit instead of dismissing the summons.

(b) Defence on the Merits. The corollary of the rule that the plaintiff must prove that he has an unanswerable case is that the defendant in order to succeed need show no more than a "triable issue": he need do no more than in the words of the order show *"that there is an issue or question in dispute which ought to be tried"*. It is not of course sufficient for the defendant to depose to his belief that he has a good defence to the action. He must set out in his affidavit the nature of his defence. It is a very good rule in practice to exhibit to the affidavit a draft defence settled by counsel showing precisely the defendant's contentions. If the defendant shows a triable issue then the master will *either*

give unconditional leave to defend and order that the costs of the application should be in cause (i.e. paid after the trial by the unsuccessful party) *or*, if he considers the plaintiff knew all the time that there was a triable issue, dismiss the summons and order the plaintiff to pay the costs forthwith.

(c) Counterclaim and Set-off. A counterclaim is a cross-action by the defendant against the plaintiff. It need *not* be connected with the plaintiff's claim in any way.

> *Example*—P sells goods to the value of £1,000 to D. D refuses to pay on the basis of defects in some machinery purchased earlier from P which have now come to light and will cost £1,500 to repair.

In such a case the defendant will not have a defence as such to the plaintiff's claim but it would clearly be unjust that the plaintiff should obtain his money when he may owe the defendant more than the amount of the claim. Accordingly the practice in such cases is for the master to give judgment for the plaintiff on his claim with costs but order that execution of the judgment be stayed pending the trial of the counterclaim.

There will however, be cases where the counterclaim is so closely linked to the plaintiff's claim that it provides a defence to the claim.

> *Example*—P sells goods to the value of £1,000 to D. They are seriously defective on delivery and D incurs expenses of £500 in putting them right.

In such a case section 53(1) of the Sale of Goods Act 1893 provides:

> "Where there is a breach of warranty by the seller, or where the buyer elects ... to treat any breach of condition on the part of the seller as a breach of warranty, the buyer ... may ... set up against the seller the breach of warranty in diminution or extinction of the price."

Where a counterclaim arising out of the same transaction as the claim can thus be used as a defence to the action it is termed a *set-off*.[1]

Where a *set-off* is relied upon in an Order 14 application it will count as a *defence* and therefore unconditional leave to defend must be given with an order that costs should be in cause (or, if the plaintiff knew full well of the matters giving rise to the set-off, e.g. by letters of complaint, the summons will be dismissed with costs).

(d) Special rules concerning cheques. To the above rule concerning set-offs there is a most important exception in the case of bills of exchange, cheques and promissory notes. For commercial reasons our courts treat such documents as equivalent to cash so that on an action for dishonour it is not a

---

[1] See p. 82, *ante*. It must be remembered that it is important to plead a set-off wherever this is possible because of the effect this has on the order for costs. Thus:

Judgment on claim and counterclaim:
   Order: Judgment for P for £1,000 and costs
            Judgment for D for £1,000 on counterclaim and costs.
   Note: Costs on the claim may be £600 but will be much lower on the counterclaim: say £300. The net result is that although the defendant owes the plaintiff nothing he may have to pay him £300 costs. He may be able to persuade the judge to make no order for costs but he certainly will not recover his costs.

Judgment where counterclaim can be set-off
   Order: P's claim dismissed with costs.
   Note: Because the counter-claim was now a defence to the claim, P failed to recover any sum and D became entitled to £600 as his costs.

defence to show that the defendant has a valid set-off nor will execution be stayed because of a counterclaim.

Example—D buys a motor car from P and pays him by a cheque for £1,700. Whilst D is driving home he notices serious defects in the vehicle and telephones his bank to stop the cheque. The cost of repairs on the vehicle will be about £200. Nonetheless P will be able to obtain summary judgment for £1,700 without any stay of execution.

The Court of Appeal have consistently held that, apart from quite exceptional cases where for instance the bill of exchange is alleged to be fraudulent or given for a consideration which has wholly failed, the court will not stay judgment in an action for its dishonour. *Per* Lord Denning M.R. in *Fielding and Platt Ltd v. Najjar*, [1969] 2 All E.R. 150, at p. 152:—

"We have repeatedly said in this court that a bill of exchange or a promissory note is to be treated as cash. It is to be honoured unless there is some good reason to the contrary."

A "good reason" for this purpose will only exist if there is an arguable case based on fraud, illegality or a total failure of consideration.

(e) Leave to defend although no clear defence shown.   Order 14, rule 3(1) provides that leave to defend shall be given either if the defendant shows a triable issue of the claim or if he satisfies the court *"that there ought for some other reason to be a trial of that claim"*. This clearly means that there will be circumstances in which summary judgment will be refused notwithstanding that there appears to be no defence. Although this is obviously a residual power intended to prevent injustice and may in the future be employed in diverse circumstances, it would seem that it is primarily aimed at the case where the facts upon which the plaintiff relies are not within the knowledge of the defendant so that fairness requires that he should be able to test the plaintiff's case by discovery and cross-examination.

Example—H sold a farmhouse to P which was occupied by H's wife W. P sued W for possession. Three days after the sale W's solicitors registered a class F land charge which was ineffective to protect her rights of occupation against purchasers prior to registration. P applied under Order 14 for possession on the basis that until registration occurred the wife had no rights against a purchaser for value unless the sale was a pure sham. Megarry J. rejected W's contention that the sale was a sham but although she could show no other arguable defence refused summary judgment (*Miles v. Bull*, [1968] 3 All E.R. 632).

The learned judge explained his decision as follows:

"the defendant can obtain leave to defend if . . . the defendant satisfies the court 'that there is an issue or question to dispute which ought to be tried or that there ought for some other reason to be a trial'. These last words seem to me to be very wide. They also seem to me to have special significance where (as here) most or all the relevant facts are under the control of the plaintiff and the defendant would have to seek to elicit by discovery, interrogatories and cross-examination those which will aid her. If the defendant cannot point to a specific issue which ought to be tried, but nevertheless satisfies the court that there are circumstances that ought to be investigated, then I think those concluding words are invoked. These are cases when the plaintiff ought to be put to strict proof of his claim, and exposed to the full investigation possible at a trial; and in such cases it would, in my judgment, be wrong to enter summary judgment for the plaintiff".

(f) Conditional leave to defend. It has already been stated that it is sufficient for a defendant to show "a triable issue" to be granted leave to defend. In the early cases it appeared that the master was not to enter into any sort of detailed examination of the merits. Thus in *Jacobs* v. *Booth's Distillery Co.* [1901] 85 L.T. 262, Lord James of Hereford said:

> "The view which I think ought to be taken of Order XIV is that the tribunal to which the application is made should simply determine 'Is there a triable issue to go before a jury or a court?' It is not for that tribunal to enter into the merits of the case at all."

Despite this dicta the practice has developed whereby the master looks beyond the mere assertion of facts entitling leave to defend and does consider the merits to the extent that if the defence seems improbable the defendant will only be permitted to defend on, for example, payment into court of part or the whole of the amount claimed. This practice was expressly approved by Devlin J. in *Fieldrank, Ltd.* v. *Stein*, [1961] 3 All E.R. 681 where at p. 682 he says:

> "The broad principle, which is founded on *Jacobs* v. *Booth's Distillery Co.* is sum-marised on p. 266 of the *Annual Practice* (1962 Edn.) in the following terms: 'The principle on which the court acts is that where the defendant can show by affidavit that there is a bona fide triable issue, he is to be allowed to defend as to that issue without condition.' If that principle were mandatory, then the concession by counsel for the plaintiffs that there is here a triable issue would mean at once that the appeal ought to be allowed; but counsel for the plaintiffs has drawn our attention to some comments that have been made on *Jacobs* v. *Booth's Distillery Co.* in the [*Annual Practice*]. It is suggested [there] that possibly the case, if it is closely examined, does not go as far as it has hitherto been thought to go; and . . . the learned editors of the *Annual Practice* have [noted]:
>> 'The condition of payment into court, or giving security, is nowadays more often imposed than formerly, and not only where the defendant consents but also where there is a good ground in the evidence for believing that the defence set up is a sham defence and the master "is prepared very nearly to give judgment for the plaintiff".'
> . . . I should be very glad to see some relaxation of the strict rule in *Jacobs* v. *Booth's Distillery Co.* I think that any judge who has sat in chambers in R.S.C. Order 14 summonses has had the experience of a case in which, although he cannot say for certain that there is not a triable issue, nevertheless he is left with a real doubt about the defendant's good faith, and would like to protect the plaintiff, especially if there is not grave hardship on the defendant in being made to pay money into court. I should be prepared to accept that there has been a tendency in the last few years to use this condition more often than it has been used in the past, and I think that that is a good tendency."

The general form of order in such a case is that the defendant bring into court within a specified time a sum representing the whole or part of the claim as security to abide the event and in default the plaintiff is to have leave to sign final judgment for such sum. It is important to note that the plaintiff is secured by such an order against the eventual bankruptcy of the defendant (*see Re Ford, ex parte Trustee* [1900] 2 Q.B. 211).

It may be convenient to summarise at this stage the various orders above discussed:

(a) If D shows case not under Order 14, or clear triable issue or set-off known to P	summons dismissed with costs
(b) If D shows technical defect	adjournment and leave to amend or file fresh evidence but P to pay D costs thrown away *or* summons dismissed with costs
(c) If D shows triable issue or set-off which P would not necessarily anticipate	unconditional leave leave to defend and costs in cause
(d) If D shows triable issue or set-off but his defence arouses suspicion	leave to defend on payment into court of whole or part of claim in x days to abide event with costs in cause; in default, final judgment and costs
(e) If D shows circumstances which although not a defence warrant putting the plaintiff's case to the test of discovery, interrogatories and cross-examination	unconditional leave to defend, costs in cause
(f) If D shows a valid counterclaim (which does not arise out of the claim and so is not also a set-off)	judgment for P with costs execution stayed until trial of counterclaim *unless* claim is for dishonoured cheque or bill of exchange
(g) If D shows no triable issue, set-off or counterclaim	judgment for P with costs

Notes: (1) As this is a chambers summons counsel must obtain a direction that the case is "fit for counsel" before his fees will be allowed on taxation.
(2) If the case is one where there is no defence as to liability but the plaintiff is claiming general damages (e.g. a personal injury case) the order is for final judgment on liability with damages to be assessed under Order 37.

DIRECTIONS AS TO FURTHER CONDUCT OF PROCEEDINGS

If leave is granted to defend the master must proceed to give directions as to the future conduct of the action.[1] Normally he will fix a time scale for service of defence, reply and discovery. It should be noted that the normal time limit for service of defence is automatically suspended if the plaintiff serves a summons under Order 14. If the master gives no specific direction, the defence must be served 14 days after the making of the order.[2] It frequently

---

[1] R.S.C. Ord. 14, r. 6.   [2] R.S.C. Ord. 18, r. 2(2).

happens at this stage that the master directs that the case be transferred to the appropriate county court for trial. There is no practicable equivalent procedure to Order 14 in the county court so litigants often commence proceedings within the county court limit in the High Court in order to avail themselves of the summary procedure. If they succeed, they are entitled to the High Court costs (notwithstanding the general rule under section 47 of the County Court Act) unless the claim is less than £150. These costs are in fact on a fixed scale.[1] If the application for summary judgment is unsuccessful and an order is made giving the defendant leave to defend with costs in cause, the successful party in the county court will obtain High Court costs up to and including the hearing of the summons and thereafter on the appropriate county court scale (*see Simmons & Son, Ltd* v. *Wiltshire*, [1938] 3 All E.R. 403).

INJUNCTIONS

An application for a final injunction (as opposed to an interlocutory injunction) may be made under Order 14 by a summons to the defendant to appear before a judge in chambers (instead of the master).

> *Example*—Shell-Mex granted the defendants a licence to operate for one year a filling station on a forecourt owned by Shell. At the expiry of the licence the defendants refused to leave. Lord Denning M.R. in the Court of Appeal referred to a note in the 1970 *Practice* to the effect that a claim for an injunction was by its nature not appropriate for Order 14 proceedings since the master had no power to grant an injunction except by consent. He said: "It is true that a master has no power to grant an injunction, but the judge has ample power. I see no reason whatever why a plaintiff cannot go straight to the judge and ask for summary judgment under R.S.C. Order 14 for an injunction". (*Shell-Mex and B.P. Ltd.* v. *Manchester Garages Ltd.*, [1971] 1 All E.R. 841 at p. 843).

CHANCERY PRACTICE

The principal difference between the hearing of an Order 14 summons before a master in the Queen's Bench Division and a Chancery master is that in the latter case the master cannot give judgment either way if one or both parties wish the matter to be referred to a judge. This practice (which applies to all chambers business in the Chancery Division and not just an Order 14 summons) is explained in *Lloyds Bank Ltd.* v. *Princess Royal Colliery Co. Ltd. (No. 2)*, (1900), 48 W.R. 427 at p. 428 as follows:

> "Byrne J., stating that he had made inquiries from judges and others of greater experience in these matters than himself, held that the right of every suitor in the Chancery Division to have any question determined by the judge was not in the nature of an appeal. All orders made in chambers are orders of the judge, though taken without the parties going before him. . . ."

In addition to the general power under Order 14 (which applies to actions commenced by writ in the Chancery Division in the same way as it does to proceedings in the Queen's Bench Division). Order 86 empowers the Chancery Division to give summary judgment where an action is commenced by writ indorsed with a claim for specific performance or rescission of an agreement, whether in writing or not, for the sale, purchase or exchange of property or for the grant or assignment of a lease. The order also includes a claim for the forfeiture or return of any deposit under such an agreement. The rule is similar to Order 14 procedure in that judgment is granted on the basis of affidavit evidence verifying the claim and alleging that there is no defence to the action. It differs from Order 14 procedure in that:

---

[1] R.S.C. Ord. 62 and Appendix 3.

(*a*) no statement of claim need be served

(*b*) no appearance need have been entered

(*c*) the summons is returnable in 4 clear days from service.

It should be noted that the plaintiff must attach to his summons full minutes of the order to which he claims to be entitled. The master may order summary judgment himself if:

(*a*) the parties consent

or (*b*) the agreement is in *writing and* the defendant is in default of appearance *or* does not attend at the hearing *or* there is clearly no defence.

In all other cases (e.g. where the agreement is oral or where the question of whether there is a triable issue is doubtful) the summons must be adjourned to the judge in chambers when the evidence filed is complete. [1]

APPEALS IN ORDER 14 PROCEEDINGS

Either party may appeal to the judge in chambers from any order made by a master or district registrar on a summons under Order 14. [2] The notice of appeal must be issued out of the Action Department of the Central Office within 5 days of the order[3] and served on the respondent 2 clear days[4] before the return date. The appeal involves a complete *rehearing* of the summons; either party may put in new evidence (subject to the other side's right to an adjournment if taken by surprise). If the judge grants unconditional leave to defend, the plaintiff cannot appeal further to the Court of Appeal (the reason being that if a judge feels there is a clear triable issue it is pointless to permit this preliminary question to be litigated further) (Judicature Act 1925, s. 31(1)c.). On the other hand if the judge gives judgment for the plaintiff, the defendant may appeal of right to the Court of Appeal (Judicature Act 1925, s. 31(2)). If the judge imposes conditions in granting defendant's leave to defend he may appeal of right against those conditions (Ibid). [5]

SQUATTERS

Special problems arise in utilising the ordinary procedure for recovery of land where the identity of the persons in occupation are not known to the owner. To meet this difficulty and to provide a speedy alternative to Order 14 where it is beyond doubt the occupants have no existing licence to occupy the land special procedures have been created by R.S.C. Order 113 and C.C.R. Order 26. The rules in the county court (which apply where the rateable value of the premises does not exceed £1,000) are to all intents and purposes identical to the provisions of the corresponding rules in the High Court. Since most such actions are commenced in the county court we shall describe the procedure under Order 26 here. The stages in the action:

(*a*) The applicant issues an *originating application* seeking recovery of possession on the grounds that he is entitled to possession and that the

---

[1] See *Practice Direction* [1970] 1 All E.R. 1183; [1970] 1 W.L.R. 762. The hearing before the judge usually takes place on a Monday morning.

[2] See page 192, *post*, where the form of notice of appeal is set out.

[3] 7 days if the appeal is from the decision of a district registrar. If the appeal is to be heard by a judge in the provinces the notice is issued out of the district registry of the trial centre where the judge will hear the appeal.

[4] 3 if a district registry case.

[5] Because of the curious and possibly unintentional wording of s. 31(2) the *plaintiff* may appeal against an order granting conditional leave to the defendant to defend and argue that there should be final judgment. (See *Gordon* v. *Cradock* [1964] 1 Q.B. 503; [1963] 2 All E.R. 121.)

persons in occupation of the premises are in occupation without licence or consent.

(*b*) He files an affidavit in support stating (i) his interest in the land (ii) the circumstances in which the land has been occupied without licence or consent and in which his claim to possession arises and (iii) if it be the case that he is unaware of the identity of some of the occupants.

(*c*) Notice of the date of hearing, a copy of the application and the affidavit are served on the persons named by (i) personal delivery or (ii) by an officer of the court leaving the documents at or posting them to the premises or (iii) by serving of a solicitor instructed to accept service by the respondent or (iv) in such other manner as the court may direct.

(*d*) If there are persons in occupation who are not identified a copy of the originating application and a notice telling them of the date of hearing and of their rights to be made parties to the application are affixed to "the main door or other conspicuous part of the premises" unless the court directs service in some other manner.

The hearing of the application must be not less than 7 clear days (including Saturdays and Sundays) from the date of service. At the hearing, if the applicant proves his title as absolute owner of the land (usually by production of a land certificate which will be conclusive proof of his title) and his intention to regain possession, the onus then falls on the respondent to prove either a tenancy or a licence which has not been determined (see *Portland Management, Ltd.* v. *Harte*, [1976] 1 All E.R. 225; [1976] 2 W.L.R. 174). If the defendant succeeds in establishing a prima facie case the judge will normally give directions for pleadings and discovery as if the application had begun as a normal action. We set out below the forms which would be used in a typical case where the identity of *some* of the occupants was not known.

In the Westminster County Court   No. 76.263

In the Matter of Premises known
as 501A Greek Street, London W.1.

Between:

Charles Henry Dickens   Applicant

and
Susie Wong (Spinster)   Respondent

I, Charles Henry Dickens of 36 Doughty Street, London WC1, apply to the Court for an Order for recovery of possession of all the premises known as and situated at 501A Greek Street, London W1. on the ground that I am entitled to possession and that the persons in occupation of the premises are in occupation without licence or consent. The person in occupation who is intended to be served personally with this application is Miss Susie Wong. There are other persons in occupation whose names I do not know.

Dated the   *Dodson and Fogg*
1st day of July 1976   Solicitors for the Applicant

In the Westminster County Court   No. 76.623

In the Matter of Premises known
as 501A Greek Street, London W.

Between:

Charles Henry Dickens

Applicant

and
Susie Wong (Spinster)

Respondent

I, Charles Henry Dickens, of 36 Doughty Street, London WC1, journalist, make oath and say as follows:

(1) I am the freehold owner of the premises situated at and known as 501A Greek Street, London W1 which is a first floor flat formerly occupied by me as my residence. There is now produced and shown to me marked "CHD 1" a copy of the entry in H.M. Land Registry under title No. LN 526357 showing my title to the said premises.

(2) In May 1975 I left the premises for an extensive stay in Italy. When I returned to this country on the 6th day of June 1976 I went immediately to the said premises to find that the locks on the outer door had been changed. It appeared that the premises were inhabited and I saw a notice on the bell push "Miss Susie Wong—professional model". I immediately contacted the police and when I returned with a uniformed constable a man of about 30 years of age opened the door and said "I am the tenant here—clear off". He said he paid his rent to a Mr. William Sikes. He refused to give his name. I have returned on a number of occasions to the premises but on each such occasion have seen the said man who has refused to disclose his identity.

(3) The persons now in occupation are there without my licence or consent and I respectfully apply to this Honourable Court for an order pursuant to Order 26 of the County Court Rules 1936 for an order requiring them to deliver up possession of the said premises forthwith.

Sworn at 26 Cheapside, London EC2 } *Charles Dickens*
this 23rd day of July 1976.
Before me,
Marmaduke Smiles
  Marmaduke Smiles LL.B.
    A Commissioner of Oaths.

INTERIM PAYMENTS

An order for interim payment (i.e. payment on account of damages likely to be awarded on final judgment) will be made in the High Court (but *not* the county court) in personal injury cases and claims under the Fatal Accidents Act wherever it appears virtually certain that the plaintiff will succeed at the trial.

Example—P is a passenger in a motor car which, whilst being driven by D, collides with a tree. P receives such serious injuries that, although his solicitors have issued a writ, they are reluctant to settle the claim until the true extent of his permanent disability is revealed. His doctors say that a final prognosis cannot be given for at least a year. In this case P's solicitors can apply for an interim payment on account of the damages he is eventually bound to recover.

The power of the High Court to award an interim payment is derived from section 20 of the Administration of Justice Act 1969 and is set out in Order 29 rules 9–17. The basic procedure is as follows:

(1) After the time for entry of appearance has expired the plaintiff issues a summons applying for an interim order. This summons must be served 10 clear days before the return date.

(2) The plaintiff serves at the same time an affidavit which (a) verifies the special damage (e.g. loss of wages) to date (b) exhibits the relevant medical reports and (c) if the claim arises under the Fatal Accidents Act sets out the statutory particulars of dependency.

(3) At the hearing of the summons the master may make an interim award provided (a) the defendant admits liability or (b) the plaintiff has obtained judgment for damages to be assessed or (c) if the action proceeded, the plaintiff would succeed on the issue of liability without any substantial reduction for contributory negligence.

(4) At the eventual trial the court (which must not be told of the interim award until it has ruled on liability and quantum) may make appropriate orders adjusting payment between defendants and even ordering repayment by the plaintiff in the rare case where the interim award was too high.

SECURITY FOR COSTS

We have seen above how a plaintiff who considers there is no credible defence to the action is able to issue a summons under Order 14 which may either result in his obtaining judgment or at least obtaining an order for a sum to be paid into court. We have now to consider the position where the defendant feels that he has a strong case but is concerned that if the action proceeds to trial and he then wins the plaintiff will not be able to pay the costs awarded against him. The basic rule is that there is nothing the defendant can do in these circumstances: the impecuniosity of the plaintiff is *not* in itself sufficient grounds for an order that he gives security for costs.[1] However in the following circumstances the court *may* on application by the defendant order security:

(1) Where the plaintiff is ordinarily resident outside the United Kingdom[2] and has no substantial property in this country.

(2) Where the plaintiff is a limited company and "it appears by credible testimony that there is reason to believe that the company will be unable to pay the costs of the defendant if successful in his defence".

Even though the above conditions are satisfied it does not automatically follow that security will be ordered. In exercising its discretion the court will take into account the following matters:

(1) Whether the plaintiff's claim is bona fide.

(2) Whether he has a reasonably good prospect of success.

(3) Whether there is an admission by the defendants on the pleadings or elsewhere that money is due.

---

[1] Except on appeal to the Court of Appeal see p. 197, *post.*

[2] R.S.C. Ord. 23. This order also provides for security against a nominal plaintiff or a plaintiff who deliberately mis-states his address on the writ or who has changed his address to evade the consequences of the litigation.

(4) Whether there is a substantial payment into court (so that the question becomes whether the plaintiff has reasonable prospects of succeeding in recovering more than the payment-in).

(5) Whether the application for security is being used oppressively, e.g. so as to stifle a genuine claim.

(6) Whether the plaintiff's want of means has been brought about by any conduct of the defendants.

(7) The stage of the proceedings at which the application is made: it should generally be made as early as possible.

It should be noted that security for costs may be ordered against a legally aided person in exceptional circumstances.[1]

In the county court, security may be ordered in the circumstances referred to above and in addition may be ordered where the defendant neither resides nor carries on business within 20 miles of the court.[2]

An application for security for costs is made in the High Court by summons to the master or district registrar with an affidavit in support. The form of order is that the action be stayed unless security be given within a specified period. In the county court, the application is on notice to the registrar (except where the plaintiff resides abroad in which case he must give security before the court will issue process unless the registrar on an ex parte application directs otherwise).

---

[1] See *Conway* v. *George Wimpey & Co. Ltd.* [1951] 1 All E.R. 56 and *Jackson* v. *John Dickinson & Co. (Bolton) Ltd.* [1952] 1 All E.R. 104.
[2] See C.C.R. Ord. 3, r. 1 and Ord. 13, r. 7.

CHAPTER FOUR

INJUNCTIONS

(The beginner is advised to read through the example appended at the end of this chapter before studying the text.)

An injunction is an order of the court restraining[1] the defendant from continuing in a course of wrongful conduct (e.g. publishing a libel) or requiring[2] him to take certain measures to abate a wrong which he has created (e.g. an order to a landlord who has wrongfully evicted his tenant by changing the locks requiring him to give the tenant free access to the premises by delivering up the new keys). In exceptional cases an injunction will be granted to prevent the commission of a threatened wrong although no actual wrong has yet been committed (e.g. a proposed infringement of copyright): this is known as a *quia timet* injunction.

Injunctions were developed by the Court of Chancery as a discretionary remedy to supplement the inadequate relief granted by the common law courts; two important characteristics of the modern law reveal the historical origin of the remedy, namely:

(a) that the grant of an injunction is discretionary and will be refused if damages would be an adequate remedy, and

(b) the enforcement of the court's order is generally by imprisonment for contempt, i.e. the court acts against the person in default rather than his property.

An injunction may be the substantive relief required in an action, i.e. the final order in the case after the trial of the action. Often however, the court will be asked to grant an *interim* injunction as a matter of urgency *before* the trial of the action. This chapter is primarily concerned with the procedure by which such interlocutory relief can be obtained. It should be noted that in many cases (especially in the Chancery Division) the action terminates with the decision as to interlocutory relief because the parties are content to accept this interim decision as representing the likely result of the trial.

APPLICATIONS IN THE QUEEN'S BENCH DIVISION

An application for an interim injunction in proceedings in the Queen's Bench Division is brought by a summons to the defendant requiring him to attend before a *judge in chambers* and setting out the terms of the order sought. The summons must be served not less than 2 clear days before the date for hearing (i.e. the "return day").[3] The plaintiff must prepare an affidavit verifying the matters which he alleges are grounds for granting an injunction. The affidavit may contain hearsay evidence provided the deponent states the source of the

---

[1] Called a *prohibitory* injunction.
[2] Called a *mandatory* injunction.
[3] Exclude day of service, return day, Saturdays, Sundays and bank holidays in calculating 2 clear days.

information.[1] The affidavit should be served at the same time as the summons; later service may result in the defendant applying for an adjournment to put in his own evidence. If, as will frequently be the case, the defendant fails to attend at the hearing of the summons, the court will proceed in his absence[2] provided the plaintiff can prove service. For this reason it is a sensible course for the plaintiff's solicitor to have an affidavit of service sworn by the process server and available at the hearing whenever it is not certain that the defendant will attend. If the defendant wishes to dispute the facts alleged in the plaintiff's affidavit he will put in an affidavit in reply. However the court at this stage is not primarily concerned with evidence and certainly cannot attempt normally to resolve conflicting issues of fact. At the most it will determine only the very limited issues which are relevant in deciding whether to make an interim order. After the hearing in chambers is concluded, the parties file their affidavits at the Central Office.

APPLICATIONS IN THE CHANCERY DIVISION

By contrast with the privacy of proceedings in the Queen's Bench Division, applications for injunctions in the Chancery Division are heard in open court. The plaintiff issues a *notice of motion* informing the defendant that the court will be moved by counsel for an interlocutory injunction in the terms specified in the notice. The notice must again be served two clear days before the motion is heard. The affidavits to be used ought to be filed at court before the hearing of the motion (although in practice it frequently happens that the parties because of lack of time are unable to do this and give an undertaking to file). The application as stated above will be heard in open court on one of the days set aside for motions in the Chancery Division (usually Tuesdays and Fridays). Frequently in contested cases the motion is adjourned on the defendant giving undertakings to preserve the status quo until the motion can be disposed of.

APPLICATIONS IN THE COUNTY COURT

The county court has *no* jurisdiction to grant an injunction if that is the *only* relief sought in the action. However section 74 of the County Courts Act 1959 provides the court with a limited power to grant an injunction as *ancillary relief* to a claim within the jurisdiction.

Example—T rents a flat at L's house. L constantly disturbs T by playing loud music late at night. If T sues in the county court for an injunction and no other relief he will find the court has no jurisdiction. Therefore he will sue for damages for nuisance and possibly breach of covenant in his lease and add a claim for an injunction as ancillary relief.

The procedure in the county court so far as interlocutory relief is concerned is that the plaintiff must serve on the defendant and file at court not less than 1 clear day before hearing a notice that the plaintiff intends to apply for an injunction.[3] The plaintiff should normally prepare a draft of the proposed order and submit the same to the registrar for his approval. If the judge grants the order, he may sign the order as settled by the registrar or with such

---

[1] R.S.C. Ord. 41, r. 5(2).
[2] R.S.C. Ord. 32, r. 5.
[3] C.C.R. Ord. 13, r. 8(2); Ord. 13, r. 1(1).

alteration as he thinks proper (see Order 13, rule 13). Although the rules provide that no affidavit is necessary on the first hearing of the application and give the judge power to "direct evidence to be adduced in such manner as he thinks fit", the normal practice where counsel or a solicitor is instructed is for an affidavit to be sworn and if possible served with the summons.

THE PRINCIPLES UPON WHICH THE COURT ACTS

The problem which the court faces when asked for interlocutory relief is that it must make a decision affecting the rights of the parties without the opportunity of a full investigation of the disputed issues in the action. The traditional approach was for the court to determine two matters:

(a) whether the plaintiff could show a prima facie case, and
(b) if so, whether he could prove that the damage he would suffer if an injunction was refused would outweigh the nuisance and inconvenience to the defendant in having his activities temporarily restricted.

If he could prove *both* these points, he would obtain an injunction restraining the defendants until the trial of the action at which the rights of the parties would be finally decided. However in *American Cyanamid* v. *Ethicon, Ltd.*, [1975] A.C. 396; [1975] 1 All E.R. 504 the House of Lords stated that it was *not* necessary for the plaintiff to establish a prima facie case to succeed; it was sufficient that there was a serious issue to be tried. Their lordships held that the court should not embark on any sort of review of the evidence. Thus Lord Diplock at p. 510 pointed out:

> "It is no part of the court's function at this stage of the litigation to try to resolve conflicts of evidence on affidavit as to facts on which the claims of either party may ultimately depend nor to decide difficult questions of law which call for detailed argument or mature considerations. These are matters to be dealt with at the trial".

In the *American Cyanamid* case the plaintiffs applied for an interim injunction to restrain the defendants from acts allegedly infringing their patent on a special sort of surgical stitch which would dissolve and be absorbed into the body. The Court of Appeal held that the plaintiffs had to show a prima facie case that the patent would be infringed and so refused the application. The House of Lords unanimously reversed this decision because, as stated above, they held that the appellants did *not* have to show a prima facie case that they would win the eventual action in order to be granted relief; they had merely to show that there was a *serious question to be tried* between themselves and the defendant (in the sense that his claim was not frivolous or vexatious). Once this was established the court had then to consider whether the balance of convenience lay in favour of granting or refusing interlocutory relief.

The correct approach appears to be for the court to consider the following questions:

(1) Has the plaintiff shown a serious question to be tried?
(2) If so, has he also shown that if he is not granted an injunction he will sustain more than direct financial loss?
(3) If both conditions are satisfied the court then looks at the defendant's position and asks whether, if he eventually wins, damages will adequately compensate him for any loss he may suffer by reason of the injunction. If so, the injunctioh should be granted.

(4) If, however, it appears that damages will not compensate him, the court should then compare the likely hardship to the plaintiff and defendant and see where the balance of convenience lies. If all else is equal the court should generally lean to preserving the status quo but it may at this stage be proper to take into account the relative strength of each party's case. Lord Diplock however emphasised this "should be done only where it is apparent on the facts disclosed by evidence as to which there is no credible dispute that the strength of one party's case is disproportionate to that of the other party. The court is not justified in embarking on anything resembling a trial of the action on conflicting affidavits in order to evaluate the strength of either party's case".

It may be helpful at this stage to consider two recent cases which show how the guidelines formulated by Lord Diplock in the *American Cyanamid* case are applied.

Example—A firm of solicitors in Walthamstow employed a young legal executive under a written contract which provided that after he left their employment he should not be employed "in the legal profession" in the area for a period of five years. Some time after he had left their employment he obtained work in the area with another firm of solicitors. His former employers issued a writ claiming damages and an injunction and sought an interim injunction restraining him from working in the district until the trial of the action. The Court of Appeal refused an interlocutory injunction. Browne L.J. approached the case by saying (1) that the plaintiffs' case showed a serious question to be tried but (2) since they failed to provide any evidence of likely damage, interlocutory relief should be refused. Sir John Pennycuick went further and analysed the defendant's position and pointed out that "the possible inconvenience to the plaintiffs in that they might lose a few clients appears to be much less than the certain inconvenience to the defendant of being prevented from continuing his present employment in Walthamstow" (*Fellowes* v. *Fisher*, [1975] 2 All E.R. 829 at p. 844).

Example 2—A firm of estate agents in Islington who had acted for property developers in the area were picketed by a group of social workers complaining at the tactics allegedly used by the developers and their agents. The plaintiffs issued a writ for nuisance and conspiracy. They alleged in the statement of claim that "the said picketing has been carried out in such a manner as substantially to interfere with the plaintiffs' enjoyment of the said premises and the conduct of their said business and so as to intimidate or deter persons wishing to transact business with the plaintiffs." The Court of Appeal approved the granting of an interlocutory injunction. Orr L.J. after holding that there was a serious question to be tried went on to say: "The next question to be asked is whether, if the plaintiffs were to succeed at the trial, they would be adequately compensated for the interim continuance of the defendant's activities. In my judgment, the answer is that they plainly would not because such continuance might well cause very serious damage to their business, and the judge was entitled, on this issue, to have regard to any doubts he might feel as to the defendants' ability to satisfy any award of damages made against them. . . . The next question to be asked is the converse question whether if the defendants were to succeed at the trial they would be adequately compensated for the interim restriction on their activities which the grant of an interlocutory injunction would have imposed. I have no doubt that they would be, since the only restriction imposed by the injunction would be in respect of activities in front of the plaintiffs' premises, leaving the defendants free to conduct their campaign by lawful means elsewhere, . . . It followed the balance of convenience lay in granting the interlocutory relief" (*Hubbard* v. *Pitt,* [1975] 3 All E.R. 1, at p. 20).

The important point to note about the principles in the *American Cyanamid* case is that they provide that the court should *not* normally consider the likely prospects of success in the action in determining whether or not to grant interlocutory relief. The advantage of the decision is that it relieves the court from the burden of considering the evidence and making a provisional assessment. The criticism which has been levied at the decision is principally directed to the fact that before this rule was promulgated in many cases (including a substantial number of leading authorities) the litigation did not continue to trial because the parties were content to accept a provisional decision on the merits by the judge hearing the interlocutory application. Thus in *Fellowes* v. *Fisher* Sir John Pennycuick pointed out (at p. 843):

> "By far the most serious difficulty, to my mind, lies in the requirement that the prospects of success in the action have apparently to be disregarded except as a last resort when the balance of convenience is otherwise even. In many classes of cases, in particular these depending in whole or in great part on the construction of a written instrument, the prospect of success is a matter within the competence of the judge who hears the interlocutory application and represents a factor which can hardly be disregarded in determining whether or not it is just to give interlocutory relief. Indeed many cases of this kind never get beyond the interlocutory stage, the parties being content to accept the judge's decision as a sufficient indication of the probable upshot of the action. ... There is also a class where immediate judicial interference is essential, e.g. to take two examples at random, trespass or the internal affairs of a company, and in which the court could not do justice without to some extent considering the probable upshot of the action if it ever came to be fought out, or in other words, the merits."

UNDERTAKING AS TO DAMAGES

Where an interlocutory injunction is granted it is the inevitable practice of the courts to extract from the applicant an undertaking to compensate the other party for any loss he may sustain in consequence of the injunction if it eventually appears at the trial that the applicant was not entitled to the relief sought.

COSTS

The normal order for costs will be as follows:

(a) If the application for an injunction succeeds, costs will be *in cause*, so that whichever party wins at the conclusion of the case will obtain the costs he has incurred in applying for or opposing the interlocutory injunction.

(b) If the application is refused it will not necessarily follow that the applicant will be ordered to pay the costs. Where for instance the balance of convenience is nearly even, the right order would be costs in cause.

Where an application for an injunction is made to a county court judge by counsel the costs of his attendance will only be allowed if he applies and the judge certifies the case as fit for counsel.

URGENT CASES

There will be cases where the need for an injunction is so urgent that the applicant will have already sustained irreparable harm if he has to wait for the other side to be served with notice of his application. In such exceptional cases both the High Court and the county court will grant temporary orders on an *ex parte* application by the plaintiff (i.e. without notice being given to the defendant). Indeed such relief may be granted notwithstanding the writ or originating summons or county court summons has not been issued. The plaintiff will present the court[1] with an affidavit as to the merits of his case and if he is successful the court will issue an injunction effective for a short period (usually five days to a week) during which the plaintiff must serve notice on the defendant of his intention to apply at the expiry of the injunction that it should be continued to trial. The plaintiff will be required to give the usual undertaking to compensate the defendant if it transpires he was not entitled to the relief sought and to issue and serve the writ or other process forthwith. Frequently the order gives the defendant liberty to apply to the court on, for instance, one day's notice to discharge the injunction. It must be emphasised that ex parte injunctions are for cases of real urgency where there has been a true impossibility of giving notice of the application. In less urgent cases, the plaintiff may apply to the court for leave to issue a summons or notice of motion with *short notice* (i.e. less than two clear days). The illustration at the end of this chapter shows how an application is made for an *ex parte* order.

INJUNCTIONS TO ASSIST EXECUTION

An injunction may be granted to restrain the defendant from disposing of his assets in such a way as to defeat any award the plaintiff is likely to obtain if he is successful in the action.

> *Example*—Japanese shipowners chartered three vessels to the defendants who allegedly failed to pay the hire charges. The defendants had substantial assets in banks in London.
> *Held:* an injunction should be issued restraining the defendants from disposing or dealing with their assets (*Nippon Yusen Kaisha v. Karageorgis* [1975] 3 All E.R. 282).

In the above case Lord Denning M.R. said (at p. 283):

> "We are told that an injunction of this kind has never been done before. It has never been the practice of the English courts to seize assets of a defendant in advance of judgment, or to restrain the disposal of them. ... It seems to me that the time has come when we should revise our practice. There is no reason why the High Court ... should not make an order such as is asked for here. It is warranted by section 45 of the Supreme Court of Judicature (Consolidation) Act 1925 which says the High Court may grant a mandamus or injunction or appoint a receiver by an inter-locutory order in all cases in which it appears to the court to be just or convenient so to do."

The limits of this novel form of order have yet to be worked out but it is suggested that (by analogy with the practice in the Family Division) there would have to be circumstances, such as evasion of service, which suggest the likelihood of the defendant disposing of his assets before the trial.[2]

SETTLEMENT OF INTERLOCUTORY PROCEEDINGS

Where the defendant is prepared to agree to the terms of the proposed

---

[1] In extreme cases where the court is not sitting application may be made to a judge at his home. The plaintiff's solicitors should telephone to the Royal Courts of Justice who will be able to put them in touch with a judge available for the hearing of urgent applications.

[2] See further *Rasu Maritima Case* (1977) *Times*, 15th March: the defendant may be able to resist the order if its effect would be to bring his business to a standstill.

injunction or offers to accept modified terms the usual practice is for him to offer formal *undertakings* to the court which does not then proceed to issue a formal injunction. An undertaking can be enforced in exactly the same method as an injunction: it merely means (*a*) that normally the court does not have to investigate the matters at all and (*b*) that there is no order which has to be served on the defendant.

Sometimes the parties will agree at the hearing of the interlocutory application on terms intended to settle the whole of the action. In these circumstances in the Queen's Bench Division and county court the parties normally draw up terms of final judgment including the appropriate permanent injunction. In the Chancery Division the common practice is to stay further proceedings in the action on terms set out in a schedule annexed to the order. This form of order (known as a *Tomlin Order* from the judge who formulated the terms) is set out as follows: "The plaintiff and the defendant having agreed to the terms set forth in the schedule hereto, it is ordered that all further proceedings in this action be stayed, except for the purpose of carrying such terms into effect. Liberty to apply as to carrying such terms into effect."

ENFORCEMENT OF INJUNCTIONS

As soon as possible after the injunction has been granted the applicant should obtain a sealed copy of the order[1] and effect personal service on the defendant. The order *must* be indorsed with a *penal notice* warning the defendant that he is liable to be committed to prison if he disobeys the order. The form of indorsement (where the injunction restrains the defendant from certain conduct) would be as follows:

> If you, the within-named Joseph Soap disobey this order, you will be liable to process of execution for the purpose of compelling you to obey the same.[2]

The order duly indorsed with the penal notice must be served personally on the defendant. If the defendant is in breach of the terms of an injunction or his undertaking to the court, the plaintiff will then apply by *notice of motion* for an order that he be committed to prison for contempt.

The procedure is regulated by R.S.C. Order 45, rules 5 to 8 and Order 52, rule 4. The notice of motion must state clearly the breach alleged and be served personally on the defendant two clear days before the hearing (a specimen motion is set out at page 119, *ante*). In the county court, Order 25, rules 6–8 provide that the registrar shall give the plaintiff's solicitors a notice addressed to the defendant requiring him to attend and show cause why an order of attachment (i.e. committal) should not be made. Once again there must be personal service not later than two clear days before the hearing. At the hearing the applicant will have to prove:

(1) *Service of the injunction together with the penal notice* (although, in the case of prohibitive injunctions, it is sufficient to prove the defendant's

---

[1] The procedure in the Queen's Bench Division is that the judge returns the summons indorsed with a short note of his decision and the plaintiff's solicitors prepare a formal order (as set out as in the example at p. 116) and take it (together with a copy for filing) to the Central Office or District Registry. In the county court, the order is drawn up by the court itself and issued on application by the plaintiff.

[2] If the order is mandatory, the notice begins "If you ... neglect to obey this order by the time limited within. ..." In the county court the penal notice reads "Take notice that unless you obey the directions contained in this order you will be guilty of contempt of court and liable to be committed to prison." Ord. 25, r. 68(1), Form 140.

presence when the order was made or that he has been notified of the order[1] and in all cases the court may dispense with service where it is just so to do[2]).

(2) *Breach* of the injunction or undertaking (this is proved by affidavit evidence).

(3) *Service* of the *notice of motion* and the *affidavits* on the defendant. This is particularly important because frequently the defendant will not attend at the application and no order can be made unless it is proved that he has had notice of the application and a copy of the affidavit. For this reason the plaintiff should *always* prepare an *affidavit of service* of the motion and affidavit of merits. The affidavits of service of the original order and the notice of motion must be sworn by the persons who effected service and must state how they identified the defendant.

If the court finds that the defendant is in breach of the injunction (or his undertaking) it may commit him to prison forthwith for his contempt. More commonly if the defendant offers suitable apologies the court will suspend the committal order so long as he thereafter complies with the terms of the injunction or original undertaking together with any new undertakings required by the court. The costs of the hearing will be awarded to the successful applicant "in any event".

EXAMPLE

In September 1976 Miss Henrietta Carlova (the internationally renowned soprano) agreed to appear at the Metropolitan Opera House for the 1976/7 Winter Season. On 1 November after a furious quarrel with the artistic director she stormed out of rehearsals for "La Boheme", which was to be the first production of the new season. On 5 November the London evening newspapers carried a story that she intended to open in a production of the "Marriage of Figaro" at a rival theatre on the following Wednesday. The Opera House consulted their solicitors who explained that although the courts will not enforce a contract of service by injunction (i.e. will not *force* an employee to work for his employer) they will enforce reasonable restrictions on the employee's right to work for rival concerns (*see Lumley* v. *Wagner* [1852] 1 De G.M. & G. 604). In the present case Miss Carlova's contract contained a clause prohibiting her appearing for any other companies during the winter season. Her solicitors therefore instructed counsel to settle as a matter of urgency a writ and an affidavit of merits. As soon as these documents were prepared they applied ex parte to a Queen's Bench judge in chambers for an interlocutory injunction.

The general indorsement of the writ read: "The plaintiffs claim damages for breach of a written contract dated the 23rd day of September 1976 whereby the defendant agreed to perform at the plaintiff's Opera House during the Winter Season 1976–77 and for an injunction restraining the defendant from appearing at any other establishment in breach of the terms of the said contract." The affidavit is set out at page 115. Note that it contains statements of hearsay evidence (paragraphs 3 and 4). These are permissible because the application is for interlocutory relief. Note also how the relevant

---

[1] R.S.C. Ord. 45, r. 7(6).
[2] Ibid., r. 7(7). In the county court strict service of the order need only be proved if the defendant fails to appear. Ord. 25, r. 68(3).

documents (i.e. the written agreement and the newspaper cutting) are exhibited to the affidavit.

The judge approached the case by finding first that there was a serious question to be tried between the parties. He then considered whether the plaintiffs would suffer harm other than direct financial loss if he refused the injunction. Clearly they sustain loss although it would be impossible to prove or quantify in money their damage if Miss Carlova was allowed to appear for a rival concern. If on the other hand she was prohibited from doing so, it might be that she would decide to honour her contract with the plaintiffs. The judge then had to consider whether the defendant would herself suffer more than financial loss if the injunction was granted and it eventually transpired that the Opera Company were not entitled to an order. It could be argued that being prevented from performing for the season in London might cause more than financial loss, in that it could cause permanent harm to her career. However, the judge felt that even if it could be said that the harm to each party was evenly balanced, at the end of the day the court should incline to preserving the status quo. Accordingly the judge granted the injunction but.:

(1) obtained an undertaking from the plaintiffs that they would issue the writ and serve it and a statement of claim forthwith,
(2) obtained an undertaking from the plaintiffs to compensate the defendant if it eventually transpired that the injunction should not have been granted,
(3) ordered that the injunction was to remain in force for only 8 days (if the plaintiffs wish it continued thereafter they should serve a summons on the defendant returnable on or before the day on which the injunction would expire),
(4) gave the defendant leave to apply on one day's notice to discharge the injunction if she was so advised.

The order is set out in document no. 2 (p. 116). Note that it is indorsed with a *penal notice* warning the defendant of the consequences of disobeying the order of the court. Document no. 3 (p. 117) shows the summons served at the same time as the injunction telling the defendant of the next hearing of the matter. Document no. 1 (the affidavit of merits) would be served at the same time since the plaintiffs would use that again at the hearing of the summons. Document no. 4 (p. 118) shows the statement of claim seeking a permanent injunction and damages.

To the plaintiffs' consternation Miss Carlova not only tore up the order when she was served but announced her intention of appearing the next day at the Empire Theatre. And indeed the very next evening she appeared in the first night of "The Marriage of Figaro". In these circumstances the plaintiffs had no option but to apply by *notice of motion* (document no. 5; p. 119) to commit her for breach of the injunction. At the hearing they would produce:

(a) an affidavit deposing to the service of the injunction (duly indorsed with the penal notice) on her,
(b) an affidavit as to the breach by her of the injunction,
(c) an affidavit proving service of the notice of motion.

It would certainly be likely that for so flagrant a breach of the court's order Miss Carlova would find herself committed to prison. Her only chance of avoiding such a fate would be to apologise abjectly and promise henceforth to obey the order.

Document 1

In the High Court of Justice   1976-T.-No. 106
Queen's Bench Division

Between:

The Metropolitan Opera Company

Plaintiffs

and

Henrietta Carlova   Defendant

I, Jeremy Sebastian Tooth, of 24a South Audley Street, London W1, a
director of the Plaintiff Company, make oath and say as follows:

1.   I am the principal casting director at the Metropolitan Opera House
and as such responsible for the engagement of artists.

2.   On the 23rd day of September, 1976 the Defendant entered into a
written agreement with the Plaintiffs to appear in the Winter
Season productions at the Opera House. There is now produced and
shown to be marked "JST 1" a true copy of the said agreement.

3.   I am informed by M. Serge Dubrovnik, the artistic director of the
company's current production of the opera "La Boheme", and verily
believe to be true, that after a rehearsal of the said opera on
the 1st day of November, 1976 the Defendant left the Opera House
stating that she had no intention of working with sub-standard
performers. I am further informed by him and verily believe to be
true that the Defendant has failed to appear at all subsequent
rehearsals at the theatre.

4.   There is now produced and shown to me marked "JST 2" an extract
from the "Evening News" dated the 5th day of November, 1976
containing an item indicating that the Defendant intends appearing
at the Empire Theatre's current season.

5.   On the 6th day of November, 1976 I spoke to the Defendant on the
telephone and asked her if this item was true. She said "I can do
what I like" and after uttering certain words of abuse replaced
the receiver.

6.   I verily believe that the Defendant will appear at the said Theatre
in breach of the terms of her agreement with the Plaintiffs unless
restrained by order of this Honourable Court from so doing.

Sworn at *Holborn*
this *6th* day of *November 1976*
Before me
Marmaduke Smiles
A Commissioner of Oaths

Jeremy Sebastian Tooth

This affidavit is filed on behalf of the Plaintiffs.

Document 2

<u>In the High Court of Justice</u>   <u>1976 -T.-No. 106</u>

<u>Queen's Bench Division</u>

Between:

The Metropolitan Opera Company
                                        <u>Plaintiffs</u>

and

Henrietta Carlova   <u>Defendant</u>

The Hon. Mr. Justice Strawberry in Chambers

UPON HEARING Counsel for the Plaintiffs

<u>ex parte</u>

AND UPON READING the affidavit of Jeremy Sebastian Tooth filed the
7th day of November, 1976

AND UPON THE PLAINTIFFS by their Counsel undertaking to issue and serve
a writ forthwith upon the Defendant and undertaking to abide by any
order this Court may make as to damages in case this Court shall
hereafter be of opinion that the Defendant shall have sustained any by
reason of this Order which the Plaintiffs ought to pay,

IT IS ORDERED THAT the Defendant be restrained and an injunction is
hereby granted restraining her from appearing as a performer at any
opera house, theatre, concert hall or public or private entertainment
whatsoever until after the hearing of a summons returnable on the 16th
day of November, 1976 next or until further order.

Dated the 8th day of November, 1976

Note: On the reverse of Document 2 would be printed the following words: Notice If you
the within named Defendant, Henrietta Carlova, disobey this order you will be liable to
process of execution to compel you to obey it.

Document 3

In the High Court of Justice
QUEEN'S BENCH DIVISION

1975.— T .—No.106.

Between

S.1
—
Judge's Summons
(General Form)

Oyez Publishing
Limited
Oyez House
237 Long Lane
London SE1 4PU
a subsidiary of
The Solicitors' Law
Stationery Society
Limited

F21247 10-5-73

The Royal Metropolitan Opera Company   Plaintiffs

AND

Henrietta Carlova   Defendant

(¹) Judge in Chambers, Central Office, or Judge in Court, as the case may be   Let all parties concerned attend the (¹) **Judge in Chambers, Room 206,** Central Office Royal Courts of Justice, Strand, London, on   **Thursday**, the 18th day of **November,** 1976, at   **10.30.** o'clock in the   forenoon, on the hearing of an application on the part of **the Plaintiffs**

for an order that the injunction granted the 8th day of November, 1976 by the Hon. Mr. Justice Strawberry whereby the Defendant was restrained from appearing or performing at any opera house, theatre, concert hall or other public or private entertainment in the British Isles until the hearing of this summons be continued until the trial hereof or further order.

Dated the   8th   day of   **November,**   1976.

To **Miss Henrietta Carlova**
Hilton Hotel
Park Lane, London W1

This Summons was taken out by

Dodson and Fogg
Freeman's Court
of   **Cornhill**
London EC3
Solicitors for the **Plaintiffs**

Document 4

In the High Court of Justice   1976.-T.-No. 106

Queens' Bench Division

  (Writ issued the 8th day of November 1976)

            Between:

                    The Metropolitan Opera Company

                                        Plaintiffs

                            and

                    Henrietta Carlova   Defendant

                    _____

                    Statement of Claim

                    _____

1.   By an agreement in writing dated the 23rd day of September, 1976
      the Defendant agreed to appear at the Plaintiffs' Opera House,
      Bow Street, London WC1 during the Winter Season 1976-77 (which
      expression denotes the period from the 3rd day of November, 1976
      to the 31st day of March, 1977).

2.   The following were inter alia express terms of the said agreement:-

      (a)   that the Defendant should attend punctually at all
             rehearsals and performance,

      (b)   that during the currency of the said agreement she
             should not appear at any other opera house, theatre,
             concert hall or public or private entertainment in the
             British Isles, without the prior written consent of
             the Plaintiffs.

3.   In breach of the aforesaid terms the Defendant has failed to attend
      at rehearsals or performances since the 1st day of November, 1976
      and has agreed to appear in current performances at the Empire
      Theatre, Haymarket, London W1.

4.   By reason of the matters aforesaid the Plaintiffs have suffered
      damage.

5.   The Defendant threatens and intends to continue to appear at the
      aforesaid Empire Theatre, unless restrained from so doing.

      And the Plaintiffs claim:-

      1.   An injunction to restrain the Defendant from appearing
            at any opera house, theatre, concert hall or other public
            or private entertainment in the British Isles, until the
            31st day of March, 1977.

      2.   Damages.

                                        Robert Jordan

Served etc.

Document 5

In the High Court of Justice   1976.-T.-No. 106
Queen's Bench Division

          Between

                    The Metropolitan Opera Company
                                        Plaintiffs

                              and

                    Henrietta Carlova   Defendant

          In the Matter of an Application on behalf of
          the Plaintiffs against the Defendant for an
          Order of Committal.

                    _____

                         Notice of Motion

                    _____

TAKE NOTICE that this Court will be moved before one of the Judges of the
High Court sitting at the Royal Courts of Justice, Strand, London WC2 on
Monday the 15th day of November, 1976 at 10.30 o'clock in the forenoon or
so soon thereafter as counsel can be heard by counsel on behalf of the
Plaintiffs for an order:

   1.   That the Defendant be committed to one of Her Majesty's Prisons
           for her contempt of court in appearing at the Empire Theatre,
           London W1 on the 9th day of November 1976 in breach of the
           injunction made by the order of the Honourable Mr. Justice
           Strawberry, dated the 8th day of November 1976.

   2.   That the said Defendant do pay to the Plaintiffs their costs
           of and incidental to this application and the order to be made
           thereon.

   3.   That such further or other order may be made as to the Court
           shall seem proper.

AND FURTHER TAKE NOTICE that the applicants herein, the said Plaintiffs,
intend to read and use in support of the application the affidavit of
Benjamin Hutchinson sworn the 10th day of November 1976 and the exhibits
thereto, a true copy of which affidavit is served together with this Notice
of Motion.

Dated the 10th day of November 1976.

To: Miss Henrietta Carlova   Dodson and Fogg
of   Freeman's Court
Hilton Hotel   Cornhill
Park Lane   London EC3
London W1   Solicitors for the Plaintiffs

CHAPTER FIVE

THIRD PARTY PROCEDURE

DEFENDANT'S RIGHT TO BRING IN THIRD PARTIES

Where a defendant wishes to claim that a person not a party to the proceedings should be responsible in whole or in part for any damages he may have to pay the plaintiff he will issue a *third party notice* which has the effect of enabling the issues between the defendant and the third party to be determined in the action proceeding between the plaintiff and the defendant.

> *Example 1*—P is a passenger in a car driven by T which is involved in a collision with a lorry driven by D. P sues D for damages for personal injuries. D can join T as a third party and claim contribution under the Law Reform Act 1935.
>
> *Example 2*—Thomas enters into a hire purchase agreement with Paramount Finance Company. His uncle, Donald, signs a guarantee. Thomas defaults in payment and the company sue Donald on the guarantee. Donald can join Thomas as a third party and claim indemnity.
>
> *Example 3*—Paul is injured whilst working a machine at Dickson's factory and brings an action claiming damages. Dickson can join the Thompson Engineering Co. who made the machine and claim damages for breach of the conditions as to fitness for purpose implied by the Sale of Goods Act.
>
> *Example 4*—David buys a second-hand car from Terry. In fact the car had originally been obtained by a rogue from Peter's garage and sold by him to Terry. Peter sues David for specific recovery of the vehicle. David can join Terry as third party and claim damages for breach of condition as to title since a common question in respect of the subject matter of both claims arises, namely did Terry have good title to pass to David.

It can be seen from the above examples that there are basically four cases where a third party notice may be issued, namely:[1]

(1) where the defendant claims *contribution*
(2) where he claims an *indemnity*
(3) where he claims against the third party *substantially the same relief* in respect of the *same subject matter* as the plaintiff claims against him.
(4) where he requires that any *question* or *issue* relating to or connected with the original subject matter of the action should be determined not only as between himself and the plaintiff but between either or both of them and a third party.

In theory in each of the above cases it would be possible to permit the defendant to bring a separate action against the third party but the issue of a third party notice saves time, expense and the possibility of the courts coming to a different conclusion on the same point.

THIRD PARTY NOTICE PROCEDURE

D. Copperfield Ltd. is a company which operates a fleet of lorries in West London. On 12 August 1976 their managing director, Mr. Green, visits the garage

---

[1] See R.S.C. Ord. 16, r. 1; C.C.R. Ord. 12, r. 1.

premises of Easy Rider Garages in Chiswick and sees a lorry for sale at £4,000. He is told by the salesman that the lorry is in excellent condition. He then agrees to take the lorry and finance is arranged by way of hire purchase agreement with the Universal Finance Company. The lorry develops serious defects and the purchasers stop paying the instalments. The finance company sue for the return of the lorry and a minimum payment under the contract or damages for breach of contract. The purchasers wish to join the garage to claim either an indemnity if they have to return the lorry or else damages for the cost of repairs.

The procedure to be followed is set out in R.S.C. Order 16. The first step is for the defendant to issue a third party notice; the procedure for issue and service is the same as in the case of a writ except that where the defendant has already served a defence, he must obtain leave by applying ex parte to a master with an affidavit setting out the nature of the case, the stage which it has reached, the basis of his claim against the third party and the name and address of the person to whom the notice is to be issued. The form of notice is set out below:

In the High Court of Justice

Queen's Bench Division

1976—U—No. 2067.

Between:

Universal Finance Company Limited	Plaintiffs
and	
David Copperfield Limited	Defendants
and	
Easy Rider Garages	Third Party
(a firm)	

Third Party Notice

Issued pursuant to the order of Master Cooper dated the 23rd day of January 1976.

To Easy Rider Garages of 206 High Street, Chiswick, London W7.

TAKE NOTICE that this action has been brought by the Plaintiffs against the Defendants. In it the Plaintiffs claim the sum of £3,569 being the balance of the hire charges and interest outstanding on a Ford motor lorry registration number "AMO 12 L" or the return of the said vehicle and damages as appears from the Writ of Summons a copy whereof is served herewith together with a copy of the Statement of Claim.

The Defendants claim against you to be indemnified against the Plaintiffs' claim and the costs of this action alternatively the following relief or remedy namely damages on the grounds that they were induced to hire purchase the said vehicle by negligent mis-statements as to its condition or quality by your servant or agent and/or that the vehicle is defective and unroadworthy in breach of a warranty collateral to the contract of hire purchase.

AND TAKE NOTICE that if you wish to dispute the Plaintiffs' claim against the Defendants, or the Defendants' claim against you, an appearance must be entered on your behalf within 14 days after the service of this notice on you, inclusive of the day of service, otherwise you will be deemed to admit the Plaintiffs' claim against the Defendant and the Defendants' claim against you and your liability to indemnify the defendant or in damages and will be bound by any judgment or decision given in the action and the judgment may be enforced against you in accordance with Order 16 of the Rules of the Supreme Court.

Dated ....

Signed

Solicitors for the Defendants

Directions for entering appearance ....

_____

Once the third party has entered an appearance, the defendant must issue a summons for "third party directions". This is served on the plaintiff and the third party and enables the master

(a) to consider whether the third party notice should stand, i.e. whether the case is appropriate for third party proceedings,

(b) to give directions as to the future conduct of the case. This will often involve an order that the defendant serves a detailed statement of his claim on the third party since the third party notice will generally only contain a short outline of the case analogous to the general indorsement on a writ.

We set out below the typical wording of a summons for third party directions which will indicate the sort of orders which will be requested:

_____

Let all parties concerned attend the Master in Chambers in Room No.   at the Central Office, Royal Courts of Justice on Friday the 23rd day of January 1976 at 11 o'clock in the forenoon for an order for third party directions, as follows:

1. That the Defendants serve a statement of their claim on the Third Party within 28 days from this date.
2. That the Third Party plead thereto within 14 days of service.
3. That the Defendants and Third Party do respectively exchange lists of documents within 14 days after these pleadings are closed and that there be inspection of documents within 7 days thereafter.
4. And that the said Third Party be at liberty to appear at the trial of this action and take such part as the Judge shall direct, and be bound by the result of the trial,

And that the question of the liability of the said Third Party to indemnity the Defendants and the said Defendants' claim for damages be tried at the trial of this action, but subsequent thereto.

5. And that the costs of this application be costs in the cause and in the Third Party proceedings.

_____

The practice in the County Court is set out in C.C.R. Order 12 and follows the High Court procedure except that since the notice[1] requires the third party (a) to file a defence within 14 days to the third party claim and (b) to attend the trial there is no special summons for third party directions.

CONTRIBUTION NOTICE

We have dealt so far with the situation where a defendant seeks an indemnity, contribution, etc. from a person who is *not* already a party to the proceedings.

_____

[1] Form 70.

We have now to consider the position where one defendant seeks an indemnity or contribution from another defendant.

Example 1—P is a passenger in a van driven by D1 which collides with a car driven by D 2. P sues both D1 and D2. D2 wishes to claim contribution from D1.

Example 2—An opera house sue one of their singers who has taken a post at another opera company in breach of her contract. They also sue the other company for inducing a breach of contract. That company wish to claim indemnity from the singer on the basis that by her contract she expressly warranted that "no other company has any enforceable rights to my services during the currency of this agreement".

In the first example above, D1 and D2 are sued as tortfeasors liable in respect of the same damage so that the court has a statutory power to apportion liability between them without the necessity of either side filing any notice.[1] If however either party wishes to obtain discovery from the other or administer interrogatories then he will have to issue a formal notice and take out a summons for third party directions.

In the second example given above, the opera company will only be able to claim indemnity if they have issued a notice of contribution upon the singer and taken out a summons for direction.[2] The form of notice reads as follows:

To the Defendant A.B. of (address).
Take notice that the Defendant C.D. claims against you to be indemnified against the Plaintiff's claim and to the costs of this action on the grounds that. . . .

INTERPLEADER SUMMONS

Where a defendant is sued by a plaintiff claiming property held by the defendant in which the defendant has no interest but which is also claimed by a third party, the defendant may take out and serve a summons[3] on both claimants for an order that the issue as to ownership be decided between them.

Example—A buys a car from a rogue R who has obtained it by a trick from the original owner O. The car is seized by the police in connection with proceedings against R. Now A has brought an action against the police claiming delivery. O has also intimated a claim.

The interpleader summons must be supported by an affidavit stating (*a*) that the defendant claims no interest in the subject matter in dispute except his charges and costs; (*b*) that he does not collude with either claimant and (*c*) that he is willing to pay or transfer the subject matter into court or dispose of it as the court directs. The effect of the summons is of course that the party interpleading drops out and the action proceeds as between the two claimants.[4]

---

[1] Law Reform (Married Women and Tortfeasors) Act 1935, s. 6(1). It is customary to serve an informal notice of intention to ask the court for an order apportioning liability: *Clayson* v. *Rolls Royce, Ltd.* [1951] 1 K.B. 746; [1950] 2 All E.R. 884.
[2] See Ord. 16, r. 8; C.C.R. Ord. 12, r. 5.
[3] R.S.C. Ord. 17; C.C.R. Ord. 28. If neither claimant has brought proceedings, the person holding the disputed vehicle may issue an originating summons for the same purpose. The rule applies equally to debts where there are two claimants.
[4] The problem of rival claimants to goods can easily arise where either sheriffs officers or the bailiffs of a county court enter premises to seize goods by way of execution. As to the special rules in such circumstances: see R.S.C. Ord. 17, rr. 2, 4, 6 and C.C.R. Ord. 28, rr. 1–15.

CHAPTER SIX

DISCLOSURE OF EVIDENCE

The basic rule in the English system of civil litigation is that each side is entitled to know in advance the allegations which they will have to meet at the trial but *not* the evidence by which the other side intend to prove their case.

Example—P sues D for damages caused to his car in a collision with D's lorry. P must set out specifically in his pleading the allegations of negligence (e.g. "Drove at too fast a speed; failed to stop at a red traffic light") but will not disclose to D that he proposes to call witnesses who will say they saw D driving at speed past the red lights. The first D will hear of this evidence is when the witnesses are called to give evidence at the trial.

This system whereby evidence is concealed until the trial is not generally followed in the Chancery or Family Division where (in, for example, originating summons procedure or custody applications) the parties are required to file and exchange affidavits in advance of the hearing. Even in the Queen's Bench Division it will be appreciated that a certain amount of evidence may be revealed in interlocutory applications (e.g. for an injunction) or on an application for summary judgment under Order 14. Nonetheless where an action is commenced by writ it is the basic rule that neither side knows the other's evidence. This chapter is concerned with the extent to which one party can compel the other to reveal his evidence—the process originally developed in the Court of Chancery and known as *discovery*. We shall see that the position can be summarised as follows:

(1) The parties are compelled to disclose all *documentary* evidence.
(2) *Expert* evidence which is to be used at the trial must be revealed to the other side.
(3) In exceptional cases one party can *cross-examine* the other before the trial by means of *interrogatories*.

We shall also consider the extent to which information can be obtained before the action is begun and the circumstances in which it can be obtained from non-parties.

PRE-ACTION DISCOVERY

As a general rule the courts will not intervene to assist a person who wants to discover information in order to bring proceedings.

Example—A collision occurs in which one driver sustains injuries and suffers amnesia. He cannot obtain an order against the other driver or witnesses to the accident requiring them to set out their recollection of the incident in order for him to decide whether it is worth suing the other driver.

There are three exceptions to this basic proposition, each designed to prevent injustice to a person who may have a valid claim.

(i) *Documents in personal injury and fatal accident cases.* Section 31 of the Administration of Justice Act 1970 empowers the court to order disclosure of relevant documents by any person who is "likely to be a party to subsequent proceedings in that court in which a claim in respect of personal injuries to a person or in respect of a person's death is likely to be made". The procedure is governed by Order 24, rule 7A. The applicant issues an *originating summons* applying for an order that the respondent disclose the relevant documents.[1] This summons must be supported by an affidavit explaining the circumstances in which it is said the respondent is likely to be a party to the eventual action, setting out the reasons why the documents in question are relevant at this stage and deposing to the applicant's belief that the respondent has the documents in his possession, custody or power.[2] An example of the working of this new system can be seen in *Dunning* v. *United Liverpool Hospital's Board of Governors* [1973] 2 All E.R. 454.

Mrs. Dunning went into Liverpool Royal Infirmary for a minor ailment but whilst there developed very serious symptoms and left hospital considerably disabled. She believed her condition was the result of negligent treatment. An independent report obtained by her solicitors stated that the hospital was probably not at fault but regretted that the hospital had failed to provide copies of the notes of her treatment. The doctor concluded "As an independent medical witness it is my opinion that this failure to reveal the hospital notes has unreasonably prolonged the litigation in this patient's case. ... It is my opinion that once these notes have been made available and their contents explained in lay terms to the plaintiffs their minds will be set at rest." Mrs. Dunning's solicitors then made an application under Order 24, rule 7A for disclosure of the hospital records. The hospital opposed the application on the grounds that in view of the doctor's report it could not be said the records were needed for a claim which was *likely* to be made. Lord Denning M.R. (at p. 457) said that "we should construe 'likely to be made' as meaning 'may' or 'may well be made' dependent on the outcome of the discovery". James L.J. at p. 460 said that section 31 "covers both the situation in which without sight of the documents in question the intending plaintiff may have ample evidence on which to found a claim, and also the situation in which the documents are the evidence essential to the claim or are evidence without which the claim is not so strong". He went on to say that in view of the medical experts qualification of his view with the comment that the absence of hospital notes made his task difficult "it leaves open the possibility that the notes ... may add to the existing evidence to support Mrs. Dunning's allegation. ... I would construe 'likely' there as meaning 'a reasonable prospect'".

It should be noted that the section does not enable the court to order the production of documents for which the respondent could claim privilege. The provisions of Order 24, rule 7A apply specifically to actions in the county court by virtue of C.C.R. Order 13, rule 15.

(ii) *Pre-action inspection of property.* By section 21(1) of the Administration of Justice Act 1969 both the High Court and the county court have power to make orders for:

"(*a*) the inspection, photographing, preservation, custody and detention of property which appears to the court to be property which may become the subject matter of subsequent proceedings in the court, or as to which any question may arise in any such proceedings, and

(*b*) the taking of samples of any such property as is mentioned in the preceding

---

[1] It is sensible where the documents are properly confidential to seek an order that the applicant's *solicitors* be permitted to inspect the documents and take copies of the relevant items.
[2] The applicant generally pays the costs in such cases even if an order is made.

paragraph and the carrying out of any experiment on or with any such property."

The expression property "includes any land, chattel or other corporeal property of any description".

Example—P is injured when he catches his hand in a press at work. In order to decide whether there has been a breach of the Factory Acts his solicitors can apply to the court for an order enabling them to inspect the machine before they finally decide whether or not to issue a writ.

The procedure is governed by Order 29, rule 7A. The applicant issues and serves an originating summons accompanied by an affidavit showing how his claim falls within the order. If an order is made the defendant is nonetheless entitled to the costs of and incidental to the application and of complying with the order unless the court directs otherwise.[1] The High Court procedure is followed where the application is made in the county court.[2]

(iii) *Discovery against innocent persons who have facilitated the wrong in question.* To the general rule stated at the beginning of this chapter that the court will not compel an innocent party to disclose information which would assist a prospective litigant in determining whether or not to bring an action, there is an exception where that person though innocent has in some way facilitated the wrong in question. This exception was laid down by the House of Lords in *Norwich Pharmacal Co.* v. *Customs and Excise Commissioners* [1973] 2 All E.R. 943 where the facts were:

The Plaintiffs owned a patent for the production and sale of a chemical fertiliser. Every importer of chemicals into the United Kingdom is required to identify the substances imported to the Customs. The Excise statistics for 1960–1970 showed 30 consignments of this chemical fertiliser had been imported into the country by persons other than the plaintiffs in breach of the plaintiffs' monopoly. The Customs refused to disclose the identity of the importers.

The House of Lords held that an *action for discovery* lay to compel the Commissioners to disclose the information. Although they had committed no tort themselves, without customs' clearance the fertiliser could not have been brought into the country and so they had unwittingly facilitated the breach of the plaintiffs' patent. Lord Reid (at p. 948) explained the principle to be applied as follows:

"if through no fault of his own a person gets mixed up in the tortious acts of others so as to facilitate their wrongdoing he may incur no personal liability but he comes under a duty to assist the person who has been wronged by giving him full information and disclosing the identity of the wrongdoers. I do not think that it matters whether he became so mixed up by voluntary action on his part or because it was his duty to do what he did. It may be that if this causes him expense the person seeking the information ought to reimburse him. But justice requires that he should co-operate in righting the wrong if he unwittingly facilitated its perpetration".

The important point to note is that the plaintiff must prove the defendant has in some way *facilitated* the wrong in question. That would seem to cover the case where A lends B his car and B (who is uninsured) is involved in an accident. It is an open question whether there would be an order in the case below:

Farmer Giles lets some close friends camp at the bottom of his meadow for their summer holiday. Next door to the meadow is the country home of Sir Roderick

[1] R.S.C. Ord. 62, r. 3(12).
[2] C.C.R. Ord. 13, r. 15(1).

Murgatroyd who at the material time had himself gone on holiday to the Continent. Unbeknown to Giles, his friends trespass on Sir Roderick's land causing extensive damage. When Sir Roderick returns from holiday he demands to know the identity of the campers. Giles refuses to tell him.

The procedure which was adopted in the *Norwich Pharmacal* case by the plaintiffs was based on the old Chancery action of discovery. A writ or originating summons is issued seeking an order "that the defendants disclose the following documents. . . ."

DISCOVERY BETWEEN PARTIES AFTER ACTION COMMENCED

(a) Inspection of documents referred to in pleadings etc.

If any document is referred to in one party's pleadings or affidavits, his opponent may serve notice on him requiring him within 4 days of receipt of the notice to notify him of a time within 7 days when he will provide facilities for inspection of the document.[1] Thus, if for example, a pleading refers to "an agreement in writing dated ..." the other side can inspect that document without waiting for the formal discovery which occurs after the pleadings are closed. Indeed the order effectively enables inspection before the other party settles any pleading in reply. If inspection is not forthcoming the applicant can issue an interlocutory summons to a master for an order.

(b) Automatic discovery by list

In actions commenced by writ in the High Court each party is required within 14 days of the close of pleadings[2] to send the other party a list of all documents relating to matters in question in the action which are or have been in his possession, custody or power. The list is divided into two schedules; the first schedule sets out details of all documents which the party has at present in his possession and is subdivided into a list of documents he is willing to disclose and those for which he claims privilege; the second schedule describes the material documents which were formerly in his possession stating when they were last in his possession, what became of them and in whose possession they now are. The list must conclude with a notice stating a place and time within 7 days of service of the list at which the documents may be inspected.[3] It is important to notice that the exchange of lists and inspection takes place without any specific order of the court, the process occurs automatically at the close of pleadings.[4]

(c) Orders for discovery

The process of automatic discovery by exchange of lists does *not* apply in the following cases:

(1) Third party procedure.
(2) Originating summons procedure (where frequently there will be no dispute on evidence).

---

[1] R.S.C. Ord. 24, r. 10. Cf. C.C.R. Ord. 14, r. 3—slightly different periods apply in the county court.
[2] Close of pleadings is defined by R.S.C. Ord. 18, r. 20 as occurring 14 days after service of reply or defence to counter-claim or if neither such reply nor defence to counter-claim is served, as the expiration of 14 days after service of the defence.
[3] The above paragraph paraphrases the provision of R.S.C. Ord. 24, rr. 1, 2, 5 and 9.
[4] The standard form used is set out at pp. 18–20, *ante*.

(3) To *defendants* in road traffic cases (since there are generally *no* relevant documents).
(4) County court proceedings.

In all the above cases however, the parties may serve on the other side a request either for discovery of all material documents or for specific documents, and, in default, apply to the court. [1]

(d) What documents are to be disclosed
There is an important difference between discovery and inspection in that on discovery one is notifying the other side of the *existence* of the document in question whilst at inspection one is *showing* the document to the other side. It should be noted that *all* relevant documents must be disclosed on discovery even though inspection will be refused on a claim for privilege:

> "The rule as to the discovery of documents is the exact contrary to that as to inspection—you must disclose every document you have in your possession, whether you are bound to produce it or not." [2]

The documents which must be disclosed are all documents "relating to any matter in question ... in the action." This expression covers not only documents which are direct evidence of the facts in issue or which one intends to use at the trial but every document which contains information which may enable one's opponent to advance his own case or damage one's own case or which "may fairly lead him to a train of inquiry which may have either of these two consequences". [3] The exact limit of this rule has however never been defined.

> *Example*—A (a rogue) sues B on an oral contract. In particulars of his pleading he sets out the precise date and time and place of the alleged agreement. B has in his possession his passport which shows he was out of the country at the relevant time. Is B bound to disclose this document?

One would have thought the answer to the above problem was clearly in the affirmative, even though the disclosure would enable A to trim his account in advance of the trial to meet the new evidence. However in *Britten* v. *Pilcher & Sons* [1969] 1 All E.R. 491[4] (where insurers in a workman's claim for personal injuries did not disclose a statement headed "for company's solicitors" and made by the plaintiff himself immediately after the accident and produced it at the trial to rebut his sworn evidence) Thesiger J. said (at p. 493):

> "The difficulty that I feel in saying that this document ought to have been disclosed ... is that this is the sort of document that is prepared ... in many cases of mining accidents, in many cases of railway accidents and in very many industrial injury cases where it is to the advantage of a potential defendant and employer to ascertain as quickly as possible what the various witnesses in and about the place can tell them as to how the accident happened. I have nowhere previously ... heard it suggested that all documents obtained under a heading like this from the various witnesses ought to be disclosed to a plaintiff in order that he can avoid calling witnesses

---

[1] In the High Court the application is by summons to the master under Ord. 24, r. 3. In the county court the procedure, which is governed by Ord. 14, r. 2, is by application to the registrar.
[2] *Gardner* v. *Irvin* [1878] 4 Ex. D. 49.
[3] *Compagnie Financière Et Commerciale Du Pacifique* v. *Peruvian Guano Co.* [1882] 11 Q.B.D. 55.
[4] This case is actually reported because the unsuccessful plaintiffs resisted an order for costs on the grounds that if the document had been disclosed they might have decided not to continue the case. Such statements from witnesses will normally be covered by legal professional privilege which protects them from inspection but not disclosure.

without giving them the opportunity of trimming the evidence they propose to give to the more contemporary document."

(e) Failure to make discovery

Suppose one party suspects the other has not revealed a relevant document in his possession. In such a case he may require that party to verify his list by affidavit.[1] The Affidavit must be served within 14 days. Alternatively (or if the procedure above has failed to produce disclosure of the document) he can apply to the master with an affidavit setting out why he believes his opponent has the document in question. The other side will be ordered to file an affidavit dealing specifically with the allegation. This affidavit is usually regarded as conclusive but the applicant can challenge the matter before the master by applying for specific production.[2]

(f) Inspection

This crucial stage of the action is described in the *Justice Report* on *Going to Law*[3] as follows:

> "'Inspection' is a lengthy meeting between representatives of both firms of solicitors at which each inspects the documents in the possession of the other. All this is painstaking and important work, on which success or failure at the trial may depend. It requires many hours of undisturbed concentration, the writing of a good many letters, and much time on the Xerox machine".

The reason of course why this stage is of such immense importance is that the most telling evidence at the trial is often not what the parties say in the witness box but what contemporary documents show they said and did at the time when the cause of action arose. It is significant that the compilers of the Justice Report found that settlements of actions are most commonly effected at the time of compilation of lists or inspection:

> "Because of the mounting expense of this phase of the proceedings often reflected in requests from the solicitors to their clients for the payment of more money on account of costs, it is a phase when many actions are settled—especially if the collection of documents for discovery shows that they will not help one's client's case, and more favourable terms of settlement can therefore be expected if the other side has not yet had a chance to see them. But there are other reasons too; inspection of documents is often the first real chance that each side has to assess the true strength of the other's case, and it provides the only occasion before the trial itself when the solicitors are bound to meet, and can casually talk about settlement, without being suspected of weakness by being the first to ask for a meeting."

(g) Documents privileged from inspection

Although the general rule is that each party is bound to show the other side all material documents in his possession the courts have held that the public interest requires that there should be exceptions to this rule where there are factors outweighing this general rule.[4] The most important ground of privilege in practice is that which protects from inspection any direct com-

---

[1] See Ord. 24, r. 2(7).
[2] See Ord. 24. r. 7. The sanction for failure to produce after an order is that the defaulting party has his claim dismissed if he is plaintiff or, if defendant, has his defence struck out and judgment entered. The equivalent procedure in the county court is set out in Ord. 14, rr. 6 and 9.
[3] Stevens 1974, p. 14.
[4] For example, documents which would expose the party in question to criminal prosecution need not be disclosed (Civil Evidence Act 1968, s. 14); nor need documents where disclosure would be contrary to the interests of the state (see *Duncan* v. *Cammel Laird* [1942] A.C. 624; [1942] 1 All E.R. 587 and *Conway* v. *Rimmer* [1968] A.C. 910; [1968] 1 All E.R. 874.

munication between a party and his legal advisers. This covers communications before any litigation has begun or was even contemplated. It extends to communications between employers and salaried solicitors employed directly by them (e.g. the legal departments of ministries and large companies). The reason for this privilege is that the courts consider they have an overriding obligation to ensure full and candid disclosure by clients to their legal advisers which would not be possible unless the clients were aware that their confidences could not be broken. Documents are also privileged if they are prepared by a third party for submission to the litigant's solicitor in order to enable him to advise his client (e.g. expert reports in a factory accident). In itself this is a fairly narrow extension of the doctrine of legal privilege but in practice it can create problems. The first point to notice is that documents prepared by a third party are only privileged if litigation was contemplated when they were written.[1] The second point to note is that the document must have been drawn up for immediate communication to legal advisers:

Example 1—A member of a trade union who thought that he had been unjustly dismissed by his employers furnished the union authorities with information in writing as to the facts of the case in order to satisfy them it was proper for them to instruct a solicitor on his behalf. His employers obtained discovery of this document on the ground that the *immediate* purpose of the document was *not* its reference to a solicitor but merely to the trade union committee.[2]

Example 2—Purchase tax was assessed on the basis of the wholesale value of amusement machines manufactured and sold by A. The Commissioners of Customs and Excise obtained substantial documentary evidence from A's customers on which they based an assessment of value for tax purposes. A challenged the assessment and demanded production of the evidence collected from his customers. The Commissioners claimed privilege on the ground that they had expected the assessment to be challenged and knew when they collected the information that they would probably be passing it to their legal advisers. The claim for privilege failed on the basis that the *immediate* purpose of the document was not its reference to a solicitor but merely to provide the Commissioners with the information for making an assessment.[3]

A limit is however placed on this rule where an intermediary receives a document which he will transmit at once to legal advisers without acting on it himself; in such a case the document remains privileged. Thus an accident claim form sent to insurers is privileged.[4] Similarly it is submitted that an accident report sent to a trade union officer for immediate despatch to the trade union's legal department or solicitors would be protected.

The third point of importance so far as this aspect of privilege is concerned is that, although the immediate communication to legal advisers must have been one reason for producing the document, it need not have been the *only* reason, provided such communication was not merely incidental.

Example 1—A fatal accident occurred on the railway. The staff present prepared a report for submission (*a*) to the Ministry of Transport (who were under a statutory duty to investigate all such accidents) and (*b*) to the railway's solicitors' department. The plaintiffs sought to obtain inspection of the report on the basis it had not been

---

[1] *Ogden* v. *London Electric Rail. Co.* [1933], 149 L.T.476—accident on platform. Report headed "For the information of Company's solicitors only" made at once. Although no claim had been intimated the very fact of the accident meant proceedings were contemplated.
[2] *Jones* v. *Great Central Rail. Co.* [1910] A.C. 4.
[3] *Alfred Crompton Amusement Machines* v. *Customs and Excise Commissioners* (No. 2) [1974]A.C. 405; [1973] 2 All E.R. 1169. Note an alternative claim based on Crown Privilege succeeded.
[4] *Westminster Airways Ltd* v. *Kuwait Oil Co. Ltd* [1951] 1 K.B. 134; [1950] 2 All E.R. 596.

prepared solely for the purpose of obtaining legal advice on contemplated proceedings. The court refused to order production on the ground that submission to legal advisers need not be the sole or even dominant purpose of the report for privilege to attach to it.[1]

Example 2—An employee was injured at work on the railway. The railway held a private court of inquiry and sent a copy of the report to various departments who were concerned with safety precautions and also to their legal department. The employee claimed to see a copy of the report; the railway claimed it was privileged. *Held*, since the substantial purpose of the report was to provide for safety measures so submission to the legal department was purely incidental, the claim for privilege failed. In order to prove privilege it must be shown that communication to legal advisers was a substantial purpose in preparing the document.[2]

DISCOVERY BETWEEN CO-DEFENDANTS

R.S.C. Order 24, rule 6 provides that a defendant is entitled to receive a copy of any list served by any other defendant on the plaintiff. In the county court, where discovery (if not mutually agreed) only takes place after an application to the registrar, a defendant may make such application against a co-defendant; discovery will be ordered if there are rights to be adjusted as between the defendants (see C.C.R. Order 14, rule 2).

DISCOVERY AGAINST NON-PARTIES

The basic rule is that the parties to an action have no right to compel persons not parties to disclose relevant documents in their possession. They can issue a *subpoena duces tecum* requiring the non-party to attend at the trial with the relevant document but they are not entitled to inspect it before the trial. To this general rule there are three exceptions:

(i) In personal injury and fatal accident cases, a party to the action can apply for an order that a person who is not a party (e.g. a hospital authority) disclose relevant documents. The application is made by summons served on
     (a) the person holding the documents, and
     (b) on all other parties to the action.
     Note this procedure can only be adopted *after* an action has begun (see section 32(1) of the Administration of Justice Act 1970; R.S.C. Order 24, rule 7A; C.C.R. Order 14, rule 15).

(ii) A similar application can be made to inspect property held by a person who is not a party to an action (see section 32(2) of the Administration of Justice Act 1970; R.S.C. Order 29, rule 7A; C.C.R. Order 13, rule 15).

(iii) It may be that an application could be made under the principle in the *Norwich Pharmacal* case (see page 126 *ante*) for an order against a person not a party but who facilitated the commission of the alleged wrong by the defendant.

(iv) Either party may apply *ex parte* to the master for an order that a bank not a party to the action be required to permit him to inspect entries in its books and take copies—section 7 Bankers' Books Evidence Act 1879. If the account in question has been held at any time by the other party a summons will be issued so he can attend at the hearing of the application.

---

[1] *Seabrook v. British Transport Commission* [1959] 2 All E.R. 15; [1959] 1 W.L.R. 509.
[2] *Longthorn v. British Transport Commission* [1959] 2 All E.R. 32; [1959] 1 W.L.R. 530.

MEDICAL EXAMINATION OF PLAINTIFF AND INSPECTION OF PROPERTY

Although nothing in the Rules provides for the compulsory medical examination of the plaintiff in a personal injury case (or other case where his health or life expectancy would be relevant) the courts will refuse to allow the plaintiff to continue his case if he will not agree to a reasonable request for medical examination on reasonable terms (e.g. including the condition that he shall be given a copy of the report[1]). In *Edmeades* v. *Thames Board Mills, Ltd.* [1969] 2 Q.B. 67; [1969] 2 All E.R. 127 Lord Denning (at p. 129) (after quoting from the Winn Committee on Personal Injuries Litigation[2]) where the committee recommended a rule that the plaintiff should be required to submit to medical examination but felt legislation would be necessary to create such a rule) said:

"I do not think legislation is necessary. This court has ample jurisdiction to grant a stay whenever it is just and reasonable so to do. It can, therefore, order a stay if the conduct of the plaintiff in refusing a reasonable request is such as to prevent the just determination of the cause."

Either party can apply by summons or notice at any stage in an action for an order permitting him to inspect premises or property in the possession of his opponent (R.S.C. Ord. 29, r. 2; C.C.R. Ord. 13, r. 11). The order may authorise him to draw plans, take samples, etc. as may be necessary.

EXPERT EVIDENCE

A report from an expert concerning the subject matter of the action and commissioned when proceedings were contemplated or after they had commenced is clearly a privileged document and inspection of it will not be ordered.

Example—Before P's solicitors issued a writ for damages for personal injuries they permitted the defendants' insurers to arrange for their doctors to examine P but omitted to take an undertaking from the insurers that copies of the medical reports would be sent to them. After the action was commenced they applied for an order against the defendants requiring them to provide copies of the reports. The order was refused on the ground that the reports were privileged. *Per* Roskill L.J.: "so long as we have an adversary system, a party is entitled not to produce documents which are properly protected by privilege if it is not to his advantage to produce them and even though their production might assist his adversary if his adversary or his solicitor were aware of their contents or might lead the court to a different conclusion from that to which the court would come in ignorance of their existence. Some may regret this; but the law always has allowed it and it is not for us to change the law in this respect."[3]

This rule if unmodified would cause very great inconvenience in practice since by its very nature opinion evidence requires reflection and careful study by the opposing advocates and experts. Indeed it would be a great injustice if an advocate was forced to cross-examine on a complex statement of expert opinion without the opportunity of digesting it and seeking advice from his own experts. For this reason Parliament has enacted that the courts shall have power to compel the disclosure of opinion evidence *which is to be put in at the trial*.[4]

---

[1] See *Clarke* v. *Martlew* [1973] Q.B. 58; [1972] 3 All E.R. 764.
[2] Cmnd. 3691 of 1968 at para. 312.
[3] *Causton* v. *Mann Egerton (Johnsons), Ltd.* [1974] 1 All E.R. 453, at p. 460.
[4] *Note* the eventual evidence may be *oral*: the section requires that the report on which oral evidence will be based should be submitted to the other side. Note also the rule does *not* apply to opinion evidence which one party has obtained (such as a medical report unfavourable to his case) which he does *not* propose to call.

"Notwithstanding any enactment or rule of law by virtue of which documents prepared for the purpose of pending or contemplated civil proceedings are ... privileged ... provision may be made by rules of court in any civil proceedings to direct ... that the parties ... shall each ... disclose to the other ... in the form of one or more expert reports the expert evidence ... which he proposes to adduce as part of his case at the trial. ..."[1]

The sanction behind the court's order is that a party will not be permitted to call expert evidence which has not been disclosed.

The relevant procedure is set out in R.S.C. Order 38, rules 35 to 42 (which are expressly applied to the county court by C.C.R. Order 20, rules 33 to 34). The procedure is based on the concept that expert evidence is only admissible by consent or by leave obtained under the rules. The procedure can be summarised as follows:

(i) *engineer's evidence as to cause of motor accident*—the party wishing to rely on such evidence must first disclose his report to the other side and then apply to the master for leave to call the evidence at the trial. The rationale of this rule seems to be that it enables the other side to argue that the expert should not be called at all because his evidence is valueless (e.g. where it consists of speculation as to the cause of the accident based on the final position of the vehicles).[2]

(ii) *medical evidence*—in the absence of agreement the party seeking to put in the evidence must apply for leave to the court which is prima facie bound to direct disclosure as a condition precedent to granting leave. There will be exceptional cases where the court will grant leave but not direct disclosure, e.g. where the report goes to the cause of the injury as opposed to the effects (i.e. proves it is or is not the defendant's fault) or the case is based on medical negligence or the report deals with an allegation of malingering (e.g. by describing false symptoms which could be tested at the trial).[3]

(iii) *other experts*—the party seeking to call the expert must apply for leave to call the evidence but this time it is for his opponent to show that pre-trial disclosure is necessary in the interests of justice.[4]

ADMISSIONS AND INTERROGATORIES

Although the effect of the rules discussed above is that each side is normally fully aware of the documentary and expert evidence which will be adduced at the trial, there is no similar procedure for compelling one's opponent to reveal in advance the oral evidence he proposes to call. There are however circumstances where one party needs to know in advance what his opponent will say on certain points in order to prepare his own case properly or to save costs.

Example—You are instructed by "Claude et Cie of Clapham" (a firm of ladies' hairdressers) who are being sued by a former client in respect of negligent permanent waving which is alleged to have caused hair loss and irritation. A medical report (dated 12 months after the treatment) says that the plaintiff suffered itchiness after the permanent waving and treated her hair with "a number of concoctions

---

[1] Civil Evidence Act 1972, s. 2(3).
[2] R.S.C. Ord. 38, r. 40.
[3] R.S.C. Ord. 38, r. 37.
[4] R.S.C. Ord. 38, r. 38.

privately purchased but they failed to improve matters and the condition deteriorated".

In the above example it is clearly of vital importance to know precisely what preparations the plaintiff put on her hair after she found her scalp was itchy (a normal consequence of permanent waving). It may be that armed with this information it will be possible to show that her condition is not attributable in any way to the defendant's conduct.

In such a case the defendant would apply by interlocutory summons (or on the summons for directions) for an order[1] that the plaintiff answers on oath a number of questions drafted by counsel designed to extract precise information as to the matters in question. In the present case the interrogatories might begin as follows:

(1) Did you not tell Doctor —— that you had applied "a number of concoctions" to your hair after the permanent wave treatment the subject of this action or some other words to that effect?

(2) If yes, what was the proprietary name of each concoction so applied to your hair, from whom and when was each concoction purchased and on how many occasions was each such concoction applied and with what results?

A copy of the proposed interrogatories is served with the summons. The master is given power to require the other party to answer by affidavit all such interrogatories as he "considers necessary either for disposing fairly of the cause or matter or for saving costs". Although the rule is *not* limited to cases where the facts of the matter are peculiarly within the knowledge of the party to be interrogated, it is unusual to find interrogatories in other cases—probably because the master "in deciding whether to give leave ... shall take into account any offer made by the party to be interrogated to give particulars or to make admissions or to produce documents relating to any matter in question". Thus although interrogatories were formerly employed to obtain specific admissions from the other side this can be more conveniently done today by serving on the other side a *notice to admit facts*. The procedure is set out in R.S.C. Order 27, rule 2:

"A party to a cause or matter may not later than 21 days after the cause or matter is set down for trial serve on any other party a notice requiring him to admit, for the purpose of that cause or matter only, the facts specified in the notice."

If the other party does not admit the facts in question but they are proven at the trial, R.S.C. Order 62, rule 3(5) provides that the cost of proving such facts shall be borne by him even if he wins the substantial action. When therefore a notice to admit evokes no response or no specific admission, one can either proceed at once to apply for interrogatories or simply set in hand the preparation of evidence to cover the matters in question in the confident knowledge that win or lose one's opponent will pay the bill of one's proving these matters.

In conclusion we set out below two cases which illustrate how interrogatories are used:

Example 1—P who had just alighted from a stationary omnibus was knocked down and injured by a motor car as she was coming from behind the omnibus. She sustained concussion and had no clear recollection of the accident. The master and the judge held that interrogatories were not proper in "running down cases". The

---

[1] R.S.C. Ord. 26, r. 1. C.C.R. Ord. 14, r. 1—the practice and principles are the same in the County Court.

Court of Appeal reversed this decision and ordered the defendant to answer precise interrogatories designed to show his course prior to the accident and the position of his vehicle at the moment of impact. *Per* Scrutton L.J.: "In most accident cases both parties are able to call witnesses, and therefore to interrogate upon small questions of fact relating to the details of the accident cannot be necessary for the fair trial of the action, and interrogatories should not be allowed. Nor should interrogatories be allowed for 'fishing' purposes[1] or to obtain the names of the opponent's witnesses. These considerations are probably sufficient to disentitle the party to interrogate in most accident cases. But there should be no other fetter" (*Griebart v. Morris* [1920] 1 K.B. 659 at p. 666).

Example 2—The following interrogatories were permitted in a case of medical negligence: "(1) Were any, and if so how many, swabs removed from the deceased prior to the conclusion of the said operation? If yes, on whose instructions were they removed and what became of them? (2) Did you or some other, and what, person, purport to remove the swabs from the deceased's abdomen? Whose duty do you allege it was to remove the swabs inserted in the deceased's abdomen? If the said swabs were removed by some person other than you, on whose instructions were they acting? (3) Was a swab measuring 10 by 8 inches left in the deceased's abdomen? If yes, how, and in what way do you say it came to be left there?" (*Mahon v. Osborne* [1939] 2 K.B. 14; [1939] 1 All E.R. 535.)

PRE-TRIAL DISCOVERY IN AMERICA

The courts in the United States of America permit a much greater freedom to interrogate than is allowed in this country. The American system is described in the *Justice Report* on *Going to Law* (para. 130) as follows:

"The Federal Rules permit inspection, discovery of documents, and interrogation much as they are permitted in England, but the most significant device for our purposes, unknown to English law is the *deposition*. Either side may examine the other party on oath on reasonable notice before an officer authorised to administer oaths without leave of the court from a time twenty days after the action is commenced. A subpoena is required for examination of witnesses not party to the action unless they consent. Examination and cross-examination proceeds as at the trial, and the deposition may always be used at the trial 'to contradict or impeach the deponent as a witness' and may also be used ... as evidence *per se*".

---

[1] I.e. trying to build up a case when one does not have the basic evidence oneself to establish a prima facie case—see *Rofe v. Kevorkian* [1936] 2 All E.R. 1334.

CHAPTER SEVEN

EVIDENCE

Once discovery has been completed the parties must put their minds to how they will prove their case in court. In a case of any substance the papers will be sent to counsel to provide an advice on evidence. In minor cases, especially in the county court, the parties cannot afford such a luxury although in those very cases, because frequently the defendant does not appear and so the rules of evidence are rigidly applied against the plaintiff, it is of vital importance to be able to produce admissible evidence which will prove every essential allegation in the pleadings. In this chapter we shall discuss the problems of evidence which most frequently give trouble in the preparation of a case. At the end of the chapter we shall consider how counsel would write an advice on evidence in two typical cases.

DOCUMENTARY EVIDENCE

The basic rule applied by our courts is that where a document is put in as evidence the original must be produced. One must therefore check that the original is available for the trial.[1] If it is *not* available then the court will only admit secondary evidence (e.g. a copy or sworn testimony as to the contents of the original document) if:

(i) The party wishing to produce the document *proves* that it has been *destroyed* or that it has been *lost* and all reasonable steps to trace it have been unsuccessful. Note that this involves calling evidence as to the destruction or loss of the document. Such evidence could be by sworn testimony or where the destruction or loss is not likely to be contested, by affidavit.[2] Secondary evidence will *not* be admitted merely because the advocate at the trial says the original document has been destroyed or is missing (unless his opponent agrees to such a course).

(ii) The original is *in the possession of the opposing party* and he has been served with *notice to produce* that original at the trial, but has failed to do so. In the High Court, where there has been discovery by list each party is deemed to have been served with notice requiring him to produce all documents he has listed as being in his possession.[3] In all other High Court cases and *in all county court actions* each party must serve on the other a specific notice to produce any original documents held by the other side which he wishes to put in as part of his case. The practice followed is that when counsel comes to the stage in his case where he wishes to put in the original document, he "calls for its production". If his opponent does not then produce the original, counsel may at once

---

[1] Copies of bank records are admitted provided the person taking the copy attends or swears an affidavit verifying the copy—Bankers' Books Evidence Act 1879, ss. 4–5.
[2] One must send a copy of the affidavit and notice of intention to use it to the other side. see R.S.C. Ord. 38, r. 2; C.C.R. Ord. 20, r. 5.
[3] See R.S.C. Ord. 27. r. 4(3).

prove its contents by, for example, producing a copy and calling evidence to show this corresponds with the original.

If the original document is in the possession of a person who is not a party to the action, he must be served with a *subpoena duces tecum*[1]; if he fails to produce it, secondary evidence does *not* become admissible—the remedy is to enforce the subpoena against him.[2]

Assuming that one can produce all the original documents necessary in one's case (or will be able to put in secondary evidence under the above rules) a question still remains as to how one proves the documents are authentic.

Example 1—In order to succeed in an action A needs to produce a lease made in 1960 and an assignment of that lease in 1963. All the parties to the lease and assignment are now dead.

Example 2—B wishes to produce a series of letters which he says were written to him by the defendant. What happens if the defendant does not appear at the trial? What would happen if the letters were written not by the defendant but by his predecessor-in-title who is now dead?

Clearly great expense would be caused if in the above cases the authenticity of the document had to be strictly proved. Of course there will be some cases where this is necessary (i.e. where it is suggested that the document is a forgery) but generally since there is likely to be no dispute about the matters the rules provide:

(a) that in High Court actions *where a list of documents is served*, the party on whom the list is served is deemed to admit the authenticity of the original documents set out in the list (and also that all copies mentioned therein are true copies) unless he serves a counter-notice to the effect that he challenges their authenticity.[3]

(b) in *all county court* cases (and all cases in the High Court where lists of documents have not been exchanged) it is necessary to serve a *notice to admit* on the other side who will be deemed to admit the authenticity of the documents (or the veracity of copied documents) unless a counter-notice is served.[4]

Where, in the above cases a counter-notice is served, the authenticity of the document must then be strictly proved. If its authenticity is so proved, the party challenging it will normally be required to pay the costs occasioned by proving this item even if he succeeds overall in the case. It should be noted that certain documents are deemed to be authentic without any notice having been served.[5]

---

[1] I.e. an order of the court directing him to produce the relevant document: see *post* p. 138.

[2] If a person under subpoena lawfully refuses to produce the original document, secondary evidence may then be given.

[3] R.S.C. Ord. 27, r. 4. The counter-notice is to be served before the expiry of 21 days from the date of inspection or after the time limited for inspection has expired.

[4] C.C.R. Ord. 20, r. 10(1) provides that notice to admit must be sent not less than 5 clear days from the date of hearing and the counter-notice must be served within 3 days of service of the notice to admit (in practice the notice served is a notice to *produce and admit*). R.S.C. Ord. 27, r. 5 provides that the notice to admit must be served within 21 days of setting down the action for trial and the counter-notice is to be served with 21 days of such service.

[5] Public documents (such as entries in public registers) are deemed to be authentic and copies duly certified by the officer in charge of the register or record are admitted without his attendance at court. Thus copy marriage certificates, records of convictions, copy entries in rent registers, adjudications of rent tribunals, land certificates, etc. generally require no proof of authenticity. See on this point *Cross on "Evidence"*, 4th edn., pp. 454 *et seq.*

ATTENDANCE OF WITNESSES

Each party must arrange to secure the attendance of all his witnesses at court. If there is the slightest doubt about the willingness of the witness to attend, an application should be made for an order requiring his attendance at the trial. In the High Court[1] the procedure is governed by Order 38, rule 14. The party wishing to secure the attendance of the witness fills in an application form (called a *praecipe*) which he delivers to the central office.[2] If the case is to be heard in open court the order called a *subpoena ad testificandum* (or, if only the production of a document is required, called a *subpoena duces tecum*) is issued of right. If the matter is proceeding in chambers, the applicant will have to obtain leave from the master and so should swear an affidavit setting out his reasons for requiring the subpoena. The subpoena may be served anywhere in the United Kingdom.[3] It is sealed like a writ and must be served personally within 12 weeks of its issue.[4] When service is effected the witness must be given conduct money (i.e. a sufficient sum to defray his expenses in coming to, attending at and returning from court).[5] Disobedience of a subpoena is punishable as contempt of court.[6]

It should be noted that if either party wishes to produce evidence of entries in a banker's ledger (and this frequently happens when there is a dispute as to whether sums were paid some considerable time ago) he can obtain an order for him to inspect the books under section 7 of the Bankers' Books Evidence Act 1879 and take a copy rather than issuing a subpoena to the bank requiring an officer to attend (see p. 131 *ante*).

WITNESSES UNABLE TO ATTEND COURT

What is the position if a crucial witness is unable to attend court? We shall see below that in some circumstances the court will receive a statement signed by the witness pursuant to the Civil Evidence Act 1968 but this course necessarily means that the other side will not have the opportunity of cross-examining the witness and therefore is not satisfactory where the evidence is important and very much contested.

Example 1—In a probate action it was highly relevant to ascertain the state of the deceased's mental health immediately prior to the execution of the will. The only relevant witness was an old lady who had been a friend of the deceased but was now bedridden and could not attend court to give evidence.
Example 2—O sues T for possession of certain property which O has just bought and in which T is living. T claims.to be a tenant. O has a statement from his predecessor in title W saying he had never granted T any tenancy.

One must distinguish between those cases where the witness is within the jurisdiction and the cases where the witness is abroad.

(a) Witness in England or Wales
In the High Court[7] the party desiring to call the evidence applies on notice to

---

[1] The relevant procedure in the county court is set out in C.C.R. Ord. 20, r. 8.
[2] Or appropriate district registry.
[3] Supreme Court of Judicature Act 1925, s. 49(1).
[4] R.S.C. Ord. 38, r. 17.
[5] Supreme Court of Judicature Act, s. 49(4).
[6] If the witness is in Scotland or Northern Ireland a certificate of default is transmitted to the Court of Session or High Court in Belfast who will then punish the contempt.
[7] R.S.C. Ord. 39, r. 1. The equivalent procedure in the county court is set out in C.C.R. Ord. 18, r. 1. Often the local district or county court registrar will act as examiner.

the master for an order that an examiner be appointed to take the sworn evidence of the witness in the form of a deposition. The application should be accompanied by an affidavit setting out the reasons why the application is made, e.g. that the witness is too old or infirm to attend court, or might die before the trial or intends to leave the country before the trial. The examiner appoints the date and place for the examination and both parties attend by counsel and proceed respectively to examine and cross-examine the witness whose answers are recorded by the examiner on a deposition.

Frequently in practice in lieu of a deposition the parties agree that a shorthand transcript should be taken. Where an objection is taken to a question, the objection is noted but the question and answer are recorded leaving the trial judge to decide whether to uphold the objection and strike out the testimony or to overrule it.

(b) *Witnesses abroad*

As a general rule it is today far less expensive to pay the air fare of a witness abroad to England than arrange for his examination overseas. The following methods[1] are however available if the party desiring to call the witness can prove that it is not practicable to bring the witness to this country:

(i) *Letters of request.* The English court issues a request to the judicial authorities abroad to arrange for the attendance of the witness and his answers to be recorded either to *viva voce* questioning or to a set of prepared interrogatories. This method is available for all countries.[2]

(ii) *Convention countries.* Various countries[3] have agreed that evidence can be taken before a British Consul. This procedure is generally however only available where the witness is willing to give evidence. In other cases letters of request should be issued. Other countries will permit the English court to nominate a *special examiner* to record the evidence of willing witnesses.[4]

EVIDENCE BY WRITTEN STATEMENT

One of the basic rules of evidence is that no evidence should be given which cannot be tested by cross-examination. Suppose P (who has no recollection of an accident) wishes to prove that D drove past a red traffic light:

(*a*) P can call W to say he saw D go past the light *but*

(*b*) P cannot give evidence to the effect that W had told him that he had seen D go past the light *nor*

(*c*) can P put in a written statement by W to that effect.

In the second and third examples it would be unfair that D should hear this damning testimony given in court when he cannot cross-examine W. This principle of the law of evidence, which is called *"the hearsay rule"*, can be roughly formulated as follows:

---

[1] See R.S.C. Ord. 39, rr. 2 and 3. Note: the county court cannot deal with the above matters so that where a witness in a county court action is abroad application has to be made to the High Court: County Court Act 1959, s. 85.

[2] This is the method generally employed for witnesses in Eire and in Commonwealth countries.

[3] E.g. France, Italy, Belgium, Netherlands, Germany.

[4] E.g. the United States of America.

No witness is allowed to give evidence in court by reference to what he has been told by somebody else about the matters in question or by producing an account of those matters written by somebody else.

This rule was sensible where the tribunal of fact consisted of a jury who might not have had the intelligence to realise the risks of accepting evidence which had not been subjected to the test of cross-examination. The rule could however work considerable injustice. Suppose the person who could give direct evidence was dead or could not be traced or was overseas (but the value of the claim could not justify paying his passage to England or issuing letters of request). Again, suppose the witness would have no real recollection of the matters any longer so that his attendance at court would be a waste of time (e.g. a clerk who prepared a formal delivery note). To deal with these problems the Civil Evidence Act 1968[1] provided that hearsay evidence should be admissible subject to certain safeguards:

> "In any civil proceedings a statement made, whether orally or in a document or otherwise, by any person ... shall, subject to this section and to rules of court, be admissible as evidence of any fact stated therein of which direct oral evidence by him would be admissible".[2]

This section amongst other things means that a party can choose to present evidence at court by submitting a written statement without calling as a witness the person who made it. This can be of great practical advantage in preparing a case.

The procedure is set out in R.S.C. Order 38, rule 20 *et seq.*[3] Any party wishing to put in hearsay evidence must serve on every other party a notice to that effect not later than 21 days from the date of setting down.[4] The notice must contain[5]:

(a) details of the date, time and place and circumstances in which the statement was made,
(b) the name of the person who made it,
(c) if oral, the substance of what was said; if in writing, a copy thereof,
(d) if the statement is to be submitted because the maker is dead, unfit by reason of his bodily or mental condition to attend as a witness, over-seas, unable to be found or identified despite the exercise of reasonable diligence, or cannot reasonably be expected to have any recollection of matters relevant to the accuracy or otherwise of the statement, then particulars as to how the case falls within one or more of these categories must be set out in the notice.[6]

---

[1] Replacing and extending the scope of earlier statutes.

[2] Section 2(1). This section also provides an exception to another rule of evidence namely that a person called in court is not allowed to give evidence of earlier consistent oral statements or documents made by him, i.e. cannot say "what I am saying is true because I have said it before". Now such evidence is in limited circumstances admissible—see s. 2(2) and s. 3.

[3] In the county court the procedure (which is substantially identical) is governed by C.C.R. Ord. 20, rr. 20–29. The notice of intention to put in hearsay evidence is to be served not less than 14 clear days before the date fixed for the hearing and the counter-notice within 7 days of service of the notice. The time limits do not apply where no defence has been served although late service of the notice may cause the other side to apply for an adjournment of the hearing.

[4] See R.S.C. Ord. 38, r. 21. In the case of an originating summons in the Chancery Division, notice must be served not later than 21 days from the date when the summons was "adjourned into court" (see *post*, p. 171).

[5] R.S.C. Ord. 38, r. 22.

[6] R.S.C. Ord. 38, r. 25; Civil Evidence Act 1968, s. 8(2)(b).

Upon receipt of the notice the other parties have 21 days in which to serve a counter-notice.[1] They *must* do this if they are attacking the credibility of the maker of the statement.[2] If the applicant is not relying on any of the reasons set out in paragraph (*d*) above, the service of the counter-notice prevents his using the hearsay evidence at the trial. If he is relying on one of those reasons, he must apply to the master for a determination of the issue whether that reason is made out.[3] If it is, he can submit the hearsay evidence *of right*.

Example—P sued D for damages for injuries after she was run over by a bus owned by D. D served notice under R.S.C. Order 38 rule 21 of intention to put in a written statement by an eye-witness to the effect that " the pedestrian walked straight out into the road without looking in either direction". D stated in the notice that the eye-witness who was Jamaican had returned home. P served a counter-notice and the issue then arose whether D could prove the witness was overseas and if so whether the court could nevertheless refuse to admit this damning evidence in the absence of the maker. Finer J. held (1) that the issue of fact was to be determined on a balance of probabilities and (2) that once any of the stated conditions was proven (e.g. that the witness was overseas) the court had no discretionary power to refuse to admit the statement.[4]

It should be observed that a statement may be admitted under the Civil Evidence Act 1968 notwithstanding a failure to follow the above rules but the party at fault will be at risk as to costs and a possible adjournment.[5]

ADVICE ON EVIDENCE

After the pleadings have been exchanged and discovery has taken place, counsel may be asked to advise on evidence. He will be sent all the proofs of evidence taken by his solicitors, the correspondence, the documents disclosed by his side on discovery and copies of the documents disclosed by the other side. In order to advise on evidence counsel should go through each allegation in the pleadings which is disputed and ask himself how he can prove each such matter. The process is vividly described in the report *Going to Law*[6] at paragraph 59:

"To write a useful advice on evidence, counsel has to rehearse in his mind's eye every possible scenario for the trial. Who will make the opening speech? What documents will have to be handed to the judge? Will the witnesses have to have a

---

[1] R.S.C. Ord. 38, r. 26.
[2] R.S.C. Ord. 38, r. 30.
[3] R.S.C. Ord. 38, r. 27.
[4] *Rasool v. West Midlands Passenger Transport Executive*, [1974] 3 All E.R. 638. The procedure is summarised by Finer J. (at p. 641) as follows: "Now the short effect of all these complicated provisions seems to be as follows: that the system of adducing a written statement in evidence without calling the maker involves the service by the party wishing to take that course on the other parties of a notice in a prescribed form. A party receiving such a notice who objects to the proposal to put in the statement can, by an appropriate counter-notice, require the witness to be called, failing which the statement (subject to an overriding discretion which the court has to admit it under rule 29) will be excluded. This right of objection, however, is modified in the case where the stated reason for desiring to put the statement in evidence without calling the witness is one or other of the five reasons mentioned in section 8(2)(*b*) of the 1968 Act and rule 25. In such a case the objecting party must, despite the assertion in the notice that the witness cannot or should not be called because he is dead, or beyond the seas, or as the case may be, state in his counter-notice that the witness can or should be called. This raises the issue as to the truth or validity of the reason relied on, and that issue will be determined ... under the procedure laid down by rule 27."
[5] Civil Evidence Act 1968, s. 8(3)(*a*). R.S.C. Ord. 38, r. 29. C.C.R. Ord. 20, r. 26.
[6] Report of Justice Committee.

bundle of correspondence to refer to? Whose job will it be to prepare these? What are the issues as defined by the pleadings? For each of these, which party has the burden of proving it? What admissible evidence is there to prove it? Do the statements of the various witnesses cover not only what they have to prove, but also the matters on which they are likely to be cross-examined? Are any documents still missing? Above all, what could go wrong during the performance, and what contingency plans need to be made to cover such eventualities".

Although it is impossible to set out here every matter which has to be considered in writing an advice on evidence, it is probably a sensible rule to commence by listing each of the separate issues in the trial and then taking each issue separately consider the following:

(a) The *burden of proof*.
(b) Whether there is any relevant *oral evidence*: if so, does it need to be supplemented: will the witness attend voluntarily or should a subpoena be issued: will the witness need to refer to documents, if so can they be agreed or will this witness or someone else produce them?
(c) Are any *witnesses unavailable*? If so notices must be served under the *Civil Evidence Act*. Similarly, is it a case where although a witness is available he would have no present recollection of matters set out in a document or his evidence is unlikely to be contradicted? In both cases it would again be right to serve notices under the Act.
(d) Are there any *original* or *copy documents* which need to be put in as evidence? If so, who has them? If the originals are in one's own possession is it necessary to serve notice to admit? It should be remembered that this will frequently be necessary in county court actions. If they are in the possession of the other side, is notice to produce necessary? If they are in the possession of a third party a *subpoena duces tecum* may be necessary.

In almost any case of complexity it is necessary for the plaintiff to prepare copies of a *bundle* of *agreed documents* which can be used by the judge, counsel and the witnesses. In order to show how an advice is prepared in practice we shall conclude this section by considering two specimen cases. Note how frequently in practice it is necessary to use the provisions of the Civil Evidence Act if matters cannot be agreed.

EXAMPLES OF ADVISING ON EVIDENCE

A POSSESSION ACTION

On 1st December 1975 P let an upstairs room in his house to D at a rent of £10 per week inclusive of rates. The terms of the tenancy were set out in a written agreement. On 20th April 1976 P's solicitors served notice to quite on D. Since P actually lived at the house, the tenancy was not "protected" under the Rent Acts, but D nevertheless had the right to refer the notice to the local rent tribunal who reduced the rent to £6 per week and directed that the notice was not to take effect until 30th November 1976. On that date arrears of rent amounted to £36. P issued a summons for possession in the local county court. No defence has been filed.

Advice on Evidence

(1) In this case the plaintiff must prove (a) the creation of the tenancy; (b) service of the notice to quit; (c) that the notice is effective; (d) the adjudication of the Rent Tribunal, (e) the amount of arrears outstanding and (f) that the defendants are still in occupation.

(2) The Plaintiff can himself give evidence to prove the tenancy. He must produce his copy of the tenancy agreement and notice to admit should be served on the defendant. He must give evidence that he (the plaintiff) lives at the premises as his residence.

(3) Those instructing me should have available at the hearing a witness who can speak as to the date of posting the notice to quit and produce the appropriate post office advice of recorded delivery. That witness should also be able to produce a copy of the notice to quit. Notice to produce the original should be sent to the defendant.

(4) The plaintiff can put in the notice of the Rent Tribunal's determination as to the rent and period of security. This would be admissible without proof of its authenticity since it is a public document.

(5) The plaintiff must give oral evidence of the rent in arrears to the date of hearing and confirm the defendant is still in occupation. The plaintiff should produce his record of payments. It would be sensible to have copies available of the relevant pages. Notice should be served on the defendant to produce his Rent Book at the hearing which should confirm the plaintiff's calculations.

A MOTOR ACCIDENT CASE

On 6 June 1976 a collision occurred on the M3 motorway when a lorry owned by D pulled across into the path of a motor car driven by P. P claims that the lorry gave no warning whatsoever of its intention to change lane. P sustained a serious fracture of the leg which has left him with considerable disabilities. He was off work for 6 months. Repairs to his vehicle cost £450. The scene was witnessed by an American tourist W who has written to P's solicitors from New York a detailed explanation of the incident exonerating P. The position of the vehicles after the accident was taken down by the police who interviewed D's driver under caution. No proceedings were however brought against D's driver.

Advice on Evidence

(1) P will have to prove (a) the collision was caused by D's negligence and (b) that as a result thereof he has sustained injuries to the extent alleged and (c) financial loss as alleged.

(2) On the issue of liability, P must give oral evidence in accordance with his proof. It is essential to have available an agreed plan and photographs of the *locus in quo* to which P can refer. The statement of the witness W is admissible under the Civil Evidence Act 1968. A copy of the statement and details of when and by whom it was made must be sent to the defendant's solicitors with notice of our intention to put in the statement and evidence without calling the maker on the grounds that he is beyond the seas (R.S.C. Order 38, rule 22). The notice must be served not later than 21 days from date of setting down. The notes of the officer who prepared the police report and took the oral statement from the defendants' driver should also be sent to the defendants' solicitors with notice of our intention to produce the same as evidence under the Act without calling the officer. If the defendants serve a counter-notice requiring the officer's attendance, then a subpoena duces tecum must be issued and served on the officer requiring his attendance at court with his original notes.

(3) So far as the medical evidence is concerned, those instructing me must obtain an up-to-date medical report setting out the extent of the plaintiff's present disabilities and the prognosis. We should agree to exchange this report together with our earlier reports detailing his treatment to date. If the defendants' solicitors will not agree to an exchange of reports, the master must be asked to give directions under Order 38, rule 37. I would hope that the various reports disclosed can be put in as an agreed bundle. If not, notice should be sent to the other side of our intention to put the disclosed reports in evidence pursuant to

the Civil Evidence Act. This does not preclude our calling one or more of the doctors to amplify his report.

(4) So far as repair costs are concerned, *if these matters cannot be agreed*, then:

(a) Serve notice under the Civil Evidence Act 1968 of the repair estimate, the repair invoice and the receipt for payment. If counter-notice is received, subpoena the appropriate persons at the garage.

(b) The Plaintiff can give evidence that the repairs done are all attributable to the accident.

(c) The insurance company's claims assessor who inspected the vehicle must state that in his expert opinion the cost of repairs was fair and reasonable. Leave to call this evidence must be obtained from the master who will no doubt direct disclosure of the report (Order 38, rule 38).

(5) So far as loss of earnings are concerned:

(a) Serve upon the defendants' solicitors a statement from P's employers setting out his total *net* loss of earnings. Notice should accompany this statement of our intention to adduce the same under the Civil Evidence Act 1968.

(b) Similarly serve a copy of the letter received from the Department of Health and Social Security detailing the National Insurance Benefits received.

CHAPTER EIGHT

PAYMENT INTO COURT AND INFANT SETTLEMENTS

PAYMENT INTO COURT

Once the pleadings are closed and discovery has taken place it may well be that the defendant will wish to make an offer of settlement to the plaintiff. In considering that offer the plaintiff will obviously take into account not only the value of his claim and his likely chance of success but also the amount he has already incurred in costs due to his solicitor. Suppose he decides not to accept the defendant's offer but to let the matter continue to trial. If he eventually is awarded only the amount offered by the defendant or a lesser sum, it would be unfair that the defendant should be liable for the costs incurred after his offer was refused. In order to solve this problem the courts permit a defendant to make a formal offer by paying the amount offered to the court to hold until either the plaintiff accepts the sum in question or the matter goes to trial. If the plaintiff does not accept the sum offered but at the end of the trial only recovers that amount or a lesser sum, the court will order that the plaintiff is only to have the costs of the action to the date of payment-in and that he is to pay the costs incurred by the defendant thereafter.

> *Example*—P sustains a serious knee injury as a result of D's negligence. Counsel advises him he is likely to recover total damages in the region of £3,000. After the summons for directions D pays into court £2,500. At that stage P's costs would tax at about £250. P can accept the payment into court and at once tax his costs—so the *total* sum received will be £2,750. Assume P refuses the offer and fights the case but is only awarded £2,500. Although he has won the action, the order for costs will be P's costs to the date of payment into court (i.e. £250) but he will have to bear his own costs thereafter (£1,000) *and* pay the taxed costs incurred by the defendant from the date of payment (£750). The net result is that he finishes with £1,500 whilst he would have had £2,750 if he had accepted the payment into court.

The High Court procedure for making and accepting a payment into court is set out in Order 22 and can be summarised as follows.

(1) At any time after an appearance has been entered a defendant may make a payment into court.

(2) He calculates the amount ignoring (*a*) interest under the Law Reform Act 1934 and (*b*) costs. If there is a claim for contractual interest however he should work out the amount due to the date of payment.

(3) He prepares a form of "notice of payment into court"; in a simple case it would set out the title of the action and then read: "Take notice that the Defendant has paid the sum of £   into court. The said £   is in satisfaction of all the causes of action in respect of which the plaintiff claims and after taking into account and satisfying the above-

named defendant's cause of action for damages in respect of which he counterclaims.[1]

(4) The defendant pays in the sum offered by producing cash or a banker's draft at the Pay Office in the Law Courts. The form of notice is then duly stamped and receipted and the payment is recorded in the court ledgers.

(5) The notice of payment-in must then be served on the plaintiff and every other defendant.[2]

(6) Within 3 days of receiving notice of payment-in the plaintiff must send an acknowledgement of its receipt to the defendant.[3]

(7) Within 21 days of the date of receipt of the notice of payment into court, the plaintiff may give notice to the defendant that he accepts the payment into court,[4] arrange for the monies to be paid out to his solicitor (who will have to retain them in a Legal Aid case to deal with the Law Society's first charge on all sums recovered by an assisted person) and within 4 days of payment out lodge his bill of costs to be taxed and sign judgment for the costs allowed within 48 hours of the taxation.[5] Once the plaintiff has accepted a payment into court all further proceedings in respect of the cause of action are stayed against the defendant who has paid into court and all other defendants.[6]

(8) After 21 days have elapsed from the date of payment-in the plaintiff may still accept the payment into court but he may be ordered to pay the costs incurred by the defendant since the date of payment-in.

(9) The defendant may increase the amount of his payment into court any time. He must serve a notice of increase on the plaintiff or any co-defendant.[7]

(10) The monies paid into court will not carry interest so that the defendant should at the earliest possible moment apply that the monies he has paid-in be transferred to the Short Term Investment Account. The interest will then accrue to the account of the defendant and may be used as he directs.[8]

(11) The plaintiff cannot take out a payment into court once the trial of the action has effectively started.[9]

(12) The defendant may pay money into court or increase the sum paid in even after the trial has begun and up to the moment when the judge commences his judgment.[10] If the plaintiff chooses to accept monies paid in or increased after the trial has begun, the question of costs is at large.[11]

(13) The fact of payment into court is not to be disclosed to the judge until he has given judgment.[12]

(14) As stated above, where the sum eventually awarded to a plaintiff who

---

[1] The relevant form is Form No. 23 of the General Forms set out as Appendix A to the R.S.C. The form makes provision for payment in to satisfy separate causes of action and for apportionment between them.
[2] R.S.C. Ord. 22, r. 1(2).
[3] Ibid.
[4] R.S.C. Ord. 22, r. 3(1).
[5] R.S.C. Ord. 62, r. 10(2).
[6] R.S.C. Ord. 22, r. 3(4) and (5).
[7] R.S.C. Ord. 22, r. 1(3).
[8] Administration of Justice Act 1965, s. 6(1).
[9] R.S.C. Ord. 22, r. 3(1).
[10] R.S.C. Ord. 22, rr. 1(1, 3(2), (3).
[11] R.S.C. Ord. 22, r. 3(2).
[12] R.S.C. Ord. 22, r. 7.

has not accepted the payment into court is no more than the amount paid in by the defendant, the plaintiff will be entitled to his costs to the date of payment in but he will be required to pay the costs incurred thereafter by the defendant.[1]

The procedure in the county court is substantially similar to that followed in the High Court.[2] It should be noted that where an action is brought on behalf of minors, payment-in cannot be accepted without the approval of the court under Order 80, rule 10.

CONTRIBUTION NOTICE

So far we have been considering the position as between plaintiff and defendant, but there will be cases where one defendant will wish to preserve his position as regards the costs he may have to pay his co-defendants as a third party.

Example 1—P, a passenger in D1's car is injured when it is in collision with a lorry owned and driven by D2. P sues both drivers.

Example 2—P sues D a shopkeeper for damages for breach of warranty in respect of certain defective goods. D issues third party proceedings against the manufacturer T who in his defence alleges that D is partly responsible for the matters in question because of his negligent storage of the goods.

In both the above cases the court will have to determine not only the issue between the plaintiff and the defendant(s) but also the extent to which each of the co-defendants (or the defendant and the third party) should contribute towards the judgment and what orders as to costs should be made as between themselves. R.S.C. Order 16, rule 10 provides that a third party or joint tortfeasor may make a written offer, without prejudice to his defence to another party to contribute to a specified extent to the debt or damages for which they may both be liable. Such an offer is known as a "notice of contribution". There is no prescribed form but the notice generally is set out with the title of the action and such words as:

"Take notice that I the above-named First Defendant pursuant to Order 16, rule 10 offer to make contribution as to – per cent of the damages and taxed costs which may be awarded to the plaintiff in this action and for which we jointly stand liable."

If this offer is rejected the trial judge will have to determine the issues as between the co-defendants[3] and decide the extent of their respective contributions *inter se*. Once he has made this determination (but *not* before) the notice will be brought to his attention and he will take the offer into account

---

[1] R.S.C. Ord. 62, r. 5 in fact merely provides: "The court in exercising its discretion as to costs shall, to such extent, if any, as may be appropriate in the circumstances take into account ... any payment of money into court and the amount of such payment". See *Brown* v. *New Empress Saloons, Ltd.*, [1937] 2 All E.R. 133. As to the position where the difference is very small, see *Tingay* v. *Harris*, [1967] 2 Q.B. 327.

[2] The procedure is set out in C.C.R. Order 11 which also deals with payment into court of the *whole* sum claimed and costs of summons (cf. procedure on payment-in of whole sum claimed on writ where only fixed costs are payable R.S.C. Ord. 6, r. 2) and payments into court of a sum on *account* of admitted liability for the whole or part. Where a payment in is made in the county court of a lesser sum in *satisfaction* of the plaintiff's claim (i.e. as an offer of settlement) care must be taken to see that the notice submitted to the registrar on payment-in specifies this; if it is not so specified it is deemed to be "on account" so that the plaintiff can take the sum out and continue with his action for the balance (C.C.R. Ord. 11, r. 2). If payment-in is made within 14 days of service of a summons for a liquidated sum one should include the fixed costs appropriate to the amount paid in: if this is done the plaintiff will generally not be entitled to any other costs if he accepts the payment-in (see C.C.R. Ord. 11, r. 7). In other cases rr. 9 and 11 specifically provide for orders as to costs where the payment-in is accepted.

[3] Or defendant and third parties.

in determining the order for costs as between the co-defendants.[1] Although the County Court Rules make no specific provision for "contribution notices" the practice is followed in the county court as in the High Court.[2]

INFANT SETTLEMENTS

Where an action is brought on behalf of an infant (or any other person who is under a disability) the defendant will wish to be certain that any settlement entered into with the infant's next friend shall be binding on the infant when he attains his majority. The next friend also may wish to be certain that any compromise he agrees cannot at a later date give rise to a claim against him by the infant and to be relieved of the responsibility of looking after the money recovered during the infant's minority. The rules[3] therefore provide that:

(a) before proceedings are commenced the approval of the court can be sought for any proposed settlement by issuing and serving an *originating summons* on the proposed defendants;

(b) after proceedings are commenced, the approval of the court *must* be obtained by an *interlocutory summons* served on the defendants.

The parties duly attend before the master who considers:

(i) The question of liability. In accident cases, each party puts his version of the facts before the master and indicates the evidence in support of his version of the case. Counsel's advice on liability should be put in. The master should then be able to have an opinion of the infant's likely chances of success if the action was fought and whether any allowance should be made for contributory negligence.

(ii) The master must then consider the question of quantum.[4] In personal injury cases he should be shown the medical reports on both sides. An up-to-date report must be available. In fatal accident claims he should be told how the dependency is calculated and the apportionment between the widow and the children.

The summons must *not* disclose the amount offered as the master must approach the matter with a fresh mind. If he feels the sum offered is not enough (and this is quite often the case) he may adjourn the summons for the parties to continue negotiating. If he approves the settlement, he will go on to give directions as to the investment of the damages.[5] This is usually achieved by ordering that the whole fund should be paid into the county court of the district in which the infant lives,[6] leaving that court the responsibility of investing and administering the fund. The infant may apply through his parent to the county court during his minority for sums to be paid out for clothing, education, holidays, etc. Once he attains the age of eighteen he is entitled to payment out to him of the balance of the fund and interest.

---

[1] See *Clarke v. E. R. Wright & Son*, [1957] 3 All E.R. 486; [1957] 1 W.L.R. 1191 and *Bragg v. Crosville Motor Services, Ltd*, [1959] 1 All E.R. 613; [1959] 1 W.L.R. 324.

[2] And would be effective by virtue of s. 103 of the County Court Act 1959 which provides that "in any case not expressly provided for by or in pursuance of this Act, the general principles of practice in the High Court may be adopted and applied in proceedings in a county court".

[3] R.S.C. Ord. 80, rr. 10 and 11. The equivalent procedure in the county court is governed by C.C.R. Ord. 5, r. 19. Note: strictly one should speak of "minors" rather than "infants".

[4] In modern times because of the rapid decrease in the value of money he will wish to know what factor in the proposed figure represents interest from the date of the writ or of the death.

[5] R.S.C. Ord. 80, r. 12.

[6] Pursuant to County Courts Act 1959, s. 174.

In infant settlement cases (as so often in considering the rules of civil procedure) the student must know the relevant provisions as to costs. These can only be understood if it is appreciated that the assessment of costs may be on one of three different bases:

(1) *Party and party costs*—here the taxing officer is only to order payment of such costs as were necessary for the conduct of the action and no more.[1]
(2) *Common-fund costs*—here the officer will order payment of such *reasonable sums as were reasonably incurred in the action*.[2]
(3) *Solicitor and own client costs*—here the officer will order payment of *all sums expended except in so far as they are of an unreasonable amount or have been unreasonably incurred*.[3]

Where an infant wishes to accept a *payment into court* by the defendant and the master approves the proposal the order for costs will be:

(a) that the costs which the infant is to pay his own solicitor are to be taxed by the taxing officer and that he is to apply the *solicitor and own client scale*;[4]
(b) that the infant's costs are also to be taxed on the *party and party basis* to the date of payment into court and the defendant is to pay those costs.[5]

The difference between these two sums will represent the amount due to the infant's solicitor and will be paid over to him by the county court administering the fund. Where there is no payment into court, but the court is merely being asked to sanction a compromise, the plaintiff's solicitor and the defendant usually agree to split the costs so as to save two taxations. The defendant pays more than he would be ordered to pay on a strict "party and party" taxation and the plaintiff's solicitor agrees to forgo some of the costs he would obtain on a "solicitor and own-client" assessment of his bill. The form of order usually agreed is that the infant's costs are to be taxed on a "common fund basis" and paid by the defendant to the plaintiff's solicitor who waives his right to any further costs.[6]

---

[1] R.S.C. Ord. 62, r. 28(2).

[2] Ibid., r. 28(4).

[3] Ibid., r. 29(1).

[4] R.S.C. Ord. 62, r. 30. Note the costs *must* be taxed—they cannot be agreed between the next friend and the solicitor. Note if the infant is an assisted person, then under the provisions of the Legal Aid Act the costs payable to his solicitor are taxed on the less generous common fund basis and *not* on the solicitor and-own client basis.

[5] See R.S.C. Ord. 62, r. 30(3). The taxing officer must certify the difference between the amount the defendant will have to pay the infant and the amount the infant will have to pay his solicitor.

[6] This order is appropriate even if the infant is legally aided since a common fund taxation is the same thing as a legal aid taxation.

CHAPTER NINE

STRIKING OUT FOR
WANT OF PROSECUTION

The Supreme Court Rules provide a timetable for the parties to follow from the moment the writ is served to the time when the action is set down for trial. In practice this timetable is never followed; almost always the solicitors on both sides, themselves harassed by the pressure of other work or simply the problems of preparing the evidence in the action, will extend each other's time for taking the necessary steps in prosecuting the action. Without this relaxation of the rules it would be impossible for most litigation to be undertaken. However it sometimes happens that the plaintiff's solicitor (who of course is the person who has the power under the rules to force the defendant to proceed expeditiously and the duty to issue the summons for directions and to set down) will allow a substantial time to elapse while the action "goes to sleep". In these circumstances the defendant may apply for a summons to the master for an order that the action be struck out.[1] In order to succeed in his application he must show:

(a) prolonged delay by the plaintiff,
(b) which is inexcusable,[2]
(c) and which prejudices the fair trial of the action.
(d) the limitation period has expired.[3]

The principles have been described by Lord Denning M.R. in the following trenchant phrases:[4]

> "The delay of justice is a denial of justice. Magna Carta will have none of it 'To no one will deny or delay right or justice'. All through the years men have protested at the law's delay and counted it as a grievous wrong, hard to bear. Shakespeare ranks it among the whips and scorns of time. Dickens tells how it exhausts finances, patience, courage, hope. To put right this wrong, we will in this court do all in our power to enforce expedition: and, if need be, we will strike out actions when there has been excessive delay. ... The principle upon which we go is clear: when the delay is prolonged and inexcusable, and is such as to do grave injustice to one side or the other or to both, the court may in its discretion dismiss the action straightaway, leaving the plaintiff to his remedy against his own solicitor who has brought him to this plight."

---

[1] This application can be brought if P fails to deliver a statement of claim (R.S.C. Ord. 19, r. 1), fails to make discovery (R.S.C. Ord. 24, r. 16), fails to comply with any order of the master as to the conduct of the suit, fails to take out a summons for directions (R.S.C. Ord. 25, r 1(4)), and fails to set down for trial (R.S.C. Ord. 34, r. 2). The county court has the same powers by virtue of County Courts Act 1959, s. 103. See *Kirkpatrick v. Salvation Army Trustee Co. Ltd.*, [1969] 1 All E.R. 388; [1968] 1 W.L.R. 1955. The application should be made at first instance to the registrar from whom appeal will be to the judge. Note that C.C.R. Ord. 13, r. 4 provides that if no application for a hearing date is made within 12 months of the date when a hearing was adjourned generally, the court itself notifies the parties that unless application is made for hearing within 14 days the action will be struck out.
[2] The plaintiff should file an affidavit setting out his reasons for the delay.
[3] See *Birkett* v. *James*, [1977] 2 All E.R. 801, H.L.
[4] *Allen* v. *Sir Alfred McAlpine & Sons, Ltd.*, [1968] 2 Q.B. 229, at pp. 245–6; [1968] 1 All E.R. 543, at pp. 546–7. The action arose out of a fatal accident in 1959. Pleadings were delivered in 1961. No further action was taken until 1967 when the defendant applied to strike the action out.

It should be noted that the power to strike out is generally exercised because the delay has caused prejudice: as time goes on memories will fade, witnesses may die or disappear and so it may become impossible for the court to reach a fair conclusion on the issues. Where, however, the case is not one where the court is going to be asked to determine disputed issues on the basis of oral testimony, it may be that although the defendant can prove inordinate and inexcusable delay on the part of the plaintiff, he will be unable to prove that he is prejudiced by the delay and in consequence the action will not be dismissed.

Example—In 1963 D failed to deliver certain goods to P Co. In 1967 P Co. issued a writ and the parties exchanged pleadings—D denying liability. No further steps were taken by P Co.: they failed to make discovery, they failed to take out a summons for directions, they in fact did nothing. In 1972 D applied for the action to be dismissed for want of prosecution. P Co. admitted that there had been inordinate and inexcusable delay after the pleadings had closed but claimed that since all the relevant evidence was totally contained in contemporary documents, the delay had not prejudiced the defendants. The Court of Appeal accepted this contention. *Per* Buckley L.J.: "The question to which the court must address its mind is whether that delay which is properly described as 'inordinate and inexcusable' has given rise to circumstances in which it is possible that a fair trial may be impossible or that the defendant may be seriously prejudiced. If the facts are such that no additional prejudice to the defendant has arisen as the result of delay after the end of that period in which delay can be said to be excusable, it cannot be right, in my judgment, for the court to dismiss the action under this rule."[1]

There is, however, one rare but important exception to the rule that the defendant must show prejudice. If he can show that the delay by the plaintiff has been *deliberate* the court may strike out the action without considering the question of prejudice, on the grounds that the plaintiff's conduct is an abuse of the process of the court.

Example—D, a minority shareholder in a company run by P, wished to expose misapplication of company funds by P. D published a circular letter alleging fraud by P. P issued a writ for libel and obtained an interlocutory injunction prohibiting D repeating the alleged libel until the trial. Having successfully silenced D, P took no real action in the next five years to bring the case to trial. The Court of Appeal held that P's action should be struck out. *Per* Lord Denning M.R.: "[the plaintiff] has made default time after time. He failed to give proper discovery. He failed to deliver a proper defence. He failed to set the action down for trial. It is obvious that he was not at all keen that the action should come to trial. It would suit him well if it dragged on for ever. So long as he could prolong the proceedings he could always say— as he so often did—'These matters are *sub judice*, so they cannot be discussed'. All things considered, it must have been plain to [him] that his best strategy was to conduct this action as if it were a war of attrition. If he fought it long enough, he might be able to break [the defendant's] nerve, exhaust his limited resources, make him give up trying, so that the case would never come to trial. ... To my mind his action was an abuse of the process of the court. His defaults ... were 'intentional and contumelious'. ... Where the court meets with such abuse, it has the means to cope with it. It will strike out the action. ..."[2]

---

[1] *William C. Parker Ltd.* v. *F. J. Ham & Son Ltd.*, [1972] 3 All E.R. 1051, at p. 1055; [1972] 1 W.L.R. 1583, at p. 1588. It was also argued that since the plaintiff had 6 years to bring his claim, delay in issuing the writ was totally irrelevant. The court held that although such delay in itself could not give rise to a right to strike out, it was relevant in considering whether delay after the issue of the writ was inordinate and inexcusable, i.e. if one leaves the issue of proceedings to the last moment, one should then pursue the suit with expedition and further delay is normally inexcusable.

[2] *Wallersteiner* v. *Moir*, [1974] 3 All E.R. 217, at p. 231. The principle in this case probably applies even if the limitation period is still running.

CHAPTER TEN

PREPARING FOR TRIAL

THE SUMMONS FOR DIRECTIONS AND SETTING DOWN

In the vast majority of all actions begun by writ in the High Court the plaintiff is bound to issue a summons within 14 days of the date fixed for discovery[1] requiring the defendant to attend an appointment[2] before the master[3] at which he will give directions as to the future conduct of the case. The standard form of summons (which is set out at p. 21) lists the following numbered paragraphs which the master may be asked to consider at this stage:

(1) That the action be consolidated with other pending cases (see p. 40).

(2) For an order that *the case be heard by an official referee* rather than by the judge. This would be appropriate for example in a building dispute where the case involved consideration of many small detailed points. The parties may also agree for the matter to be tried by a master.

(3)–(4) That the *action be transferred* to *the county court.* This would be appropriate where the plaintiff felt he was unlikely to recover a sum in excess of £1,200 and so would suffer the sanctions in costs provided by section 47 of the County Courts Act (see p. 38)

(5)–(7) Application for *leave to amend the writ or pleadings* (see pp. 83–85, *ante*).

(8)–(10) Applications for further and better particulars of pleadings (see pp. 85–86, *ante*).

(11) The defendant may ask for the proceedings to be stayed unless the plaintiff gives *security for costs* (see p. 104, *ante*).

(12)–(14) The master in cases where there is no automatic discovery may be asked to order *discovery*; in other cases he may be asked to resolve disputes concerning discovery, e.g. an application by one party that the other disclose a document not shown on his list or for an order for inspection of a document claimed to be privileged (see pp. 129–131, *ante*).

(15)–(16) Either side may apply at this stage for leave to serve *interrogatories on his opponent (see p. 133, ante).*

---

[1] R.S.C. Ord. 25, rr. 1 and 3. The rule is that if the case is one where automatic discovery takes place under Ord. 24, r. 2 the summons is to be issued 14 days after the date fixed by the rules for the exchange of lists or such later date as the parties may agree. If there is no automatic discovery, then the summons is to be issued within 14 days of the close of pleadings. The pleadings are deemed to be closed 14 days after the defence is served unless a reply or defence to counterclaim has to be served in which case the close of pleadings occurs 14 days after service of those documents (see R.S.C. Ord. 18, r. 20). If the plaintiff fails to issue the summons for directions, the defendant may do so himself or apply for the action to be dismissed for want of prosecution (R.S.C. Ord. 25, r. 1(4)).

[2] The summons is returnable in not less than 14 days from the date of *issue.*

[3] Or district registrar; in commercial list cases, the summons is heard by the Commercial Judge. See R.S.C. Ord. 72, r. 2.

(17) An application may be made for the *custody and inspection* of property pending the trial (see p. 132, *ante*).

(18) Either side may apply under the *Civil Evidence Act 1968* for an order that a statement may be admitted at the trial without calling the maker as a witness (see p. 139, *post*).

(19)–(20) The master may be asked to direct that evidence should be admitted by *affidavit* or by *hearsay evidence*.

(21) Either side may apply that it be recorded that he or his opponent *admits* certain facts or that his opponent has *refused to admit* such facts. The point is that if facts not admitted are subsequently proven at the trial, the party refusing to make the admission may be ordered to pay the costs involved notwithstanding that he wins the action (see p. 134, *ante*).

(22) That the evidence of a witness who cannot attend the trial *be taken on examination* (see p. 138, *post*).

(23)–(24) That if *medical* and *expert* evidence cannot be agreed, each side is to be limited as to the number of expert witnesses they may call at the trial. The master will also have to consider the new rules about the exchange of expert reports (see p. 132, *ante*).

(25)–(26) That provision be made for *plans* and *photographs* to be available at the trial.

(27) The parties may agree to *limit their rights* as to *appeal*.

(29) That directions should be given as to the mode of trial (i.e. with or without jury) and the *place* at which it is to be heard and for the setting down of the action.

The practice is for the plaintiff to strike out on his summons the matters which he does not wish the master to deal with. The defendant (or if there are several, each defendant) must serve not less than 7 days before the hearing of the summons notice of all other matters which he may wish should be dealt with at the summons.

It will be appreciated that the purpose of the summons for directions is two-fold:

(a) It enables the court to deal at one and the same time with all interlocutory matters in dispute thus saving the costs of numerous applications. Indeed R.S.C. Order 25, rule 7 provides that it is the duty of the parties so far as is practicable to make all interlocutory applications at this stage; the sanction for issuing a separate summons being in theory an order for costs.

(b) It should provide a "stock-taking" process at which the master can consider whether the case is ready for trial and check that consideration has been given to the provision of all evidence (and e.g. plans, photographs) which could assist the court.

In practice the position is very different. When a serious dispute arises as to interlocutory matters, the parties generally brief counsel to attend the master on a straightforward interlocutory summons raising that point and nothing else[1] so that, unless there is agreement between the parties it is *not* the general rule that the matters set out above are decided at one time on the summons for directions. Normally on the summons for directions the parties are obtaining

---

[1] Alternatively counsel may attend at an adjourned hearing of the summons for directions again to argue this specific point.

the official sanction of the court to courses they have already chosen. The position is accurately described by the Justice Committee in *Going to Law* as follows:[1]

> "Instead of the 'stock-taking'which the summons for directions was designed to achieve, it is more often a two-minute formality, in which two very junior clerks from the respective firms of solicitors appear before the master, themselves knowing little if anything about the case, and with no authority to agree any orders which might provoke a sense of urgency, or involve extra expense, in the pursuit of the litigation. The master too, is under pressure: although he will be handed the pleadings at the hearing, he will not have seen them before and will certainly not have time to read them in detail. Nine times out of ten, he will be asked only to make an agreed order for 'trial by judge alone at Middlesex, set down for forty-two days after inspection, costs in cause'. He initials the form, the two clerks disappear, the next pair take their place. Even if he had wanted to, he could not have made any order which was not asked for by at least one of the parties."

It follows therefore that the primary use of the summons for directions today is in practice to obtain the order of the master as to the place and mode of trial. So far as the place of trial is concerned, the court considers the convenience of the parties and their witnesses and the date at which the trial can take place.[2] The normal method of trial is by judge alone except for cases falling within section 6(1) of the Administration of Justice Act 1933 which provides:

> "If on the application of any party to an action to be tried in the Queen's Bench Division of the High Court, the court ... is satisfied that—
> (a) a charge of fraud against that party; or
> (b) a claim in respect of libel, slander, malicious prosecution, or false imprisonment is in issue, the action shall be ordered to be tried with a jury unless the court ... is of opinion that the trial thereof requires any prolonged examination of documents or accounts or any scientific or local investigation which cannot conveniently be made with a jury...."

Although this section goes on to preserve the inherent discretion of the court to order trial by jury in other cases, it is in fact confined today to cases falling with the section.[3]

If the action is to be tried in the Queen's Bench Division in London the master must assign the case to the appropriate list of actions (usually the Non-Jury List).[4] The master must also direct the period within which the case is to be *set down* for trial. An action is set down by lodging with the court[5] two bundles each comprising top copies of the following documents:

---

[1] *Op. cit.*, para. 55.

[2] See R.S.C. Ord. 35, r. 1. The Queen's Bench judges sit at "trial centres" to hear actions at Birmingham, Lincoln, Nottingham, Stafford, Warwick, Leeds, Newcastle upon Tyne, Sheffield, Teesside, Carlisle, Liverpool, Manchester, Preston, Norwich, Caernarvon, Cardiff, Chester, Mold, Swansea, Bodmin, Bristol, Exeter and Winchester. Chancery actions may be heard at Leeds, Liverpool, Manchester, Newcastle and Preston.

[3] See *Ward* v. *James*, [1966] 1 Q.B. 273; [1965] 1 All E.R. 568 (jury trial not appropriate in personal injury cases) and *Williams* v. *Beesley*, [1973] 3 All E.R. 144; [1973] 1 W.L.R. 1295 (House of Lords held jury trial not to be ordered in action involving allegations of negligence by solicitor's articled clerk).

[4] The seven separate lists of Queen's Bench action are—Jury List, Non-Jury List, Short Cause List (i.e. actions likely to take less than 2 hours), Commercial List, Revenue List, Motions for Judgment List, and the Special Paper List (principally trial of preliminary issues of fact as points of law).

[5] See R.S.C. Ord. 34, r. 3. If the trial is to be in the Queen's Bench Division in London the documents are delivered or posted to the Head Clerk, Crown Office and Associates Department (Room 478), Central Office. In the Chancery Division, they are lodged with the Cause Clerk, Chancery Registrar's Office (Room 136). If the trial is to be out of London, they are lodged with the district registrar for the district where the trial is to be held.

(i)   the writ,
(ii) the pleadings including any request or order for particulars and the particulars given
(iii) all orders made on the summons for directions and
(iv) all notices of issue and amendment of Legal Aid certificates.

One of the two bundles is used by the judge at the trial; the other bundle is stamped to show the appropriate fee on setting down has been paid and is retained by the court officers as the official record. The names, addresses and telephone numbers of the parties solicitors (or the parties themselves if they are appearing in person) must be indorsed on the record bundle. The plaintiff must notify all other parties within twenty-four hours that he has set down the action for trial. An action set down in the non-jury list is initially put into a general list of actions pending where it waits its turn for hearing. Either party may however apply to the Clerk of the Lists for a fixed date for hearing (in which case the action is removed from the general list since it has become a fixture).[1]

How does the solicitor tell when an action in the general list is likely to come on for trial? He will be able to get rough guidance from the court as to the position of the action in the general list but in practice well before the action could come on both solicitors will have warned the clerks to counsel briefed in the action. Eventually (and this may well not be for many months) the clerks will find the case appears in the daily bulletin issued by the court showing the sittings arranged for the next day and the actions fixed for hearing or which are likely to be heard within the next week. The actual list of actions for each day's sittings is compiled the previous afternoon by the Clerk of the Lists. For this reason as soon as a case appears in the warned list counsel's clerks attend each day before the Clerk of the Lists to check whether or not the action in which they are involved is to be listed for hearing next day. If, as often happens, counsel briefed will not be available, the clerks will wish the case not to be listed the next day and will seek to persuade the Clerk of the Lists to put the action over. Normally they will succeed on a first or second occasion but eventually they will be forced to accept the decision of the Clerk of the Lists. If counsel is still unavailable, this will result in the brief being *returned*, i.e. given to another member of the bar who will have to prepare the brief hurriedly for the trial and who will not have had any opportunity of seeing the client in conference. Not unnaturally this causes intense resentment on the part of the client as well as distress and embarrassment to the instructing solicitor. The only method of avoiding a last minute transfer is to apply for a fixture.[2]

Where a case has been assigned a fixed date or is currently listed in the week's list any party may apply to the judge in charge of the non-jury list to

---

[1] In actions ordered to be tried outside London, the plaintiff's solicitor must file a certificate of readiness stating whether the orders made on the summons for directions have been complied with, the estimated length of trial, a statement that the plaintiff is ready for the action to be brought for trial, names and addresses and telephone numbers of the solicitors and of any party in person and a statement that he has given each defendant 7 days notice of his intention to file the certificate. The registrar then marks the action as ready for trial and informs the parties of the likely date of trial. The parties may apply for a fixed date or for the case not to be tried before a certain date.

[2] This should ensure that if the brief has to be returned it is referred to the barrister who will in fact appear in reasonable time for preparation. In practice this does not always work because counsel's clerk will keep the brief until the last moment in the hope that counsel will be free.

vacate the date or stand the case out. Such applications, unless supported by very convincing explanations, inevitably incur considerable judicial displeasure and are by no means automatically granted.

PRE–TRIAL REVIEW

In the county court the equivalent procedure to the High Court summons for directions is the "pre-trial review".[1] This is held by the registrar wherever the action is proceeding by ordinary summons or the defendant has put in a defence to a default summons.[2] The registrar will deal with all interlocutory matters and will fix a date for the hearing of the trial. The table opposite sets out the relevant orders which can be made at this stage in the case of an ordinary action. It will be remembered that in the case of an ordinary action the summons specifies the date for hearing or pre-trial review.[3]

---

[1] See C.C.R. Ord. 21.

[2] Note if the defendant does not file a defence within 14 days of service of a default summons (i.e. in an action for a debt or liquidated demand) the plaintiff may have judgment entered in default of defence (C.C.R. Ord. 10, r. 2). If he does file a defence the registrar will either appoint a day for pre-trial review or, if the dispute is so simple that directions need not be given, he may fix at once a date for hearing.

[3] See pp. 63 *et seq.*

CIRCUMSTANCES WHICH MAY ARISE ON A PRE-TRIAL REVIEW IN AN ORDINARY ACTION

Circumstances	How to be dealt with	Relevant provision in C.C.R.
1. Defendant files defence and appears	Unless defendant withdraws defence or defence is struck out, registrar gives directions for trial and fixes date of hearing, or, if appropriate, refers to arbitration or for inquiry or report.	Ord. 21, rr. 1 and 9. Ord. 19, rr. 1 and 2.
2. Defendant files defence but does not appear.	(a) Registrar may strike out defence and give judgment (interlocutory unless plaintiff ready to prove damages). (b) Plaintiff may elect to prove his claim and get judgment. (c) Otherwise, directions for trial and adjourn.	Ord. 13, r. 6; Ord. 21, r. 4; Ord. 24, r. 10. Ord. 21, r. 8. See 1.
3. Defendant does not file defence or appear.	(a) Registrar may direct defendant to file defence with judgment in default. (b) Registrar may enter judgment (interlocutory unless plaintiff ready to prove damages).	Ord. 9, r. 4. (8); Ord. 21, 4. 4; Ord. 24, r. 10. Ord. 21, r. 7; Ord. 24, r. 10.
4. Defendant does not file a defence but appears.	(a) If defendant seems to have a defence, he may be ordered to file one with judgment in default. (b) By consent of parties and if registrar (having jurisdiction) agrees, appointment may be treated as trial of action (and adjourned into court). (c) If defendant admits claim (or part which plaintiff accepts), registrar may enter judgment and make any necessary instalment order.	See 3 (a). Ord. 21, r. 6.
5. Defendant files an admission but there is a dispute— (a) as to mode of payment. (b) as to quantum.	(a) Registrar makes order for payment. (b) (i) If defendant does not appear, plaintiff may elect to prove his damages and get judgment. (ii) In any case, treat as a defended action unless defence as to quantum is struck out.	Ord. 21, r. 6. Ord. 21, r. 8. See 1 and 2 (a).

CHAPTER ELEVEN

THE TRIAL

THE TRIBUNAL

The rules of court were originally drafted when civil cases were frequently tried by jury; in modern times (except for some defamation cases) trial is by a judge alone. Accordingly in this chapter we shall deal only with trial by a judge.

It should be noted that in the county court the registrar may be given power by the judge to try contested cases. If such authority has been given to him he can hear claims not exceeding £200 if neither party objects and claims in excess of that limit if both parties consent.[1]

FAILURE OF ONE PART TO APPEAR

On rare occasions in the High Court but frequently in the county court, the plaintiff attends on the day appointed for the hearing only to find that the defendant has not appeared. If the defendant has not supplied any satisfactory explanation of his absence to the court, the plaintiff will be entitled to prove his case and obtain judgment.[2] If the case is proceeding in the county court and no defence or form of admission has been received, the plaintiff will have to prove service on the defendant.[3] It is worth noting that the plaintiff who has to prove his case in the absence of the defendant is held strictly to the rules of evidence: matters which might be admitted for the sake of convenience if the defendant were present will have to be strictly proved. Thus, for example, the plaintiff's witnesses must not give hearsay evidence (unless the requisite notices under the Civil Evidence Act have been served) nor will the court permit the production of copies of original documents in the defendant's possession (unless notice to produce has been served).[4] In county court actions where a money judgment is obtained in the absence of the defendant no fee is normally allowed for counsel's attendance unless the defendant has filed a defence to the action.[5] Normally however in such a case in any event one asks the county court judge or registrar hearing the case to "assess" the costs which the defendant is to pay to save, in what is probably a relatively small claim, the extra costs and bother of a taxation.[6] Even where the plaintiff

---

[1] C.C.R. Ord. 23, r. 1. He also may hear contested possession actions with leave of the judge—see Rent Act 1965, s. 35(2).

[2] R.S.C. Ord. 35, r. 1; C.C.R. Ord. 23, r. 4.

[3] Service in the county court is usually effected in the first instance by the court bailiff who indorses details of service on the court copy of the summons. This indorsement is in itself sufficient proof of service—County Courts Act 1959, s. 186. If therefore the defendant does not appear one should check with the court staff to see the indorsement on the copy summons. If the bailiff is unable to effect service, the registrar will send notice of non-service on the plaintiff's solicitors who must then arrange service themselves. Such service is proved by affidavit.

[4] Thus, for example, in a possession action the plaintiff may find himself wholly unable to prove the contents of the notice to quit since the copy returned by his solicitor will be inadmissible unless notice to produce the original has been served.

[5] C.C.R. Ord. 47, r. 20. Note this only applies to *money* claims. Counsel's attendance is always a proper item where some other relief is sought, e.g. a possession action.

[6] The costs to be allowed are set out in Appendix E, C.C.Rules 1936.

obtains judgment in the absence of the defendant his problems may not be over because the defendant may apply to have the judgment set aside.[1] The application to set aside would be accompanied by an affidavit explaining the absence of the defendant and setting out the nature of his defence. If this is credible the judgment will normally be set aside on terms that the defendant pays the costs thrown away; if the merits of the defence are not convincing, a condition may be imposed that the defendant pays the amount of the judgment into court.

When the plaintiff fails to attend at the hearing of an action in the High Court the defendant may apply for judgment dismissing the claim with costs;[2] in the county court, he should apply for the action to be struck out.[3] It should be noted that if the plaintiff has some reasonable excuse for his failure to attend, then the court will on application set aside the judgment[4] or re-instate the action.[5]

APPLICATION FOR AN ADJOURNMENT

It frequently happens that when an action is about to be heard one side wishes the case to be adjourned. An adjournment will only be granted in such circumstances either by consent or because the party seeking the adjournment can show compelling reasons why the action should not proceed to trial.[6] The applicant will inevitably be ordered to pay the costs thrown away "in any event" (i.e. whether he wins or loses the action). Where the application is made by the defendant and there is reason to believe that he is merely stalling for time the plaintiff should ask the judge to make it a condition of the granting of an adjournment that the defendant pay into court within a stated number of days the whole or part of the sum claimed and that in default there should be judgment entered for the plaintiff with costs.

OFFERS OF SETTLEMENT

When a man knows that his action is about to be tried "it concentrates his mind wonderfully" so that at the court door the most intransigent litigants begin to appreciate the merits of the case on the other side. Regrettably under our present system of procedure it is frequently only at this stage that counsel meet each other and discuss terms of settlement. Accordingly a very large number of actions are settled in the rushed atmosphere outside the court—possibly with the judge sending out messages to the helpless advocates that unless some progress towards settlement is reported he intends to come into court and start the case. Despite the pressure on the advocates it is extremely important that settlements made at court should be clearly understood by the parties themselves before they are accepted and that the eventual

---

[1] R.S.C. Ord. 35, r. 2. The application is to be made by summons to attend the judge issued (unless time is extended) within 7 days of the trial. C.C.R. Ord. 37, r. 2. No period is counted for the notice of application but the defendant must proceed with expedition once he has notice of the judgment.
[2] R.S.C. Ord. 35, r. 1(2).
[3] C.C.R. Ord. 23, r. 2(1).
[4] R.S.C. Ord. 35, r. 2(1) the application should be made within 7 days but may be made later with leave.
[5] C.C.R. Ord. 23, r. 2(2).
[6] For example the absence through ill health of a crucial witness.

order should effectively realise the intention of both parties. There are two[1] different methods which are commonly employed where the parties have come to terms:

(1) Counsel draft out the proposed order of the court which is headed "by consent",[2] approved by the judge and made an order of the court which can be enforced like any other judgment.

(2) Counsel agree that the action should be dismissed on the terms of settlement endorsed on their briefs. This order is useful where the parties do not wish publicity to be given to the agreed terms but it has the serious disadvantage that if either party does not comply with the terms of settlement a new action will have to be brought to enforce the agreement—as if it were a contract.[3]

The advocate, in considering any proposed terms of settlement, should be careful to check that the proposal order includes such terms as to costs as will properly safeguard his client. In cases where the plaintiff is legally aided it must be remembered that the Fund has a charge on any sum or property recovered or preserved so that when the defendant has agreed to judgment in a specific sum and to pay costs, the plaintiff will only receive the amount awarded on judgment after his solicitors have made a deduction of the difference between the costs incurred by the legal aid authority and the costs it will receive from the defendant.[4] Again terms of settlement however apparently attractive are worthless if there is little chance of execution succeeding: for this reason where a defendant offers terms but the plaintiff is doubtful as to his willingness to pay, it is worthwhile obtaining security for payment (e.g. by the defendant consenting to the registration of a charge on land owned by him to secure the payment of the judgment debt).

OPENING SPEECH

The hearing of the case begins with an opening speech by counsel for the plaintiffs.[5] The opening of the case is of vital importance because the judge will generally be totally unaware until the case is opened of what the case is about and unless the points which the plaintiff wishes to make are clearly explained at this stage he will lose the initiative in the trial. The function of the opening address has been explained as follows:

"It is a matter of constant surprise to laymen—and to many lawyers from other countries—that an English judge traditionally sets out on the trial of an action without knowing anything about it beforehand except the names of the parties in the printed cause list (he has the pleadings, but he does not always read them). It is therefore the job of counsel ... to explain the whole case to the judge: to read the pleadings, the letters and other documents, out loud *verbatim*, and to summarise what all the witnesses he is calling will say, and how his client views the issue."[6]

---

[1] A third method employed in the Chancery Division is the Tomlin Order whereby proceedings are stayed on the terms set out in a schedule with liberty to the parties to apply as to the enforcement of the terms. See *post*, p. 111.

[2] Except in county court possession cases where the practice has developed of omitting such words because some local authorities will not rehouse a tenant who has vacated by consent.

[3] See *Green* v. *Rozen*, [1955] 2 All E.R. 797; [1955] 1 W.L.R. 741.

[4] Solicitors, counsel and judges sometimes erroneously suppose that the Law Society has a discretion to waive the charge and settlements are made on this assumption. In fact where the charge applies it has statutory force and cannot be waived even if it produces severe hardship.

[5] Exceptionally, where the onus of proof lies on the defence, counsel for the defendants opens the case—e.g. where a bailee is sued for the loss of a chattel belonging to the plaintiff so that to escape liability he must prove the loss occurred without negligence on his part. See R.S.C. Ord. 35, r. 7 and C.C.R. Ord. 20, r. 16 and *Mills* v. *Barber* (1836), 1 M. & W. 425.

[6] *Justice Report Going to Law*, para. 16.

In making his opening speech counsel will normally adopt the following procedure:

(a) He sets out in chronological order the events which give rise to the case. In many cases he will have to give the judge the plan or photographs which will later be formally put in evidence so that he can follow the speech.

(b) He then takes the judge through the pleadings, summarising the formal parts of the pleading but pointing out carefully the paragraphs which show the real issues between the parties.

(c) He then refers the judge to the documentary evidence which is agreed. The plaintiff's solicitor should have prepared an agreed bundle of correspondence for the court containing all the relevant letters which have not been marked "without prejudice". The value of a clear letter before action becomes apparent at this stage because the judge then has a written summary setting out the plaintiff's case in much greater detail than the formalised pleadings. Counsel will also normally at this stage put in the medical and other reports which have been agreed and take the judge through those reports emphasising the relevant passages.

Once the opening is concluded, the plaintiff proceeds at once to call his evidence; under our system the defendant does not have the right to address the court at this stage of the proceedings.

THE EVIDENCE

The plaintiff's counsel calls his witnesses in turn and examines them *in chief* from the proofs of evidence which have been prepared by his solicitor. Since *examination in chief* is designed to elicit evidence favourable to one's own case, two important restrictions are placed on the advocate:

(i) He must not ask *leading questions* on contentious matters. A question is leading if it is so framed as to suggest a particular answer.

(ii) *He must not contradict the testimony* of his own witness by reference to his proof of evidence or to any prior inconsistent statement. Thus if the witness says something different from what is contained in counsel's proof of evidence, he must accept the answer given, and is not allowed to refer him to what he said when the proof was taken.[1] It must be understood that counsel is forbidden to speak to any witness other than his own client or an expert and so it is by no means uncommon for him to be faced with an answer at variance with his proof.

Once the *examination in chief* of a witness has been concluded, counsel for

---

[1] Although it is open to counsel to apply to the judge at the conclusion of examination-in-chief to put in the conflicting statement under s. 2(2) of the Civil Evidence Act 1968, which provides that:

"Where in any civil proceedings a party desiring to give a statement in evidence by virtue of this section has called or intends to call as a witness in the proceedings the person by whom the statement was made, the statement (a) shall not be given in evidence by virtue of this section on behalf of that party without the leave of the court; and (b) without prejudice to paragraph (a) above shall not be given in evidence by virtue of this section on behalf of that party before the conclusion of the examination-in-chief of the person by whom it was made, except—
   (i) where before that person is called the court allows evidence of the making of the statement to be given on behalf of that party by some other person; or
   (ii) in so far as the court allows the person by whom the statement was made to narrate it in the course of his examination-in-chief on the ground that to prevent him from doing so would adversely affect the intelligibility of his evidence."
In practice where the situation arises the party calling the witness will not normally have served the notices required by the rules and thus the Act itself provides that the statement will only be admitted if the court gives leave.

the opposing party will *cross-examine* the witness in an attempt to discredit the answers he has given or to elicit testimony favourable to his own client. He is entitled to ask as many leading questions as he chooses and of course can refer the witness to any contradictory statement he has made.

In cross-examination defence counsel must put to each witness the points where his evidence will be challenged when the defendant and his witnesses give evidence. When the cross-examination is concluded, the plaintiff's advocate has the right to re-examine his witness on matters arising out of the cross-examination.

Where the witness produces a document or plan or photograph or other object as original evidence it becomes an *exhibit* in the case and is marked and kept by the associate.[1] Wherever the witness wishes to produce a copy document the party calling him will have to prove that the original has been destroyed or cannot be traced unless the opposing party waives objection to its admissibility or himself holds the original and has failed to comply with a notice to produce.

Although the judge can and will ask questions of the witnesses it is a basic characteristic of our system that the introduction and testing of testimony is principally the function of counsel and not of the court. The rule of the judge in our system has been explained by Denning L.J. (as he then was)[2] as follows:

> "If a judge, said Lord Greene, should himself conduct the examination of witnesses, 'he so to speak, descends into the arena and is liable to have his vision clouded by the dust of conflict': see *Yuill v. Yuill*.[3] ... [He] must keep his vision unclouded. It is all very well to paint justice blind, but she does better without a bandage around her eyes. She should be blind indeed to favour or prejudice, but clear to see which way lies the truth: and the less dust there is about the better.... [The] judge is not allowed in a civil dispute to call a witness whom he thinks might throw some light on the facts. He must rest content with the witnesses called by the parties: see *Re Enoch and Zaretsky, Bock & Co's Arbitration*.[4] So also it is for the advocates, each in his turn, to examine the witnesses, and not for the judge to take it on himself lest by so doing he appear to favour one side or the other.... And it is for the advocate to state his case as fairly and strongly as he can, without undue interruption, lest the sequence of his argument be lost.... The judge's part in all this is to hearken to the evidence, only himself asking questions of witnesses when it is necessary to clear up any point that has been overlooked or left obscure; to see that the advocates behave themselves seemly and keep to the rules laid down by law; to exclude irrelevancies and discourage repetition; to make sure by wise intervention that he follows the points that the advocates are making and can assess their worth; and at the end to make up his mind where the truth lies. If he goes beyond this, he drops the mantle of a judge and assumes the robe of an advocate; and the change does not become him well. Lord Chancellor Bacon spoke right when he said that:[5] 'Patience and gravity of hearing is an essential part of justice; and an over-speaking judge is no well-tuned cymbal'."

SUBMISSION OF NO CASE AND NON SUIT

In criminal trials, it often happens that at the conclusion of the case for the prosecution, counsel for the defence will submit that there is "no case to

---

[1] R.S.C. Ord. 35, r. 11. The plaintiff's exhibits are normally marked P1, P2, P3, etc. In the county court, the exhibits are kept by the clerk of the court.

[2] *Jones v. National Coal Board*, [1957] 2 Q.B. 55, at pp. 63–64. In that case the Court of Appeal allowed a re-trial because of persistent interruptions of counsel's cross-examination.

[3] [1945], P. 15, at p. 20.

[4] [1910] 1 K.B. 327.

[5] *Essays on Counsels Civil and Moral:* "Of Judicature."

answer" either in the sense that the prosecution have failed to call any evidence to prove an essential ingredient of the offence charged or on the ground that the prosecution evidence is so weak or has been so discredited by cross-examination that no reasonable jury could convict. If this submission succeeds, the accused is entitled to be acquitted and no appeal will lie from the ruling.

In civil cases, it is also possible for counsel for the defendant to make such a submission to the judge sitting alone. However if the judge rules in favour of the submission and gives judgment dismissing the plaintiff's claim, the plaintiff can appeal. If the plaintiff succeeds in the Court of Appeal, the defendant will doubtless ask for the matter to be remitted for the trial judge to hear the defence evidence. This means that a great deal of costs will have been incurred and time wasted because of the initial wrong ruling. To prevent this happening, civil judges normally refuse to rule on a submission of no case unless the defendant agrees to stand by the submission and call no evidence in the event of the submission being rejected.[1]

Submissions of no case can (subject to the above-mentioned condition that the defendant must elect to call no evidence) be made in either the High Court or county court. If the submission succeeds the defendant is entitled to have judgment entered dismissing the claim and the matter can never be litigated again. In the county court, where litigants frequently appear in person, the plaintiff may well fail on a technical ground, for example because he has produced no admissible evidence to prove an essential point (e.g. he only has a copy notice to quit and no notice to produce has been given). In such a case the court instead of dismissing the claim may *non suit* the plaintiff which has the effect of striking out the case but preserving the plaintiff's right to have the matter heard again when his tackle is in order.[2] It should be noted that there is no power to *non-suit* a plaintiff in High Court proceedings.

DEFENCE CASE, VIEWS AND CLOSING SPEECHES

Counsel for the defendant has the right if he is calling evidence to open his case.[3] In the county court this right is seldom exercised—possibly because if counsel elects to open the defence case he is not entitled to make a closing speech except with leave of the court. The defence evidence is presented in exactly the same manner as the plaintiff's evidence and is subject to the same rules.

It may happen at any stage in the trial and frequently at the conclusion of the evidence that the judge will wish to view the scene of the events in question.[4] If the view involves any display of machinery or reconstruction of the events the parties and their legal representatives should attend; if the view only involves visual observation of a public place, the judge may attend alone but he should state that he has done so before delivering judgment so that the parties may point out to him any changes in the *locus in quo* or other material differences between the conditions at the time of the view and the trial of the

---

[1] See *Alexander v. Rayson*, [1936] 1 K.B. 169.

[2] C.C.R. Ord. 23, r 3(1). Where the evidence has not been completed the plaintiff may claim to be non-suited of right but thereafter the matter is for the court's discretion. See *Clack v. Arthur's Engineering Ltd.*, [1959] 2 All E.R. 503.

[3] R.S.C. Ord. 35, r. 7(4).

[4] The power of the court to inspect any place or thing with respect to which any question arises in the cause or matter is set out in R.S.C. Ord. 35, r. 8 and C.C.R. Ord. 23, r. 14. Note that in the county court the expenses of such a view are to be paid *in the first instance* by the party on whose application the inspection is made or ordered, or if made or ordered without application, by the plaintiff, but are subsequently borne by the unsuccessful party unless the judge otherwise orders.

action.[1] Once the evidence is concluded counsel for the defendant addresses the court. Counsel for the plaintiff then summarises his submissions and answers his opponent's arguments—unless the judge has already decided to find for him on all points—in which case he will indicate that counsel need not trouble to address him. It would be impossible to set out here all the matters which should be borne in mind by the advocate in addressing the court but perhaps the following suggestions may prove helpful:

(a) The novice often irritates the court by not understanding how a legal argument should be advanced—for example, the advocate should never state his own personal opinion on any matter: therefore it is unprofessional to say "I think"—one should always use the expression "in my submission" or "I submit ...".

(b) Again one should learn the correct method of referring to a law report: "I would refer your Lordship to *X and X* reported in the second volume of the Queen's Bench Reports for 1963 at page 206 as authority for the proposition that. ..." It is quite pointless for the advocate to read a report unless he has first told the judge what legal proposition he claims can be derived from it. Some judges dislike reference to current text-books; however the most conservative judge will be prepared to listen if the text-book is properly introduced into the speech by the advocate "*adopting* the argument of the learned author at page. ..."

(c) In actions claiming general damages, counsel must not suggest to the judge the amount which should be awarded although he may and indeed should refer to any point in the evidence that is relevant in assessing quantum. It follows that unless counsel is invited so to do it is not proper for him to refer the court in personal injury cases to reports of awards in *Kemp & Kemp: Quantum of Damages in Personal Injury and Fatal Accident Cases*[2] or *Current Law* or in the *Times* reports. Of course in all cases where there has been a payment into court, care must be taken by the advocate not to mention this matter to the judge.

JUDGMENT

In every civil case the judge is bound to deliver a reasoned judgment setting out his findings of fact on the evidence and his conclusions thereon. Where he is uncertain as to where the truth lies on any issue he must find against the party bearing the onus of proof since that party will have failed to establish the matter on a balance of probabilities.[3] The judge will normally give an opinion

---

[1] See *Salsbury* v. *Woodland*, [1970] 1 Q.B. 324; [1969] 3 All E.R. 863 where the principles are discussed. *Per* Sachs s L.J. at p. 879: "Knowing how plans and photographs may give an incomplete impression of a place, it may, indeed, often be wise to go and have a look in order to get a first-hand impression of the locality as a whole—to obtain a clearer and three-dimensional picture, so that, in effect the evidence falls into place. It must be remembered that all he is doing is to appreciate the evidence already given in the light of a static background. Such visits by judges alone have a long history.... Widgery L.J. has ... mentioned the visit paid by Lord Goddard C.J. to Euston Station—and there can be but few who had more practical experience of such matters, both as a 'circuiteer' and as a judge. He gave no advance notice of his going to Euston Station.... It is, of course, wise, when practicable, to give advance notice of a visit. It is wise if there has been a visit before closing speeches, to inform counsel of that; but it is not always practicable; and it would be no credit to the law if judges were not allowed to visit public places without an expensive legal panoply accompanying them."
[2] 1975, Sweet and Maxwell.
[3] It should be remembered that the standard of proof in civil litigation is quite different from the standard in criminal cases; in a civil action it suffices that the judge concludes that the fact to be proved is "more likely than not", i.e. is the most likely explanation on a balance of probabilities. In criminal cases the prosecution have to prove their case so as to destroy all rational likelihood of any explanation other than guilt (i.e. prove its case beyond reasonable doubt).

on every issue which would be relevant in the event of appeal succeeding against any one of his findings (for example, in a personal injury case, if he finds against the plaintiff on the issue of liability he will nevertheless give his decision on quantum to save the expense of a re-trial if the Court of Appeal uphold an appeal on the question of liability). The judgment in the High Court is transcribed by an official short-hand reporter (or tape-recorded): in the county court, where such facilities are not available, it is the duty of counsel on both sides to take a full note of the judgment since this will be the only record available to the Court of Appeal.

At the conclusion of the oral judgment, counsel for the successful party asks formally for

(a) judgment[1] (e.g. "judgment for the plaintiff for £2,000" or "that there be judgment for the defendant and the claim be dismissed"),
(b) interest, if appropriate (see below), and
(c) costs.

We shall discuss the appropriate orders as to costs in the next chapter. The rules as to interest deserve attention and are set out below.

INTEREST

Interest may be claimed in any action:

(a) on the basis of a right by contract or special statute (e.g. the Bills of Exchange Act 1882) or
(b) generally under the discretionary provisions of the Law Reform (Miscellaneous Provisions) Act 1934.

In personal injury and fatal accident cases the court *must* award interest under its general statutory power if the sum awarded exceeds £200 unless there are special reasons justifying the refusal of an award. The principles to be applied when awarding interest in personal injury claims are set out in the Court of Appeal's decision in *Jefford* v. *Gee* [1970] 2 Q.B. 130; [1970] 1 All E.R. 1202[2] as follows:

(i) interest on special damage should be awarded at half the rate formerly allowed on general damages from the date of the accident to the trial;
(ii) interest on general damage for pain and suffering or under the Fatal Accidents Acts should not be awarded;
(iii) no interest is to be awarded on that part of general damages which is awarded for loss of future earnings.

The "appropriate rate" is the average rate of interest allowed on money in court placed on the Short Term Investment Account[3] over the period for which interest is awarded.[4]

---

[1] Note the judgment may be for payment in a foreign currency; see *Miliangos* v. *George Frank (Textiles) Ltd.*, [1975] 3 All E.R. 801, H.L.

[2] As modified in *Cookson* v. *Knowles* (1977), *Times*, 26th May, where the Court of Appeal held that the former practice of awarding interest on awards of general damages for pain and suffering or under the Fatal Accidents Act should be discontinued because of the current level of inflation.

[3] See p. 146, *ante*.

[4] The relevant rates in recent years are
   From 1 April, 1971—7½ per cent.
   From 1 March, 1973—8 per cent.
   From 1 March, 1974—9 per cent.
   From 1 February, 1977—10 per cent.

DRAWING UP THE JUDGMENT

In proceedings in the Queen's Bench Division the solicitor of the successful party draws up the terms of the judgment on a form purchased from the court and takes this with the writ to the Judgement Department where it is formally sealed.[1] The court itself has a record of the judgment in the form of a certificate drawn up by the associate.[2] In the county court the court staff themselves draw up and issue the record of the judgment. The forms of judgment are set out in the *County Court Practice.* By way of example we set out below the form of order which would be drawn up by the court where at the conclusion of a possession action where a suspended order is made under the Rent Act 1968:[3]

In the Shoreditch County Court

Plaint No. 77. 3064

Between:

Grand Metropolitan and Suburban
Property Company Limited

Plaintiffs

and
Wilkins Micawber

Defendant

IT IS ADJUDGED that the Plaintiff is entitled to recover against the defendant possession of the land mentioned in the particulars annexed to the summons in this action, that is to say 123 City Road, London E.C.1, the rent of the said land amounting to £150 being in arrear and the Plaintiff having a right of re-entry or forfeiture in respect thereof.

AND IT IS ADJUDGED that the Plaintiff do recover against the Defendant the sum of £150 for the arrears of rent aforesaid and the sum of £25 for costs, amounting together to the sum of £175.

AND IT IS ORDERED that the Defendant do pay the said sum of £175 to the Registrar of this Court on or before the 16th day of May 1977, and that, unless payment is made by the said date, the Defendant do thereupon give possession of the land to the Plaintiff.

AND IT IS FURTHER ORDERED that execution on such order be suspended for so long as the Defendant punctually pays to the Plaintiff or his agent the sum of £175 by instalments of £5 per week commencing on the 20th day of April 1977, in

---

[1] R.S.C. Ord. 42, r. 5. The procedure in the Chancery Division is set out at R.S.C. Ord. 42, rr. 6–7.

[2] R.S.C. Ord. 35, r. 10.

[3] In practice the beginner needs to know before appearing on a possession summons the four different types of order which can be made since the judge or registrar may refer to the order by the following form numbers:

135 Order for possession—this would be appropriate where notice to quit has been served by a resident landlord on a non-protected tenant.

136 Judgment for plaintiff for arrears of rent, forfeiture of lease, and possession within a period not less than 28 days—this applies to premises *not* protected under the Rent Act. The tenant can prevent the forfeiture by paying the sum due or applying for relief under County Courts Act 1959, s. 191.

136A Judgment for arrears and forfeiture but no order for possession–this means the contractual tenancy has been forfeited but the tenant can remain in possession as a statutory tenant under the Rent Act.

136B Judgment for arrears, forfeiture of lease and order for possession is not less than 28 days but suspended so long as the tenant pays rent and instalments off the arrears.

addition to the current rent of £8 per week and that no execution shall issue on such order when the said sum of £175 has been paid.

Dated this 18th day of April 1977   Jonathan Wedgwood
                                                  REGISTRAR

NOTICE

If you pay the arrears of rent and costs by the date mentioned in the third paragraph above or within such further time as the court may order, you will be entitled to hold the land according to the lease without any new lease. If you do not pay the arrears of rent and costs as aforesaid, you will be barred from all relief against forfeiture of the lease while this order remains unreversed, but the order will not be enforceable against you so long as you comply with the terms mentioned in the fourth paragraph above. If you become ill or out of work, ask your landlord to suspend the order until you are better or back at work. If he will not do so, you should ask the court officials to help you prepare an application to the Court.

CHAPTER TWELVE

COSTS

At the conclusion of nearly every case, the court will have to deal with an application for costs,[1] including the costs of interlocutory proceedings which have been "reserved" to the trial judge. Although the question of costs is in the discretion of the judge, the basic rule which must be followed, unless there are special factors "justifying the exercise of his discretion" otherwise, is that "costs follow the event", i.e. the winner is entitled to an order that the loser pays the costs he has incurred in the litigation. It is important to bear in mind that in a High Court action this by no means indemnifies the winner for all the costs he has paid or will have to pay to his solicitor. This is because the loser pays to the winner costs taxed by a Taxing Master on a *party and party*[2] basis covering only the essential costs of the litigation whilst the winner will have to pay his solicitor fees calculated on a *solicitor and own client basis*[3] in which he can be charged for all the work done unless he can show his solicitor was acting unreasonably. The position is exactly the same in county court litigation[4] where the winner will recover an amount on a *party and party* taxation on the appropriate scale[5] which may be far less than he has to pay his own solicitor. The fundamental point therefore for the beginner to keep in mind is that the person who obtains an order for costs will still be out of pocket so far as his own indebtedness to his solicitor is concerned. We shall now consider the most important points on costs which the advocate must understand if he is to be capable of conducting civil litigation.

COUNTY COURT COSTS

In county court cases the costs awarded to a successful party will either be

(a) *taxed*—i.e. a bill will be submitted to the registrar and the unsuccessful party will be able to challenge items he thinks are unjustified or inordinate; or

---

[1] The importance of this application can only be appreciated if one realises the proportion costs are likely to bear to the actual award of damages. In June 1975 Mr. Michael Zander published in the *Guardian Gazette* (vol. 72, no. 23) the results of research on data collected by Mr. David Abbott from a sample of 650 bills presented for taxation in the Queen's Bench Division in London and at four major trial centres. The results showed:

Median Award	£	Median Costs	£
Contested cases	3,748	Contested cases	806
Settled cases including settled at court	1,500	Settled before trial Settled at court	435 977

The *median* figure (i.e. the point at which there are as many cases above as below the figure is shown because the average figure may be distorted by exceptionally high or low cases. It is to be noted that 94 per cent of the cases in the sample were personal injury claims. In the eventual taxation only 15 per cent or less was taxed off the bill in 78 per cent of the cases.

[2] R.S.C. Ord. 62, r. 28.
[3] R.S.C. Ord. 62, r. 29.
[4] See C.C.R. Ord. 47, rr. 38 and 40.
[5] See the section on county court scales below.

(b) *assessed*—i.e. at the conclusion of the trial the judge or registrar hearing the case will make an immediate assessment based in part on fixed tables set out in the *County Court Practice* and in part on his own impression of the complexity of the case.

Assessed costs will always be less than the costs which would be awarded on taxation but in fact successful parties often ask for such an assessment to save the time and expense of drawing up a bill for taxation, especially where they are doubtful about the possibilities of eventually recovering the costs awarded. Thus for example many courts in London have a fixed sum (often £25) which will be awarded as assessed costs in simple possession actions to the plaintiff's solicitor who will ask for such an assessment because he knows he is unlikely in any event to recover such costs and is more interested in simply getting an order to evict his tenant.

The amount awarded as costs in the county court will vary according to the nature of the action and the amount of money or damages involved. Where the action is for a specific sum of money or damages, the costs awarded are on a scale governed in the case of a successful plaintiff by the amount awarded and in the case of a successful defendant by the amount claimed. The appropriate scales are set out below:

Sum of money	*Scale applicable*
Exceeding £5 and not exceeding £50	Lower Scale
Exceeding £50 and not exceeding £200	Scale 1
Exceeding £200 and not exceeding £500	Scale 2
Exceeding £500 and not exceeding £1,000	Scale 3
Exceeding £1,000	Scale 4

The above rule is, however, subject to the important principle that where the plaintiff recovers no more than £100 or where the defendant successfully resists a claim for no more than £100 *no solicitors' charges shall be allowed as between party and party.* This rule is intended to encourage litigants in small claims to employ arbitration rather than formal proceedings. There are certain exceptions to this general rule which the advocate in county court litigation must remember:

(a) If the sum involved exceeds £5 then a successful plaintiff will be entitled to the fixed costs stated on the summons and the costs of enforcing the judgment.

(b) If one party has behaved unreasonably in his conduct of the case, the court may order him to pay the costs incurred as a result of his conduct (thus where a defendant in a road traffic case persisted in a defence which was found to be a complete fabrication, the registrar would order him to pay the costs occasioned by his forcing the plaintiff to prove a case which he knew was true).

(c) If the court certifies that the case involves a question of fact or law of exceptional complexity it may award costs on such scale as it thinks fit.

(d) If a claim for damages exceeding £5 for personal injuries is made in the case then costs are to be awarded to include solicitors' fees.

For practical purposes the position is that in claims involving £100 or less and nothing else the successful litigant will recover virtually nothing of the bill he will have to pay his own solicitor. It must be remembered, however, that if the plaintiff is claiming some other relief as well as the money claimed, e.g. possession of land or an injunction, costs will be awarded which will normally then cover a much greater part of his solicitor's bill.

HIGH COURT COSTS

It has already been explained (p. 38, *ante*) that a successful plaintiff in the High Court will obtain no order for costs if his claim is in contract or tort and the amount he recovers is less than £350.[1] If he recovers £350 or more but less than £1,200 his costs will be taxed on the appropriate county court scale. In assessing the amount awarded any deduction for contributory negligence is *ignored* (i.e. one takes the figure on the basis of full liability). The court may order High Court costs if either it considers that the plaintiff had reasonable grounds for thinking his claim was worth more than £2,000 or that there was some other reason, such as the complexity of the law involved, to justify commencing the action in the High Court.[2] It should be remembered that where a person takes proceedings under the Rent Act in the High Court which he could have taken in the county court he is not entitled to recover *any* costs at all. Generally proceedings under the Rent Acts may be commenced in the county court notwithstanding that the premises have a rateable value exceeding £1,000.

LEGAL AID CASES

Where a litigant who has been issued with a certificate under the Legal Aid Act 1974 wins he is entitled to the normal order for *party and party* costs against his opponent and in addition the court will order a special taxation of his own solicitor's costs (called a *legal aid taxation*) so as to determine the amount the solicitor is to recover from the fund. The legal aid taxation is made on a *common fund* basis, i.e. the taxing officer will order payment of such "reasonable sums as were reasonably incurred in the action".[3] It should be noted that the Law Society have a first charge on any sum awarded to a successful assisted litigant. This means he will not receive his damages until the costs ordered on the Legal Aid taxation have been paid.[4]

Where an assisted person is the unsuccessful party to an action only a restricted order for costs can be made by the court against *him* (as opposed to the legal aid authority whose position is considered below). This is the effect of section 8(1) (*c*) of the Legal Aid Act 1974 which provides that:

> "Where a person receives legal aid in connection with any proceedings his liability by virtue of an order for costs made against him with respect to the proceedings *shall not exceed the amount (if any) which is a reasonable one for him to pay* having regard to all the circumstances, including the *means* of all the parties and their *conduct* in connection with the dispute."

---

[1] County Courts Act 1959, s. 47.

[2] Rent Act 1968, s. 105. Note this rule does not apply to cases where the landlord if he proves his case *must* recover, i.e. where there is overcrowding under s. 17 or the case falls under Pt. 2 of Schedule III.

[3] Contrast the *solicitor and own client* basis which is appropriate where the litigant is not legally aided and where all costs are allowed except those which are unreasonable.

[4] Legal Aid Act 1974, s. 9(6). Legal Aid (General) Regulations 1971, reg. 18.

The effect of this provision can be understood by considering a simple personal injury claim.

> *Example*—P who is privately represented sues D for damages for injuries received in a road accident. P loses. D will have to pay his solicitor £1,200 costs but will recover £800 costs from P. Now assume instead that P is legally aided with a contribution to the fund of £100. The court is bound to consider his means and is most unlikely to order him to pay more than the amount he has already paid to the Law Society as his contribution towards his own costs. This means that D, though he wins, will still be the worse off by £1,000.

If one bears in mind that over 45 per cent of all plaintiffs prosecuting accident claims are legally aided it will be realised that there is often a strong incentive to the defendant to settle however meritorious he may consider his own case.

To a certain extent the harshness of the provision is mitigated by section 13 of the Act which provides that the court may order the Legal Aid Fund to pay the costs of the successful party provided:

(a) he is not assisted himself,
(b) he did not begin the case,
(c) the court has already considered the liability of the assisted litigant to contribute towards the costs,
(d) it would be just and equitable to make an order, and
(e) the successful party would incur "severe financial hardship" if an order was not made.

The last condition was considered by the Court of Appeal in the case of *Hanning* v. *Maitland No. 2*, [1970] 1 Q.B. 580; [1970] 1 All E.R. 812.

> In April 1966 the defendant was on a walking tour in Hertfordshire. On a dark, wet night the plaintiff, who was a member of a cycling club, rode into him. The plaintiff obtained legal aid and brought an action alleging negligence, i.e. that the walker should have carried lights or been on the other side of the road. The defendant, who was 54 and of limited income applied for legal aid to defend the case. His application was refused because his savings, though small, took him outside the limit. He won the case but was refused an order for costs against the Legal Aid Fund on the grounds of his own capital. The Court of Appeal reversed this decision and ordered the fund to pay his costs. Lord Denning M.R. said that the rule that the successful defendant must show "severe financial hardship" is designed to prevent costs being awarded against the Fund to "insurance companies, commercial concerns who are in a considerable way of business and wealthy folk who can meet the costs without feeling it".[1]

COSTS WHERE DEFENDANT SUCCESSFULLY COUNTERCLAIMS

We have already seen (p. 82, *ante*) that where a defendant counterclaims damages which arise out of the same transactions as the plaintiff's claim he may *set-off* the damages he recovers against the plaintiff's claim. If the set-off extinguishes the claim then, since a set-off is in law a complete defence to the claim, the plaintiff's claim will be dismissed and he will be ordered to pay the defendant's costs.

---

[1] Since this decision the door is open for all save insurance companies and *very* wealthy persons to claim against the Fund. The profession however is only slowly waking up to the important change made by this case.

Example—P agrees to service D's machinery and claims £500 being the cost of overhauling the equipment. D refuses to pay on the ground that part of the equipment was wrongly re-fitted and this caused damage to the machine which cost £500 to repair. If D proves his case the order will be: "Plaintiff's case dismissed: plaintiff to pay defendant's costs."

Where a successful counterclaim does not arise out of the same transaction as the claim it cannot be set-off as a defence so that the order for costs *may* be:

    (i) Judgment for P on claim with costs.
    (ii) Judgment for D on counterclaim with costs.

In this case the costs of P and D are set off so that D will pay less than if he had not raised the counterclaim but nonetheless there is almost always a substantial balance of costs in favour of the plaintiff (because the defendant is only entitled to recover the costs exclusively referable to the counterclaim, i.e. only the amount by which the costs of the proceedings have been increased by the counterclaim[1]).

COSTS AFTER PAYMENT INTO COURT

We have also already discussed the position where a defendant pays money into court as an offer to the plaintiff to settle (see p. 145, *ante*). If the plaintiff does not accept the sum offered but at the end of the trial is awarded no more than the sum paid into court,[2] then the order for costs is:[3]

    (i) D to pay P costs to date of payment-in.
    (ii) P to pay D's costs thereafter.

As we have already explained, since the bulk of the costs is usually incurred at the trial stage the plaintiff is likely to have his damages reduced so as to pay the balance of costs outstanding to the defendant.

BULLOCK AND SANDERSON ORDERS

There will be many cases where a plaintiff is placed in a dilemma as to which of two parties should be sued:

Example—P is a passenger in a vehicle driven by D1 which collides with a car driven by D2. D1 and D2 blame each other. At the trial D1 is held to be solely to blame for the accident.

In such circumstances the successful defendant is entitled to look for his costs from the plaintiff since he is blameless and the plaintiff decided to bring the action against him. However, the plaintiff was forced into this action by the intransigence of the unsuccessful defendant in refusing to admit liability and in insisting that the innocent defendant was to blame; it therefore follows that the plaintiff should be indemnified in the costs he has to pay the successful defendant by the unsuccessful defendant. This form of order known as a *Bullock Order*[4] involves an order in the following terms:

---

[1] See *Medway Oil and Storage Co.* v. *Continental Contractors*, [1929] A.C. 88; [1928] All E.R. Rep. 33a.
[2] The test is to look at the sum awarded *after* any set-off has been deducted but before any sum due by counterclaim is considered; see *Chell Engineering Ltd.* v. *Unit Tool Co.*, [1950] 1 All E.R. 378.
[3] Unless possibly the difference is so small that the de minimis rule applies; see *Tingay* v. *Harris*, [1967] 2 Q.B. 327.
[4] From the case of *Bullock* v. *London General Omnibus Co.*, [1907] 1 K.B. 264 where the facts were similar to those in the example above.

(i)   Judgment for P against D1 with costs.
(ii) Claim against D2 dismissed; P to pay D2's costs.
(iii) D1 to pay to P costs so paid by P to D2.

This order safeguards the innocent defendant provided the plaintiff has the means to pay. If, however, the plaintiff is insolvent or legally aided in circumstances where the successful defendant will not recover costs from the Legal Aid Fund, the defendant may well prefer an order for costs against the unsuccessful defendant directly. This form of order is known as a *Sanderson Order*[1] and involves:

(i)   Judgment for P against D1 with costs.
(ii) Claim against D2 dismissed; D1 to pay D2's costs.

---

[1] From the case of *Sanderson v. Blyth Theatre Co.*, [1903] 2 K.B. 533, when, confusingly, the order in fact made was a Bullock Order. A Sanderson Order is the form of order suggested in the Court of Appeal in that case as more suitable where the plaintiff is unlikely to be able to pay the innocent defendant's costs.

CHAPTER THIRTEEN

ORIGINATING SUMMONS PROCEDURE

So far we have discussed proceedings which have been commenced by the issue of a writ out of the High Court or by filing a praecipe for a summons in the county court. The characteristics of such proceedings (technically "actions") are that (1) the parties exchange pleadings, (2) witnesses are called to give oral evidence at the trial and (3) various default procedures are available. Such procedure tends to be unnecessarily expensive and time-consuming where the principal issue is one of the law or the construction of a written instrument, and where there is no substantial issue on the facts. In such cases proceedings may be begun by what in the High Court is called an originating summons; its counterpart (though not identical) in the county court is an originating application. R.S.C. Order 5, rule 4(2) provides the basic test as to which cases should be begun by originating summons.

"Proceedings—
  (a) in which the sole or principal question at issue is, or is likely to be, one of the construction of an Act or of any instrument made under an Act, or any deed, will, contract or other document, or some other question of the law, or
  (b) in which there is likely to be any substantial dispute of fact are appropriate to be begun by originating summons."

One could add to the above rule a third category—namely cases brought under the provisions of particular statutes (such as the Landlord and Tenant Act 1954 in relation to business tenancies, the Married Women's Property Act 1882, the Inheritance (Provision for Family and Dependants) Act 1975, the Variation of Trusts Act 1958, or applications for inspection of property before proceedings under the Administration of Justice Act 1969). It will be appreciated that although the originating summons procedure is used principally in the Chancery Division, it is by no means the only procedure employed in that division: thus, for example an originating summons would be inappropriate in any case where there was an allegation of dishonest breach of trust, fraud or undue influence.[1] Probate actions must be begun by writ: R.S.C. Order 76, rule 2.

CHANCERY DIVISION PROCEDURE

We shall take as an illustration for this chapter a problem arising out of the provision of a will.

Example—On 31 October 1971, Jeremiah Jarndyce made a will by which he appointed his brothers Sebastian and Nathaniel executors and left his entire estate after payment of debts and tax to them "in the assured confidence that they will

---

[1] If proceedings are begun by originating summons which should have been commenced by writ, the court can direct that they shall continue and the parties may be ordered to exchange pleadings. Frequently an affidavit already lodged on behalf of the plaintiff will be ordered to stand as a statement of claim. Thereafter the proceedings will continue as if commenced by writ (R.S.C. Ord. 28, r. 8).
The position is similar in the county court—see C.C.R. Ord. 7.

distribute the same amongst societies for the suppression of pornography". He died on 3 November 1975. Probate was granted on 2 February 1976. Jeremiah left a widow, Florence, but no issue, parent, brother or sister or issue of a brother or sister. (The widow is therefore absolutely entitled to any assets passing on intestacy.)

The problems which face Sebastian and Nathaniel in this case can be summarised as follows:

(1) do the words "in the assured confidence" impose a trust which binds the executors, or are they merely expressing his hopes as to what will be done?

(2) If they are apt to impose a binding trust, is such trust valid? It will be remembered that a trust for a specific purpose is only valid if the object is "charitable". Is the "suppression of pornography" a charitable purpose? If it is not, then the residuary property will be held by the trustee for the persons entitled to take on an intestacy.

The executors will want to get the court's determination on those questions so that they can be sure of distributing the estate in accordance with law and without incurring personal risk; they will therefore apply by way of originating summons to the court. We set out below the form of summons. Note that in all Chancery proceedings the title of the action should include a reference to any relevant deed, will or statute. The widow will argue for intestacy; the Attorney-General will argue that the gift is charitable and good in law.

In the High Court of Justice
1976—J—No. 2075

Chancery Division

Group B

In the Matter of the Will dated the 31st day of October 1971 of Jeremiah Jarndyce, deceased.

Between:

Sebastian Jarndyce and
Nathaniel Jarndyce   Plaintiffs

and

Florence Jarndyce (Widow) and
Her Majesty's Attorney General   Defendants

To Florence Jarndyce of 23 Garden Walk, Aldershot, in the County of Hampshire, Widow and Her Majesty's Attorney General:

Let the Defendants, within 14 days after the service of this summons upon them, inclusive of the day of service, cause an appearance to be entered to this summons which is issued on the application of the Plaintiffs Sebastian Jarndyce of 26 Trinity Street, Cambridge and Nathaniel Jarndyce of 10 High Street, Trumpington in the County of Cambridge (who are the executors of the Will abovementioned having proved the same in the Principal Registry of the Family Division of this Honourable Court on the 2nd day of February 1976).

By this summons the Plaintiffs seek the following relief namely:

(1) That it may be determined whether upon a true construction of the said Will and in the events which have happened the Plaintiffs hold the residuary estate of the above-named Jeremiah Jarndyce:

(*a*) upon trust to distribute the same amongst societies for the suppression of
    pornography; or

(*b*) upon trust for the First Defendant absolutely; or

(*c*) upon some other and if so what trusts.

(2) That if, and so far as is necessary, there may be an order for the administration
    of the trusts of the said Will by this Honourable Court.

(3) That provision may be made for the costs of this application.

(4) That such further or other relief may be granted as to this Honourable Court
    shall seem fit.

If the Defendants do not enter an appearance, such judgment may be given or
order made against or in relation to them as the court may think just and expedient.

Dated the 22nd of May 1976.

This summons may not be served later than 12 calendar months beginning with
the above date unless renewed by order of the court.

This summons was taken out by Tulkinghorn and Co., Solicitors, of Lincoln's
Inn Fields, London W.C.2, Solicitors for the Plaintiffs (*Here summons continues with
directions for entering an appearance.*)

Once the summons has been drafted the procedure to be followed is:

(1) Two top copies of the summons are taken to the Central Office (or
    local district registry), both are sealed, a revenue stamp is affixed to one
    copy which is retained and the other is returned to the plaintiff[1]. Notice
    that all persons interested who are not themselves plaintiffs but whom
    it is desired should be bound by the order of the court should be added
    as defendants. A guardian *ad litem* will be appointed to watch over the
    interests of infant defendants. Where beneficiaries are unborn or unas-
    certained (e.g. the possible future children or issue of living persons) a
    representation order is made appointing one of the defendants to
    represent their interests.

(2) The plaintiff serves the summons in the same manner as a writ.

(3) If any defendant wishes to contest or support the summons he must
    cause an appearance to be entered by submitting the appropriate forms
    to the court with 14 days of service.[2]

(4) Once all the defendants have entered an appearance or the time limited
    for appearance has expired the plaintiff obtains a "notice of appoint-
    ment" which he must serve on every defendant who has entered an
    appearance at least 4 clear days before the appointment.[3]

(5) Any evidence which the plaintiff intends to adduce must be sworn in
    one or more affidavits and lodged in chambers. (In our example the
    executors would make an affidavit referring to the will, the probate, the
    assets of the estate, the state of the deceased's family and any other facts
    which would be relevant—such as the deceased's connection with
    anti-pornography campaigns. The probate itself (and the will annexed)
    is lodged at the court: being technically an order of the court it does not
    need to be proved.) Copies of the affidavits must be served on the
    defendants at least 4 days before the first appointment.

---

[1] See R.S.C. Ord. 7, r. 5.

[2] Note there are a few cases where an appearance need not be entered and the summons fixes
the date of the first appointment—e.g. an originating summons for the approval of an infant
settlement where proceedings have not been commenced. See R.S.C. Ord. 7, r. 2.

[3] R.S.C. Ord. 28, rr. 2 and 3.

(6) At the first appointment, the master will give directions for the lodging of further evidence, etc. Although in certain cases he has jurisdiction to make final orders, normally his function is to see the case is properly prepared before it is referred for decision to the judge. It should be noted that any party has the right to have *any* matter or direction (including matters upon which the master could make a final order) referred to the judge for his determination.[1]

(7) When all is in order, the master will adjourn the summons into court to be heard by the judge.

The procedure at the hearing is that the plaintiff opens his case, the affidavits are read, if any deponent has been ordered to attend for cross-examination his evidence is taken, and each defendant addresses the court. On the hearing of an originating summons the plaintiff can normally address the court only once and so he will usually deal with questions of law in his opening (although the judge has a discretion to allow a reply and sometimes does so on particular points of law or authorities cited by the other side). It should be noted that the common law principle that costs follow the event is seldom applicable to cases brought by originating summons where the question in issue is as to the proper application of a trust fund. Thus, for instance, in the problem above one would expect the costs of the executors to be taxed on a "trustee basis" and the costs of the defendants to be taxed on a "common fund basis"[2] and paid out of the estate: the reason for this is that the parties have really been brought before the court by the testator making a will the effect of which was unclear.

COUNTY COURT PROCEDURE

In the county court, proceedings which would be brought by originating summons in the High Court are brought by way of originating application under C.C.R. Order 6, rule 4. The application differs from an originating summons in that it sets out not only the relief claimed but also the grounds upon which it is claimed. The facts as set out in the application are not supported by an affidavit. The application is served together with a plaint note and notice of the day upon which the registrar will conduct the pre-trial review. Usually he will direct the respondent to file an answer setting out his case. The evidence when the case comes on for hearing will normally be oral rather than by affidavit. This form of procedure is frequently used in disputes between husband and wife where the court has unlimited jurisdiction under the Married Women's Property Act 1882. It is also employed where a business tenant applies for a new tenancy under Part II of the Landlord and Tenant Act 1954.[3] We set out below an illustration of the type of case which might be brought by originating summons. It is important to note that the

---

[1] See p. 100, *ante.*

[2] When costs are granted to a litigant on 'trustee basis' he is entitled to recover all his expenditure except in so far as the costs or any part thereof should not, in accordance with the duty of a trustee or personal representative, have been incurred or paid or should for that or any other reason be borne personally by him: R.S.C. Ord. 62, r. 31(2). Costs on a 'common fund basis' enable the party in question to recover a reasonable amount in respect of all costs reasonably incurred— see R.S.C. Ord. 62, r. 32 and see p. 170, *ante.*

[3] A special procedure is set out in C.C.R. Ord. 40, r. 8(1). The application must be set out in the prescribed form (Form 335) and an answer (in Form 336) must be filed within 14 days of service.

county court equity jurisdiction is limited by the size of the fund or property concerned.[1]

> *Example*—In 1974 Polly and Tony who were living together but were not married decided to purchase a small garret flat in Bloomsbury. The purchase price was £12,000 of which £10,000 was obtained by way of mortgage and the balance was contributed by each of them in equal shares. In order more easily to obtain a mortgage they decided that the house should be conveyed into Tony's name. Polly has now left Tony but he refuses to give her a half share in the flat. The present value of the flat is £14,000 and the equity is £6,000.

In the Marylebone and Bloomsbury   No. of Application

County Court

In the matter of the Law of Property Act 1925
And in the matter of Flat 3, 6 Ampton Street
in the Lond Borough of Camden

Between:

Polly Browne   Applicant
and
Anthony Brockhurst   Respondent

I, Polly Browne of 31 Lamb's Conduit Street, London W.C.1 the above-named Applicant, apply to the Court for an order in the following terms:

(1) That it may be declared that the Respondent holds the leasehold premises situated at and known as Flat 3, 6 Ampton Street, in the London Borough of Camden on trust for himself and for me in equal shares or in such shares as this Honourable Court shall determine.

(2) That the Respondent may be ordered to sell the said premises and pay to me out of the net proceeds of sale thereof one-half or such other proportion as may represent my interest therein.

(3) That the Respondent may be ordered to pay the costs of this application.

(4) That I may be granted such further or other relief as may be just.

The grounds on which I claim to be entitled to this order are as follows:

(1) On the 1st day of September 1974 the Respondent and I purchased a lease for 99 years of the aforesaid property for the sum of £12,000 of which £10,000 was obtained by way of mortgage with the Sunnyhomes Building Society. The Respondent and I each contributed £1,000 to make up the balance of the purchase price out of our savings.

(2) The said property was conveyed into the sole name of the Respondent.

(3) I cohabited with the Respondent at the above address until April 1977. During that period we pooled our resources and the mortgage repayments were made out of our joint bank account.

(4) Since we separated the Respondent has refused to acknowledge my interest in the said property or to compensate me therefore.

(5) The said premises subject to the aforesaid trust do not exceed in value £15,000.

The name and address of the person upon whom it is intended to serve this application is:

---

[1] County Courts Act 1959, s. 52. At the present the limit is £15,000.

Anthony Brockhurst
c/o his solicitors: Dodson and Fogg
Freeman's Court, Cornhill, London E.C.3

The applicant's address for service is:

c/o her solicitors Evans and Bartlam
5 South Square, Gray's Inn, London W.C.1

Dated this 12th day of May 1977.

Signed *Evans and Bartlam*
      [Solicitors for the Applicant.

CHAPTER FOURTEEN

INDUSTRIAL TRIBUNALS

Today most litigation solicitors and common law barristers can expect to be asked to appear for clients in proceedings for unfair dismissal[1] or redundancy pay[2] before an industrial tribunal. It therefore seems sensible in a book concerned with civil claims to set out in outline the procedure by which such claims are brought before the industrial tribunals.

COMMENCEMENT

Proceedings are commenced by originating application with the applicant invariably using the standard questionnaire (form IT1) available at all employment exchanges. The form effectively asks him to set out details to show the date his employment began and terminated, his earnings, reasons given for his dismissal and the nature of his claim. Note that even though an employee is suing on the basis that he was redundant it is usually right to include a claim in the alternative for unfair dismissal. Proceedings must be brought within the following time limits:

(a) Unfair dismissal claims—within 3 months of the effective date of dismissal unless it was not reasonably practicable to bring the claim in time.[3]

(b) Redundancy cases—within 6 months of the effective date of dismissal (but the tribunal has power to extend the period for a further 6 months if it is "just and equitable" so to do).[4]

Proceedings are commenced when the completed form is sent to the Central Office of Industrial Tribunals. That office registers the application and sends a copy by post to the respondent together with a blank form of appearance. It should be noted that although solicitors will advise under the Green Form Scheme (see p. 47, *ante*) as to the merits of an application, legal aid is not available for representation before the tribunal.

APPEARANCE

The respondent must enter an appearance within 14 days of service stating whether or not he intends to resist the application and if so on what grounds.

---

[1] Under Schedule 1 of the Trade Union and Labour Relations Act 1974, as amended by Employment Protection Act 1975.

[2] Under Redundancy Payment Act 1965.

[3] Sch. 1, para. 2(b) of the Trade Union and Labour Relations Act 1974. Sch. 16, Pt. III, para. 21 of the Employment Protection Act 1975.

[4] Redundancy Payments Act 1965, s. 21 and Employment Protection Act 1975, Sch. 16, Pt. I, para. 9.

This is an important document from the point of view of the applicant since he will frequently have only an imperfect appreciation of the reasons for his dismissal.[1] The purpose of the appearance is to show the employee precisely the nature of the case to be presented against him at the tribunal. If, as frequently happens, the employer sets out his grounds in only the vaguest terms the employee should not hesitate to write to the tribunal asking for further and better particulars of the grounds stated.[2]

EVIDENCE

Both sides are entitled to apply by letter to the Central Office of Tribunals or the local area office for discovery and for orders requiring the attendance of witnesses or the production of documents. The parties' advisers should consider carefully:

(1) Whether there are any documents likely to be in the possession of the other side which could assist in the presentation of their case. For example, copies of the form setting out reasons for dismissal which is sent to the employment exchange, personal files, and minutes of management meetings may all be of assistance in a claim for unfair dismissal; in redundancy cases one would ask in addition for production of trading figures, balance sheets and the minutes of any relevant board meetings. It is always sensible, so as to avoid surprise, to ask for discovery of any documents which the other side intends to produce at the hearing.

(2) Whether any witnesses should be summoned to attend: for instance, an employee's workmates, who can sometimes give valuable evidence in his favour, will normally prefer to be summoned to attend rather than give evidence voluntarily against their employer.

In addition to the above an applicant should take with him to the hearing the following documents:

(a) the contract of employment and all other documents relating to the terms of his contract,
(b) details of his pay whilst employed by the respondents,
(c) details of pay at his new job, and any other benefits (such as car allowances) he receives and of any pension schemes,
(d) details of any expenses caused by having to look for new work,
(e) details of all unemployment benefit and social security benefit received.

THE HEARING

The party upon whom the burden of proof rests commences; this will normally be the employer unless the actual fact of dismissal is in dispute. The evidence consists principally of the sworn testimony of witnesses as to matters within their personal knowledge although the tribunals are not obliged to follow the strict rules of evidence.[3] Proceedings for unfair dismissal are normally in two stages:

---

[1] Although he has a right under Employment Protection Act 1975, s. 70 to require his employer to give him a written statement of the reasons for his dismissal.
[2] See Industrial Tribunal Rules, r. 5 and *White* v. *Manchester University*, [1976] I R.L.R. 218.
[3] Note a party may submit written representations instead of attending but this is very seldom done.

(1) The issue of whether the dismissal is unfair; if it is held unfair the tribunal will normally recommend re-instatement or re-engagement and adjourn.

(2) If the employer does not take the employee back (or the tribunal decide in the first hearing that such a recommendation is impracticable), the tribunal must determine compensation. In order to save the expense of the parties attending twice, many tribunals prefer to obtain precise evidence of the employee's loss at the first hearing, so both parties should have, at that stage, clear evidence available of the employee's earnings[1] and the amount which they contend should be awarded as the basic award[2] and the compensatory award.[3]

The tribunal generally makes no order as to costs unless it can be shown that a party has acted frivolously or vexatiously.[4] An appeal will lie from the decision of a tribunal to the Employment Appeals Tribunal but *on a point of law only*. The appeal must be brought within 42 days of the date on which the decision is entered in the Register. Legal aid although not available for representation before an industrial tribunal is available on appeal.

We set out in the appendix below the forms of originating application and appearance together with the rules at present in force.

---

[1] The mode of calculation is set out in Employment Protection Act 1975, Sch. 4.
[2] Employment Protection Act 1975, ss. 74–75 calculated by reference to the length of service.
[3] Ibid., s. 76 and see the headings in *Norton Tool Co., Ltd.* v. *Tewson*, [1973] 1 All E.R. 183; [1973] 1 W.L.R. 45.
[4] Travel and subsistence allowances and also loss of earnings up to £9.80 per day are payable out of public funds to the parties and witnesses and to anyone representing the parties (unless the representative is a barrister, solicitor or full-time official of a workers' or employers' association).

ORIGINATING APPLICATION TO AN INDUSTRIAL TRIBUNAL

UNDER ONE OR MORE OF THE FOLLOWING ACTS:—

TRADE UNION AND LABOUR RELATIONS ACT 1974
REDUNDANCY PAYMENTS ACT 1965
CONTRACTS OF EMPLOYMENT ACT 1972
EQUAL PAY ACT 1970
SEX DISCRIMINATION ACT 1975
EMPLOYMENT PROTECTION ACT 1975
RACE RELATIONS ACT 1976

	For Official Use
Case Number	

IMPORTANT: DO NOT FILL IN THIS FORM UNTIL YOU HAVE READ THE NOTES FOR GUIDANCE. THEN COMPLETE ITEMS 1, 2, 4 AND 13 AND ALL OTHER ITEMS RELEVANT TO YOUR CASE

To:— The Secretary of the Tribunals
Central Office of the Industrial Tribunals (England and Wales)
93, Ebury Bridge Road, London SW1W 8RE

Telephone: 01—730—9161

1   I hereby apply for a decision of a tribunal on the following question (*State here question to be decided by the Tribunal and explain the grounds overleaf*)

     Whether my dismissal by the Respondents was unfair

2   My name (*surname in block capitals first*) is Mr/~~Mrs/Miss~~. . . . . . . WILLIAM SIKES . . . . OR

2(A)   our title (*if company or organisation*) is. . . . .

2 and 2(A)   address . 236 Western Road, Southall

                         Telephone no. . . . .

3   If a representative has agreed to act for you in this case please give his name and address below and note that further communications will be sent to him and not to you (*See Note 2*)

     Name   Frederick Engels

     Address and telephone no.   National Society of Machine Operators, Unity House, 121 Euston Road, NW1

4   **(a)**   Name of respondent(s) (*in block capitals*) ie the employer, person or body against whom a decision is sought (*See Note 3*)

         Address(es) and telephone no.(s)   WEST MIDDLESEX SALVAGE COMPANY LIMITED

                 201 Uxbridge Road, Southall.

   (b)   Respondent's relationship to you for the purpose of the application (*eg employer, trade union, employment agency, employer recognising the union making application, etc.*)

     EMPLOYER

5   Date of birth . . . . . . 15. 9. 35 . . . .

6   Place of employment to which this application relates, or place where act complained about took place.   201 Uxbridge Road, Southall.

7   Occupation or position held/applied for, or other relationship to the respondent named above (*eg user of a service supplied by him*)   Machine Operator

8   Employment began on . . . . 26. 3. 70 . . . . . and (*if appropriate*) ended on . . . . 13. 12. 76 . . . .

9   Basic wages/salary . . . . £60 per week . . . .

10   Other pay or remuneration . . . . None . . . .

11   Normal basic weekly hours of work . . . . . . 40 . . . .

12   (In an application under the Sex Discrimination Act or the Race Relations Act) Date on which action complained of took place or first came to my knowledge. . . . .

Please continue overleaf

IT 1 (Revised April 1977)
(2781) Dd543059 100,000 5/77 JC&SLtd Gp3615

13   The grounds of this application are as follows: (*See Note 4*)

I was unfairly dismissed by the Respondents.

14   (If dismissed) If you wish to state what in your opinion was the reason for your dismissal, please do so here.

I was dismissed because of the way I gave evidence in a case concerning safety precautions at the Respondents' premises.

15   If the Tribunal decides that you were unfairly dismissed, what remedy would you prefer? (Before answering this question please consult the Notes for Guidance for the remedies available and then write one only of the following in answer to this question: reinstatement, re-engagement or compensation)

Reinstatement

Signature........ *William Giles* .... Date.... *1.3.77* ....

FOR OFFICIAL USE

	Code	ROIT	Inits

Industrial Tribunals

NOTICE OF APPEARANCE BY RESPONDENT

To the Secretary of the Tribunals

Case Number............................

FOR OFFICIAL USE	
Date of receipt	Initials

REGIONAL OFFICE OF THE INDUSTRIAL TRIBUNALS
LONDON (SOUTH)
93 EBURY BRIDGE ROAD
LONDON SW1W 8RE
Telephone: 01-730-9161

1 I *do/~~do not~~ intend to resist the claim made by William Sikes

2 *~~My~~/Our Name is *~~Mr/Mrs/Miss~~/title (if company or organisation) West Middlesex Salvage Company Limited

   address 201 Uxbridge Road
        Southall
        Middlesex

   telephone number 01-583-4673

3 If you have arranged to have a representative to act for you, please give his name and address below and note that further communications will be sent to him and not to you.

   name Mr. Bertram Fogg

   address Dodson and Fogg,
        Freeman's Court,
        Cornhill,
        London EC3

   telephone number

4 a Was the applicant dismissed? *YES/~~NO~~

   b If YES, what was the reason for the dismissal? Redundancy

   c Are the dates given by the applicant as to his period of employment correct? *YES/~~NO~~

   d If NO, give dates of commencement .... and termination ....

5 If the claim is resisted, please state the grounds on which you intend to resist:—

      We were forced to make Mr. Sikes redundant because of a reduction of work coupled with the introduction of new plant necessitating fewer staff. He has been paid the appropriate redundancy payment.

Signature ....Dodson and Fogg...................   Date ....8.3.77............

           Delete inappropriate items

IT 3   181 527130 25M 1/77 HGW 752

APPENDIX TO CHAPTER 14

INDUSTRIAL TRIBUNALS (LABOUR RELATIONS) REGULATIONS 1974, S.I. 1974, NO. 1386 (as amended by S.I. 1976, No. 661).

RULES OF PROCEDURE

Originating application

1.—(1) Proceedings for the determination of any matter by a tribunal shall be instituted by the applicant (or in a matter falling under sub-paragraph (*d*) of this paragraph, by a court) sending to the Secretary of the Tribunals an originating application which shall be in writing and shall set out:—

(*a*) the name and address of the applicant; and

(*b*) the names and addresses of the person or persons against whom relief is sought or of the parties to the proceedings before the court (as the case may be); and

(*c*) the grounds on which that relief is sought; or

(*d*) the question for determination under section 51 of the 1966 Act and, except where the question is referred by a court, the ground on which relief is sought.

(2) Where the Secretary of the Tribunals is of the opinion that the originating application does not seek or on the facts stated therein cannot entitle the applicant to a relief which a tribunal has power to give, he may give notice to that effect to the applicant stating the reasons for his opinion and informing him that the application will not be registered unless he states in writing that he wishes to proceed with it.

(3) An application as respects which a notice has been given in pursuance of the preceding paragraph shall not be treated as having been received for the purposes of Rule 2 unless the applicant intimates in writing to the Secretary of the Tribunals that he wishes to proceed with it; and upon receipt of such an intimation the Secretary of the Tribunals shall proceed in accordance with that Rule.

(4) Where the applicant does not intimate in writing to the Secretary of the Tribunals that he wishes to proceed with the application the non-registration of the application shall be without prejudice to any right of the applicant to make a further application to a tribunal.

Action upon receipt of originating application

2.—(1) Upon receiving an originating application the Secretary of the Tribunals shall enter particulars of it in the Register and shall forthwith send a copy of it to the respondent ... and inform the parties in writing of the case number of the originating application entered in the Register (which shall thereafter constitute the title of the proceedings) and of the address to which notices and other communications to the Secretary of the Tribunals shall be sent. Every copy of the originating application sent by the Secretary of the Tribunals under this paragraph shall be accompanied by a written notice which shall include information, as appropriate to the case, about the means and time for entering an appearance, the consequences of failure to do so, and the right to receive a copy of the decision. The Secretary of the Tribunals shall also notify the parties that in all cases under the provisions of any enactment providing for conciliation the services of a conciliation officer are available to them.

(2) In proceedings falling under the 1965 Act, the Secretary of the Tribunals shall forthwith send copies of all documents and notices to the Secretary of State notwithstanding the fact that he may not be a party to such proceedings.

(3) ...

(4) In all cases under the provisions of any enactment providing for conciliation, the Secretary of the Tribunals shall forthwith send copies of all documents and notices to a conciliation officer who in the opinion of the Secretary is an appropriate officer to receive them.

Appearance by respondent

3.—(1) A respondent shall within 14 days of receiving the copy originating application enter an appearance to the proceedings by sending to the Secretary of the Tribunals a written notice of appearance setting out his full name and address and stating whether or not he intends to resist the application and, if so, on what grounds. Upon receipt of a notice of appearance the Secretary of the Tribunals shall forthwith send a copy of it to any other party.

(2) A respondent who has not entered an appearance shall not be entitled to take any part in the proceedings except—

(i) to apply under Rule 12(1) for an extension of the time appointed by this Rule for entering an appearance;
(ii) to be called as a witness by another person;
(iii) to be sent a copy of a decision or specification of reasons or corrected decision or specification in pursuance of Rules 8(3), 8(7) or 9(5); and
(iv) to make an application under Rule 9(1)(b),

and accordingly (without prejudice to the generality of this provision) he shall not be entitled—

(a) to make an application under Rule 4;
(b) to submit representations in writing for consideration by the tribunal in pursuance of Rule 6(3);
(c) to be heard or to be represented at the hearing in pursuance of Rule 7;
(d) to apply for directions in pursuance of Rule 12(2) or to receive a notice in pursuance of Rule 12(4); or
(e) to make an application under Rule 9, except under paragraph (1)(b) of that Rule.

(3) A notice of appearance which is sent to the Secretary of the Tribunals after the time appointed by this Rule for entering appearance shall be deemed to include an application under Rule 12(1) (by the respondent who has sent the notice of appearance) for an extension of the time so appointed. Without prejudice to Rule 12(4), if the tribunal grants the application (which it may do notwithstanding that the grounds of the application are not stated) the Secretary of the Tribunals shall forthwith send a copy of the notice of appearance to any other party. The tribunal shall not refuse an extension of time under this Rule unless it has given the person wishing to enter an appearance an opportunity to show cause why the extension should be granted.

Power to require further particulars and attendance of witnesses and to grant discovery

4.—(1) Subject to Rule 3(2), a tribunal may on the application of a party to the proceedings (or ... the Secretary of State (whether or not a party)) made either by notice to the Secretary of the Tribunals or at the hearing of the originating application—

(a) require a party ... to furnish in writing to the person making the application further particulars of the grounds on which he or it relies and of any facts and contentions relevant thereto;
(b) grant to the person ... making the application such discovery or inspection of documents as might be granted by a county court; and

(c) require the attendance of any person (including a party to the proceedings) as a witness or require the production of any document
relating to the matter to be determined, wherever such witness may be
within Great Britain;

and may appoint the time at or within which or the place at which any act
required in pursuance of this Rule is to be done.

(2) A party on whom a requirement has been made under paragraph (1 (*b*)
of this Rule on an *ex parte* application and a person on whom a requirement
has been made under paragraph (1)(*c*) thereof may apply to the tribunal to
vary or set aside the requirement.

(3) No such application to vary or set aside shall be entertained in a case
where a time has been appointed under paragraph (1) of this Rule in relation
to the requirement unless it is made before the time or, as the case may be,
expiration of the time so appointed. Notice of the application in accordance
with Rule 11(3) shall be given to the party on whose application the requirement was made.

(4) Every document containing a requirement under paragraph (1)(*b*) or
paragraph (1)(*c*) of this Rule shall contain a reference to the fact that under
paragraph 21(6) of Part III of Schedule 1 to the 1974 Act any person who
without reasonable excuse fails to comply with any such requirement shall be
liable on summary conviction to a fine not exceeding £100.

(5) If the requirement under paragraph (1)(*a*) of this Rule is not complied
with, a tribunal, before or at the hearing, may dismiss the application, or, as
the case may be, strike out the whole or part of the notice of appearance, and,
where appropriate, direct that a respondent shall be debarred from defending
altogether.

Time and place of hearing and appointment of assessor

5.—(1) The President or a nominated chairman shall fix the date, time and
place of the hearing of the originating application and the Secretary of the
Tribunals shall not less than 14 days (or such shorter time as may be agreed by
him with the parties) before the date so fixed (subject to Rule 3(2)) send to
each party a notice of hearing which shall include information and guidance as
to attendance at the hearing, witnesses and the bringing of documents (if any),
representation by another person and written representations.

(2) ...

(3) Where in the case of any proceedings it is provided for one or more
assessors to be appointed the President or a nominated chairman may, if he
thinks fit, appoint a person or persons having special knowledge or experience in relation to the subject matter of the originating application to sit with
the tribunal as assessor or assessors.

The hearing

6.—(1) Any hearing of or in connection with an originating application
shall take place in public unless in the opinion of the tribunal a private hearing
is appropriate for the purpose of hearing evidence which relates to matters of
such a nature that it would be against the interests of national security to allow
the evidence to be given in public or hearing evidence from any person which
in the opinion of the tribunal is likely to consist of—

(a) information which he could not disclose without contravening a pro-
hibition imposed by or under any enactment; or

(b) any information which has been communicated to him in confidence,
of which he has otherwise obtained in consequence of the confidence
reposed in him by another person; or

(c) information the disclosure of which would cause substantial injury to
any undertaking of his or any undertaking in which he works for
reasons other than its effect on negotiations with respect to any of the
matters mentioned in section 29(1) of the 1974 Act.

(2) In cases to which the foregoing provisions of this Rule apply, a member of the Council on Tribunals shall be entitled to attend the hearing in his capacity as such member.

(3) Subject to Rule 3(2), if a party shall desire to submit representations in writing for consideration by a tribunal at the hearing of the originating application that party shall send such representations to the Secretary of the Tribunals not less than 7 days before the hearing and shall at the same time send a copy of it to the other party or parties (... or the Secretary of State (if not parties)).

(4) Where a party has failed to attend or be represented at the hearing (whether or not he has sent any written representations) the contents of his originating application or, as the case may be, of his entry of appearance may be treated by a tribunal as representations in writing.

(5) The Secretary of State if he so elects shall be entitled to appear as if he were a party and be heard at any hearing of or in connection with an originating application in proceedings which may involve payments out of the Redundancy Fund under the provisions of any enactment.

(6) Subject to Rule 3(2), at any hearing of or in connection with an originating application a party and any person entitled to appear may appear before the tribunal and may be heard in person or be represented by counsel or by a solicitor or by a representative of a trade union or an employers' association or by any other person whom he desires to represent him.

Procedure at hearing

7.—(1) Subject to Rule 3(2), at the hearing of the originating application a party, and the Secretary of State if he is not a party and he elects to appear under Rule 6(5) and any person entitled to appear shall be entitled to make an opening statement, to give evidence, to call witnesses, to cross-examine any witnesses called by the other party (or by the Secretary of State if he is not a party) and to address the tribunal.

(2) If a party shall fail to appear or to be represented at the time and place fixed for the hearing, the tribunal may dispose of the application in the absence of that party or may adjourn the hearing to a later date: Provided that before disposing of any application in the absence of a party the tribunal shall consider any representations submitted by that party in pursuance of Rule 6(3).

(3) A tribunal may require any witness to give evidence on oath or affirmation and for that purpose there may be administered an oath or affirmation in due form.

Decision of tribunal

8.—(1) A decision of a tribunal may be taken by a majority thereof and, if the tribunal shall be constituted of two members only, the chairman shall have a second or casting vote.

(2) The decision of a tribunal shall be recorded in a document signed by the chairman which shall contain the reasons for the decision.

(3) The clerk to the tribunal shall transmit the document signed by the chairman to the Secretary of the Tribunals who shall as soon as may be enter it in the Register and shall send a copy of the entry to each of the parties and to the persons entitled to appear who did so appear and where the originating application was sent to a tribunal by a court, to that court.

(4) The specification of the reasons for the decision shall be omitted from the Register in any case in which evidence has been heard in private and the tribunal so directs and in that event a specification of the reasons shall be sent to the parties and to any superior court in any proceedings relating to such decision together with the copy of the entry.

(5) The Register shall be kept at the Office of the Tribunals and shall be open to the inspection of any person without charge at all reasonable hours.

(6) The chairman of a tribunal shall have power by certificate under his hand to correct in documents recording the tribunal's decisions clerical mistakes or errors arising therein from any accidental slip or omission.

(7) The clerk to the tribunal shall send a copy of any document so corrected and the certificate of the chairman to the Secretary of the Tribunals who shall as soon as may be make such correction as may be necessary in the Register and shall send a copy of the corrected entry or of the corrected specification of the reasons, as the case may be, to each of the parties and to the persons entitled to appear who did so appear and where the originating application was sent to a tribunal by a court, to that court.

(8) If any decision is—

(a) corrected under paragraph (6) of this Rule; or
(b) reviewed, revoked or varied under Rule 9; or
(c) altered in any way by order of a superior court,

the Secretary of the Tribunals shall alter the entry in the Register to conform with any such certificate or order and shall send a copy of the new entry to each of the parties and to the persons entitled to appear who did so appear and where the originating application was sent to the tribunal by a court, to that court.

Review of tribunal's decisions

9.—(1) A tribunal shall have power to review and to revoke or vary by certificate under the chairman's hand any of its decisions in a case in which a county court has power to order a new trial on the grounds that—

(a) the decision was wrongly made as a result of an error on the part of the tribunal staff; or
(b) a party did not receive notice of the proceedings leading to the decision; or
(c) the decision was made in the absence of a party or person entitled to be heard; or
(d) new evidence has become available since the making of the decision provided that its existence could not have been reasonably known of or foreseen; or
(e) the interests of justice require such a review.

(2) An application for the purposes of paragraph (1) of this Rule may be made at the hearing. If the application is not made at the hearing, such application shall be made to the Secretary of the Tribunals at any time from the date of the hearing until 14 days after the date of the entry of a decision in the Register and must be in writing stating the grounds in full.

(3) An application for the purposes of paragraph (1) of this Rule may be refused by the President or by the chairman of the tribunal which decided the case or by a nominated chairman if in his opinion it has no reasonable prospect of success.

(4) If such an application is not refused under paragraph (3) of this Rule, it shall be heard by the tribunal and if it is granted the tribunal shall either vary its decision or revoke its decision and order a re-hearing.

(5) The clerk to the tribunal shall send to the Secretary of the Tribunals the certificate of the chairman as to any revocation or variation of the tribunal's decision under this Rule. The Secretary of the Tribunals shall as soon as may be make such correction as may be necessary in the Register and shall send a copy of the entry to each of the parties and to the persons entitled to appear who did so appear and where the originating application was sent to a tribunal by a court, to that court.

Costs

10.—(1) Subject to paragraphs (2) and (3) of this Rule, a tribunal shall not normally award costs but where in its opinion a party to any proceedings (and if he is a respondent whether or not he has entered an appearance) has acted frivolously or vexatiously the tribunal may make—

(a) an order that that party shall pay to another party (or to the Secretary of State, where appropriate, if he is not a party) either a specified sum in respect of the costs incurred by that other party (or, as the case may be, by the Secretary of State), or, in default of agreement, the taxed amount of those costs;

(b) ...

(2) Notwithstanding the provisions of paragraph (1) of this Rule where—

(a) on the application of a party to the proceedings the tribunal has postponed the day or time fixed for the hearing or has adjourned the hearing, the tribunal may make orders against that party or, as the case may be, in favour of that party as at paragraph (1)(a) and (b) of this Rule as respects any costs incurred or any allowances paid as a result of the postponement or adjournment; or

(b) any postponement or adjournment of the hearing has been caused by the respondent where (in accordance with paragraph 21(3A) of Schedule 1 to the 1974 Act in relation to a complaint of unfair dismissal)—

  (i) the employee has expressed a wish to be reinstated or re-engaged which has been communicated to the employer at least 7 days before the hearing of the complaint; or

  (ii) the proceedings arise out of the employer's failure to permit the employee to return to work after an absence due to pregnancy or confinement,

the tribunal shall, in the absence of a special reason for his failure to adduce reasonable evidence as to the availability of the job from which the employee was dismissed, or, as the case may be, which she held before her absence, or of comparable or suitable employment, make orders against that respondent as at paragraph (1)(a) and (b) of this Rule as respects any costs incurred or any allowances paid as a result of the postponement or adjournment.

(3) ...

(4) Any costs required by an order under this Rule to be taxed may be taxed in the county court according to such of the scales prescribed by the county court rules for proceedings in the county court as shall be directed by the order.

Miscellaneous powers of tribunal

11.—(1) Subject to the provisions of these Rules, a tribunal may regulate its own procedure.

(2) A tribunal may, if it thinks fit,—

(a) subject to Rule 4(3), extend the time appointed by these Rules for doing any act notwithstanding that the time appointed may have expired;

(b) postpone the day or time fixed for, or adjourn, any hearing;

(c) if the applicant shall at any time give notice of the withdrawal of his originating application, dismiss the proceedings;

(d) except in proceedings under the 1966 Act, if both or all the parties (and the Secretary of State, where appropriate, if he is not a party) agree in writing upon the terms of a decision to be made by the tribunal, decide accordingly;

(e) at any stage of the proceedings order to be struck out or amended any originating application or notice of appearance or anything in such application or notice of appearance on the ground that it is scandalous, frivolous or vexatious.

(3) A tribunal, may, if it thinks fit, before granting an application under Rule 4 or Rule 12 require the party (or, where appropriate, . . . the Secretary of State (whether or not a party)) making the application to give notice of it to the other party or parties (and, where appropriate, to . . . the Secretary of State (whether or not a party)). The notice shall give particulars of the application and indicate the address to which and the time within which any objection to the application shall be made being an address and time specified for the purposes of the application by the tribunal.

(4) Any act other than the hearing of an originating application or the making of an order under Rule 9(1) required or authorised by these Rules to be done by a tribunal may be done by, or on the direction of, the President, the chairman of the tribunal or a nominated chairman.

(5) Rule 10 shall apply to an order dismissing proceedings under paragraph (2)(c) of this Rule.

(6) Any functions of the Secretary of the Tribunals other than that mentioned in Rule 1(2) may be performed by an Assistant Secretary of the Tribunals.

Extension of time and directions

12.—(1) An application to a tribunal for an extension of the time appointed by these Rules for doing any act may be made by a party (or, where appropriate, . . . by the Secretary of State (whether or not a party)) either before or (subject to Rule 4(3)) after the expiration of any time so appointed.

(2) Subject to Rule 3(2), a party (or, where appropriate, . . . the Secretary of State (whether or not a party)) may at any time apply to a tribunal for directions on any matter arising in connection with the proceedings.

(3) An application under the foregoing provisions of this Rule shall be made by sending to the Secretary of the Tribunals a notice of application, which shall state the title of the proceedings and shall set out the grounds of the application.

(4) Subject to Rule 3(2), the Secretary of the Tribunals shall give notice to both or all the parties of any extension of time granted under Rule 11(2)(a) or any directions given in pursuance of this Rule.

Joinder of parties and representative proceedings

13.—(1) A tribunal may be any time upon the application of any person, whether an applicant or respondent or not, or of its own motion, direct that any person appearing to the tribunal to be directly interested in the subject of the originating application be added as a respondent, and give such consequential directions as it considers necessary.

(2) A tribunal may likewise, either upon such application or of its own motion, order that any respondent named in the originating application or subsequently added, who shall appear to the tribunal not to have been, or to have ceased to be, directly interested in the subject of the originating application, be dismissed from the proceedings.

(3) Where there are numerous persons having the same interest in an originating application, one or more of them may be cited as the person or persons against whom relief is sought, or may be authorised by the tribunal, before or at the hearing, to defend on behalf of all the persons so interested.

Notices, etc.

14.—(1) Any notice given under these Rules shall be in writing and all notices and documents required or authorised by these Rules to be sent or given to any person hereinafter mentioned may be sent by post (subject to paragraph (3) of this Rule) or delivered to or at—

(a) in the case of a document directed to the Secretary of the Tribunals, the Office of the Tribunals or such other office as may be notified by the Secretary of the Tribunals to the parties;

(b) in the case of a document directed to the Secretary of State in proceedings to which he is not a party, the offices of the Department of Employment at 8, St. James's Square, London, SW1Y 4JB or such other office as may be notified by the Secretary of State;

(c) in the case of a document directed to the Board, the principal office of the Board;

(d) in the case of a document directed to a court, the office of the clerk of the court;

(e) in the case of a document directed to a party, his address for service specified in the originating application or in a notice of appearance or in a notice under paragraph (2) of this Rule or (if no address for service is so specified), his last known address or place of business in the United Kingdom or, if the party is a corporation, the corporation's registered or principal office;

(f) in the case of a document directed to any person (other than a person specified in the foregoing provisions of this paragraph), his address or place of business in the United Kingdom, or if such a person is a corporation, the corporation's registered or principal office;

and if sent or given to the authorised representative of a party shall be deemed to have been sent or given to that party.

(2) A party may at any time by notice to the Secretary of the Tribunals and to the other party or parties (and, where appropriate, to the Secretary of State if he is not a party or, as the case may be, to the appropriate conciliation officer) change his address for service under these Rules.

(3) Where a document or notice is not delivered, the recorded delivery service shall be used in the following circumstances—

(a) if under Rule 2(1) a second set of documents or notices is sent to a respondent who has not entered an appearance under Rule 3(1);

(b) if an order is made under Rule 4(1)(c).

(4) Where for any sufficient reason service of any document or notice cannot be effected in the manner prescribed under this Rule, the President or a nominated chairman may make an order for substituted service in such manner as he may deem fit and such service shall have the same effect as service in the manner prescribed under this Rule.

(5) In relation to the matters specified in Rule 3(1), Rule 5, paragraphs (3), (4), (7) and (8) of Rule 8 and Rule 9(5), the Secretary of the Tribunals shall also send copies of all documents and notices (where appropriate) to the Secretary of State notwithstanding the fact that he may not be a party to the proceedings, or (as the case may be) to the appropriate conciliation officer.

(6) In relation to the matters specified in paragraphs (3), (4), (7) and (8) of Rule 8 and Rule 9(5), the Secretary of the Tribunals shall also send copies of the relevant documents to the Commission in all cases under the Equal Pay Act 1970 or the Sex Discriminations Act 1975.

CHAPTER FIFTEEN

APPEAL SYSTEMS

INTERLOCUTORY APPEALS: HIGH COURT

Where any order is made by a master or district registrar on any one of the procedural applications discussed in this book or on an application for summary judgment under R.S.C. Order 14, either party may appeal against his decision to a judge in chambers.

> *Example*—D fails to enter an appearance within the prescribed period and P signs judgment in default of appearance under R.S.C. Order 13. D takes out a summons for the judgment to be set aside and for leave to enter an appearance out of time but at the hearing of the application the master refuses to set the judgment aside. D can appeal of right to the judge in chambers.

The procedure is governed by R.S.C. Order 58. The appellant drafts a notice of appeal in the form set out below and takes it to the Action Department at the Law Courts[1] where it is sealed and issued. The notice must be issues within 5 days[2] of the order appealed against and served not less than 2 clear days before the return day. It should be noted this notice does *not* state the grounds of appeal since the appeal is by way of a complete rehearing of the case (although the appellant will open the case).

NOTICE OF APPEAL TO JUDGE IN CHAMBERS

In the High Court of Justice   1976—W—No. 206

Queen's Bench Division

Between:

John Wellington Wells   Plaintiff

and

St. Mary Axe Novelty Company Limited   Defendants

TAKE NOTICE that the above-named Defendants intend to appeal against the decision of Master Cooper given on the 29th day of April, 1976 refusing to set aside the judgment for £2,000 and £25 costs entered herein by the Plaintiffs on the 6th day of March, 1976 in default of appearance and ordering the Defendants to pay the costs of the application.

AND further take notice that you are required to attend before the Judge in Chambers at the Central Office, Royal Courts of Justice, Strand on Friday the 28th day of May, 1976 at 10.30 o'clock on the forenoon, on the hearing of an application

---

[1] Or to the district registry.
[2] Discount the day of the order and Saturdays and Sundays in computing 5 days—see Ord. 3, r. 2. In the district registry the period is 7 days. Note that the court has power in any event to extend the time.

by the said Defendants that the said judgment be set aside and that the Defendants be granted unconditional leave to defend this action and that the said order for costs be set aside and the Plaintiffs do pay to the Defendants the costs of this appeal and of the said application.

AND further take notice that it is the intention of the said Defendants to attend by Counsel.

Dated this 4th day of May, 1976.   *Dodson and Fogg*
                                                    Solicitors for Defendants
To

    Evans and Bartlam,
    10, Holborn Court,
    Gray's Inn,
    Solicitors for the Plaintiff.

Either side may ask the judge to consider affidavit evidence not produced to the master although, if notice of this new evidence has not been given in advance, the other side may ask for an adjournment to consider the evidence and for an order for the costs thrown away. The appeal is therefore a complete rehearing so that although the judge "will of course give the weight it deserves to the previous decision of the master . . . he is in no way bound by it".[1] The successful party at the hearing must ask for the costs of the appeal and of the appearance below since they will not be costs in the cause and neither party will get them unless an order is made. An appeal to the Court of Appeal will lie from the decision of the judge with leave[2] (either from the judge himself or from the Court of Appeal) *except* where the judge has granted a defendant unconditional leave to defend.[3]

APPEALS TO COUNTY COURT JUDGE

In the county court appeal lies to the judge under C.C.R. Order 13, rule 1(h) from any decision of the registrar on an interlocutory order by filing and serving a notice of application one clear day before the hearing. The principles discussed above apply equally in the county court. An appeal also lies to a judge against any final order or judgment by the registrar[4] by notice served within 6 days of the judgment or order in question. The judge may make any of the following orders:

(a) he may set aside or vary the judgment, or
(b) he may give some other judgment having heard the appeal, or
(c) he may remit the action to the registrar for retrial or further consideration, or
(d) he may order a new trial to take place before himself or another judge of the court on a day to be fixed.[5]

---

[1] *Per* Lord Atkin in *Evans v. Bartlam*, [1937] A.C. 473, at p. 478.
[2] No leave is required to appeal against an order under R.S.C. Ord. 14—see Supreme Court of Judicature Act 1925, s. 31(2).
[3] Ibid., s. 31(1)(c). The point is that a further appeal is a waste of time—it is better that the plaintiff proceed with the action in the normal way.
[4] It should be remembered that the registrar has extensive jurisdiction over minor claims—see p. 158, *ante*.
[5] C.C.R. Ord. 37, r. 5.

APPEALS TO THE COURT OF APPEAL

Appeal lies to the Court of Appeal from the High Court and the county court. In some circumstances it is necessary for the proposed appellant to obtain leave to appeal, thus:

(1) where the appeal is from a consent order or against the exercise of the judge's discretion as to costs, leave must be obtained from the trial judge;[1]

(2) where the appeal is from the decision of a county court judge on a point of law on a claim involving a sum or property worth less than £20[2] leave must be obtained from the judge.

(3) where the appeal is from an interlocutory order, leave must be given either by the judge who made the order or by the Court of Appeal.[3]

It is to be noted that there is *no* appeal from a decision of a county court on a question of *fact* alone where the value of the claim does not exceed £200 or the rateable value of the land in question does not exceed £500.[4] It should also be noted that in the county court (but *not* in the High Court) either party can apply to the judge for a new trial if there has been a serious irregularity at the original hearing or if there is fresh evidence. The procedure is governed by C.C.R. Order 37.

Where a party desires to appeal he must issue within the prescribed period a *notice* of *appeal*. The relevant periods[5] are:

(1) appeals from interlocutory orders (including judgment under Order 14)—14 days;

(2) cases concerning bankruptcy or the winding up of a company—21 days;

(3) all other appeals—6 weeks.

The notice of appeal will follow the form set out opposite:

---

[1] Judicature Act 1925, s. 31(1)(h). Where it is contended that the judge has applied the wrong principles of law in deciding the question of costs, so that the Court of Appeal is being asked to do more than review the exercise of discretion, leave is not required: see *Donald Campbell & Co. Ltd.* v. *Pollak*, [1927] A.C. 732 and *Evans* v. *Bartlam*, [1937] A.C. 473. If the application for leave is not made at the original hearing the party desiring leave should ask the judge's clerk to arrange for the matter to be listed before the judge and give notice of the day fixed to the other parties.

[2] County Courts Act 1959, s. 108.

[3] Judicature Act 1925, s. 31(1)(i). The test whether an order is interlocutory or final is determined by considering whether the order sought from the Court of Appeal would have the effect of continuing the litigation. Thus appeals from a judgment under Ord. 14 or against an order striking out for want of prosecution are regarded as interlocutory. See *Salter Rex & Co.* v. *Ghosh*, [1971] 2 All E.R. 865. *Per* Lord Denning M.R. at p. 866, "This question of 'final' or 'interlocutory' is so uncertain that the only thing for practitioners to do is to look up the practice books and see what has been decided upon the point."

[4] County Courts Act 1959, s. 109.

[5] Ord. 59, r. 4. The court has power to extend the time on application under Ord. 3, r. 5. The court below may also extend the time period before it has elapsed Ord. 59, r. 15.

In the Court of Appeal   Plaint No. 76 0356

On appeal from the Clerkenwell County Court

Between:

Martha Bardell   Plaintiff

(Widow)
and
Samuel Pickwick   Defendant

Notice of Appeal

TAKE NOTICE that the Court of Appeal will be moved so soon as counsel can be heard on behalf of the above-named Defendant by way of appeal from the whole of the judgment and order of His Honour Judge Barker given on the 4th day of December 1976 (whereby it was adjudged and ordered that the Defendant should deliver up possession of the first and second floors at 32 Goswell Street, London EC2 to the Plaintiff on the 3rd day of January 1977) for an order that the said judgment and order may be set aside and that the Plaintiff may be ordered to pay to the Defendant his costs of this action and of this appeal to be taxed or in the alternative that a new trial may be ordered.

AND FURTHER TAKE NOTICE that the grounds of this appeal are:

(1) The learned judge wrongly permitted the Plaintiff to amend her pleadings at the trial so as to allege that the said premises were not protected under the provisions of the Rent Act 1968 and thereafter wrongly refused the Defendant an adjournment.

(2) The learned judge wrongly admitted in evidence the testimony of one Jackson to the effect that he had been informed by a person not called as a witness that the notice to quit had been served on the Defendant before the 1st day of October 1976.

(3) The learned judge improperly interrupted the Defendant's evidence-in-chief to indicate his disbelief of the Defendant's testimony and impatience at the amount of time the evidence was taking.

(4) The learned judge erred in law and fact in holding that the Plaintiff was resident at the said premises.

AND FURTHER TAKE NOTICE that the Defendant proposes to apply to set down this appeal in the County Courts Final and New Trial List.

Dated the 30th day of December 1976.

To the above-named Plaintiff and to   *Parker and Co.* of
Messrs. Dodson and Fogg, her Solicitors   2 Holborn Court, Gray's Inn.
and to the Registrar of the Clerkenwell   Solicitors for the Defendant.
County Court.

NOTE

No notice as to the date on which this appeal will be in the list for hearing will be given: it is the duty of solicitors to keep themselves informed as to the state of the lists. A respondent intending to appear in person should inform the Appeal Clerk, Room 136, Royal Courts of Justice, Strand, London W.C.2. of that fact and give his address; if he does so, he will be notified by telegram to the address he has given of the date when the appeal is expected to be heard.

PROCEDURE ON APPEAL TO COURT OF APPEAL

The procedure to be followed is set out below:

(1) The notice of appeal must be served on every party affected and, in county court cases, also on the county court registrar. Ordinary service (i.e. by leaving the notice at the respondent's address or sending it by post) is sufficient.

(2) Within 7 days after service, the appellant must produce at Room 136 Royal Courts of Justice the judgment of the court below and deposit a copy of that judgment, two copies of the notice of appeal and an office copy of the list of exhibits.

(3) The court then sets down the appeal for hearing in the relevant group of appeals (e.g. the Queen's Bench Division Interlocutory List, and Queen's Bench Division Final and New Trial List, the County Court Interlocutory List, the County Court Final and New Trial List).

(4) Within 2 days of setting down the appellant must give notice thereof to all the parties stating in which list the appeal has been set down.

(5) The respondent must within 21 days of service serve a 'respondent's notice' if he wishes to contend that the judgment below should be varied (either in any event or only on the appeal being allowed). If the appeal is against an interlocutory order the respondent's notice must be served within 7 days of service of the notice of appeal.

(6) If the appellant receives such a respondent's notice he must within two days of service, send two copies to the court.

(7) Not less than 7 days before the appeal is likely to be listed for hearing the appellant must lodge three copies of the following documents:
   (a) The notice of appeal.
   (b) The respondent's notice, if any.
   (c) Any supplementary notice.
   (d) The judgment or order of the court below.
   (e) The pleadings (including further and better particulars).
   (f) In High Court appeals, so much of the shorthand note of the judgment and so much of the note of the evidence as is relevant. In county court appeals, a note of the judgment (usually prepared by counsel who have a duty to take down the oral judgment and submit it to the county court judge for his approval).[1] If any passage of evidence is relevant counsel will normally submit a copy of their notes to the county court judge and request him to approve the note or furnish a copy of his own note on the point.
   (g) The list of exhibits.
   (h) Such affidavits or exhibits as are relevant to the appeal.

Where an appeal is taken there are a number of points which may arise for decision before the appeal can be heard:

(1) *Stay of execution:* the appellant may apply on notice to the judge at first instance for a stay pending the determination of the appeal; if this is refused he may make application to the Court of Appeal.[2] Where the judgment is for payment of money, the general principle is that a stay will not be granted unless the appellant is able to produce evidence to

---

[1] In theory an advocate in the county court can ask the judge to make a specific note on any point of law under s. 112 of the County Courts Act but this is seldom done in practice.
[2] See R.S.C. Ord. 59, rr. 13 and 19(5).

show that if the damages are paid there is no reasonable possibility of getting them back if the appeal succeeds.

(2) *Security for costs:* the respondent may apply to the Court of Appeal in *special circumstances* for an order requiring the appellant to provide security for the costs of the appeal. Security might be ordered if the appellant was ordinarily resident abroad and had no property in the jurisdiction *or* was an insolvent company or in the other circumstances laid down in R.S.C. Order 23, rule 1.[1] It would also probably be ordered even where the appellant was legally aided[2] if it could be shown that he had not the means to pay the costs ordered below.

(3) *Fresh evidence:* if the appellant desires to place new evidence before the Court of Appeal he must apply on notice for leave to do so before the appeal comes on for hearing. If the appeal is from a decision of the county court this application will not normally be entertained unless he has applied to the trial judge for a new trial been refused.[3] Leave will only be granted by the Court of Appeal if the following conditions are satisfied: "first, it must be shown that the evidence could not have been obtained with reasonable diligence for use at the trial; secondly, the evidence must be such that, if given, it would probably have an important influence on the result of the case, though it need not be decisive; thirdly, the evidence must be such as is presumably to be believed, or, in other words, it must be apparently credible though it need not be uncontrovertible".[4]

The appeal will come on for hearing before three Lords Justices of Appeal sitting at the Royal Courts of Justice.[5] Counsel must leave a list of authorities with the Chief Usher not later than 10 a.m. on the day of the hearing. The appeal is generally opened by counsel for the appellant explaining the case in outline, referring to the pleadings and reading the judgment and any relevant passages of evidence before dealing specifically with his argument. It should be carefully noted that the appellant will not be permitted to raise any point in the Court of Appeal which was not taken below unless the court "is in possession of all the material necessary to enable it to dispose of the matter finally, without injustice to the other party, and without recourse to a further hearing below".[6] The Court of Appeal has power to make any order that could have been made by the court below so that, if it decides to allow an appeal, it will generally endeavour to determine all the issues then arising between the parties. Where however the appeal is allowed because of a substantial miscarriage of justice in the court below or because of new evidence then the court will order a re-trial.[7]

APPEAL TO THE HOUSE OF LORDS

An appeal will lie from any decision of the Court of Appeal to the House of Lords if *leave* is granted by the Court of Appeal or by the House on a petition

---

[1] R.S.C. Ord. 59, r. 10(5).
[2] See *Bampton v. Cook*, [1954] 1 All E.R. 457; *Wyld v. Silver*, [1962] 2 All E.R. 809.
[3] C.C.R. Ord. 37, r. 1.
[4] *Per* Denning L.J. in *Ladd v. Marshall*, [1954] 1 W.L.R. 1489, at p. 1491.
[5] Two Lords Justices instead of three may determine interlocutory appeals.
[6] *Per* Widgery L.J. in *Wilson v. Liverpool City Council*, [1971] 1 All E.R. 628, at p. 633.
[7] Note: where a litigant in a county court desires a new trial on the ground, for example, of new evidence he should apply under C.C.R. Ord. 37, r. 1 to the county court judge for a new trial and only if the application is refused appeal to the Court of Appeal.

lodged within one month of the decision of the court.[1] An appeal will also lie to the House of Lords from the decision of a single judge of the High Court if with the consent of the parties he certifies that a point of law of public importance is involved relating either to a point of construction or to a point of law upon which there is binding authority in the Court of Appeal *and* the House then grants leave to appeal.[2]

REFERENCE TO THE EUROPEAN COURT OF JUSTICE[3]

Where a question arises in a case before either the High Court or the county court as to the validity or interpretation of any acts of the institutions of the E.E.C. or as to the interpretation of the Treaty of Rome and a ruling on that question is necessary to determine that case the court *may*[4] refer the question to the European Court for a preliminary ruling. The rules as to the circumstances where such a reference should be made have been formulated by the Court of Appeal in its decision in *H. P. Bulmer, Ltd.* v. *J. Bollinger S.A.*, [1974] Ch. 401;[5] [1974] 2 All E.R. 1226.

> Producers of champagne in France brought proceedings in the Chancery Division to prohibit English cider manufacturers marketing their product as "Champagne perry". They claimed this infringed a community regulation dealing with the application of geographical descriptions. The issue was whether the regulation applied to wine only or to all forms of drink. The manufacturers applied for the judge to refer this question to the European Court. The judge refused on the ground that such a reference was not necessary in order to enable him to give judgment.

The Court of Appeal upheld his decision and ruled:

(a) That before a reference was made it had to be shown that a ruling on the point of law was *necessary* to enable the English court to give judgment. It would only be necessary if (i) the facts of the case had been determined and it was clear that the point had to be decided in order to give judgment and (ii) the point of law was not already covered by clear authority or so straightforward that the English court could readily decide the matter itself.

(b) Even if such a ruling was necessary the court should still consider whether to save time and cost it should not exercise its discretion to rule on the matter itself. Only points of real difficulty and importance should be referred to the European Court.

---

[1] Administration of Justice (Appeals) Act 1934, s. 1.
[2] Administration of Justice Act 1969, ss. 12 *et seq*.
[3] Article 117 of the Treaty of Rome; R.S.C. Ord. 114; C.C.R. Ord. 19, r. 3.
[4] Except in the case of the House of Lords which being the final court of appeal *must* make a reference if the determination of the point of law is necessary.
[5] See also *Application Des Gaz S.A.* v. *Falks Veritas, Ltd.*, [1974] Ch. 381; [1974] 3 All E.R. 51.

CHAPTER SIXTEEN

ENFORCEMENT OF JUDGMENTS

When judgment has been delivered the layman is apt to assume that the case is then effectively finished; in fact, nothing could be further from the truth, for the judgment does nothing more than declare the respective rights of the parties and says nothing about how the order of the court is to be executed. After the judgment has been delivered the successful party must then consider how his judgment is to be enforced. This chapter deals with the means by which the courts will assist a successful litigant to realise the fruits of his victory.

DISPOSAL OF PROPERTY BEFORE JUDGMENT

It is of little value to a plaintiff to succeed in his claim if the defendant has lost or disposed of all his property before trial in such a manner that it is no longer amenable to the enforcement procedure. The student should therefore remember the following methods of freezing the defendant's assets:

(1) An application under Order 14 is often made with the express purpose of obtaining an order that the defendant shall only be permitted to defend if he pays the whole or part of the claim into court to abide the event. Once this has been done the plaintiff is in the position of a secured creditor (see p. 98 *ante*).

(2) Where the plaintiff can show that the defendant is withdrawing his assets from the jurisdiction or disposing of them with intent to evade judgment, the court will grant an injunction to restrain him even though the rights of the parties have not been finally determined (*Nippon Yusen Kaisha* v. *Karageorgis*, [1975] 3 All E.R. 282; [1975] 1 W.L.R. 1093).

(3) Where the plaintiff has an interest in a fund held by the defendant (e.g. partnership property) he may apply by summons or motion for the appointment of a *receiver* (i.e. an independent person appointed to manage the property pending the trial under the supervision of the court).[1]

(4) Where the plaintiff is suing to enforce any interest on land he should register a "notice of pending action" at the Land Registry so that if the owner sells the land before the case has been decided the purchaser will be bound by the claim.[2]

INSTALMENT ORDERS

A High Court money judgment normally takes effect from the day on which it is pronounced[3] but the court has the power on the application of the

---

[1] R.S.C. Ord. 30, r. 1. C.C.R. Ord. 30, r. 1.
[2] Land Charges Act 1972.
[3] R.S.C. Ord. 42, r. 3.

defendant to stay execution of the judgment on terms that he pays the judgment debt by such instalments as the court deems appropriate.[1] This application can be made immediately after judgment to the trial judge or subsequently by summons to a master. The court will examine the debtor as to his means in order to determine whether an instalment order should be made at all (it clearly would not be made if he had ample assets to enable him to pay the debt at once) and, if so, how much he should be ordered to pay in each instalment. The order of the court typically runs:

"... stay of execution so long as the defendant pays the judgment debt and costs by instalments at the rate of £— per month, the first instalment to commence on the — day of —— 197–, provided that if he should make default in the payment of the said instalments or any part thereof on the due date, the stay be forthwith removed in respect of the whole outstanding balance at the time of such default and the plaintiff be then at liberty forthwith to issue execution by writ of *fi fa* on the said judgment and costs".

The county court is given express power to make an instalment order on the application of either party[2] and stay all execution until default occurs.[3]

EFFECT OF BANKRUPTCY OF JUDGMENT DEBTOR

The successful litigant remains at risk that the debtor will become bankrupt before he has actually completed the process of enforcing the judgment. Once a petition has been presented, the creditor cannot proceed to execution but must prove on the debtor's bankruptcy and take a proportionate share with the other creditors. Section 40 Bankruptcy Act 1914 provides that where a creditor has:

(*a*) issued execution against the goods or lands of the debtor, or
(*b*) taken garnishee proceedings against a debt due to the debtor,

the creditor is not entitled to retain the benefit of the execution against the trustee in bankruptcy unless the execution was completed[4] before:

(i) the date of the receiving order, *and* before
(ii) notice of the presentation of the petition or any available act of bankruptcy.

Similarly sections 325–6 of the Companies Act 1948 provide that the creditor cannot retain the benefit of an execution unless it is complete before the commencement of the winding up of the company or the date of notice of the meeting at which a resolution for voluntary winding up was to be proposed. The position has been summarised by Pennycuick J. as follows

"The basic scheme of these provisions is that unsecured creditors rank *pari passu*, and that an execution creditor who has not completed execution at the com-

---

[1] Execution Act 1844 s. 61; R.S.C. Ord. 47, r. 1. In formal terms the court stays execution against the debtors *goods* but since every other form of order for execution requires leave of the court it can effectively protect the judgment debtor so long as he complies with the order of the court.
[2] County Courts Act 1959, s. 99.
[3] Ibid., s. 121.
[4] Execution is *completed* when *goods* taken have been sold by the sheriff or bailiff; when *land* has been charged and a receiver has been appointed to enforce the charge; and when a garnishee has paid over the debt to the creditors.

mencement of the [bankruptcy or winding-up proceedings] is for this purpose in the same position as any other unsecured creditor".[1]

The moral of course is that a judgment creditor should proceed speedily to enforce his judgment if there is the slightest risk of the insolvency of the debtor.

DISCOVERY IN AID OF EXECUTION

The judgment creditor may have little or no knowledge of the income or capital of the debtor. Since the methods of enforcement differ according to the nature of the asset in question it will be necessary for him to discover something about the debtor's financial position if he is to choose the appropriate remedy. This of course can be done informally (e.g. by the employment of an inquiry agent), but in addition the Rules provide for the debtor to be summoned for an examination as to his means before an officer of the court.[2] In the High Court, the creditor applies ex parte on affidavit to the master for an order requiring the attendance of the debtor. He then obtains a date for the hearing which is indorsed on the order together with a penal notice warning the debtor that he is liable to be committed for contempt if he fails to attend. The order must then be served *personally* (i.e. in the same manner as a writ) and the debtor must be tendered a sum sufficient to cover the cost of his attendance. The procedure in the county court follows the same broad lines except that the application commences by filing a request for an order for oral examination.[3] When the debtor appears the creditor is entitled to conduct the most exhaustive inquiry into his means and assets:

"As I understand the rule, the examination is to be 'as to whether any and what debts are owing to the judgment debtor' ... Any question, therefore, fairly pertinent to the subject matter of the inquiry, which means put with a view to ascertain as far as possible, by discovery from a reluctant defendant, what debts are owing to him, ought to be answered by the defendant. ... He must answer all questions fairly directed to ascertain from him what amount of debts are due, from whom due, and to give all necessary particulars to enable the plaintiffs to recover under a garnishee order."[4]

THE METHODS AVAILABLE FOR ENFORCING A MONEY JUDGMENT

Before we consider in detail the procedure adopted in the case of the different methods of execution open to the judgment creditor it may be convenient to set out in tabular form the complete range of remedies.

---

[1] *Re Redman (Builders), Ltd.*, [1964] 1 All E.R. 851 at p. 855.
[2] R.S.C. Ord. 46, r. 1; C.C.R. Ord. 25, r. 2. Note the examination of a debtor under a High Court judgment may be undertaken by an officer of the local county court at the request of the master.
[3] Form 149.
[4] *Per* Sir George Jessel M.R. in *Republic of Costa Rica* v. *Strousberg* (1880), 16 Ch. D. 8. And see *per* James L.J. at p. 12: "The examination is not only intended to be an examination, but to be a cross-examination, and that of the severest kind."

METHODS OF ENFORCEMENT

Asset	Method	High Court	County Court
(1) Goods, leases, cheques	Seizure and sale	Writ of *fi. fa.* R.S.C. Ord. 47	Warrant of execution, C.C.R. Ord. 25, r. 13
(2) Land, stocks and shares partner-ship, property and profits	Register charge and obtain order for receiver and sale	Administration of Justice Act 1956, s. 35	County Court Act 1959, s. 141
(3) Bank accounts and other debts due to judg-ment debtor	Garnishee order	Attachment R.S.C. Ord. 49	C.C.R. Ord. 27
(4) Sums due at future date e.g. rent, royalties on book, rever-sionary interest under trust, insurance policies and building society deposit accounts	Appointment of receiver	R.S.C. Ord. 51	C.C.R. Ord. 30
(5) Salary	Instalment order followed by attachment of earnings if debtor defaults	Transfer to county court	Attachment of Earnings Act 1971, s. 24
(6) Debtor runs a business and debt exceeds £200	Bankruptcy notice and petition	Bankruptcy Act 1914, s. 98. Insolvency Act 1976 Schedule I	Out of London certain county courts have bankruptcy jurisdiction
(7) Debtor is a limited company and debt exceeds £200	Serve statutory demand and present petition to wind-up company	Companies Act 1948, s. 224	Where share capital does not exceed £120,000— Companies Act 1948, s. 218

EXECUTION AGAINST CHATTELS

The courts provide the means by which a judgment creditor can obtain the seizure and sale of chattels owned by the debtor so to satisfy the judgment. Although in theory an effective remedy, in practice as we shall see the creditor may find this method of enforcement fails because the assets in question are the property of someone other than the debtor.

> *Example*—D, an allegedly impecunious plumber against whom judgment for £2,000 has been entered, runs a Jaguar motor car, has two colour television sets and a cabin cruiser.

The practice in respect of a High Court judgment[1] is that the creditor applies for a writ of fieri facias (*fi. fa.*) by delivering a formal request (*praecipe*) at the court together with office copies of the judgment and certificate for costs in the action, pays the appropriate fee and submits two copies of the writ of *fi. fa.* The writ is then sealed and delivered to the under-sheriff of the county (bailiwick) where the assets are to be found. The form of writ is shown on p. 204. It will be noted that the writ is a command to the sheriff to seize and sell sufficient of the debtor's goods to discharge his own costs and the judgment debt and cost.

The writ is executed by the sheriff's officers.[2] It is to be noted that the following property is exempt from execution:

(a) wearing apparel } of the debtor or his family,
(b) bedding
(c) tools and implements of his trade,

to a total value of £50.[3] A more important restriction in practice is that it may transpire that no goods worth seizing are found on the premises[4] or that goods apparently belonging to the debtor are claimed by someone else. In the example above, it may be that the car and the cabin cruiser are being bought on hire purchase whilst the colour television sets may belong to rental companies. Clearly in such cases the property cannot be seized. What is the position where a claim is made by a third party to goods found in the debtor's possession but the judgment creditor insists the goods really belong to the debtor and so should be seized? In such a case the sheriff retains possession and issues an interpleader summons so that both claimants can be brought before the court which can determine their respective rights.[5] In the case of a claim by the debtor's wife the creditor is often well advised to dispute the claim because the assertion is easily made but often is untrue or incapable of proof.

Where the value of the goods exceeds £20 the sheriff must sell them by public auction unless either party applies to the court for an order permitting

---

[1] See R.S.C. Ord. 46, r. 7. Note if the debt is for less than £350 no costs will be allowed on the claim or execution so the solicitor will normally use the county court procedure of issuing an execution warrant.

[2] The officers may enter the debtor's house provided they do not break any outer doors. They do not have to remove the goods at once: instead they may enter into "walking possession" of the goods in which case the debtor will sign an agreement that in consideration of the bailiff not removing the goods he will not dispose of the goods or permit them to be removed from the premises. See *Abingdon Rural District Council* v. *O'Gorman*, [1968] 3 All E.R. 79, at p. 81.

[3] Small Debts Act 1845, s. 8. Administration of Justice Act 1956, s. 37. County Courts Act 1959, s. 124.

[4] This is particularly the case where county court bailiffs are seeking to execute a warrant of execution, there is a substantial risk in such a case that the creditor will be faced with a "nil return".

[5] R.S.C. Ord. 17, see p. 123 *ante*.

Writ of Fieri Facias

In the High Court of Justice

QUEEN'S BENCH　　　　　DIVISION

19 74.– M .–No. 2075

F.1
—
Writ of
Fieri Facias
(0.45, r.12)

Oyez Publishing
Limited
Oyez House
237 Long Lane
London SE1 4PU
a subsidiary of
The Solicitors' Law
Stationery Society
Limited

F23343 29-9-76
✸✸✸✸

Between

Murdstone and Grinby (Blackfriars) Ltd　　　　Plaintiff

and

Wilkins Micawber　　　　Defendant

ELIZABETH THE SECOND, by the Grace of God, of the United Kingdom of Great Britain and Northern Ireland and of Our other realms and territories Queen, Head of the Commonwealth, Defender of the Faith.

To the Sheriff of **the County of Kent**　　　　greeting:

Whereas in the above-named action it was on the　　**10th**　　day of **November**, 19 75 , (¹) adjudged that that the Defendant (²) **Wilkins Micawber**

(1) "adjudged" or "ordered".

do pay the Plaintiffs (³)　**Murdstone and Grinby (Blackfriars) Limited**

(2) Name of Defendant.

of £ 2000　　　　and　　　　[costs] [costs to be taxed, which

costs have been taxed and allowed at £ 500　　　　as appears by the

(3) Name of Plaintiff.

certificate of the taxing officer dated the 15th　　　　day of

April　19 76]:

WE COMMAND YOU that of the goods, chattels and other property of (²)　**the said Wilkins Micawber**

in your County authorised by law to be seized in execution you cause to be made the sum[s] of £ 2500　　　†[and £ 8.40　　　　for costs of

†The words in this set of square brackets are to be omitted where the judgment or order is for less than £150 and does not entitle the Plaintiff to costs against the person against whom the writ is issued.

execution] and also interest on £ 2500　　　at the rate of £10.00 per centum per annum from the　　**10th**　　day of　**November**, 19 75, until payment †[together with Sheriff's poundage, officers' fees, costs of levying and all other legal, incidental expenses] and that immediately after execution of this writ you pay (⁴)

[**the said Murdstone and Grinby (Blackfriars) Limited**

(4) Name of Plaintiff, or, if Exchange Control Act 1947, applies and a certificate has not been given under Order 46, Rule 7(2), delete words in this set of square brackets and substitute "into our High Court of Justice in pursuance of Rules of Court made under the Exchange Control Act 1947, and in manner provided by the Supreme Court Funds Rules".

in pursuance of the said (⁵)　　　judgment　　　] the amount levied in respect of the said sums and interest.

AND WE ALSO COMMAND YOU that you indorse on this writ immediately after execution thereof a statement of the manner in which you have executed it and send a copy of the statement to (³)　　**the said Murdstone and Grinby (Blackfriars) Limited.**

WITNESS　　Frederick Baron Elwyn-Jones

Lord High Chancellor

(5) "judgment" or "order".

of Great Britain, the　　20th　　day of　September, 19 76.

[Note: on the reverse is set out the name and address of the person issuing the writ and the debtor's place of residence.]

sale under private contract.[1] During this period the judgment debtor may apply by summons pursuant to Order 47, rule 1 to the court for an order staying the execution.

The rules above stated apply equally to the enforcement by the county court of a warrant of execution.[2] It should be noted that the county court has power to issue such a warrant to enforce a judgment given in the High Court.[3] In practice, whilst the sheriff's officers enforce a High Court writ with considerable vigour, the county court bailiffs are far less efficient and for this reason many solicitors experienced in debt-collection prefer to use the High Court machinery.

CHARGING ORDER ON LAND OR SECURITIES

The High Court is given power under section 35 of the Administration of Justice Act 1956 to impose a charge on any freehold or leasehold land owned by a judgment debtor so as to provide security for payment of the judgment debt. This can be a very effective remedy but before it can be employed the creditor has to obtain prima facie proof of the ownership of the land in question. (One method by which this can be done is to require the attendance of the debtor for oral examination and to question him as to the identity of any land held by him and the nature of his interest.[4]) The creditor applies[5] ex parte by affidavit setting out the amount of the judgment unpaid, the land proposed to be charged and verifying that the land belongs to the debtor alone.[6] The master will make an *order nisi*, i.e. an order that the land is to stand charged until the hearing on notice of the application. The effect of the order is that the creditor may register the charge[7] (or in the case of registered land, lodge a caution[8]) so that any person dealing with the land thereafter can only take subject to the creditor's rights to enforce his security. In very urgent cases where it is thought that the debtor might attempt to dispose of the land before registration, the master may grant an injunction restraining dealings with the land. Once the order is made a copy stating the date and time of further consideration of the matter must be served on the debtor. Generally this order must be served at least 7 days before the appointment. At the subsequent hearing the master shall "unless it appears (whether on the representation of the judgment debtor or otherwise) that there is sufficient cause to the contrary, make the order absolute".[9]

The effect of such an order when registered is that it inhibits any dealings with the property by the debtor. This in itself may be sufficient incentive to the debtor to pay off the debt. It must however be noted that:

(a) If the debtor becomes bankrupt the creditor is in exactly the same

---

[1] See R.S.C. Ord. 47, r. 6.
[2] The judgment creditors produce the plaint note and an application for a warrant in Form 156. No sale is allowed until 5 days have elapsed from the date of seizure. County Courts Act 1959, s. 128.
[3] County Courts Act 1959, s. 139. C.C.R. Ord. 25, r. 13A.
[4] Note a judgment creditor on production of evidence of his judgment and of ownership by the debtor of the land in question may apply by summons to the court for an order that the register of title be produced to the creditor without the authority of the debtor, Land Registration Rules 1967, r. 3 and 4.
[5] R.S.C. Ord. 50, r. 1.
[6] If the debtor is a joint tenant e.g. he owns the house jointly with his wife an order cannot be made (unless they are joint debtors). See *Irani Finance, Ltd.* v. *Singh*, [1971] Ch. 59, [1970] 3 All E.R. 199.
[7] Land Charges Act 1972, s. 6.
[8] Land Registration Act 1925, s. 59(3).
[9] R.S.C. Ord. 50, r. 1(6).

position as any other creditor since he has not *completed* the execution and so has no secured interest in the land against other creditors. In effect the charging order is then worthless. To avoid this embarrassment the judgment creditor frequently asks in his application for a charging order for the *appointment of a receiver* by way of equitable execution. This has the vitally important effect of placing the creditor in the same position as a secured creditor (such as a mortgagee) on the bankruptcy of the debtor—see *Barclays Bank* v. *Moore*, [1967] 3 All E.R. 34; [1967] 1 W.L.R. 1201.

(b) If the creditor wishes to enforce the charge he must apply for an order for sale under R.S.C. Order 88 as if he was a mortgagee of the land. These proceedings however cannot be brought for a period of 6 months from the date of the order nisi. Presumably the court hearing an application under R.S.C. Order 88 for sale of a house will consider the wide powers granted to it under section 36(2) of the Administration of Justice Act 1970 to adjourn the proceeedings or stay or suspend its order if it appears that the debtor is likely within a reasonable time to pay any of the sum secured by the charge.

It may be convenient to set out these complex provisions in summary form:

(1) Creditor (C) files an affidavit ex parte asking for (a) charging order and possibly (b) injunction and (c) appointment of a receiver.
(2) Order nisi. Register at once. Serve order.
(3) Appointment for further consideration. Order absolute.
(4) 6 months later C can apply for an order for sale.

The procedure in the county court is effectively the same save that there is no order nisi stage: see section 141–142 of the County Courts Act and C.C.R. Order 25, rule 7. The procedure in respect of securities (i.e. stocks and shares) which is substantially the same is set out in R.S.C. Order 50, rules 2–6 and C.C.R. Order 25, rule 6A.

As to the procedure in respect of charging a partner's interest in partnership property and profits—see R.S.C. Order 81; C.C.R. Order 25, rule 4.

Example—Murdstone and Grinby Ltd. obtain judgment for £2,000 against Micawber. They issue a writ of *fi. fa.* but the sheriff is unable to seize any goods worth selling. They now learn that Micawber owns a house in Canterbury. It appears that he is about to sell the house in order to stave off his creditors who are threatening to serve a bankruptcy notice. We set out opposite the form of affidavit which could be used on an *ex parte* application to impose a charge on the land and for the appointment of a receiver and for an injunction to restrain the sale.

In the High Court of Justice   1974—M—No. 2075

Queen's Bench Division

Between

Murdstone and Grinby
(Blackfriars) Limited   Plaintiffs

and

Wilkins Micawber   Defendant

I, Samuel Jackson of 236 City Road, London E.C.1, a clerk in the employ of Dodson and Fogg, Freeman's Court, Cornhill, London E.C.3, Solicitors for the Plaintiffs herein, make oath and say as follows:

(1) Subject to the supervision of my principals, I have the conduct of this action on behalf of the Plaintiffs.

(2) On the 10th day of November 1975 it was adjudged by this Honourable Court that the Defendant do pay the Plaintiffs the sum of £2,000 and costs to be taxed, which costs have been taxed and allowed at £500 as appears by the certificate of the taxing officer dated the 15th day of April 1976. The said judgment remains wholly unsatisfied.

(3) On the 20th day of September 1976 the Plaintiffs sued out a writ of fieri facias directed to the Sheriff of the County of Kent for having execution of the said judgment. From a copy of the indorsement made by the Sheriff on the said writ, showing the manner in which he executed it, dated the 12th day of October 1976 and now produced and shown to me marked "S.J.1" it appears that the Defendant has no property available for execution under the said writ.

(4) Upon his oral examination in these proceedings the defendant admitted that he was the owner of the freehold interest in the house and premises situated at 26 St. Alphege's Lane, Canterbury in the County of Kent. I have caused a search to be made in H.M. Land Registry against the title number of the said premises and such search revealed a charge against the said property in the name of Friendly Homes Building Society to secure the sum of £5,000. A copy of the said entry is now produced and shown to me marked "S.J.2".

(5) I am informed by Mr. Edward Murdstone a director of the Plaintiff Company and verily believe to be true that the Defendant has already instructed estate agents to offer the said premises for sale and that unless he is restrained from so doing by order of this Honourable Court intends to sell or otherwise dispose of the said premises so that the Plaintiffs lose the benefit of their judgment herein.

(6) I have further been informed by the Defendant himself that he is unable to pay this judgment debt and is liable to be adjudicated bankrupt. In order to enable the Plaintiffs to obtain the benefit of the Charging Order sought herein as against the trustee in bankruptcy if the defendant should be adjudicated bankrupt, it is essential that a Receiver be appointed to enforce the said charging order.

(7) I have for ten years or thereabouts known and been well acquainted with Mr. U. Heep of 30 St. Peter's Street, Canterbury aforesaid who is a Chartered Auctioneer and Estate Agent. The said Mr. Heep is a respectable and responsible person and of good credit and integrity and in my judgment he is a fit and proper person to be appointed Receiver as aforesaid.

(8) In the circumstances, I respectfully request that an order be made imposing a charge on the said house and premises of the judgment debtor and that the said Mr. U. Heep be appointed the Receiver to enforce the said charge and that an injunction do issue meanwhile restraining the Defendant by himself, his servants or agents, howsoever, from selling or otherwise disposing of the said house and premises.

Sworn, etc.

GARNISHEE ORDERS

Suppose the judgment creditor knows that the judgment debtor is owed money by a third party; in such a case it is obviously an effective method of execution to obtain an order from the court diverting the payment from the judgment debtor to the judgment creditor. This process is known as *attachment* and the order is known as a *garnishee order*. It is most commonly used in order to obtain money standing to the credit of a debtor in his bank account.[1] It can also be a very effective means of execution where the creditor knows that a solicitor is holding monies in a client account for the debtor, e.g. upon the sale of a house.

The procedure followed in the High Court can be summarised as follows:

(1) The creditor applies ex parte by affidavit for an order addressed to the third party (called a garnishee) forbidding him from paying the debt over to the judgment debtor and requiring them to attend before the master to show cause why the monies should not be paid to the judgment creditor. This order is called a *garnishee order nisi*. The application is made ex parte to prevent the debtor having the time to obtain payment to himself and thus frustrate the procedure.

(2) The order is drawn up (see form at end of this section) and served on the garnishee and on the judgment debtor at least 7 days before the time appointed for the further consideration of the matter.

(3) At the hearing if the court is satisfied that the garnishee is indebted to the judgment debtor and no other persons have prior claims to the monies, it will order the garnishee to pay over the debt to the judgment creditor. This is called a *garnishee order absolute*.[2]

A similar procedure is available in the county court for the enforcement of both county court and High Court judgments.[3]

We conclude this section by setting out (a) the form of order which is drawn up by the creditor's solicitors once the order *nisi* has been made and (b) the form of order when the order is made absolute:

---

[1] It will be remembered that a bank is in the position of debtor to its customers who are in credit. By Administration of Justice Act 1956, s. 38 and County Courts Act 1959, s. 143 a sum on deposit is attachable by a garnishee order notwithstanding that there must be notice before withdrawal, personal application, etc. Note the section does not apply to National Savings or the Trustee Savings Banks but a creditor can apply to the Registrar of Friendly Societies for a direction that monies held be transferred to the creditor. See *Ministry of Pensions and National Insurance* v. *Jones*, [1965] 1 Q.B. 484; [1965] 2 All E.R. 428.

[2] The practice described above is set out in R.S.C. Ord. 49.

[3] The procedure is set out in C.C.R. Ord. 27. It should be noted that in the county court the garnishee is required to pay the sum claimed into court within 8 days of the order nisi.

(a) Order Nisi

In the High Court of Justice

Queen's Bench Division

Master Cooper in Chambers
    Between:

Murdstone and Grinby (Blackfriars) Limited	Judgment Creditors
and	
Wilkins Micawber	Judgment Debtor
and	
Midland Bank Limited	Garnishee

Upon reading the affidavit of Benjamin Wickes filed on the 16th day of February 1977.

IT IS ORDERED by Master Cooper that all debts due or accruing due from the above named garnishee to the above-named judgment debtor (in the sum of £1,206) be attached to answer a judgment recovered against the said judgment debtor by the above-named judgment creditor in the High Court of Justice on the 10th day of November 1975, for the sum of £2,000 debt and £500 costs (together with the costs of the garnishee proceedings) on which judgment the sum of £2,500 remains due and unpaid.

AND IT IS FURTHER ORDERED that the said garnishee attend Master Cooper in Chambers in Room No. 206, Central Office, Royal Courts of Justice, Strand, London on Monday the 8th day of March 1977 at half past 10 o'clock in the forenoon, on an application by the said judgment creditor that the said garnishee do pay to the said sum to the said judgment debtor, or so much thereof as may be sufficient to satisfy the said judgment, together with the costs of the garnishee proceedings.

DATED the 17th day of February 1977.

To the above-named Garnishee

And to the Judgment Debtor.

(b) Order absolute

(Title as above)

Upon hearing the solicitors for the judgment creditor and garnishee and upon hearing the judgment debtor in person, and upon reading the affidavit of Benjamin Wicks filed herein and the order to show cause herein dated the 17th day of February 1977, whereby it was ordered that all debts owing or accruing due from the above-named garnishee to the above-named judgment debtor should be attached to answer a judgment recovered against the said judgment debtor by the above-named judgment creditor in the High Court of Justice on the 10th day of November 1975 for the sum of £2,000 debt and £500 costs (together with the costs of the garnishee proceedings) on which judgment the sum of £2,500 remained due and unpaid.

IT IS ORDERED that the said garnishee (after deducting therefrom £25 for his costs of this application) do forthwith pay[1] to the said judgment creditor £1,206 the debt due from the said garnishee to the said judgment debtor. And that the sum of £40 the costs of the judgment creditor of this application be added to the judgment debt and be retained out of the money recovered by the said judgment creditor under this order and in priority to the amount of the judgment debt.

Dated the 8th day of March 1977.

---

[1] If the garnishee's debt exceeds the judgment debt the order runs "£   being so much of the debt due .... as is sufficient to satisfy the judgment debt......."

EQUITABLE EXECUTION

A receiver may be appointed by way of equitable execution where:

(a) The creditor wishes whilst charging the land of the debtor to obtain preference over all other creditors if the debtor becomes bankrupt. In such a case the receiver's functions are limited until the court orders a sale.[1]

(b) The debtor will be in receipt of income which cannot conveniently be attached by the usual methods of execution (e.g. where he receives rent from tenants), so that it is necessary that an independent person collects the income.

(c) The debtor holds property jointly (e.g. partners[2] or husband and wife holding house in joint names), so that execution cannot be effected by a charging order on the property itself.

Since this is an expensive mode of execution the remedy is discretionary and the court is expressly required "in determining whether it is just and convenient that the appointment should be made" to "have regard to the amount claimed by the judgment creditor, to the amount likely to be obtained by the receiver, and to the probable costs of his appointment and may direct an inquiry on any of these matters or any other matter before making the appointment".[3]

The practice is for the creditor to apply by summons or motion for the appointment of a suitable person as receiver. In urgent cases this may be done ex parte.[4] In all cases an affidavit is required setting out the judgment debtor's interest in the property and the fitness of the proposed receiver. It should also show that the creditor has taken all other convenient steps to execute the judgment without success.[5] If the receiver is appointed the court will normally require him to give security for the proper execution of his duties. We set out opposite the form of order drawn up in the High Court[6] where the receiver is to receive income from land held by the debtor. Study this form carefully because it explains precisely how the receiver is to operate.

---

[1] We have already discussed such an appointment—see p. 206 *ante*.
[2] See R.S.C. Ord. 81, r. 10 and the Partnership Act 1890, s. 23.
[3] R.S.C. Ord. 51, r. 1(1) C.C.R. Ord. 30, r. 11.
[4] See R.S.C. Ord. 51, r. 3, Ord. 30, r. 1(3); C.C.R. Ord. 30, r. 1.
[5] See affidavit p. 211 *post*.
[6] The procedure in the county court is governed by C.C.R. Ord. 30.

In the High Court of Justice

Queen's Bench Division

Master Cooper in Chambers
Between:

Murdstone and Grinby
(Blackfriars) Limited   Plaintiffs

and

Wilkins Micawber   Defendant

Upon hearing the solicitors for the Plaintiffs and the Defendant in person

And upon reading the affidavit of Samuel Jackson sworn the 20th day of April 1977:

IT IS ORDERED that Septimus Wickfield of 30 High Street, Rochester, in the County of Kent, on first giving security to the satisfaction of a Master of the Supreme Court, be and is hereby appointed to receive the rent, profits and monies receivable in respect of the above-named Defendant's interest in the following premises, namely all that office block known as 25/30 Station Road, Rochester aforesaid.

AND IT IS ORDERED that this appointment shall be without prejudice to the rights of any prior incumbrancers upon the said property who may think proper to take possession of or receive the same by virtue of their respective securities or, if any prior incumbrancer is in possession, then without prejudice to such possession.

AND that the tenants of premises comprised in the said property do attorn and pay their rents in arrear and growing rents to the receiver.

AND that the receiver have liberty, if he shall think proper (but not otherwise), out of the rents, profits and monies to be received by him to keep down the interest upon the prior incumbrances, according to their priorities, and be allowed such payments, if any, in passing his accounts.

AND that the receiver shall on the 9th day of September 1977 and at such further and other times as may be ordered by the Master leave and pass his accounts and shall on the 9th day of October 1977 and at such further and other times as may be hereafter ordered by the Master pay the balance or balances appearing due on the accounts so left, or such part thereof as shall be certified as proper to be paid, such sums to be paid in or towards satisfaction of what shall for the time being be due in respect of the judgment given on the 10th day of November 1975 for the sum of £2,000 and £500 costs, making together the sum of £2,500.

AND that the costs of the receiver (including his remuneration) the costs of obtaining his appointment, of completing his security, of passing his accounts and of obtaining his discharge shall not exceed 10 per cent of the amount due under the said judgment or the amount recovered by the receiver, whichever is the less, provided that not less than £5 be allowed unless otherwise ordered. Such costs shall be taxed unless assessed by the Master and shall be primarily payable out of the sums received by the receiver, but if there shall be no sums received or the amount shall be insufficient, then upon the certificate of the Master being given stating the amount of the deficiency, the amount of the deficiency so certified shall be paid by the Defendant to the Plaintiff.

IT IS ALSO ORDERED that the balance (if any) remaining in the hands of the receiver, after making the several payments aforesaid, shall unless otherwise directed by the Master forthwith be paid by the receiver into court to the credit of this action, subject to further order.

AND that any of the parties be at liberty to apply to the Master in Chambers as there may be occasion.

Dated the 9th day of June 1977.

ATTACHMENT OF EARNINGS ORDERS

Where a debtor has a regular job but no substantial assets the court will normally order him to pay the judgment debt by weekly or monthly instalments appropriate to his means and liabilities. What happens if he defaults? Formerly the practice was to apply for an order committing him to prison (usually suspended on terms that he paid the remainder of the debt and the arrears by instalments). This procedure has now for all practical purposes been abolished and instead the judgment creditor will apply to the county court for the district in which the debtor resides for an *attachment of earnings order*.[1] Only the debtor's local county court has power to make such an order but that court has power to enforce judgments given in the High Court[2] or any other county court. It is important to note that before an order will be made two conditions must be satisfied:

(1) The debtor must have defaulted in one or more instalments under a judgment ordered to be paid by such instalments.
(2) The debtor must be in employment. This covers the man who regularly subcontracts his labour to one employer (e.g. lump workers on building sites) but does not cover the man who regularly hires his services to different persons.

The creditor files at court an application for an order together with a copy of the application for service on the debtor. If the order to be enforced was made in the High Court the creditor must also file an affidavit verifying the amount due and setting out any details known to him of the debtor's employment. To this end, solicitors sometimes employ an enquiry agent who will attempt to interview the debtor and ascertain his employment position. The application and a copy of any affidavit are sent to the debtor together with (*a*) notice of the date of the hearing of the application, and (*b*) a questionnaire designed to elicit details of his means which he is required to answer on pain of imprisonment and fine. The form is set out below.

N.B. Answer *all* the following questions. Do not leave blanks. The answers you give may be checked with your employer.

Section 1 (Employment)

(*a*) What is your full name?   ....

(*b*) By whom are you employed?
(If you have more than one employer give answers in respect of each of them. If you are not employed, say so and give the name of your last employer, if any.)   ....

(*c*) Where are you employed?   ....

(*d*) In what capacity are you employed?   ....

(*e*) What is the address of your employer's Head Office if different from (*c*) above?   ....

---

[1] Attachment of Earnings Act 1971; C.C.R. Ord. 25, r. 77 *et seq.*
[2] The High Court has no power to make such an order in civil actions as opposed to matrimonial disputes.

(*f*) What is your
     Works Number?   ....
Pay reference?   ....

Section 2 (Pay and Income)

(*a*) What is your basic pay before deduc-
     tions?   £..........per week/month

(*b*) What overtime, bonuses, fees, allow-
     ances or commission do you receive?   ....

(*c*) What deductions are normally made
     from your pay?   £..........per week/month

(*d*) What is your usual take-home pay?   £..........per week/month

(*e*) Do you receive a pension or any other
     income? Please give details.   ....

Section 3 (Liabilities)

(*a*) What persons, if any, are financially
     dependent on you? Please give details
     (including the ages of any dependent
     children) and mention any con-
     tribution they make to your household
     expenses.   ....

(*b*) What rent or mortgage instalments do
     you have to pay?   £..........per week/month

(*c*) What rates, if any, do you have to pay?   £..........per week/month

(*d*) Do you have to pay under any other
     Court orders? Please give details.   ....

(*e*) What other regular payments have you
     to make?   ....

(*f*) Have you any other liabilities which
     you would like the Court to take into
     account? Please give details.   ....

Section 4 (Proposal for payment)

What sum would you be prepared to have
deducted from your earnings to satisfy the
Plaintiff's judgment?   £..........per week/month

Signed   *Defendant*

Address

On receipt of a copy of the completed questionnaire the creditor may apply
to the registrar for an order that the debtor's employer give to the court a
signed statement of the debtor's earnings. At the hearing of the application
the registrar may proceed at once to make an order or, if the debtor has not
appeared, adjourn and issue an order requiring his attendance at the adjourned
hearing.[1] At the hearing the registrar has to determine:

---

[1] Disobedience is contempt and can be punished with imprisonment, Attachment of Earnings
Act 1971, s. 23(1); County Courts Act 1959, s. 144.

(i) *A normal deduction rate*—i.e. the rate at which the court thinks the debtor's earnings should be used to satisfy the judgment.

(ii) *A protected earnings rate*—a man's income may well fluctuate from week to week according to the availability of overtime, short working, etc. In making the order the court sets a minimum sum necessary to provide for the debtor and his dependants and directs that the order is not to be applied so as to reduce his earnings below that level.

The order when made is addressed to the debtor's employer and requires him on penalty of fine to take all reasonable steps to ensure that the appropriate deduction is made from the debtor's wages and paid to the court. It should be noted that both the debtor and his employer are required to notify the court if his employment ceases.

BANKRUPTCY PROCEEDINGS

Bankruptcy is the process by which the court through a receiver takes over the debtor's business and supervises the distribution of his assets amongst his creditors. The primary purpose of the procedure is to ensure that every creditor shall receive a fair share of whatever is available for distribution. It might be thought that such proceedings would be very much a matter of last resort. In fact, since the consequences of bankruptcy proceedings is to stop a debtor carrying on his business, until recently the procedure was often initiated as a very effective means of forcing a recalcitrant debtor to settle with his creditor. Indeed the procedure was so effective that when the judgment debtor was a tradesman or in business it was often quite pointless to employ the methods of execution discussed above because the threat of bankruptcy and the consequential closure of his business would inevitably induce him to pay up if he had funds available. Since December 1976 the Bankruptcy Rules require the petitioner to deposit £90 on account of costs in addition to paying the fees on the petition. This has had the effect of discouraging the use of this method of enforcement. Although we need not attempt to consider the general law of bankruptcy, it is necessary to have a general knowledge of the use of bankruptcy as a method of execution.

A bankruptcy petition can only be filed if the debtor has committed an *act of bankruptcy*; one such act is failure to comply with a statutory notice requiring payment of a judgment debt exceeding £200. Section 1(1)(g) of the Bankruptcy Act 1914 provides that:

> "If a creditor has obtained a final judgment or order against a [debtor] for any amount, and, execution thereon not having been stayed, has served on him a bankruptcy notice under this Act and he does not, within ten days after service of the notice ... either comply with the requirements of the Notice or satisfy the court that he has a counterclaim, set off or cross demand which equals or exceeds the amount of the judgment debt or sum ordered to be paid, and which he could *not* set up in the proceedings in which the judgment was obtained [he shall be deemed to have committed an act of bankruptcy]."

The bankruptcy notice is issued by the court[1] on formal application by the creditor. The notice is set out opposite:

---

[1] The appropriate court is the High Court if the debtor has resided or carried on business in the London area in the last 6 months or is not resident in England or his residence is not known; otherwise the creditor must issue his notice in the county court having bankruptcy jurisdiction over the area where the debtor carries on business or resides.

In the High Court of Justice   No. 2067 of 1977

In Bankruptcy

Re the estate of Wilkins Micawber

Ex parte Murdstone and Grinby (Blackfriars) Limited

To Wilkins Micawber of 103 Goswell Street, London E.C.2.

TAKE NOTICE that within ten days after service of this Notice on you, excluding the day of such service, you must pay to Murdstone and Grinby (Blackfriars); Limited whose business address is 3 Puddle Dock, London EC4 or to Dodson and Fogg, of Freeman's Court, Cornhill, London EC3 their agents duly authorised the sum of £2,500 claimed by Murdstone and Grinby (Blackfriars) Limited as being the amount due on a Final Judgment or Order obtained by them against you in the High Court of Justice dated the 10th day of November, 1975, whereon execution has not been stayed, or you must secure or compound for the said sum to their satisfaction or to the satisfaction of their said agent or to the satisfaction of this Court; or you must satisfy this Court that you have a Counterclaim, Set-off or Cross-demand against them which equals or exceeds the sum claimed by them and which you could not set up in the Action or other proceedings in which the Judgment or Order was obtained.
Dated this 12th day of May 1977

BY THE COURT
R. L. Ellis
Registrar

YOU ARE SPECIALLY TO NOTE:
That the consequences of not complying with the requisitions of this Notice are that you will have committed an Act of Bankruptcy, on which Bankruptcy proceedings may be taken against you.

If, however, you have a Counterclaim, Set-off or Cross-demand which equals or exceeds the amount claimed by Murdstone and Grinby (Blackfriars) Limited in respect of the Judgment or Order, and which you could not set up in the Action or other proceedings in which the said Judgment or Order was obtained, you must within *three* days apply to this Court to set aside this Notice, by filing with the Registrar an Affidavit to the above effect.

Dodson and Fogg,
Freeman's Court,
Cornhill, London EC3.
Solicitors for the Creditor.

As indicated above the normal effect of such a notice if the debtor has funds available is that he will pay the creditor. If payment is not forthcoming the creditor will then have to consider issuing a bankruptcy petition. A petition may be issued wherever the debt due to the petitioner is £200 or more. The petition leads initially to an order appointing the Official Receiver to take the debtor's property into his custody and control. The Receiver conducts a preliminary interview of the debtor and then orders him to submit a detailed statement of his affairs which will be forwarded to each of his creditors. A First Meeting of Creditors will be held to determine whether to accept a scheme of arrangement or composition or to obtain the adjudication of the debtor as bankrupt. The creditors may delay this decision until a Public Examination has been held as to his means and assets. If his creditors will not agree upon a scheme of arrangement or composition and the debts remain outstanding, the debtor will be adjudicated bankrupt and his property will vest in the Official Receiver (or a trustee in bankruptcy appointed by him) for distribution amongst the creditors.

WINDING-UP PROCEEDINGS

A limited company cannot be made bankrupt; however any creditor has the right to petition the court for the company to be wound-up if a formal demand for payment of a debt exceeding £200 has not been satisfied within 3 weeks of service[1] and this is "a proper as well as effective mode of enforcing payment of a debt due from a company".[2] The petition is presented by delivering two copies for sealing by the Registrar of the Companies Court. The petition is stamped with a notice stating the time, date and place for the hearing of the petition. A typical petition is set out opposite:

Once the petition has been presented, the petitioner must then take the following steps:

(1) Serve the petition at the company's registered office and swear and file at court an affidavit of service.
(2) Within 4 days after the presentation of the petition swear and file an affidavit in standard form verifying the contents of the petition.
(3) Cause notice of the petition and the date of hearing and the rights of creditors and contributories to oppose or support the petition to be advertised in the London Gazette and one daily morning London newspaper[3] (outside London, one local newspaper). The advertisement must appear seven clear days before the hearing.

Before the petition is heard the petitioner must attend at an appointed day before the registrar and satisfy him that the above requirements have been satisfied.

---

[1] Companies Act 1948, s. 222. A company may also be wound up if execution issued on a judgment in favour of a creditor is returned unsatisfied in whole or in part.
[2] Palmer: *Company Law* paras 81–2. The procedure followed in the Companies Court is lucidly set out in the subsequent sections of Palmer.
[3] In practice the advertisements are usually inserted in the "Morning Star" because its rates are one-third of other national papers.

In the High Court of Justice   No. 005761 of 1977

Chancery Division

Companies Court

In the Matter of:
> West Middlesex Salvage Company Limited
> and
In the Matter of The Companies Act 1948

To Her Majesty's High Court of Justice
    The *Humble Petition* of Oliver Twist of 25 Acacia Gardens, Ealing, London W5, Clerk (hereinafter called "the Petitioner") *showeth* as follows:

(1) West Middlesex Salvage Company Limited (hereinafter called "the Company") was incorporated on the 20th day of September 1968 under the Companies Act 1948.
(2) The Registered Office of the Company is situate at 20, Uxbridge Road, Southall.
(3) The nominal capital of the Company is £100 divided into 100 Ordinary Shares of £1.00 each; the amount of capital paid up or credited as paid up is £98.00p.
(4) The objects for which the Company was established are as follows:
To carry on the business of salvage and waste paper merchants and other objects set forth in the Memorandum of Association thereof.
(5) By a judgment of the Queen's Bench Division of the High Court of Justice dated the 12th day of December 1976 it was adjudged that the Company pay to the Petitioner the sum of £11,000 together with costs to be taxed which said costs have been taxed at £600 as appears by the certificate of the taxing officer dated the 10th day of March 1977. Despite repeated applications by the Petitioner the Company has failed to pay the said sum of £11,600 or any part thereof.
(6) The Company is unable to pay its debts.
(7) In the circumstances it is just and equitable that the Company should be wound up.
    Your Petitioner therefor humbly prays as follows:
    (1) That West Middlesex Salvage Company Limited may be wound up by the Court under the provisions of the Companies Act 1948.
    (2) Or that such other Order may be made on the premises as shall be just.
Note: It is intended to serve this Petition on West Middlesex Salvage Company Limited.

Any creditor or contributory of the company is entitled to require a copy of the petition from the petitioner. If he desires to appear in support of the proposed order or to oppose it he *must* give notice of his intention to the petitioner and may file an affidavit setting out his reasons. Notice of intention to appear must be served (or posted to reach the petitioner by ordinary post) not later than 4 p.m. on the day prior to the hearing. The petitioner immediately before the hearing must provide the court with a list showing in prescribed form in columns the following information in respect of each person who has given notice:

(1) his name,
(2) his address,

(3) the name and address of his solicitor,
(4) the amount of debt if he is a creditor,
(5) the number of his shares if he is a contributory,
(6) whether he is opposing or supporting the petition.

If no one has given notice of intention to appear then a form is put in to that effect and the court is told the list is "negative".

The effect of a winding-up petition will be to stimulate the debtor into action and frequently the petitioning creditor will agree to an adjournment to see whether funds will be forthcoming. If the debt cannot be paid however then normally the petitioner is entitled to have the company wound-up *ex debito justitiae*. The "usual" order for costs is that the petitioner, the company, the creditors, and the contributories supporting the petition are given costs to be paid in the first instance out of the company's assets.

OTHER METHODS OF ENFORCEMENT

We have discussed above the methods of enforcement applicable to money judgments. It should be remembered that:

(a) An order in the form of an injunction is enforced by committal (which is discussed at p. 112 *ante*). Such an order can also be enforced against rich and powerful bodies by writ of sequestration whereby commissioners are appointed to seize the defendants' assets until they have purged their contempt. Thus, for example, in 1973 the property of the A.E.U. was made subject to such a writ by the National Industrial Relations Court for refusal to obey an order of the court.[1]

(b) Judgment for possession of land or the specific delivery of goods is enforced by the sheriff or county court bailiffs under writs or warrants of possession or specific delivery.[2]

---

[1] *Eckman* v. *Midland Bank*, [1973] Q.B. 519; [1973] 1 All E.R. 609.
[2] See R.S.C. Ord. 45, r. 3 and 4. C.C.R. Ord. 25, r. 71–76.

APPENDIX

STATUTES AND RULES
(incorporating amendments up
to 1 May 1977)

THE CIVIL EVIDENCE ACT 1968

1. Hearsay evidence to be admissible only by virtue of this Act and other statutory provisions, or by agreement.

(1) In any civil proceedings a statement other than one made by a person while giving oral evidence in those proceedings shall be admissible as evidence of any fact stated therein to the extent that it is so admissible by virtue of any provision of this Part of this Act or by virtue of any other statutory provision or by agreement of the parties, but not otherwise.

(2) In this section "statutory provision" means any provision contained in, or in an instrument made under, this or any other Act, including any Act passed after this Act.

2. Admissibility of out-of-court statements as evidence of facts stated.

(1) In any civil proceedings a statement made, whether orally or in a document or otherwise, by any person, whether called as a witness in those proceedings or not, shall, subject to this section and to rules of court, be admissible as evidence of any fact stated therein of which direct oral evidence by him would be admissible.

(2) Where in any civil proceedings a party desiring to give a statement in evidence by virtue of this section has called or intends to call as a witness in the proceedings the person by whom the statement was made, the statement—

(a) shall not be given in evidence by virtue of this section on behalf of that party without the leave of the court; and

(b) without prejudice to paragraph (a) above, shall not be given in evidence by virtue of this section on behalf of that party before the conclusion of the examination-in-chief of the person by whom it was made, except—

    (i) where before that person is called the court allows evidence of the making of the statement to be given on behalf of that party by some other person; or

    (ii) in so far as the court allows the person by whom the statement was made to narrate it in the course of his examination-in-chief on the ground that to prevent him from doing so would adversely affect the intelligibility of his evidence.

(3) Where in any civil proceedings a statement which was made otherwise than in a document is admissible by virtue of this section, no evidence other than direct oral evidence by the person who made the statement or any person who heard or otherwise perceived it being made shall be admissible for the purpose of proving it:

Provided that if the statement in question was made by a person while giving oral evidence in some other legal proceedings (whether civil or criminal), it may be proved in any manner authorised by the court.

3. Witness's previous statement, if proved, to be evidence of facts stated.

(1) Where in any civil proceedings—

(*a*) a previous inconsistent or contradictory statement made by a person called as a witness in those proceedings is proved by virtue of section 3, 4 or 5 of the Criminal Procedure Act 1865; or

(*b*) a previous statement made by a person called as aforesaid is proved for the purpose of rebutting a suggestion that his evidence has been fabricated,

that statement shall by virtue of this subsection be admissible as evidence of any facts stated therein of which direct oral evidence by him would be admissible.

(2) Nothing in this Act shall affect any of the rules of law relating to the circumstances in which, where a person called as a witness in any civil proceedings is cross-examined on a document used by him to refresh his memory, that document may be made evidence in those proceedings; and where a document or any part of a document is received in evidence in any such proceedings by virtue of any such rule of law, any statement made in that document or part by the person using the document to refresh his memory shall by virtue of this subsection be admissible as evidence of any fact stated therein of which direct oral evidence by him would be admissible.

4. Admissibility of certain records as evidence of facts stated.

(1) Without prejudice to section 5 of this Act, in any civil proceedings a statement contained in a document shall, subject to this section and to rules of court, be admissible as evidence of any fact stated therein of which direct oral evidence would be admissible, if the document is, or forms part of, a record compiled by a person acting under a duty from information which was supplied by a person (whether acting under a duty or not) who had, or may reasonably be supposed to have had, personal knowledge of the matters dealt with in that information and which, if not supplied by that person to the compiler of the record directly, was supplied by him to the compiler of the record indirectly through one or more intermediaries each acting under a duty.

(2) Where in any civil proceedings a party desiring to give a statement in evidence by virtue of this section has called or intends to call as a witness in the proceedings the person who originally supplied the information from which the record containing the statement was compiled, the statement—

(*a*) shall not be given in evidence by virtue of this section on behalf of that party without the leave of the court; and

(*b*) without prejudice to paragraph (*a*) above, shall not without the leave of the court be given in evidence by virtue of this section on behalf of that party before the conclusion of the examination-in-chief of the person who originally supplied the said information.

(3) Any reference in this section to a person acting under a duty includes a reference to a person acting in the course of any trade, business, profession or other occupation in which he is engaged or employed or for the purposes of any paid or unpaid office held by him.

5. Admissibility of statements produced by computers.

(1) In any civil proceedings a statement contained in a document produced by a computer shall, subject to rules of court, be admissible as evidence of any fact stated therein of which direct oral evidence would be admissible, if it is shown that the conditions mentioned in subsection (2) below are satisfied in relation to the statement and computer in question.

(2) The said conditions are—

(a) that the document containing the statement was produced by the computer during a period over which the computer was used regularly to store or process information for the purposes of any activities regularly carried on over that period, whether for profit or not, by any body, whether corporate or not, or by any individual;

(b) that over that period there was regularly supplied to the computer in the ordinary course of those activities information of the kind contained in the statement or of the kind from which the information so contained is derived;

(c) that throughout the material part of that period the computer was operating properly or, if not, that any respect in which it was not operating properly or was out of operation during that part of that period was not such as to affect the production of the document or the accuracy of its contents; and

(d) that the information contained in the statement reproduces or is derived from information supplied to the computer in the ordinary course of those activities.

* * * * *

8. Rules of court.

(1) Provision shall be made by rules of court as to the procedure which, subject to any exceptions provided for in the rules, must be followed and the other conditions which, subject as aforesaid, must be fulfilled before a statement can be given in evidence in civil proceedings by virtue of section 2, 4 or 5 of this Act.

(2) Rules of court made in pursuance of subsection (1) above shall in particular, subject to such exceptions (if any) as may be provided for in the rules—

(a) require a party to any civil proceedings who desires to give in evidence any such statement as is mentioned in that subsection to give to every other party to the proceedings such notice of his desire to do so and such particulars of or relating to the statement as may be specified in the rules, including particulars of such one or more of the persons connected with the making or recording of the statement or, in the case of a statement falling within section 5(1) of this Act, such one or more of the persons concerned as mentioned in section 6(3)(c)[1] of this Act as the rules may in any case require; and

(b) enable any party who receives such notice as aforesaid by counter-notice to require any person of whom particulars were given with the notice to be called as a witness in the proceedings unless that person is dead, or beyond the seas, or unfit by reason of his bodily or mental condition to attend as a witness, or cannot with reasonable diligence be identified or found, or cannot reasonably be expected (having regard to the time which has elapsed since he was connected or concerned as aforesaid and to all the circumstances) to have any recollection of matters relevant to the accuracy or otherwise of the statement.

(3) Rules of court made in pursuance of subsection (1) above—

(a) may confer on the court in any civil proceedings a discretion to allow a statement falling within section 2(1), 4(1) or 5(1) of this Act to be given in evidence notwithstanding that any requirement of the rules affecting

---

[1] I.e. "any person concerned with the supply of information to that computer, or with the operation of that computer or any equipment by means of which the document containing the statement was produced by it".

the admissibility of that statement has not been complied with, but except in pursuance of paragraph (*b*) below shall not confer on the court a discretion to exclude such a statement where the requirements of the rules affecting its admissibility have been complied with;

(*b*) may confer on the court power, where a party to any civil proceedings has given notice that he desires to give in evidence—

   (i) a statement falling within section 2(1) of this Act which was made by a person, whether orally or in a document, in the course of giving evidence in some other legal proceedings (whether civil or criminal);

   (ii) a statement falling within section 4(1) of this Act which is contained in a record of any direct oral evidence given in some other legal proceedings (whether civil or criminal),

to give directions on the application of any party to the proceedings as to whether, and if so on what conditions, the party desiring to give the statement in evidence will be permitted to do so and (where applicable) as to the manner in which that statement and any other evidence given in those other proceedings is to be proved; and

(*c*) may make different provision for different circumstances, and in particular may make different provision with respect to statements falling within section 2(1), 4(1) and 5(1) of this Act respectively;

and any discretion conferred on the court by rules of court made as aforesaid may be either a general discretion or a discretion exercisable only in such circumstances as may be specified in the rules.

(4) ...

(5) In deciding for the purposes of any rules of court made in pursuance of this section whether or not a person is fit to attend as a witness, a court may act on a certificate purporting to be a certificate of a fully registered medical practitioner.

*   *   *   *   *

11. Convictions as evidence in civil proceedings.

(1) In any civil proceedings the fact that a person has been convicted of an offence by or before any court in the United Kingdom or by a court-martial there or elsewhere shall (subject to subsection (3) below) be admissible in evidence for the purpose of proving, where to do so is relevant to any issue in those proceedings, that he committed that offence, whether he was so convicted upon a plea of guilty or otherwise and whether or not he is a party to the civil proceedings; but no conviction other than a subsisting one shall be admissible in evidence by virtue of this section.

(2) In any civil proceedings in which by virtue of this section a person is proved to have been convicted of an offence by or before any court in the United Kingdom or by a court-martial there or elsewhere—

(*a*) he shall be taken to have committed that offence unless the contrary is proved; and

(*b*) without prejudice to the reception of any other admissible evidence for the purpose of identifying the facts on which the conviction was based, the contents of any document which is admissible as evidence of the conviction, and the contents of the information, complaint, indictment or charge-sheet on which the person in question was convicted, shall be admissible in evidence for that purpose.

(3) Nothing in this section shall prejudice the operation of section 13[1] of this Act or any other enactment whereby a conviction or a finding of fact in any criminal proceedings is for the purposes of any other proceedings made conclusive evidence of any fact.

(4) Where in any civil proceedings the contents of any document are admissible in evidence by virtue of subsection (2) above, a copy of that document, or of the material part thereof, purporting to be certified or otherwise authenticated by or on behalf of the court or authority having custody of that document shall be admissible in evidence and shall be taken to be a true copy of that document or part unless the contrary is shown.

---

[1] This provides that convictions shall be treated as conclusive evidence in defamation actions.

LIMITATION ACT 1939

1. Part I to be subject to provisions of Part II relating to disability, acknowledgment, fraud, etc.

The provisions of this Part of this Act shall have effect subject to the provisions of Part II of this Act which provide for the extension of the periods of limitation in the case of disability, acknowledgment, part payment, fraud and mistake.

2. Limitation of actions of contract and tort, and certain other actions.

(1) The following actions shall not be brought after the expiration of six years from the date on which the cause of action accrued, that is to say:

(*a*) actions founded on simple contract or on tort;

(*b*) actions to enforce a recognisance;

(*c*) actions to enforce an award, where the submission is not by an instrument under seal;

(*d*) actions to recover any sum recoverable by virtue of any enactment, other than a penalty or forfeiture or sum by way of penalty or forfeiture.

(2) An action for an account shall not be brought in respect of any matter which arose more than six years before the commencement of the action.

(3) An action upon a speciality shall not be brought after the expiration of twelve years from the date on which the cause of action accrued:

Provided that this subsection shall not affect any action for which a shorter period of limitation is prescribed by any other provision of this Act.

(4) An action shall not be brought upon any judgment after the expiration of twelve years from the date on which the judgment became enforceable, and no arrears of interest in respect of any judgment debt shall be recovered after the expiration of six years from the date on which the interest became due.

(5) An action to recover any penalty or forfeiture, or sum by way of penalty or forfeiture, recoverable by virtue of any enactment shall not be brought after the expiration of two years from the date on which the cause of action accrued:

Provided that for the purposes of this subsection the expression "penalty" shall not include a fine to which any person is liable on conviction of a criminal offence.

(6) Subsection (1) of this section shall apply to an action to recover seamen's wages, but save as aforesaid this section shall not apply to any cause of action within the Admiralty jurisdiction of the High Court which is enforceable in rem.

(7) This action shall not apply to any claim for specific performance of a contract or for an injunction or for other equitable relief, except in so far as any provision thereof may be applied by the Court by analogy in like manner

as the corresponding enactment repealed by this Act has heretofore been applied.

(8) This section has effect subject to section 2A below.

2A. Time limit for personal injuries.

(1) This section applies to any action for damage for negligence, nuisance or breach of duty (whether the duty exists by virtue of a contract or of provision made by or under a statute or independently of any contract or any such provision) where the damages claimed by the plaintiff for the neg-ligence, nuisance or breach of duty consist of or include damages in respect of personal injuries to the plaintiff or any other person.

(2) Section 2 of this Act shall not apply to an action to which this section applies.

(3) Subject to section 2D below, an action to which this section applied shall not be brought after the expiration of the period specified in subsections (4) and (5) below.

(4) Except where subsection (5) applies, the said period is three years from—

(a) the date on which the cause of action accrued, or
(b) the date (if later) of the plaintiff's knowledge.

(5) If the person injured dies before the expiration of the period in sub-section (4) above, the period as respects the cause of action surviving for the benefit of the estate of the deceased by virtue of section 1 of the Law Reform (Miscellaneous Provisions) Act 1934 shall be three years from—

(a) the date of death, or
(b) the date of the personal representative's knowledge,

whichever is the later.

(6) In this section, and in section 2B below, references to a person's date of knowledge are references to the date on which he first had knowledge of the following facts—

(a) that the injury in question was significant, and
(b) that that injury was attributable in whole or in part to the act or omission which is alleged to constitute negligence, nuisance or breach of duty, and
(c) the identity of the defendant, and
(d) if it is alleged that the act or omission was that of a person other than the defendant, the identity of that person and the additional facts sup-porting the bringing of an action against the defendant,

and knowledge that any acts or omissions did or did not, as a matter of law, involve negligence, nuisance or breach of duty is irrelevant.

(7) For the purposes of this section an injury is significant if the plaintiff would reasonably have considered it sufficiently serious to justify his institut-ing proceedings for damages against a defendant who did not dispute liability and was able to satisfy a judgment.

(8) For the purposes of the said sections a person's knowledge includes knowledge which he might reasonably have been expected to acquire—

(*a*) from facts observable or ascertainable by him, or

(*b*) from facts ascertainable by him with the help of medical or other appropriate expert advice which it is reasonable for him to seek,

but a person shall not be fixed under this subsection with knowledge of a fact ascertainable only with the help of expert advice so long as he has taken all reasonable steps to obtain (and, where appropriate, to act on) that advice.

(9) For the purposes of this section "personal representative" includes any person who is or has been a personal representative of the deceased, including an executor who has not proved the will (whether or not he has renounced probate) but not anyone appointed only as a special personal representative in relation to settled land; and regard shall be had to any knowledge acquired by any such person while a personal representative or previously.

(10) If there is more than one personal representative, and their dates of knowledge are different, subsection (5)(*b*) above shall be read as referring to the earliest of those dates.

2B Time limit for actions under Fatal Accidents Act[s] 1846 [and 1976].[1]

(1) This section has effect subject to section 2D below.

(2) An action under the Fatal Accidents Act 1846 shall not be brought if the death occurred when the person injured could no longer maintain an action and recover damages in respect of the injury (whether because of a time limit in this Act or in any other Act, or any other reason).

Where any such action by the injured person would have been barred by the time limit in section 2A above, no account shall be taken of the possibility of that time limit being overridden under section 2D of this Act.

(3) An action under the Fatal Accidents Act 1846 shall not be brought after the expiration of three years—

(*a*) the date of death, or

(*b*) the date of knowledge of the person for whose benefit the action is brought,

whichever is the later.

(4) Subsection (3) above shall not apply to an action for which a period of limitation is prescribed by or under any Act other than this Act, and section 2A above shall not apply to an action under the Fatal Accidents Act 1846.

(5) An action under the Fatal Accidents Act 1846 shall be one to which section 22 of this Act (persons under disability) applied, but otherwise Part II and Part III of this Act shall not apply to the action.

2C. Dependants subject to different time limits.

(1) This section applies where there is more than one person for whose benefit an action under the Fatal Accidents Act is brought.

(2) Section 2B(3)(*b*) shall be applied separately to each of them, and if that would debar one or more of them, but not all, the court shall direct that any person who would be so debarred shall be excluded from those for whom the action is brought unless it is shown that if the action were brought exclusively for the benefit of that person it would not be defeated by a defence of

---

[1] See the Fatal Accidents Act 1976, Sch. 1, para. 3, which provides that references to the 1846 Act are to be construed as including a reference to the 1976 Act.

limitation (whether in consequence of section 22 of this Act (persons under disability), or an agreement between the parties not to raise the defence, or otherwise).

2D. Court's power to override time limits.

(1) If it appears to the court that it would be equitable to allow an action to proceed having regard to the degree to which—

(a) the provisions of section 2A or 2B of this Act prejudice the plaintiff or any person whom he represents, and
(b) any decision of the court under this subsection would prejudice the defendant or any person whom he represents,

the court may direct that those provisions shall not apply to the action, or shall not apply to any specified cause of action to which the action relates.

(2) The court shall not under this section disapply section 2B(2) except where the reason why the person injured could no longer maintain an action was because of the time limit in section 2A.

If, for example, the person injured could at his death no longer maintain an action under the Fatal Accidents Act 1846 because of the time limit in Article 29 in Schedule 1 to the Carriage by Air Act 1961, the court has no power to direct that section 2B(2) shall not apply.

(3) In acting under this section the court shall have regard to all the circumstances of the case and in particular to—

(a) the length of, and the reasons for, the delay on the part of the plaintiff;
(b) the extent to which, having regard to the delay, the evidence adduced or likely to be adduced by the plaintiff or the defendant is or is likely to be less cogent than if the action had been brought within the time allowed by section 2A or as the case may be 2B;
(c) the conduct of the defendant after the cause of action arose, including the extent if any to which he responded to requests reasonably made by the plaintiff for information or inspection for the purpose of ascertaining facts which were or might be relevant to the plaintiff's cause of action against the defendant;
(d) the duration of any disability of the plaintiff arising after the date of the accrual of the cause of action;
(e) the extent to which the plaintiff acted promptly and reasonably once he knew whether or not the act or omission of the defendant, to which the injury was attributable, might be capable at that time of giving rise to an action for damages;
(f) the steps, if any, taken by the plaintiff to obtain medical, legal or other expert advice and the nature of any such advice he may have received.

(4) In a case where the person injured died when, because of section 2A, he could no longer maintain an action and recover damages in respect of the injury, the court shall have regard in particular to the length of, and the reasons for, the delay on the part of the deceased.

(5) In a case under subsection (4) above, or any other case where the time limit, or one of the time limits, depends on the date of knowledge of a person other than the plaintiff, subsection (3) above shall have effect with appropriate modifications, and shall have effect in particular as if references to the plaintiff included references to any person whose date of knowledge is or was relevant in determining a time limit.

(6) A direction by the court disapplying the provisions of section 2B(2) shall operate to disapply the provisions to the same effect in section 1 of the Fatal Accidents Act 1846.

(7) In this section "the court" means the court in which the action has been brought.

(8) References in this section to section 2A include references to that section as extended by any provision of Parts II and III of this Act.

* * * * *

PART II

EXTENSION OF LIMITATION PERIODS IN CASE OF DISABILITY
ACKNOWLEDGMENT, PART PAYMENT, FRAUD AND MISTAKE

22. Extension of limitation period in case of disability.

(1) If on the date when any right of action accrued for which a period of limitation is prescribed by this Act, the person to whom it accrued was under a disability, the action may be brought at any time before the expiration of six years . . . from the date when the person ceased to be under a disability or died, whichever event first occurred, notwithstanding that the period of limitation has expired:

Provided that—

(a) this section shall not affect any case where the right of action first accrued to some person (not under a disability) through whom the person under a disability claims;

(b) when a right of action which has accrued to a person under a disability accrues, on the death of that person while still under a disability, to another person under a disability, no further extension of time shall be allowed by reason of the disability of the second person;

(c) no action to recover land or money charged on land shall be brought by virtue of this section by any person after the expiration of thirty years from the date on which the right of action accrued to that person or some person through whom he claims;

(d) . . .; and

(e) this section shall not apply to any action to recover a penalty or forfeiture, or sum by way thereof, by virtue of any enactment, except where the action is brought by an aggrieved party.

(2) If the action is one to which section 2A or 2B(3) of this Act applies subsection (1) of this section shall have effect as if for the words "6 years" there were substituted the words "3 years".

(3) Where this section applies by virtue of section 4(3) of the Limitation Act 1963 (contribution between tortfeasors)[1] subsection (1) of this section shall have effect as if for the words "6 years" there were substituted the words "2 years".

* * * * *

26. Postponement of limitation period in case of fraud or mistake.

Where, in the case of any action for which a period of limitation is prescribed by this Act, either—

---

[1] Section 4 of the 1963 Act provides that a torfeasor must claim contribution from another tortfeasor within 2 years of the relevant judgment or admission of liability.

(a) the action is based upon the fraud of the defendant or his agent or of any person through whom he claims or his agent, or

(b) the right of action is concealed by the fraud of any such person as aforesaid, or

(c) the action is for relief from the consequences of a mistake.

the period of limitation shall not begin to run until the plaintiff has discovered the fraud or the mistake, as the case may be, or could with reasonable diligence have discovered it:

Provided that nothing in this section shall enable any action to be brought to recover, or enforce any charge against, or set aside any transaction affecting, any property which—

(i) in the case of fraud, has been purchased for valuable consideration by a person who was not a party to the fraud and did not at the time of the purchase know or have reason to believe that any fraud had been committed, or

(ii) in the case of mistake, has been purchased for valuable consideration, subsequently to the transaction in which the mistake was made, by a person who did not know or have reason to believe that the mistake had been made.

COUNTY COURTS ACT 1959

39. General jurisdiction in actions of contract and tort.

(1) A county court shall have jurisdiction to hear and determine any action founded on contract or tort where the debt, demand or damage claimed is not more than £2,000, whether on balance of account or otherwise:

Provided that a county court shall not, except as in this Act provided, have jurisdiction to hear and determine,—

(a) any action for the recovery of land; or
(b) any action in which the title to any hereditament or to any toll, fair, market or franchise is in question; or
(c) any action for libel, slander, or seduction.

(2) A county court shall have jurisdiction to hear and determine any action where the debt or demand claimed consists of a balance not exceeding £2,000 after a set-off of any debt or demand claimed or recoverable by the defendant from the plaintiff, being a set-off admitted by the plaintiff in the particulars of his claim or demand.

47. Costs of actions of contract or tort commenced in High Court which could have been commenced in county court.

(1) Where an action founded on contract or tort is commenced in the High Court which could have been commenced in the county court, then, subject to subsection (3) of this section, the plaintiff—

(a) if he recovers a sum less than £1,200, shall not be entitled to any more costs of the action than those to which he would have been entitled if the action had been brought in the county court; and
(b) if he recovers a sum less than £350, shall not be entitled to any costs of the action;

so, however, that this section shall not affect any question as to costs if it appears to the High Court or a judge thereof (or where the matter is tried before a referee or officer of the Supreme Court, to that referee or officer) that there was reasonable ground for supposing the amount recoverable in respect of the plaintiff's claim to be in excess of the amount recoverable in an action commenced in the county court.

For the purposes of paragraphs (a) and (b) of this subsection, a plaintiff shall be treated as recovering the full amount recoverable in respect of his claim without regard to any deduction made in respect of contributory negligence on his part or otherwise in respect of matters not falling to be taken into account in determining whether the action could have been commenced in the county court.

(1A) In relation to an action brought to enforce a right to recover possession of goods, or to enforce such a right and to claim payment of a debt or other demand or damages, subsection (1) of this section shall have effect as if—

(a) in paragraph (a) of that subsection, for the words "he recovers a sum less than £1,200" there were substituted the words "the aggregate amount recovered by him in the action, including the value of any goods ordered in the action to be delivered to him, is less than £1,200", and

(b) In paragraph (b) of that subsection, for the words "he recovers a sum less than £350" there were substituted the words "the aggregate amount recovered by him in the action, including the value of any goods ordered in the action to be delivered to him, is less than £350",

and as if, in the words so substituted, any reference to an order for the delivery of goods to the plaintiff included a reference to an order to deliver goods to the plaintiff or to pay their value to him.

(2) Where a plaintiff is entitled to costs on a county court scale only, the taxing master shall have the same power of directing on what county court scale costs are to be allowed, and of allowing any items of costs, as the judge would have had if the action had been brought in a county court.

(3) In any such action as aforesaid, whether founded on contract or tort, the High Court or a judge thereof (or where the matter is tried before a referee or officer of the Supreme Court, that referee or officer), if satisfied—

(a) that there was sufficient reason for bringing the action in the High Court; or
(b) that the defendant or one of the defendants objected to the transfer of the action to a county court;

may make an order allowing the costs or any part of the costs thereof on the High Court scale or on such one of the county court scales as he may direct.

(4) [*Repealed by the Administration of Justice Act 1969, s. 35(2) and Sched. 2.*]

(5) This section applies only to the costs of the proceedings in the High Court, and shall have effect subject to the provisions of section sixty of this Act.

(6) This section shall not apply in the case of any proceedings by the Crown.

74. General ancillary jurisdiction.

(1) Every county court, as regards any cause of action for the time being within its jurisdiction, shall—

(a) grant such relief, redress or remedy or combination of remedies, either absolute or conditional; and
(b) give such and the like effect to every ground of defence or counter-claim equitable or legal (subject to the provisions of section sixty-five of this Act);

as ought to be granted or given in the like case by the High Court and in as full and ample a manner.

(2) For the purposes of this section it shall be assumed (notwithstanding any enactment to the contrary) that any proceedings which can be commenced in a county court could be commenced in the High Court.

COUNTY COURT RULES 1936

1. Actions generally.

(1) Except where by any Act or Rule it is otherwise provided, an action may be commenced—

(a) in the court for the district in which the defendant or one of the defendants resides or carries on business; or

(b) subject to the succeeding paragraphs of this Rule, in the court for the district in which the cause of action wholly or in part arose.

(2) Where the plaintiff sues as assignee of a debt or other legal thing in action, the action may be commenced in any court in which the assignor might have commenced the action but for the assignment, and not elsewhere.

(3) Where the plaintiff's claim—

(a) is founded on a hire-purchase agreement but is not for the delivery of goods, or

(b) is founded on a contract for the sale or hire of goods under which the purchase price or rental is payable otherwise than in one sum,

paragraph (1)(b) of this Rule shall have effect as if for the words "the cause of action wholly or in part arose" there were substituted the words "the defendant or one of the defendants resided or carried on business when the contract was made".

(4) Where the plaintiff's claim is founded on tort and the defendant or each of the defendants does not reside or carry on business in England or Wales, paragraph (1)(a) of this Rule shall have effect as if for the words "the defendants or one of the defendants" there were substituted the words "the plaintiff or one of the plaintiffs".

(5) Where a plaintiff desires to commence an action by virtue of paragraph (1)(b) of this Rule, he shall file a præcipe in Form 8 or Form 11, stating the facts on which he relies as giving the court jurisdiction under this Rule to entertain the action, and if the facts stated to the præcipe do not show that the court has such jurisdiction, the plaint shall not be entered, or if owing to a misstatement in the præcipe the plaint is entered, the action may be dealt with as provided by Order 16, Rule 4.

2. Recovery of land, etc.

Proceedings—

(a) for the recovery of land; or

(b) [Revoked, 1954]

(c) foreclosure or redemption of any mortgage or for enforcing any charge or lien on land; or

(d) for the recovery of money secured by a mortage or charge on land;

shall be commenced in the court for the district in which the land or any part thereof is situate.

Provided that proceedings for enforcing a charge imposed on land under section 141 of the Act, shall be commenced in the court in which the order imposing the charge was made.

ORDER 5
PARTIES

21. Partners may sue and be sued in the name of their firm.

(1) Two or more persons claiming or alleged to be liable as partners and carrying on business within England or Wales may sue or be sued in the name of the firm in which they were partners when the cause of action arose.

(2) Where partners sue or are sued in the name of their firm in accordance with this Rule, a statement that the plaintiffs are suing or the defendants are sued as a firm shall be included in the praecipe and in the title of the action.

(3) Where partners sue or are sued in the name of their firm, the partners shall, on demand made in writing by or on behalf of any other party, forthwith deliver to the party making the demand, and file in the court office, a statement of the names and places of residence of all the persons constituting the firm.

(4) If the partners fail to comply with the demand, the court may, on application by any other party, order them to furnish and verify by oath or otherwise a statement of the names and places of residence of the persons who were partners in the firm when the cause of action arose.

(5) If the partners fail to comply with the order, the court may—

(a) if the partners are plaintiffs, direct all proceedings to be stayed until the order is obeyed; and

(b) if the partners are defendants, order that they be debarred from defending the action.

(6) When the names and places of residence of the partners have been stated, the proceedings shall continue in the name of the firm.

24. Business in name other than own.

A person carrying on business in a name other than his own, may be sued in that name as if it were a firm name, and so far as the nature of the case will permit, all the provisions of these Rules relating to actions against firms shall apply.

ORDER 8
SERVICE
PART I—GENERALLY

1. Registrar's duty to serve.

Except as otherwise provided by these Rules, the registrar shall serve or cause to be served by bailiff all process issued by him or sent to him for service from another court.

2. Personal service.

Where by any Act or Rule personal service of any document is required for the purpose of any proceedings in a county court, the following provisions shall apply:—

(a) Service shall be effected by delivering the document to the person to be served in any district in which he may be found.

(b) The document may be served by—

    (i)   a bailiff of the court, or, if the defendant attends at the office of the court, any other officer of the court; or

    (ii) a party to the proceedings or some person in his permanent and exclusive employ; or

    (iii) the solicitor of a party or a solicitor acting as an agent for such solicitor or some person employed by either solicitor to serve the document.

(c) The person effecting service shall—

    (i)   if he is an officer of the court indorse on a copy of the document a note of the date and place of service and of any conduct money paid or tendered and a statement that he had served the document on the person to be served personally, and shall sign the indorsement and file the copy of the document in the court office; and

    (ii) if he is not an officer of the court, file in the court office within three days of the day of service or such further time as may be allowed by the registrar a copy of the document and an affidavit (in these Rules called "an affidavit of service") in such one of the Forms in the Appendix as is applicable to the case.

(d) A bailiff who has failed to effect service shall indorse on the document a note of the reason why service has not been effected, and shall sign the indorsement and file the document in the court office, and the registrar of the court of which he is a bailiff shall send to the person at whose instance the document was issued notice of non-service in Form 36.

(e) Where a document or copy thereof has been filed in the court office pursuant to paragraph (c)(i) or (d) of this Rule, the registrar shall, if the document was received from another court, return the document or copy to the registrar of the court.

(f) Where at any time upon or after the issue of a document for personal service, the party at whose instance the document was issued desires service to be effected otherwise than by bailiff, the document and any necessary copies thereof shall, on request, be delivered to him for service.

6. Substituted service

(1) Subject to the provisions of paragraph (3) of this Rule, where for any sufficient reason service of any summons, originating application, petition, notice, order or other document cannot be effected in the manner prescribed by these Rules, the court may, upon an affidavit showing grounds, make an order giving leave for steps to be taken to bring the document to the knowledge of the person to be served by sending it by post addressed to him at his last known residence or place of business or by advertisement or in some other manner.

(2) Where any such order has been carried out, the steps taken may be called substituted service, and such service shall have the same effect as service of the document in the manner prescribed otherwise than by this Rule:

Provided that—

(a) the indorsement or affidavit of service (if any) shall show that the terms of the order for substituted service have been complied with; and

(b) the document shall be deemed to have been served—

    (i)   where the order is for service by post, at the time when the letter would have been delivered in the ordinary course of post; and

    (ii) in any other case, at such time as the order may direct.

(3) Where the court has power under any other Rule to cause the document to be served by post by an officer of the court,—

(i) no order for substituted service by post shall be made in respect of the document; and

(ii) no order for substituted service by advertisement or in any other manner shall be made in respect of the document, unless the court considers that service cannot be effected by post.

(4) Where a summons to be served by bailiff cannot be served in accordance with Rule 8 of this Order, the registrar for the district in which the summons is to be served shall, if so requested, take such steps as may be necessary to enable the plaintiff to apply for an order for substituted service.

PART II—ORDINARY AND DEFAULT SUMMONS

8. Mode of service.

(1) Subject to the provisions of any Act and the following paragraphs of this Rule, and Rules 11 to 26 and Rule 30 of this Order, service of an ordinary or default summons shall be effected—

(*a*) by delivering the summons to the defendant personally; or

(*b*) by a bailiff of the court delivering the summons to some person apparently not less than 16 years old, at the residence of the defendant or, where the defendant is the proprietor of a business, at his place of business.

(2) Where the plaintiff or his solicitor gives a certificate for postal service in Form 6, the summons shall, unless the registrar otherwise directs, be served by an officer of the court sending it by ordinary post to the defendant named in the certificate at the address stated in the præcipe.

(3) Where it appears to the bailiff by whom a summons is to be served that there is a reasonable probability that the summons if delivered at the address stated in the præcipe will come to the defendant's knowledge in sufficient time—

(*a*) in the case of an ordinary summons, for the defendant to appear at the hearing; or

(*b*) in the case of a default summons, for the defendant to deliver a defence, admission or counterclaim within the time prescribed by those Rules,

the summons may, with the general or special leave of the registrar, be served by—

(i) an officer of the court sending the summons by ordinary post to the defendant at that address; or

(ii) the bailiff inserting the summons, enclosed in an envelope addressed to the defendant, in the letterbox at that address.

(4) Service of an ordinary summons shall be effected not less than 21 clear days before the return-day:

Provided that service may be effected at any time before the return-day on the plaintiff satisfying the registrar by affidavit that a defendant is about to remove from the address stated in the præcipe.

9. Indorsement or affidavit of service of summons.

(1) Where a summons is to be served by bailiff, he shall indorse on the copy of the summons retained by him—

(a) the date and place of service; and

(b) the mode of service showing that the provisions applicable have been complied with; and

(c) any statement made by the person who received the summons and any other circumstances from which it may be inferred that the summons has come to the knowledge of the defendant; or

(d) where service is effected under Rule 8(3) of this Order, a note of the reasons for supposing that the summons was likely to come to the defendant's knowledge; or

(e) if he has failed to effect service, a note of the reason why service has not been effected;

and shall sign the indorsement, add the name of the court of which he is a bailiff and return the indorsed copy of the summons and any unserved summons to the registrar.

(2) Where a summons is served by post pursuant to paragraph (2) or (3) of Rule 8 of this Order, the officer of the court shall indorse on the copy of the summons retained in the court office the date of posting and the address written on the letter, and shall sign the indorsement and add the name of the court of which he is an officer.

11. Solicitor accepting service.

Where a solicitor indorses on the copy of an ordinary or default summons which is to be retained by the person effecting service a memorandum signed and dated by the solicitor, stating that he accepts service of the summons on behalf of a defendant and giving an address for service, the summons shall be deemed to have been duly served on that defendant and to have been so served on the date on which the indorsement was made.

12. Presumed service of summons.

Where a summons has not been served in accordance with Rule 8 of this Order but the registrar receives from the defendant a defence, admission or counterclaim, the action may proceed as if the summons had been duly served.

13. Person under disability.

(1) Where a defendant is a person under disability, an ordinary summons shall be served—

(a) in the case of an infant who is not also a mental patient, on his father or guardian or, if he has no father or guardian, on the person with whom he resides or in whose care he is;

(b) in the case of a mental patient, on the person (if any) who is authorised under Part VIII of the Mental Health Act, 1959, to conduct in the name of the mental patient or on his behalf the proceedings in connection with which the summons is to be served or, if there is no person so authorised, on the person with whom he resides or in whose care he is.

(2) Notwithstanding anything in the foregoing paragraph, the court may order that any summons which has been, or is to be, served on the person

under disability or on a person other than a person mentioned in that paragraph shall be deemed to be duly served on the person under disability.

14. Partners

(1) Subject to the following paragraphs of this Rule, where partners are sued in the name of their firm, service of a summons shall be good service on all the partners, whether any of them is out of England and Wales or not, if the summons is delivered—

(*a*) to a partner personally, or

(*b*) at the principal place of the partnership business within the district within which the summons is to be served, to any person having, or appearing to have, at the time of service, the control or management of the business there.

Provided that, where the partnership has to the knowledge of the plaintiff been dissolved before the commencement of the action, the summons shall be served upon every person within England and Wales sought to be made liable.

(2) Where the plaintiff or his solicitor gives a certificate for postal service in Form 6 the summons shall, unless the registrar otherwise directs, be served by an officer of the court sending it by ordinary post to the firm at the address stated in the præcipe.

(3) Rule 8(3) of this Order shall apply to the service of the summons as if for the reference to the defendant's knowledge there was substituted a reference to the knowledge of one of the persons to whom the summons may be delivered in accordance with paragraph (1) of this Rule and as if for the references in sub-paragraphs (*a*) and (*b*) of Rule 8(3) to the defendant there were substituted references to one of the partners.

(4) Where a person carrying on a business in a name other than his own, is sued in that name as if it were a firm name, the summons may be served in accordance with the foregoing provisions of this Rule as if he were a partner sued in the name of a firm and his business were a partnership business.

15. Indorsement, etc. of service on partner.

Where a summons is served under the last preceding Rule, the indorsement or affidavit of service shall state whether the person served was served—

(*a*) as a partner; or

(*b*) as a person carrying on business in a name other than his own; or

(*c*) as a person having, or appearing to have, the control or management of the business; or

(*d*) as a person occupying a dual capacity;

and shall be in Form 33 or Form 35 whichever is applicable.

39. Mode of service.

Where in any proceedings in a county court any document is required to be served on any person and no other mode of service is prescribed by any Act or Rule, the following provisions shall apply:—

(*a*) Where the person to be served is acting in person, service shall be effected—

    (i) by delivering the document to him or at his residence or by sending the document by prepaid post to his last known residence; or

    (ii) if he is a proprietor of a business, by delivering the document at his place of business or sending it by prepaid post to his last known place of business.

(*b*) Where the person to be served is acting by a solicitor, service shall be effected by delivering the document at or sending it by prepaid post to the solicitor's address for service.

(*c*) Where the document is sent by post, it shall, unless the contrary be proved, be deemed to have been served at the time when the letter containing it would have been delivered in the ordinary course of post, and in proving service of the document it shall be sufficient to prove that it was properly addressed, prepaid and posted.

ORDER 9

ORDINARY ACTIONS

Admission, Defence and Counterclaim

1. Admission and request for time.

(1) A defendant in an ordinary action who admits his liability for the whole or part of any claim but desires time for payment, shall within 14 days of the service of the summons on him, inclusive of the day of service, deliver at the court office an admission for which the form appended to the summons may be used.

(2) The registrar shall upon the receipt by him of the admission send notice thereof to the plaintiff in Form 60.

(3) If the plaintiff elects to accept the amount admitted in satisfaction of his claim and the proposal as to time of payment, he shall within 8 days of the receipt by him of the notice of admission send notice of acceptance to the registrar, who shall as soon as practicable enter judgment accordingly.

(4) If the plaintiff does not elect to accept the amount admitted and the proposal as to time of payment, he shall within 8 days of the receipt by him of the notice of admission send notice of non-acceptance to the registrar and to the defendant, and the action shall be dealt with on the return day in the ordinary way.

(5) Where the amount admitted is £40 or upwards and the plaintiff does not accept the defendant's proposal as to mode of payment, he may, when giving the registrar notice of non-acceptance, request that the defendant be required to give evidence of his means on the return day, and in any such case—

(*a*) the registrar shall send the defendant a notice in Form 88;

(*b*) the defendant's admission shall not be treated as evidence of his means, unless the court otherwise orders; and

(*c*) if in the opinion of the court it is not reasonably practicable for the defendant to appear on the return day to give evidence of his means, evidence by affidavit shall be admissible on his behalf without the notice required by Order 20, Rule 5(1), having been given.

(6) If a defendant or plaintiff fails to deliver an admission or a notice of acceptance within the time limited by paragraph (1) or paragraph (3) of this Rule, he may nevertheless deliver an admission or a notice of acceptance at any time before the return day, and, if time permits, the procedure prescribed in paragraphs (2), (3), and (4) of this Rule shall be followed, but the court may order him to pay any costs properly incurred in consequence of his delay.

2. Admission in action for recovery of land.

(1) A defendant in an action for the recovery of land who admits the plaintiff's right to recover possession of the land may at any time before the return day deliver at the court office an admission thereof.

(2) The registrar shall, as soon as practicable after the receipt of the admission by him, send notice thereof to the plaintiff in Form 62, and no costs incurred after the receipt of such notice in respect of the proof of any matters admitted therein shall be allowed against the defendant who has made the admission.

3. Admission by letter.

Where a defendant in an ordinary action has not delivered an admission, the court may accept as an admission of the claim or any part thereof any letter addressed to the court which the court is satisfied was written by or with the authority of the defendant.

4. Defendant to deliver notice of defence if claim disputed.

(1) A defendant in an ordinary action who disputes his liability for the whole or part of any claim shall within 14 days of the service of the summons on him, inclusive of the day of service, deliver at the court office a defence for which the form appended to the summons may be used.

(2) On receipt of a defence on the form the registrar shall make and send a copy thereof to the plaintiff.

(3) If a defence is delivered otherwise than on the form, it shall be accompanied by as many copies thereof as there are plaintiffs and on receipt of the defence and copies the registrar shall send a copy to every plaintiff.

(4) Subject to paragraph (8) of this Rule and paragraph (2) of Order 14, Rule 3, if a defendant fails to deliver a defence within the time limit by paragraph (1) of this Rule, he may nevertheless deliver a defence any time before the return-day and if time permits the procedure prescribed by paragraph (2) of this Rule shall be followed, or the defendant may without delivering a defence appear on the return day and dispute the plaintiff's claim, but the court may order him to pay any costs properly incurred in consequence of his delay or failure.

(5) If a defendant fails to deliver a defence within the time limited by paragraph (1) of this Rule, the court may at any time before the trial order the defendant to deliver a defence.

(6) If the plaintiff requires further particulars of the defence—

(a) he may file a notice specifying what further particulars he requires, and deliver a copy thereof to the defendant, and

(b) the defendant shall within 5 days of the service of the notice, file the further particulars and within the same time deliver a copy thereof to the plaintiff.

(7) If the defendant does not within 5 days after receipt of the notice file further particulars and deliver a copy thereof to the plaintiff, or if the further particulars are still insufficient, the court may, if satisfied that the plaintiff is thereby prejudiced, order the defendant to file and deliver further particulars of his defence.

(8) On or at any time after the making of an order under paragraph (5) or (7) of this Rule the court may direct that the defendant shall be debarred from defending altogether, or that anything in the defence of which further particulars have been ordered shall be struck out, unless the order is obeyed within such time as the court may allow.

(9) Where the defence is tender before action, the defendant shall pay onto court at the time of delivering the defence the amount alleged to have been tendered, and if he fails to do so, the tender shall not be available as a defence unless and until the payment into court has been made.

(10) The delivery by a defendant of a defence shall not relieve him from the obligation imposed by the summons to appear at court on the return-day.

ORDER 10
DEFAULT ACTIONS

Defence and Counterclaim, Admission and Judgment in Default

1. Defence, request for time, etc.

A defendant in a default action who disputes his liability for the whole or part of any claim or desires time for payment or desires to set up a counterclaim, shall within 14 days of the service of the summons on him, inclusive of the day of service, deliver at the court office

(a) the form appended to the summons completed according to the circumstances of his case and signed by him or by some person on his behalf; or

(b) a defence or an admission and a request for time for payment (in this Order called an admission) or a counterclaim otherwise than on the form, signed as aforesaid and accompanied by as many copies thereof as there are plaintiffs.

2. Judgment in default.

If the defendant does not within 14 days of the service of the summons on him, inclusive of the day of service, pay into court the total amount of the claim and costs or deliver at the court office a defence or an admission or a counterclaim, the service being duly proved, the plaintiff may, upon filing a præcipe in Form 30 and producing the plaint-note, have judgment entered against the defendant for the amount of the claim and costs, and the order shall be for payment forthwith, or at such time or times as the plaintiff may request:

Provided that if the defendant delivers at the court office a defence or an admission or a counterclaim after the said period of 14 days has expired and before judgment has been entered, judgment shall not be entered under this paragraph but the procedure prescribed by Rule 3 or Rule 4 of this Order shall be followed.

3. Defence or counterclaim.

If within the period of 14 days prescribed by Rule 1 of this Order, or before judgment has been entered, the defendant delivers at the court office a defence not accompanied by an admission of any part of the claim or delivers a counterclaim, the registrar shall fix a day for the preliminary consideration of the action under Order 21 or, if he thinks fit, a day for the hearing of the action and shall give not less than 8 clear days' notice thereof to the plaintiff and the defendant in Form 27, annexing to the notice given to the plaintiff a copy of the defence or counterclaim.

ORDER 14

APPLICATIONS AND DIRECTIONS IN THE COURSE OF
PROCEEDINGS

1. General procedure.

(1) Where by any Act or Rule any application in the course of an action or matter before or after judgment is expressly or by implication authorised to be made to the court or to the judge or to the registrar, then, subject to the provisions of the particular Act or Rule applicable thereto and so far as not inconsistent therewith, the following provisions shall apply:—

(a) The application may be made either in or out of court and either *ex parte* or on notice.

(b) Where made on notice—
   (i) the notice shall be in writing and shall be served on the opposite party and filed in the court office not less than one clear day before the hearing of the application unless the judge or registrar dispenses with notice or gives leave for shorter notice; and
   (ii) the party serving the notice shall be responsible for ascertaining that the judge or registrar will be available to hear the application on the day, at the time and in the place for which notice is served.

(c) No affidavit shall be necessary in the first instance, but the judge or registrar may direct evidence to be adduced in such manner as he thinks fit.

(d) Upon the hearing of the application the judge or registrar may make such order as may be just.

(e) If the registrar has power to hear and determine the application, the applicant shall, unless the judge otherwise orders, make the application to the registrar in the first instance.

(f) Where the application is made to the registrar, the registrar may, if in doubt as to the proper order to be made, refer the application to the judge forthwith or at the next convenient opportunity, and the judge may hear the application and make such order as may be just.

(g) The costs of interlocutory applications shall not be taxed until the general taxation of the costs of the action or matter unless the judge or registrar otherwise orders, and where an earlier taxation is ordered, Order 47 shall apply as if the word "claimed" were substituted for the word "recovered" wherever it occurs.

(h) Where the registrar has made an order to which this Rule applies, any party who is dissatisfied therewith may apply to the judge on notice to vary or rescind the order, and on the hearing of the application the judge may vary or rescind the order and may make such order as may be just.

(2) The jurisdiction of the court to hear and determine any application in the course of an action or matter before judgment may be exercised by the registrar, unless there is a provision to the contrary in any Act or Rule.

2. Power to impose terms.

The court may, as a condition of granting any application, impose such terms and conditions as it thinks fit, and, without prejudice to the generality of the foregoing provisions, may make orders requiring any party to—

(*a*) give security; or
(*b*) give an undertaking; or
(*c*) pay money into court; or
(*d*) pay all or any part of the costs of the proceedings; or
(*e*) give a power of re-entry.

3. Directions.

(1) In any action or matter the court may at any time on the application on notice of any party or of its own motion give such directions as it thinks proper.

(2) Without prejudice to the generality of the last preceding paragraph, the court may at any time on the application on notice of any party to an action or matter or of its own motion order any party to file or deliver any pleading, particulars or answer which the court thinks necessary for defining the issues in the proceedings and may at the same or any subsequent time direct that the action or matter shall be dismissed or, as the case may be, the defendant shall be debarred from defending altogether, or that anything in any pleading of which particulars have been ordered shall be struck out, unless the order is obeyed within such time as the court may allow.

(3) An order for directions shall be in Form 368.

8. Application for injunction.

(1) An application for the grant of an injunction may be made to the judge by any party to an action or matter before or after the trial or hearing whether or not a claim for the injunction was included in that party's particulars of claim, originating application, petition, counter-claim or third party notice, as the case may be.

(2) Where the applicant is the plaintiff and the case is one of urgency, the application may be made *ex parte* on affidavit but, except as aforesaid, the application must be made on notice.

(3) The plaintiff may not make an application before the issue of the summons, originating application or petition by which the action or matter is to be commenced except where the case is one of urgency and in that case—

(*a*) the affidavit on which the application is made shall show that the action or matter is one which the court to which the application is made has jurisdiction to hear and determine, and

(*b*) the injunction applied for shall, if granted, be on terms providing for the issue of the summons, originating application or petition in the court granting the application and on such other terms, if any, as the judge thinks fit.

ORDER 15
AMENDMENT

1. Generally.

The court may, at any time—

(*a*) amend any defects and errors in any proceedings whether the defect or error is that of the party applying to amend or not; and

(*b*) add, strike out or substitute any person either as plaintiff or defendant;

and all such amendments as may be necessary for the purpose of determining the real question in controversy between the parties shall be made, if duly applied for, and the proceedings shall continue in all respects as if they had been commenced in the form in which they appear after the amendment has been made:

Provided that no person shall be added as a plaintiff without his consent in writing, or in the case of a person under disability without the consent in writing of the next friend or other person acting on behalf of the person under disability.

4. Amendment of particulars, etc.

A plaintiff may file and deliver amended particulars of claim, and a defendant may file and deliver an amended notice of defence or particulars of counter-claim, at any time before the return day without any order, and any party may increase the amount of his claim or counter-claim on payment of the difference between the fees paid and those payable on the larger amount, but the court on the return day for any sufficient cause may disallow the amendment or give effect thereto on such terms as may be just.

ORDER 16
TRANSFER OR PROCEEDINGS

1. Generally.

(1) If the judge or registrar of any court is satisfied that any proceedings in that court can be more conveniently or fairly tried in some other court, he may order them to be transferred to the other court.

(2) Without prejudice to the generality of the last preceding paragraph, where an action has been commenced in a county court against a defendant who does not reside or carry on business within the district of that court, and the defendant desires the action to be transferred to the court for the district in which he resides or carries on business, he may apply *ex parte* in writing without fee to the court in which the action was commenced for an order transferring the action to the other court, and the judge or registrar of the court in which the action was commenced may, if after considering the application and the question whether the claim is disputed he thinks that it would be a hardship on the defendant for the action to proceed in the court in which it was commenced, order the action to be transferred to the other court:

Provided that the judge or registrar may, if he thinks fit, before dealing with the application, cause notice to be given to the plaintiff that the application has been made and of a day and hour when the plaintiff may attend and be heard, and if necessary may adjourn the hearing of the action.

4. Where proceedings commenced in the wrong court.

Where proceedings are commenced in the wrong court the judge or registrar may either—

(*a*) transfer the proceedings to the court in which they ought to have been commenced; or
(*b*) order that the proceedings shall continue in the court in which they were commenced; or
(*c*) order the proceedings to be struck out.

ORDER 20
EVIDENCE

4. Power to order proof by affidavit, &c.

The judge or registrar may at any time order that—

(*a*) any particular fact or facts may be proved by affidavit or

(*b*) the affidavit of any witness may be read at the hearing on such conditions as the judge thinks reasonable; or

(*c*) any witness whose attendance in court ought for some sufficient cause to be dispensed with be examined by interrogatories or before an examiner:

    (i) provided that, where it appears to the judge or registrar that any party *bona fide* desires the production of a witness for cross-examination and that the witness can be produced, an order shall not be made authorising his evidence to be given by affidavit; and

    (ii) Nothing in any order so made shall affect the power of the judge at the hearing to refuse to admit evidence tendered in accordance with any such order if in the interests of justice he should think fit to do so.

5. Use of affidavit without order.

(1) Where a party desires to use at the hearing an affidavit by any witness as to particular facts, as to which no order has been made, he may, not less than 5 clear days before the hearing, give notice, accompanied by a copy of the affidavit, to the party against whom it is to be used, and unless the last mentioned party, not less than 2 clear days before the hearing, gives notice to the other party that he objects to the use of the affidavit, he shall be taken to have consented to the use thereof and the affidavit may be used at the hearing unless the judge otherwise orders.

(2) Where in an ordinary action the defendant has not delivered a defence to the action within the time limited by Order 9, Rule 4(1), evidence by affidavit shall be admissible on behalf of the plaintiff without the notice required by the preceding paragraph of this rule having been given, unless the court otherwise orders.

ORDER 22
REGISTRARS' COURTS

6. Transfer to judge's court.

Where an action has been entered or fixed for hearing at a registrar's court, and

(*a*) the claim exceeds £200 and is disputed; or

(*b*) the claim is disputed and any party objects to the action being heard by the registrar; or

(*c*) an order is made for trial with a jury; or

(*d*) any defendant files a third-party notice or sets up a counterclaim exceeding £200,

the registrar shall unless he is given jurisdiction to hear and determine the action pursuant to sub-paragraph (*b*) of Order 23, rule 1(1) transfer the action to a court to be held by the judge and give notice of the day fixed for the hearing to the parties in Form 71.

ORDER 23
HEARING OF ACTION OR MATTER

1. Hearing by registrar.

The registrar shall have power to hear and determine—

(*a*) by leave of the judge and in the absence of objection by any of the parties, any action or matter in which the sum claimed or the amount involved does not exceed £200 or in which the claim is for the return of goods not exceeding £200 in value or of goods let under a hire-purchase agreement where the unpaid balance of the hire-purchase price does not exceed £200;

(b) by leave of the judge and with the consent of the parties, any other action or matter.

(2) Nothing in this Rule shall prejudice any power conferred by any Act or Rule on the registrar to hear and determine any other action or matter or authorise the registrar to exercise any jurisdiction conferred by any Act or Rule on the judge alone.

2. Where plaintiff does not appear.

(1) If in any action or matter the plaintiff does not appear on the return day, then, except as otherwise provided in this Rule, the proceedings shall be struck out, and where an order for costs is made against the plaintiff, the registrar shall send him a notice in Form 128.

(2) Where any proceedings have been struck out under this Rule, the court may reinstate them for hearing on the same or any subsequent day.

(3) Where the plaintiff does not appear on the return day but the court has received from him an affidavit which is admissible in evidence by virtue of any Act or Rule, the proceedings shall not be struck out but the plaintiff shall be deemed to have appeared on the return day and to have tendered the evidence in the affidavit.

4. Judgment where defendant does not appear.

(1) If the defendant does not appear at the hearing the judge, upon proof of service and of facts entitling the plaintiff to relief, may give such judgment or make such order as may be just:

Provided that an endorsement of service or an affidavit of service may be accepted as proof of service.

(2) The powers conferred upon the judge by paragraph (1) of this rule may with the leave of the judge be exercised by the registrar, whatever may be the cause of action and notwithstanding that the sum claimed or the amount involved exceeds £200.

ORDER 26
SUMMARY PROCEEDINGS FOR THE RECOVERY OF LAND OR RENT

1. Proceedings to be by originating application.

(1) Where a person claims possession of land which he alleges is occupied solely by a person or persons (not being a tenant or tenants holding over after the termination of the tenancy) who entered into or remained in occupation without his licence or consent or that of any predecessor in title of his, the proceedings may be brought by originating application in accordance with the provisions of this Order.

(2) The originating application shall be in Form 398.

(3) Where the applicant does not know the name of every person occupying the land for the purpose of making him a respondent, the conclusion of Form 26 shall be in Form 399 instead of Form 3.

2. Affidavit in support.

The applicant shall file in support of the originating application an affidavit stating—

(*a*) his interest in the land;
(*b*) the circumstances in which the land has been occupied without licence or consent and in which his claim to possession arises; and
(*c*) in a case to which rule 1(3) relates, that he does not know the name of any person occupying the land who is not named in the originating application.

3. Service of originating application.

(1) Where any person in occupation of the land is named in the originating application, the application shall be served on him—

(*a*) by delivering to him personally a copy of the originating application, together with a notice in Form 26 and a copy of the affidavit in support, or
(*b*) by an officer of the court leaving the documents mentioned in sub-paragraph (*a*), or sending them to him, at the premises, or
(*c*) in accordance with Order 8, rule 11, as applied to originating applications by Order 6, rule 4(2), or
(*d*) in such other manner as the court may direct.

(2) In a case to which Rule 1(3) relates, the originating application shall, in addition to being served on the named respondents (if any) in accordance with paragraph (1), be served, unless the court otherwise directs, by—
(*a*) affixing a copy of the originating application to the main door or other conspicuous part of the premises, and
(*b*) if practicable, inserting through the letterbox at the premises a copy of the originating application enclosed in a sealed envelope addressed to "the occupiers."

4. Application by occupier to be made a party.

Without prejudice to Order 15, rule 1, any person not named as a respondent who is in occupation of the land and wishes to be heard on the question whether an order for possession should be made may apply at any stage of the proceedings to be joined as a respondent.

5. Hearing of originating application.

(1) Except in case of urgency and by leave of the court, the day fixed for the hearing of the originating application shall not be less than 5 clear days after the day of service.
(2) Notwithstanding anything in Order 23, rules 4 and 5, no order for possession shall be made on the originating application except by the judge.
(3) An order for possession in proceedings under this Order shall be in Form 400.

6. Warrant of possession.

(1) Subject to paragraph (3), a warrant of possession to enforce an order for possession under this Order may be issued at any time after the making of the order.
(2) The warrant of possession shall be in Form 401.
(3) No warrant of possession shall be issued after the expiry of 3 months from the date of the order without the leave of the court, and an application for such leave may be made *ex parte* unless the court otherwise directs.

7. Setting aside order.

The judge may, on such terms as he thinks just, set aside or vary any order made in proceedings under this Order.

ORDER 37
NEW TRIAL, SETTING ASIDE, AND APPEAL FROM REGISTRAR

1. New trial.

(1) The judge shall in every case have the power to order a new trial to be had upon such terms as he thinks reasonable, and in the meantime to stay the proceedings.

(2) An application for a new trial under this Rule may be made on the day of the trial if both parties are present, or at the first court held next after the expiration of 12 days from the day of trial, or by leave of the judge at any subsequent court.

(3) Except where the application is made on the day of the trial the applicant shall, not less than 6 clear days before the hearing of the application, file in the court office and give to the opposite party notice in writing of the application, stating the grounds thereof.

(4) The notice shall not operate as a stay of proceedings, unless the court otherwise orders.

(5) On receipt of the notice the registrar shall, unless otherwise ordered, retain any money in court until the application has been heard.

(6) A new trial may be ordered on any question without interfering with the finding or decision on any other question.

(7) An order for a new trial shall be in Form 320.

2. Setting aside judgment given in absence of defendant.

(1) Where a defendant to an action or matter or a defendant to a counter-claim does not appear at the hearing and a judgment or order is given or made against him in his absence, the judgment or order and any execution thereon may on application be set aside and a new trial may be granted.

(2) The application may, if the parties are present, be made on the day on which the judgment or order was given or made, and in any other case shall be made on notice.

(3) The application shall be made to the judge if the judgment or order was given or made by the judge and in any other case to the registrar.

3. Setting aside judgment entered in default of defence.

(1) Where in a default action judgment is entered in default of delivery of a defence or counter-claim, and the defendant satisfactorily explains his default and satisfies the court that he has a defence or counter-claim which ought to be heard, the court may, on application made on notice, set aside the judg-ment and execution thereon, or, where only a counter-claim remains to be tried, stay execution on the judgment pending the trial of the counter-claim.

(2) The court may stay execution under the judgment pending the hearing of the application.

4. Non-compliance with Rules.

(1) Where there has been a failure to comply with any requirement of these rules, the failure shall be treated as an irregularity and shall not nullify the proceedings, but the court may set aside the proceedings wholly or in part or exercise its powers under these rules to allow such amendments, if any, and to give such directions, if any, as it thinks fit.

(2) No application to set aside any proceedings for irregularity shall be granted unless made within a reasonable time, nor if the party applying has taken any step in the proceedings after knowledge of the irregularity.

(3) Where any such application is made, the objections intended to be relied upon shall be stated in the notice.

(4) The expression "proceedings" in paragraph (1), and where it first occurs in paragraph (2), includes any step taken in the proceedings and any document, judgment or order therein.

5. Appeal from registrar.

(1) Any party affected by a judgment or final order of the registrar may, except where he has consented to the terms thereof, appeal therefrom to the judge, who may upon such terms as he thinks just—

(a) set aside or vary the judgment or order or any part thereof, or

(b) give any other judgment to make any other order in substitution therefor, or

(c) Remit the action or matter or any question therein to the registrar for re-trial or further consideration, or

(d) order a new trial to take place before himself or another judge of the court on a day to be fixed.

(2) The appeal shall be made on notice stating the grounds of the appeal and the notice shall be served within 6 days of the judgment or order appealed from.

(3) The court may stay execution under the judgment or order pending the hearing of the appeal and may in consequence of any order made on the appeal suspend or set aside any warrant of execution issued in the proceedings.

ORDER 47
COSTS

5. Scales of cost.

(3) The Scale of Costs applicable to a sum of money only shall be as follows:—

Sum of money	*Scale applicable*
Exceeding £5 and not exceeding £50	Lower Scale
Exceeding £50 and not exceeding £200	Scale 1
Exceeding £200 and not exceeding £500	Scale 2
Exceeding £500 and not exceeding £1,000	Scale 3
Exceeding £1,000	Scale 4

(4) Where the sum of money does not exceed £100, no solicitors' charges shall be allowed as between party and party unless—

(a) a certificate is granted under rule 13 of this Order;

(b) the sum exceeds £5, in which case there may be allowed—

   (i) in respect of the charges of the plaintiff's solicitor, the costs stated on the summons;

   (ii) the costs of enforcing any judgment or order;

   (iii) such costs as are certified by the court to have been incurred through the unreasonable conduct of the opposite party in relation to the proceedings or the claim made therein;

(*c*) a claim is made in the proceedings for damages for personal injuries exceeding £5.

6. Recovery of money.

(1) Subject to rules 7, 8, 9 and 13 of this Order, the Scale of costs in an action for the recovery of a sum of money only shall be determined—

(*a*) as regards the costs of the plaintiff, by the amount recovered; and
(*b*) as regards the costs of the defendant, by the amount claimed; and
(*c*) as regards costs payable to a third party, by the amount claimed against him; and
(*d*) as regards costs payable by a third party, by the amount recovered against him.

(2) This rule shall not apply to actions under the equity jurisdiction of the court or to admiralty actions or actions in which the title to hereditaments comes in question.

7. Counterclaim.

(1) Subject to the next succeeding paragraph, rule 6 of this Order shall apply to a counterclaim as it applies to a claim.
(2) Where in one action a claim for a sum of money only and counterclaim for a sum of money only are tried—

(*a*) if the plaintiff is awarded costs on both claim and counterclaim, the costs shall be on the Scale applicable to the amount which he recovers on the claim, but if such amount is less than the counterclaim, the costs subsequent to the filing of the counterclaim shall be on the Scale applicable to the amount of the counterclaim; and
(*b*) if the defendant is awarded costs on both claim and counterclaim, the costs shall be on the Scale applicable to the amount which he recovers on the counterclaim or the amount of the plaintiff's claim, whichever is the larger, but the costs prior to the filing of the counterclaim shall be on the Scale applicable to the amount of the claim:

13. Difficult questions of law or fact.

In any proceedings in which the judge certifies that a difficult question of law or a question of fact of exceptional complexity is involved, he may award costs on such scale as he thinks fit.

16. Discretionary increases.

All charges or disbursements which are discretionary shall, unless otherwise provided, be allowed at the discretion of the registrar, who, in the exercise of such discretion, shall take into consideration the other charges and disbursements to the solicitor and counsel, if any, in respect of the work to which the fee or allowance applies, the nature and importance of the action or matter, the amount involved, the interest of the parties, the general conduct and costs of the proceedings and all other circumstances.

19. Counsel in interlocutory application.

Where costs are on one of the Higher Scales, no fee for counsel shall be allowed on taxation in respect of an interlocutory application, unless the judge or registrar certifies that the application is fit for counsel.

20. Counsel where claim admitted or not disputed.

Unless the judge otherwise orders, no fee for counsel with brief shall be allowed in an action for the recovery of a sum of money only—

   (a) where the defendant has admitted the whole or part of the claim within the time limited by Order 9, rule 1(1)[1] or Order 10, rule 1,[2] and the plaintiff recovers judgment for a sum not exceeding the amount admitted; or
   (b) Where no defence has been delivered and the defendant does not appear at the hearing to resist the claim.

27. Where Counsel disallowed.

Where a party appearing by counsel is awarded costs, but the costs of employing counsel are not allowed, he may be allowed such costs as he might have been allowed if he had appeared by a solicitor and not by counsel.

29. Compensation for loss of time.

(1) Subject to paragraph (2), where on the hearing of an action or matter a party to the proceeding or any other person attends the court as a witness of fact, or as a witness producing a document, there may be allowed in respect of his attendance such sum as the judge or registrar thinks reasonable, not exceeding the sum prescribed in Column 2 of Appendix C[3] for a person of the class to which he belongs:
Provided that the sum allowed shall not, unless the court otherwise orders, exceed the sum prescribed in Column 1 of Appendix C[4] where—

   (a) a witness or party has lost no wages, earnings or other income in attending court; or
   (b) the period during which the witness has been away from home or in respect of which he has lost wages, earnings or other income by reason of his attendance does not exceed 4 hours.

(2) Where the costs are on Scale 2, 3 or 4, the registrar on taxing or fixing and allowing the costs may, if satisfied that the sum specified in Appendix C may be inadequate in the circumstances, allow such larger sum as he thinks reasonable, notwithstanding that, in the case of a sum prescribed in column 1, no order has been made under the proviso to paragraph (1).

30. Expert witnesses.

(1) Where a person attends the court as an expert witness, or attends as a witness of fact and, being called upon to do so, gives in evidence his opinion as an expert, a fee may be allowed in respect of his attendance and in addition, if the judge or registrar thinks fit, a fee for qualifying to give evidence:
Provided that no fee as an expert witness may be allowed in respect of a person attending the court only to prove the correctness of a plan, drawing, chart, photograph or model.

(2) Subject to paragraph (5) the fee for qualifying to give evidence shall be such sum as the registrar thinks reasonable, not being more than £10, and the fee for attending the court shall be such sum as the registrar thinks reasonable, not being more than £20 nor less than the sum appearing in Appendix C as

---

[1] See p. 240, *ante*.
[2] See p. 242, *ante*.
[3] I.e. £7 for police officers and £10 for all other persons.
[4] I.e. £4.

compensation for loss of time for a person of the class to which the expert witness belongs.

(3) The judge or registrar may, if he thinks fit, allow the fee for qualifying to give evidence, notwithstanding that the witness does not attend the trial.

(4) Subject to paragraph (5), where a report in writing has been obtained from an expert witness who is not entitled to a qualifying fee, the registrar may if he thinks such a report was reasonably necessary allow a fee of not exceeding £10, therefor.

(4A) Where the costs of the proceedings are on scale 4, paragraphs (2) and (4) of this rule shall have effect as if for "£10" and "£20", wherever they appear, there were substituted "£20" and "£40" respectively.

(5) If in any particular case—

(a) the judge certifies that the fee for qualifying to give evidence or for a report in writing or for attending court ought not to be limited as aforesaid, or

(b) the costs of the proceedings are on scale 2, 3 or 4 and the registrar considers that any of the fees mentioned in subparagraph (a) ought not to be limited as aforesaid but no certificate has been given under sub-paragraph (a) and no direction has been given by the judge that this sub-paragraph shall not apply.

the fee to be allowed on taxation shall be such larger sum as the registrar thinks fit.

(6) Rule 21(4) of this Order shall apply to an application for a certificate under paragraph (5) of this rule as it applies to an application for a certificate under that rule.

ORDER 48
GENERAL PROVISIONS

10. Computation of time.

(1) Where anything is required by these rules or by any judgment, order or direction to be done within a specified period of or after the happening of a particular event, the period shall be computed from the end of the day on which the event happens unless the period is expressed to be inclusive of such day.

(2) Where anything is required by these rules or by any judgment, order or direction to be done within a period not exceeding 3 days or where a period not exceeding 3 days is required by these rules to elapse between the doing of an act and the happening of a particular event, no Sunday and no day on which the court office is closed shall be included in the computation of that period.

(3) Where the time fixed for doing any act expires on a Sunday or any other day on which the court office is closed and by reason thereof the act cannot be done on that day, the act shall be in time if done on the next day on which the court office is open.

RULES OF THE SUPREME COURT 1965

1. "Month" means calendar month

Without prejudice to section 3 of the Interpretation Act, 1889, in its application to these rules, the word "month," where it occurs in any judgment, order, direction or other document forming part of any proceedings in the Supreme Court, means a calendar month unless the context otherwise requires.

2. Reckoning periods of time.

(1) Any period of time fixed by these rules or by any judgment, order or direction for doing any act shall be reckoned in accordance with the following provisions of this rule.

(2) Where the act is required to be done within a specified period after or from a specified date, the period begins immediately after that date.

(3) Where the act is required to be done within or not less than a specified period before a specified date, the period ends immediately before that date.

(4) Where the act is required to be done a specified number of clear days before or after a specified date, at least that number of days must intervene between the day on which the act is done and that date.

(5) Where, apart from this paragraph, the period in question, being a period of 7 days or less, would include a Saturday, Sunday or bank holiday, Christmas Day or Good Friday, that day shall be excluded.

In this paragraph "bank holiday" means a day which is, or is to be observed as, a bank holiday, or a holiday, under the Bank Holidays Act, 1871, or the Holidays Extension Act, 1875, in England and Wales.

3. Long Vacation excluded from time for service, etc. of pleadings

Unless the Court otherwise directs, the period of the Long Vacation shall be excluded in reckoning any period prescribed by these rules or by any order or direction for serving, filing or amending any pleading.

4. Time expires on Sunday, etc.

Where the time prescribed by these rules, or by any judgment, order or direction, for doing any act at an office of the Supreme Court expires on a Sunday or other day on which that office is closed, and by reason thereof that act cannot be done on that day, the act shall be in time if done on the next day on which that office is open.

5. Extension, etc. of time.

(1) The Court may, on such terms as it thinks just, by order extend or abridge the period within which a person is required or authorised by these rules, or by any judgment, order or direction, to do any act in any proceedings.

(2) The Court may extend any such period as is referred to in paragraph

(1) although the application for extension is not made until after the expiration of that period.

(3) The period within which a person is required by these rules, or by any order or direction, to serve, file or amend any pleading or other document may be extended by consent (given in writing) without an order of the Court being made for that purpose.

(4) In this rule references to the Court shall be construed as including references to the Court of Appeal.

6. Notice of intention to proceed after year's delay

Where a year or more has elapsed since the last proceeding in a cause or matter, the party who desires to proceed must give to every other party not less than one month's notice of his intention to proceed.

A summons on which no order was made is not a proceeding for the purpose of this rule.

ORDER 10

SERVICE OR ORIGINATING PROCESS: GENERAL PROVISIONS

1. General provisions.

(1) Subject to the provisions of any Act and these rules, a writ must be served personally on each defendant by the plaintiff or his agent.

(2) Where a defendant's solicitor indorses on the writ a statement that he accepts service of the writ on behalf of that defendant, the writ shall be deemed to have been duly served on that defendant and to have been so served on the date on which the indorsement was made.

(3) Where a writ is not duly served on a defendant but he enters an unconditional appearance in the action begun by the writ, the writ shall be deemed to have been duly served on him and to have been so served on the date on which he entered the appearance.

(4) Where a writ is duly served on a defendant otherwise than by virtue of paragraph (2) or (3), then, subject to Order 11, rule 5,[1] unless within three days after service the person serving it indorses on it the following particulars, that is to say, the day of the week and date on which it was served, where it was served, the person on whom it was served, and, where he is not the defendant, the capacity in which he was served, the plaintiff in the action begun by the writ shall not be entitled to enter final or interlocutory judgment against that defendant in default of appearance or in default of defence.

ORDER 12

ENTRY OF APPEARANCE TO WRIT OR ORIGINATING SUMMONS

1. Mode of entering appearance

(1) Subject to paragraph (2) and to Order 80, rule 2,[2] a defendant to an action begun by writ may (whether or not he is sued as a trustee or personal representative or in any other representative capacity) enter an appearance in the action and defend it by a solicitor or in person.

(2) Except as expressly provided by any enactment, a defendant to such an action who is a body corporate may not enter an appearance in the action or defend it otherwise than by a solicitor.

(3) An appearance is entered by properly completing the requisite documents, that is to say, a memorandum of appearance, as defined by rule 3, and a

---

[1] Which deals with service abroad.
[2] Which deals with service on infants and mental patients.

copy thereof, and handing them in at, or sending them by post to, the appropriate office.

(4) If two or more defendants to an action enter an appearance by the same solicitor and at the same time, only one set of the requisite documents need be completed and delivered for those defendants.

2. Place for entering appearance

(1) Where a writ is issued out of the Central Office, the appropriate office for entering an appearance is in all cases the Central Office.

(2) Where a writ is issued out of a District Registry, and there is indorsed on the writ a statement that any cause of action in respect of which relief is claimed by the writ wholly or in part arose in a place in the district of that Registry, the appropriate office for entering an appearance is in all cases the District Registry.

(3) Where a writ is issued out of a District Registry, the appropriate office for the entry of appearance by a defendant who is an individual residing or carrying on business, or a body corporate having a registered office or carrying on business, in the district of that Registry is the District Registry.

(4) Except as provided by paragraphs (2 and (3), the appropriate office for entering an appearance in an action begun by a writ issued out of a District Registry is the Central Office or the District Registry at the defendant's option.

(5) Where a writ is issued out of a District Registry, a memorandum of appearance for a particular defendant shall not be accepted by the Central Office unless it states—

(a) where the defendant is an individual, that he does not reside or carry on business in the district of that Registry;

(b) where the defendant is a body corporate, that it does not have a registered office or carry on business in that district; and

(c) in either case, that the writ is not indorsed with a statement that a cause of action in respect of which relief is claimed by the writ wholly or in part arose in a place in that district.

5. Time limited for appearing

References in these rules to the time limited for appearing are references—

(a) in the case of a writ served within the jurisdiction, to 14 days after service of the writ (including the day of service) or, where that time has been extended by or by virtue of these rules, to that time as so extended; and

(b) in the case of a writ, or notice of a writ, served out of the jurisdiction, to the time limited under Order 10, rule 2(2), Order 11, rule 1(3), or Order 11, rule 4(4),[1] or, where that time has been extended as aforesaid, to that time as so extended.

6. Late appearance

(1) A defendant may not enter an appearance in an action after judgment has been entered therein except with the leave of the Court.

(2) Except as provided by paragraph (1), nothing in these rules or any writ or order thereunder shall be construed as precluding a defendant from entering an appearance in an action after the time limited for appearing, but if a defendant enters an appearance after that time, he shall not, unless the Court otherwise orders, be entitled to serve a defence or do any other thing later than if he had appeared within that time.

---

[1] I.e. for service on agent of an overseas principal and for service of the writ or notice of the writ out of the jurisdiction.

7. Conditional appearance

(1) A defendant to an action may with the leave of the Court enter a conditional appearance in the action.

(2) A conditional appearance, except by a person sued as a partner of a firm in the name of that firm and served as a partner, is to be treated for all purposes as an unconditional appearance unless the Court otherwise orders or the defendant applies to the Court, within the time limited for the purpose, for an order under Rule 8[1] and the Court makes an order thereunder.

ORDER 13

DEFAULT OF APPEARANCE TO WRIT

1. Claim for liquidated demand

(1) Where a writ is indorsed with a claim against a defendant for a liquidated demand only, then, if that defendant fails to enter an appearance, the plaintiff may, after the time limited for appearing, enter final judgment against that defendant for a sum not exceeding that claimed by the writ in respect of the demand and for costs, and proceed with the action against the other defendants, if any.

(2) A claim shall not be prevented from being treated for the purposes of this rule as a claim for a liquidated demand by reason only that part of the claim is for interest accruing after the date of the writ at an unspecified rate, but any such interest shall be computed from the date of the writ to the date of entering judgment at the rate of 5 per cent.

2. Claim for unliquidated damages

Where a writ is indorsed with a claim against a defendant for unliquidated damages only, then, if that defendant fails to enter an appearance, the plaintiff may, after the time limited for appearing, enter interlocutory judgment against that defendant for damages to be assessed and costs, and proceed with the action against the other defendants, if any.

3. Claim in detinue.

Where a writ is indorsed with a claim against a defendant relating to the detention of goods only, then, if that defendant fails to enter an appearance, the plaintiff may, after the time limited for appearing, at his option enter either—

(a) interlocutory judgment against that defendant for the delivery of the goods or their value to be assessed and costs; or

(b) interlocutory judgment for the value of the goods to be assessed and costs,

and proceed with the action against the other defendants, if any.

7.. Proof of service of writ.

(1) Judgment shall not be entered against a defendant under this Order unless—

(a) an affidavit is filed by or on behalf of the plaintiff proving due service of the writ or notice of the writ on the defendant; or

(b) the plaintiff produces the writ indorsed by the defendant's solicitor

---

[1] I.e. to set aside the writ or service of the writ or notice.

with a statement that he accepts service of the writ on the defendant's behalf.

(2) Where, in an action begun by writ, an application is made to the Court for an order affecting a party who has failed to enter an appearance, the Court hearing the application may require to be satisfied in such manner as it thinks fit that the party is in default of appearance.

8. Action in district registry: time for entering judgment.

Where by virtue of Order 12, rule 2(4), a defendant may, at his option, enter an appearance in the Central Office or a District Registry, judgment shall not be entered under this Order against that defendant until after such time as a letter addressed to the plaintiff would, in the ordinary course of post, have been delivered to him if it had been posted in London early enough on the day on which the time limited for appearing expires for delivery to him on the following morning.

9. Setting aside judgment.

The Court may, on such terms as it thinks just, set aside or vary any judgment entered in pursuance of this Order.

ORDER 14

SUMMARY JUDGMENT

1. Application by plaintiff for summary judgment.

(1) Where in an action to which this rule applies a statement of claim has been served on a defendant and that defendant has entered an appearance in the action, the plaintiff may, on the ground that that defendant has no defence to a claim included in the writ, or to a particular part of such a claim, or has no defence to such a claim or part except as to the amount of any damages claimed, apply to the Court for judgment against that defendant.

(2) Subject to paragraph (3), this rule applies to every action in the Queen's Bench Division (including the Admiralty Court) or Chancery Division begun by writ other than one which includes—

(*a*) a claim by the plaintiff for libel, slander, malicious prosecution, false imprisonment, seduction or breach of promise of marriage, or

(*b*) a claim by the plaintiff based on an allegation of fraud.

(*c*) An Admiralty action *in rem*.

(3) This Order shall not apply to an action to which Order 86 applies.

2. Manner in which application under rule 1 must be made

(1) An application under rule 1 must be made by summons supported by an affidavit verifying the facts on which the claim, or the part of a claim, to which the application relates is based and stating that in the deponent's belief there is no defence to that claim or part, as the case may be, or no defence except as to the amount of any damages claimed.

(2) Unless the Court otherwise directs, an affidavit for the purposes of this rule may contain statements of information or belief with the sources and grounds thereof.

(3) The summons, a copy of the affidavit in support and of any exhibits referred to therein must be served on the defendant not less than 10 clear days before the return day.

3. Judgment for plaintiff.

(1) Unless on the hearing of an application under rule 1 either the Court dismisses the application or the defendant satisfies the Court with respect to the claim, or the part of a claim, to which the application relates that there is an issue or question in dispute which ought to be tried or that there ought for some other reason to be a trial of that claim or part, the Court may give such judgment for the plaintiff against that defendant on that claim or part as may be just having regard to the nature of the remedy or relief claimed.

(2) The Court may by order, and subject to such conditions, if any, as may be just, stay execution of any judgment given against a defendant under this rule until after the trial of any counterclaim made or raised by the defendant in the action.

4. Leave to defend.

(1) A defendant may show cause against an application under rule 1 by affidavit or otherwise to the satisfaction of the Court.

(2) Rule 2(2) applies for the purposes of this rule as it applies for the purposes of that rule.

(3) The Court may give a defendant against whom such an application is made leave to defend the action with respect to the claim, or the part of a claim, to which the application relates either unconditionally or on such terms as to giving security or time or mode of trial or otherwise as it thinks fit.

(4) On the hearing of such an application the Court may order a defendant showing cause or, where that defendant is a body corporate, any director, manager, secretary or other similar officer thereof, or any person purporting to act in any such capacity—

(a) to produce any document;
(b) if it appears to the Court that there are special circumstances which make it desirable that he should do so, to attend and be examined on oath.

7. Costs.

(1) If the plaintiff makes an application under rule 1 where the case is not within this Order or if it appears to the Court that the plaintiff knew that the defendant relied on a contention which would entitle him to unconditional leave to defend, then, without prejudice to Order 62, and, in particular, to rule 4(1) thereof, the Court may dismiss the application with costs and may, if the plaintiff is not an assisted person, require the costs to be paid by him forthwith.

10. Relief against forfeiture.

A tenant shall have the same right to apply for relief after judgment for possession of land on the ground of forfeiture for non-payment of rent has been given under this Order as if the judgment had been given after trial.

11. Setting aside judgment.

Any judgment given against a party who does not appear at the hearing of an application under rule 1 or rule 5 may be set aside or varied by the Court on such terms as it thinks just.

4. Joinder of parties.

(1) Subject to rule 5(1), two or more persons may be joined together in one action as plaintiffs or as defendants with the leave of the Court or where—

(a) if separate actions were brought by or against each of them, as the case may be, some common question of law or fact would arise in all the actions, and

(b) all rights to relief claimed in the action (whether they are joint, several or alternative) are in respect of or arise out of the same transaction or series of transactions.

(2) Where the plaintiff in any action claims any relief to which any other person is entitled jointly with him, all persons so entitled must, subject to the provisions of any Act and unless the Court gives leave to the contrary, be parties to the action and any of them who does not consent to being joined as a plaintiff must, subject to any order made by the Court on an application for leave under this paragraph, be made a defendant.

This paragraph shall not apply to a probate action.

(3) Where relief is claimed in an action against a defendant who is jointly liable with some other person and also severally liable, that other person need not be made a defendant to the action; but where persons are jointly, but not severally, liable under a contract and relief is claimed against some but not all of those persons in an action in respect of that contract, the Court may, on the application of any defendant to the action, by order stay proceedings in the action until the other persons so liable are added as defendants.

6. Misjoinder and nonjoinder of parties.

(1) No cause or matter shall be defeated by reason of the misjoinder or nonjoinder of any party; and the Court may in any cause or matter determine the issue or questions in dispute so far as they affect the rights and interest of the persons who are parties to the cause or matter.

(2) At any stage of the proceedings in any cause or matter the Court may on such terms as it thinks just and either of its own motion or on application—

(a) order any person who has been improperly or unnecessarily made a party or who has for any reason ceased to be a proper or necessary party, to cease to be a party;

(b) order any of the following persons to be added as a party, namely—

(i) any person who ought to have been joined as a party or whose presence before the Court is necessary to ensure that all matters in dispute in the case or matter may be effectually and completely determined and adjudicated upon, or

(ii) any person between whom and any party to the cause or matter there may exist a question or issue arising out of or relating to or connected with any relief or remedy claimed in the cause or matter which in the opinion of the Court it would be just and convenient to determine as between him and that party as well as between the parties to the cause or matter;

but no person shall be added as a plaintiff without his consent signified in writing or in such other manner as may be authorised.

(3) An application by any person for an order under paragraph (2) adding him as a party must, except with the leave of the Court, be supported by an affidavit showing his interest in the matters in dispute in the cause or matter

or, as the case may be, the question or issue to be determined as between him and any party to the cause or matter.

12. Representative proceedings.

(1) Where numerous persons have the same interest in any proceedings, not being such proceedings as are mentioned in rule 13, the proceedings may be begun, and, unless the Court otherwise orders, continued, by or against any one or more of them as representing all or as representing all except one or more of them.

(2) At any stage of proceedings under this rule the Court may, on the application of the plaintiff, and on such terms, if any, as it thinks fit, appoint any one or more of the defendants or other persons as representing whom the defendants are sued to represent all, or all except one or more, of those persons in the proceedings; and where, in exercise of the power conferred by this paragraph, the Court appoints a person not named as a defendant, it shall make an order under rule 6 adding that person as a defendant.

(3) A judgment or order given in proceedings under this rule shall be binding on all the persons as representing whom the plaintiffs sue or, as the case may be, the defendants are sued, but shall not be enforced against any person not a party to the proceedings except with the leave of the Court.

(4) An application for the grant of leave under paragraph (3) must be made by summons which must be served personally on the person against whom it is sought to enforce the judgment or order.

(5) Notwithstanding that a judgment or order to which any such application relates is binding on the person against whom the application is made, that person may dispute liability to have the judgment or order enforced against him on the ground that by reason of facts and matters particular to his case he is entitled to be exempted from such liability.

(6) The Court hearing an application for the grant of leave under paragraph (3) may order the question whether the judgment or order is enforceable against the person against whom the application is made to be tried and determined in any manner in which any issue or question in an action may be tried and determined.

13. Representation of interested persons who cannot be ascertained, etc.

(1) In any proceedings concerning—

(a) the administration of the estate of a deceased person, or
(b) property subject to a trust, or
(c) the construction of a written instrument, including a statute,

the Court, if satisfied that it is expedient so to do, and that one or more of the conditions specified in paragraph (2) are satisfied, may appoint one or more persons to represent any person (including an unborn person) or class who is or may be interested (whether presently or for any future, contingent or unascertained interest) in or affected by the proceedings.

(2) The conditions for the exercise of the power conferred by paragraph (1) are as follows:—

(a) that the person, the class or some member of the class, cannot be ascertained or cannot readily be ascertained;
(b) that the person, class or some member of the class, though ascertained, cannot be found;
(c) that, though the person or the class and the members thereof can be ascertained and found, it appears to the Court expedient (regard being

had to all the circumstances, including the amount at stake and the degree of difficulty of the point to be determined) to exercise the power for the purpose of saving expense.

(3) Where in any proceedings to which paragraph (1) applies, the Court exercises the power conferred by that paragraph, a judgment or order of the Court given or made when the person or persons appointed in exercise of that power are before the Court shall be binding on the person or class represented by the person or persons so appointed.

(4) Where, in any such proceedings, a compromise is proposed and some of the persons who are interested in, or who may be affected by, the compromise are not parties to the proceedings (including unborn or unascertained persons) but—

(a) there is some other person in the same interest before the Court who assents to the compromise or on whose behalf the Court sanctions the compromise, or

(b) the absent persons are represented by a person appointed under paragraph (1) who so assents,

the Court, if satisfied that the compromise will be for the benefit of the absent persons and that it is expedient to exercise this power, may approve the compromise and order that it shall be binding on the absent persons, and they shall be bound accordingly except where the order has been obtained by fraud or non-disclosure of material facts.

14. **Representation of beneficiaries by trustees, etc.**

(1) Any proceedings, including proceedings to enforce a security by foreclosure or otherwise, may be brought by or against trustees, executors or administrators in their capacity as such without joining any of the persons having a beneficial interest in the trust or estate, as the case may be; and any judgment or order given or made in those proceedings shall be binding on those persons unless the Court in the same or other proceedings otherwise orders on the ground that the trustees, executors or administrators, as the case may be, could not or did not in fact represent the interests of those persons in the first-mentioned proceedings.

(2) Paragraph (1) is without prejudice to the power of the Court to order any person having such an interest as aforesaid to be made a party to the proceedings or to make an order under rule 13.

ORDER 16

THIRD PARTY AND SIMILAR PROCEEDINGS

1. **Third party notice.**

(1) Where in any action a defendant who has entered an appearance—

(a) claims against a person not already a party to the action any contribution or indemnity; or

(b) claims against such a person any relief or remedy relating to or connected with the original subject-matter of the action and substantially the same as some relief or remedy claimed by the plaintiff; or

(c) requires that any question or issue relating to or connected with the original subject-matter of the action should be determined not only as between the plaintiff and the defendant but also as between either or both of them and a person not already a party to the action;

then, subject to paragraph (2), the defendant may issue a notice in Form No. 20 or 21 in Appendix A, whichever is appropriate (in this Order referred to as a third party notice), containing a statement of the nature of the claim made against him and, as the case may be, either of the nature and grounds of the claim made by him or of the question or issue required to be determined.

(2) A defendant to an action may not issue a third party notice without the leave of the Court unless the action was begun by writ and he issues the notice before serving his defence on the plaintiff.

(3) Where a third party notice is served on the person against whom it is issued, he shall as from the time of service be a party to the action (in this Order referred to as a third party) with the same rights in respect of his defence against any claim made against him in the notice and otherwise as if he had been duly sued in the ordinary way by the defendant by whom the notice is issued.

2. Application for leave to issue third party notice.

(1) Application for leave to issue a third party notice may be made *ex parte* but the Court may direct a summons for leave to be issued.

(2) An application for leave to issue a third party notice must be supported by an affidavit stating—

(*a*) the nature of the claim made by the plaintiff in the action;

(*b*) the stage which proceedings in the action have reached;

(*c*) the nature of the claim made by the applicant or particulars of the question or issue required to be determined, as the case may be, and the facts on which the proposed third party notice is based; and

(*d*) the name and address of the person against whom the third party notice is to be issued.

4. Third party directions.

(1) If the third party enters an appearance, the defendant who issued the third party notice must, by summons to be served on all the other parties to the action, apply to the Court for directions.

(2) If no summons is served on the third party under paragraph (1), the third party may, not earlier than 7 days after entering an appearance, by summons to be served on all the other parties to the action, apply to the Court for directions or for an order to set aside the third party notice.

(3) On an application for directions under this rule the Court may—

(*a*) if the liability of the third party to the defendant who issued the third party notice is established on the hearing, order such judgment as the nature of the case may require to be entered against the third party in favour of the defendant; or

(*b*) order any claim, question or issue stated in the third party notice to be tried in such manner as the Court may direct; or

(*c*) dismiss the application and terminate the proceedings on the third party notice;

and may do so either before or after any judgment in the action has been signed by the plaintiff against the defendant.

(4) On an application for directions under this rule the Court may give the third party leave to defend the action, either alone or jointly with any defendant, upon such terms as may be just, or to appear at the trial and to take such part therein as may be just, and generally may make such orders and give such directions as appear to the Court proper for having the rights and liabilities of the parties most conveniently determined and enforced and as to

the extent to which the third party is to be bound by any judgment or decision in the action.

(5) Any order made or direction given under this rule may be varied or rescinded by the Court at any time.

5. Default of third party, etc.

(1) If a third party does not enter an appearance or, having been ordered to serve a defence, fails to do so—

    (a) he shall be deemed to admit any claim stated in the third party notice and shall be bound by any judgment (including judgment by consent) or decision in the action in so far as it is relevant to any claim, question or issue stated in that notice; and

    (b) the defendant by whom the third party notice was issued may, if judgment in default is given against him in the action, at any time after satisfaction of that judgment and, with the leave of the Court, before satisfaction thereof, enter judgment against the third party in respect of any contribution or indemnity claimed in the notice, and, with the leave of the Court, in respect of any other relief or remedy claimed therein.

ORDER 18

PLEADINGS

12. Particulars of pleading.

(1) Subject to paragraph (2), every pleading must contain the necessary particulars of any claim, defence or other matter pleaded including, without prejudice to the generality of the foregoing words—

    (a) particulars of any misrepresentation, fraud, breach of trust, wilful default or undue influence on which the party pleading relies; and

    (b) where a party pleading alleges any condition of the mind of any person, whether any disorder or disability of mind or any malice, fraudulent intention or other condition of mind except knowledge, particulars of the facts on which the party relies.

(2) Where it is necessary to give particulars of debt, expenses or damages and those particulars exceed 3 folios, they must be set out in a separate document referred to in the pleading and the pleading must state whether the document has already been served and, if so, when, or is to be served with the pleading.

(3) The Court may order a party to serve on any other party particulars of any claim, defence or other matter stated in his pleading, or in any affidavit of his ordered to stand as a pleading, or a statement of the nature of the case on which he relies, and the order may be made on such terms as the Court thinks just.

(4) Where a party alleges as a fact that a person had knowledge or notice of some fact, matter or thing, then, without prejudice to the generality of paragraph (3), the Court may, on such terms as it thinks just, order that party to serve on any other party—

    (a) where he alleges knowledge, particulars of the facts on which he relies, and

    (b) where he alleges notice, particulars of the notice.

(5) An order under this rule shall not be made before service of the defence unless, in the opinion of the Court, the order is necessary or desirable to enable the defendant to plead or for some other special reason.

(6) Where the applicant for an order under this rule did not apply by letter for the particulars he requires, the Court may refuse to make the order unless

of opinion that there were sufficient reasons for an application by letter not having been made.

13. Admissions and denials.

(1) Subject to paragraph (4), any allegation of fact made by a party in his pleading is deemed to be admitted by the opposite party unless it is traversed by that party in his pleading or a joinder of issue under rule 14[1] operates as a denial of it.

(2) A traverse may be made either by a denial or by a statement of non-admission and either expressly or by necessary implication.

(3) Subject to paragraph (4), every allegation of fact made in a statement of claim or counterclaim which the party on whom it is served does not intend to admit must be specifically traversed by him in his defence or defence to counterclaim, as the case may be; and a general denial of such allegations, or a general statement of non-admission of them, is not a sufficient traverse of them.

(4) Any allegation that a party has suffered damage and any allegation as to the amount of damages is deemed to be traversed unless specifically admitted.

19. Striking out pleadings and indorsements.

(1) The Court may at any stage of the proceedings order to be struck out or amended any pleading or the indorsement of any writ in the action, or anything in any pleading or in the indorsement, on the ground that—

(a) it discloses no reasonable cause of action or defence, as the case may be; or
(b) it is scandalous, frivolous or vexatious; or
(c) it may prejudice, embarrass or delay the fair trial of the action; or
(d) it is otherwise an abuse of the process of the court;

and may order the action to be stayed or dismissed or judgment to be entered accordingly, as the case may be.

(2) No evidence shall be admissible on an application under paragraph (1)(a).

(3) This rule shall, so far as applicable, apply to an originating summons and a petition as if the summons or petition, as the case may be, were a pleading.

ORDER 20

AMENDMENT

3. Amendment of pleadings without leave.

(1) A party may, without the leave of the Court, amend any pleading of his once at any time before the pleadings are deemed to be closed and, where he does so, he must serve the amended pleading on the opposite party.

5. Amendment of writ or pleading with leave.

(1) Subject to Order 15, rules 6, 7 and 8[2] and the following provisions of this rule, the Court may at any stage of the proceedings allow the plaintiff to amend his writ, or any party to amend his pleading, on such terms as to costs or otherwise as may be just and in such manner (if any) as it may direct.

(2) Where an application to the Court for leave to make the amendment

---

[1] R.S.C. Ord. 18, r. 4, provides that if there is no reply served to a defence there is an implied joinder of issue.
[2] Which deal with the misjoinder and nonjoinder of parties and change of parties by reason of death.

mentioned in paragraph (3), (4) or (5) is made after any relevant period of limitation current at the date of issue of the writ has expired, the Court may nevertheless grant such leave in the circumstances mentioned in that paragraph if it thinks it just to do so.

(3) An amendment to correct the name of a party may be allowed under paragraph (2) notwithstanding that it is alleged that the effect of the amendment will be to substitute a new party if the Court is satisfied that the mistake sought to be corrected was a genuine mistake and was not misleading or such as to cause any reasonable doubt as to the identity of the person intending to sue or, as the case may be, intended to be sued.

(4) An amendment to alter the capacity in which a party sues (whether as plaintiff or as defendant by counterclaim) may be allowed under paragraph (2) if the capacity in which, if the amendment is made, the party will sue is one in which at the date of issue of the writ or the making of the counter-claim, as the case may be, he might have sued.

(5) An amendment may be allowed under paragraph (2) notwithstanding that the effect of the amendment will be to add or substitute a new cause of action if the new cause of action arises out of the same facts or substantially the same facts as a cause of action in respect of which relief has already been claimed in the action by the party applying for leave to make the amendment.

ORDER 29

INTERLOCUTORY INJUNCTIONS, INTERIM PRESERVATION OF PROPERTY, ETC.

1. Application for injunction.

(1) An application for the grant of an injunction may be made by any party to a cause or matter before or after the trial of the cause or matter, whether or not a claim for the injunction was included in that party's writ, originating summons, counterclaim or third party notice, as the case may be.

(2) Where the applicant is the plaintiff and the case is one of urgency such application may be made *ex parte* on affidavit but, except as aforesaid, such application must be made by motion or summons.

(3) The plaintiff may not make such an application before the issue of the writ or originating summons by which the cause or matter is to be begun except where the case is one of urgency, and in that case the injunction applied for may be granted on terms providing for the issue of the writ or summons and such other terms, if any, as the Court thinks fit.

2. Detention, preservation, etc. of subject-matter of cause or matter.

(1) On the application of any party to a cause or matter the Court may make an order for the detention, custody or preservation of any property which is the subject-matter of the cause or matter, or as to which any question may arise therein, or for the inspection of any such property in the possession of a party to the cause or matter.

(2) For the purpose of enabling any order under paragraph (1) to be carried out the Court may by the order authorise any person to enter upon any land or building in the possession of any party to the cause or matter.

(3) Where the right of any party to a specific fund is in dispute in a cause or matter, the Court may, on the application of a party to the cause or matter, order the fund to be paid into court or otherwise secured.

(4) An order under this rule may be made on such terms, if any, as the Court thinks just.

(5) An application for an order under this rule must be made by summons or by notice under Order 25, rule 7[1].

(6) Unless the Court otherwise directs, an application by a defendant for such an order may not be made before he enters an appearance.

---

[1] I.e. on the summons for directions.

3. **Power to order samples to be taken, etc.**

(1) Where it considers it necessary or expedient for the purpose of obtaining full information or evidence in any cause or matter, the Court may, on the application of a party to the cause or matter, and on such terms, if any, as it thinks just, by order authorise or require any sample to be taken of any property which is the subject-matter of the cause or matter or as to which any question may arise therein, any observation to be made on such property or any experiment to be tried on or with such property.

(2) For the purpose of enabling any order under paragraph (1) to be carried out the Court may be the order authorise any person to enter upon any land or building in the possession of any party to the cause or matter.

(3) Rule 2(5) and (6) shall apply in relation to an application for an order under this rule as they apply in relation to an application for an order under that rule.

ORDER 32
APPLICATIONS AND PROCEEDINGS IN CHAMBERS

1. **Mode of making application.**

Except as provided by Order 25, rule 7,[1] every application in chambers not made *ex parte* must be made by summons.

2. **Issue of summons.**

(1) Issue of a summons by which an application in chambers is to be made takes place on its being sealed by an officer of the appropriate office.

(2) A summons may not be amended after issue without the leave of the Court.

(3) In this rule "the appropriate office" means—

(*a*) in relation to a summons in a cause or matter proceeding in a district registry, that registry;

(*b*) in relation to a cause or matter in the Chancery Division which is not proceeding in a district registry, the judge's chambers;

(*c*) in relation to a summons in a cause or matter proceeding in the principal registry of the Family Division, that registry;

(*d*) in relation to a summons in an Admiralty cause or matter which is not proceedings in a district registry, the Admiralty Registry;

(*e*) in relation to a summons in any other cause or matter, the Central Office.

For the purposes of this paragraph, a cause or matter in which any jurisdiction is to be exercised by virtue of Order 34, rule 5(4),[2] by a master or by the registrar of a district registry shall be treated, in relation to that jurisdiction, as proceeding in the Central office or in that district registry respectively.

3. **Service of summons.**

A summons asking only for the extension or abridgment of any period of time may be served on the day before the day specified in the summons for the hearing thereof but, except as aforesaid and unless the Court otherwise orders or any of these rules otherwise provides, a summons must be served on every other party not less than two clear days before the day so specified.

---

[1] I.e. which provides that so far as is practicable all interlocutory applications are to be dealt with on the summons for directions.

[2] This deals with the position where the trial is not held at the district registry where the action was proceeding or where an action originally proceeding in London is set down out of London.

4. Adjournment of hearing.

(1) The hearing of a summons may be adjourned from time to time, either generally or to a particular date, as may be appropriate.

(2) If the hearing is adjourned generally, the party by whom the summons was taken out may restore it to the list on 2 clear days' notice to all the other parties on whom the summons was served.

5. Proceeding in absence of party failing to attend.

(1) Where any party to a summons fails to attend on the first or any resumed hearing thereof, the Court may proceed in his absence if, having regard to the nature of the application, it thinks it expedient so to do.

(2) Before proceeding in the absence of any party the Court may require to be satisfied that the summons or, as the case may be, notice of the time appointed for the resumed hearing was duly served on that party.

(3) Where the Court hearing a summons proceeded in the absence of a party, then, provided that any order made on the hearing has not been perfected, the Court, if satisfied that it is just to do so, may re-hear the summons.

(4) Where an application made by summons has been dismissed without a hearing by reason of the failure of the party who took out the summons to attend the hearing, the Court, if satisfied that it is just to do so, may allow the summons to be restored to the list.

6. Order made "ex parte" may be set aside.

The Court may set aside an order made *ex parte*.

ORDER 38
EVIDENCE

21. Notice of intention to give certain statements in evidence.

(1) Subject to the provisions of this rule, a party to a cause or matter who desires to give in evidence at the trial or hearing of the cause or matter any statement which is admissible in evidence by virtue of section 2, 4 or 5 of the Act must—

> (a) in the case of a cause or matter which is required to be set down for trial or hearing or adjourned into court, within 21 days after it is set down or so adjourned, or within such other period as the Court may specify, and
>
> (b) in the case of any other cause or matter, within 21 days after the date on which an appointment for the first hearing of the cause or matter is obtained, or within such other period as the Court may specify,

serve on every other party to the cause or matter notice of his desire to do so, and the notice must comply with the provisions of rule 22, 23 or 24, as the circumstances of the case require.

22. Statement admissible by virtue of section 2 of the Act: contents of notice.

(1) If the statement is admissible by virtue of section 2 of the Act and was made otherwise than in a document, the notice must contain particulars of—

(*a*) the time, place and circumstances at or in which the statement was made;

(*b*) the person by whom, and the person to whom, the statement was made; and

(*c*) the substance of the statement or, if material, the words used.

(2) If the statement is admissible by virtue of the said section 2 and was made in a document, a copy or transcript of the document, or of the relevant part thereof, must be annexed to the notice and the notice must contain such (if any) of the particulars mentioned in paragraph (1)(*a*) and (*b*) as are not apparent on the face of the document or part.

(3) If the party giving the notice alleges that any person, particulars of whom are contained in the notice, cannot or should not be called as a witness at the trial or hearing for any of the reasons specified in rule 25, the notice must contain a statement to that effect specifying the reason relied on.

25. Reasons for not calling a person as a witness.

The reasons referred to in rule 22(3) are that the person in question is dead, or beyond the seas or unfit by reason of his bodily or mental condition to attend as a witness or that despite the exercise of reasonable diligence it has not been possible to identify or find him or that he cannot reasonably be expected to have any recollection of matters relevant to the accuracy or otherwise of the statement to which the notice relates.

26. Counter-notice requiring person to be called as a witness.

(1) Subject to paragraphs (2) and (3), any party to a cause or matter on whom a notice under rule 21 is served may within 21 days after service of the notice on him serve on the party who gave the notice or a counter-notice requiring that party to call as a witness at the trial or hearing of the cause or matter any person (naming him) particulars of whom are contained in the notice.

(2) Where any notice under rule 21 contains a statement that any person particulars of whom are contained in the notice cannot or should not be called as a witness for the reason specified therein, a party shall not be entitled to serve a counter-notice under this rule requiring that person to be called as a witness at the trial or hearing of the cause or matter unless he contends that that person can or, as the case may be, should be called, and in that case he must include in his counter-notice a statement to that effect.

(3) Where a statement to which a notice under rule 21 relates is one to which rule 28[1] applies, no party on whom the notice is served shall be entitled to serve a counter-notice under this rule in relation to that statement, but the foregoing provision is without prejudice to the right of any party to apply to the Court under rule 28 for directions with respect to the admissibility of that statement.

(4) If any party to a cause or matter by whom a notice under rule 21 is served fails to comply with a counter-notice duly served on him under this rule, then, unless any of the reasons specified in rule 25 applies in relation to the person named in the counter-notice, and without prejudice to the powers of the Court under rule 29,[2] the statement to which the notice under rule 21 relates shall not be admissible at the trial or hearing of the cause or matter as evidence of any fact stated therein by virtue of section 2, 4 or 5 of the Act, as the case may be.

---

[1] This deals with settlements made in previous proceedings.

[2] Which provides a general discretion to admit statements notwithstanding that the rules have not been satisfied.

27. Determination of question whether person can or should be called as a witness.

(1) Where in any cause or matter a question arises whether any of the reasons specified in rule 25 applies in relation to a person particulars of whom are contained in a notice under rule 21, the Court may, on the application of any party to the cause or matter, determine that question before the trial or hearing of the cause or matter or give directions for it to be determined before the trial or hearing and for the manner in which it is to be so determined.

(2) Unless the Court otherwise directs, the summons by which an application under paragraph (1) is made must be served by the party making the application on every other party to the cause or matter.

(3) Where any such question as is referred to in paragraph (1) has been determined under or by virtue of that paragraph, no application to have it determined afresh at the trial or hearing of the cause or matter may be made unless the evidence which it is sought to adduce in support of the application could not with reasonable diligence have been adduced at the hearing which resulted in the determination.

ORDER 45
ENFORCEMENT OF ORDERS

5. Enforcement of judgment to do or abstain from doing any act.

(1) Where—

(*a*) a person required by a judgment or order to do an act within a time specified in the judgment or order refuses or neglects to do it within that time or, as the case may be, within that time as extended or abridged under Order 3, rule 5, or

(*b*) a person disobeys a judgment or order requiring him to abstain from doing an act,

then, subject to the provisions of these rules, the judgment or order may be enforced by one or more of the following means, that is to say—

(i)	with the leave of the Court, a writ of sequestration against the property of that person;

(ii)	where that person is a body corporate, with the leave of the Court, a writ of sequestration against the property of any director or other officer of the body;

(iii)	subject to the provisions of the Debtors Acts, 1869 and 1878, an order of committal against that person or, where that person is a body corporate, against any such officer.

(2) Where a judgment or order requires a person to do an act within a time therein specified and an order is subsequently made under rule 6 requiring the act to be done within some other time, references in paragraph (1) of this rule to a judgment or order shall be construed as references to the order made under rule 6.

(3) Where under any judgment or order requiring the delivery of any goods the person liable to execution has the alternative of paying the assessed value of the goods, the judgment or order shall not be enforceable by order of committal under paragraph (1), but the Court may, on the application of the person entitled to enforce the judgment or order, make an order requiring the first mentioned person to deliver the goods to the applicant within a time specified in the order, and that order may be so enforced.

6. Judgment, etc. requiring act to be done: order fixing time for doing it.

(1) Notwithstanding that a judgment or order requiring a person to do an act specifies a time within which the act is to be done, the Court shall, without prejudice to Order 3, rule 5, have power to make an order requiring the act to be done within another time, being such time after service of that order, or such other time, as may be specified therein.

(2) Where, notwithstanding Order 42, rule 2(1), or by reason of Order 42, rule 2(2), a judgment or order requiring a person to do an act does not specify a time within which the act is to be done, the Court shall have power subsequently to make an order requiring the act to be done within such time after service of that order, or such other time, as may be specified therein.

(3) An application for an order under this rule must be made by summons and the summons must, notwithstanding anything in Order 65, rule 9, be served on the person required to do the act in question.

7. Service of copy of judgment, etc. prerequisite to enforcement under rule 5.

(1) In this rule references to an order shall be construed as including references to a judgment.

(2) Subject to Order 24, rule 16(3).[1] Order 26, rule 6(3),[2] and paragraphs (6) and (7) of this rule, an order shall not be enforced under rule 5 unless—

(a) a copy of the order has been served personally on the person required to do or abstain from doing the act in question, and

(b) in the case of an order requiring a person to do an act, the copy has been so served before the expiration of the time within which he was required to do the act.

(3) Subject as aforesaid, an order requiring a body corporate to do or abstain from doing an act shall not be enforced as mentioned in rule 5(1)(ii) or (iii) unless—

(a) a copy of the order has also been served personally on the officer against whose property leave is sought to issue a writ of sequestration or against whom an order of committal is sought, and

(b) in the case of an order requiring the body corporate to do an act, the copy has been so served before the expiration of the time within which the body was required to do the act.

(4) There must be indorsed on the copy of an order served under this rule a notice informing the person on whom the copy is served—

(a) in the case of service under paragraph (2), that if he neglects to obey the order within the time specified therein, or, if the order is to abstain from doing an act, that if he disobeys the order, he is liable to process of execution to compel him to obey it, and

(b) in the case of service under paragraph (3), that if the body corporate neglects to obey the order within the time so specified or, if the order is to abstain from doing an act, that if the body corporate disobeys the order, he is liable to process of execution to compel the body to obey it.

(5) With the copy of an order required to be served under this rule, being an order requiring a person to do an act, there must also be served a copy of any order made under Order 3, rule 5, extending or abridging the time for doing the act and, where the first-mentioned order was made under rule 5(3) or 6 of this Order, a copy of the previous order requiring the act to be done.

---

[1] Service on a party's solicitor to be sufficient service of an order for discovery to ground a committal.

[2] Similarly service on a solicitor is sufficient in the case of an order to answer interrogatories.

(6) An order requiring a person to abstain from doing an act may be enforced under rule 5 notwithstanding that service of a copy of the order has not been effected in accordance with this rule if the Court is satisfied that, pending such service, the person against whom or against whose property it is sought to enforce the order has had notice thereof either—

(*a*) by being present when the order was made, or
(*b*) by being notified of the terms of the order, whether by telephone, telegram or otherwise.

(7) Without prejudice to its powers under Order 65, rule 4, the Court may dispense with service of a copy of an order under this rule if it thinks it just to do so.

ORDER 58
APPEALS FROM MASTERS, REGISTRARS, REFEREES AND JUDGES

1. Appeals from certain decisions of masters, etc. to judge in chambers.

(1) Except as provided by rule 2,[1] an appeal shall lie to a judge in chambers from any judgment, order or decision or a master of the Queen's Bench Division, the Admiralty Registrar or a registrar of the Family Division.

(2) The appeal shall be brought by serving on every other party to the proceedings in which the judgment, order or decision was given or made a notice to attend before the judge on a day specified in the notice.

(3) Unless the Court otherwise orders, the notice must be issued within 5 days after the judgment, order or decision appealed against was given or made and served not less than 2 clear days before the day fixed for hearing the appeal.

(4) Except so far as the Court may otherwise direct, an appeal under this rule shall not operate as a stay of the proceedings in which the appeal is brought.

4. Appeals from district registrars.

(1) An appeal shall lie from any judgment, order or decision of a district registrar in any cause or matter in any Division in the same circumstances and, except as provided by paragraph (2), subject to the same conditions as if the judgment, order or decision were given or made by a master or registrar in that cause or matter in that Division, and the provisions of these rules with respect to appeals shall apply accordingly.

(2) In relation to an appeal from a judgment, order or decision of a district registrar, rule 1 shall have effect subject to the modification that for the references therein to 5 days and 2 clear days there shall be substituted references to 7 days and 3 clear days respectively.

7. Appeal from judge in chambers.

(1) Subject to section 31 of the Act and section 15(2) of the Administration of Justice Act, 1960 (which restrict appeals), and to Order 53, rule 12,[2] and without prejudice to section 13 of the said Act of 1960 (which provides for an appeal in cases of contempt of court), in the Queen's Bench Division (including the Admiralty Court) an appeal shall lie to the Court of Appeal from any judgment, order or decision of a judge in chambers.

(2) Subject to the said sections 31 and 15(2), and without prejudice to the said section 13, in the Chancery Division and in the Family Division an appeal

---

[1] Which provides that in certain cases, e.g. assessment of damages, determination of interpleader or garnishee proceedings, appeal lies direct to the Court of Appeal.
[2] This deals with applications for *certiorari*, *mandamus*, etc.

shall lie to the Court of Appeal from any judgment, order or decision of a judge in Chambers either—

    (*a*) with the leave of the judge or the Court of Appeal, or

    (*b*) after an application to set aside or discharge the judgment, order or decision has been made to the judge sitting in court and has been refused.

and not otherwise.

ORDERS 65

SERVICE OF DOCUMENTS

1. When personal service required.

(1) Any document which by virtue of these rules is required to be served on any person need not be served personally unless the document is one which by an express provision of these rules or by order of the Court is required to be so served.

(2) Paragraph (1) shall not affect the power of the Court under any provision of these rules to dispense with the requirement for personal service.

2. Personal service: how effected.

Personal service of a document is effected by leaving a copy of the document with the person to be served and, if so requested by him at the time when it is left, showing him—

    (*a*) in the case where the document is a writ or other originating process, the original, and

    (*b*) in any other case, the original or an office copy.

3. Personal service on body corporate.

Personal service of a document on a body corporate may, in cases for which provision is not otherwise made by any enactment,[1] be effected by serving it in accordance with rule 2 on the mayor, chairman or president of the body, or the town clerk, clerk, secretary, treasurer or other similar officer thereof.

4. Substituted service.

(1) If, in the case of any document which by virtue of any provision of these rules is required to be served personally on any person, it appears to the Court that it is impracticable for any reason to serve that document personally on that person, the Court may make an order for substituted service of that document.

(2) An application for an order for substituted service may be made by an affidavit stating the facts on which the application is founded.

(3) Substituted service of a document, in relation to which an order is made under this rule, is effected by taking such steps as the Court may direct to bring the document to the notice of the person to be served.

5. Ordinary service: how effected.

(1) Service of any document, not being a document which by virtue of any provision of these rules is required to be served personally, may be effected—

---

[1] E.g. the Companies Act 1948, s. 437.

(*a*) by leaving the document at the proper address of the person to be served, or

(*b*) by post, or

(*c*) in such other manner as the Court may direct.

(2) For the purposes of this rule, and of section 26 of the Interpretation Act, 1889, in its application to this rule, the proper address of any person on whom a document is to be served in accordance with this rule shall be the address for service of that person, but if at the time when service is effected that person has no address for service his proper address for the purposes aforesaid shall be—

(*a*) in any case, the business address of the solicitor (if any) who is acting for him in the proceedings in connection with which service of the document in question is to be effected, or

(*b*) in the case of an individual, his usual or last known address, or

(*c*) in the case of individuals who are suing or being sued in the name of a firm, the principal or last known place of business of the firm within the jurisdiction, or

(*d*) in the case of a body corporate, the registered or principal office of the body.

(3) Nothing in this rule shall be taken as prohibiting the personal service of any document or as affecting any enactment which provides for the manner in which documents may be served on bodies corporate.

7. Effect of service after certain hours.

Any document (other than a writ of summons or other originating process) service of which is effected under rule 2 or under rule 5(1)(*a*) between 12 noon on a Saturday and midnight on the following day or after 4 in the afternoon on any other weekday shall, for the purpose of computing any period of time after service of that document, be deemed to have been served on the Monday following that Saturday or on the day following that other weekday, as the case may be.

8. Affidavit of service.

An affidavit of service of any document must state by whom the document was served, the day of the week and date on which it was served, where it was served and how.

9. No service required in certain cases.

Where by virtue of these rules any document is required to be served on any person but is not required to be served personally, and at the time when service is to be effected that person is in default as to entry of appearance or has no address for service, the document need not be served on that person unless the Court otherwise directs or any of these rules otherwise provides.

10. Service of process on Sunday.

(1) No process shall be served or executed within the jurisdiction on a Sunday except, in case of urgency, with the leave of the Court.

(2) For the purposes of this rule "process" includes a writ, judgment, notice, order, petition, originating or other summons or warrant.

ORDER 81
PARTNERS

1. Actions by and against firms within jurisdiction.

Subject to the provisions of any enactment, any two or more persons claiming to be entitled, or alleged to be liable, as partners in respect of a cause of action and carrying on business within the jurisdiction may sue, or be sued, in the name of the firm (if any) of which they were partners at the time when the cause of action accrued.

2. Disclosure of partners' names.

(1) Any defendant to an action brought by partners in the name of a firm may serve on the plaintiffs or their solicitor a notice requiring them or him forthwith to furnish the defendant with a written statement of the names and places of residence of all the persons who were partners in the firm at the time when the cause of action accrued; and if the notice is not complied with the Court may order the plaintiffs or their solicitor to furnish the defendant with such a statement and to verify it on oath or otherwise as may be specified in the order, or may order that further proceedings in the action be stayed on such terms as the Court may direct.

(2) When the names of the partners have been declared in compliance with a notice or order given or made under paragraph (1), the proceedings shall continue in the name of the firm but with the same consequences as would have ensued if the persons whose names have been so declared had been named as plaintiffs in the writ.

(3) Paragraph (1) shall have effect in relation to an action brought against partners in the name of a firm as it has effect in relation to an action brought by partners in the name of a firm but with the substitution, for references to the defendant and the plaintiffs, of references to the plaintiff and the defendants respectively, and with the omission of the words "or may order" to the end.

3. Service of writ.

(1) Where by virtue of rule 1 partners are sued in the name of a firm, the writ may, except in the case mentioned in paragraph (2), be served—

(a) on any one or more of the partners, or
(b) at the principal place of business of the partnership within the jurisdiction, on any person having at the time of service the control or management of the partnership business there;

and where service of the writ is effected in accordance with this paragraph, the writ shall be deemed to have been duly served on the firm, whether or not any member of the firm is out of the jurisdiction.

(2) Where a partnership has, to the knowledge of the plaintiff, been dissolved before an action against the firm is begun, the writ by which the action is begun must be served on every person within the jurisdiction sought to be made liable in the action.

(3) Every person on whom a writ is served under paragraph (1) must at the time of service be given a written notice stating whether he is served as a partner or as a person having the control or management of the partnership business or both as a partner and as such a person; and any person on whom a writ is so served but to whom no such notice is given shall be deemed to be served as a partner.

4. Entry of appearance in an action against firm.

(1) Where persons are sued as partners in the name of their firm, appearance may not be entered in the name of the firm but only by the partners thereof in their own names, but the action shall nevertheless continue in the name of the firm.

(2) Where in an action against a firm the writ by which the action is begun is served on a person as a partner, that person, if he denies that he was a partner or liable as such at any material time, may enter an appearance in the action and state in his memorandum of appearance that he does so as a person served as a partner in the defendant firm but who denies that he was a partner at any material time.

An appearance entered in accordance with this paragraph shall, unless and until it is set aside, be treated as an appearance for the defendant firm.

(3) Where an appearance has been entered for a defendant in accordance with paragraph (2), then—

(a) the plaintiff may either apply to the Court to set it aside on the ground that the defendant was a partner or liable as such at a material time or may leave that question to be determined at a later stage of the proceedings;

(b) the defendant may either apply to the Court to set aside the service of the writ on him on the ground that he was not a partner or liable as such at a material time or may at the proper time serve a defence on the plaintiff denying in respect of the plaintiff's claim either his liability as a partner or the liability of the defendant firm or both.

(4) The Court may at any stage of the proceedings in an action in which a defendant has entered an appearance in accordance with paragraph (2) on the application of the plaintiff or of that defendant, order that any question as to the liability of that defendant or as to the liability of the defendant firm be tried in such manner and at such time as the Court directs.

(5) Where in an action against a firm the writ by which the action is begun is served on a person as a person having the control or management of the partnership business, that person may not enter an appearance in the action unless he is a member of the firm sued.

5. Enforcing judgment or order against firm.

(1) Where a judgment is given or order made against a firm, execution to enforce the judgment or order may, subject to rule 6, issue against any property of the firm within the jurisdiction.

(2) Where a judgment is given or order made against a firm, execution to enforce the judgment or order may, subject to rule 6 and to the next following paragraph, issue against any person who—

(a) entered an appearance in the action as a partner, or

(b) having been served as a partner with the writ of summons, failed to enter an appearance in the action, or

(c) admitted in his pleading that he is a partner, or

(d) was adjudged to be a partner.

(3) Execution to enforce a judgment or order given or made against a firm may not issue against a member of the firm who was out of the jurisdiction when the writ of summons was issued unless he—

(a) entered on appearance in the action as a partner, or

(b) was served within the jurisdiction with the writ as a partner, or

(c) was, with the leave of the Court given under Order 11, served out of the jurisdiction with the writ, or notice of the writ, as a partner;

and, except as provided by paragraph (1) and by the foregoing provisions of this paragraph, a judgment or order given or made against a firm shall not render liable, release or otherwise affect a member of the firm who was out of the jurisdiction when the writ was issued.

(4) Where a party who has obtained a judgment or order against a firm claims that a person is liable to satisfy the judgment or order as being a member of the firm, and the foregoing provisions of this rule do not apply in relation to that person, that party may apply to the Court for leave to issue execution against that person, the application to be made by summons which must be served personally on that person.

(5) Where the person against whom an application under paragraph (4) is made does not dispute his liability, the Court hearing the application may, subject to paragraph (3), give leave to issue execution against that person, and, where that person disputes his liability, the Court may order that the liability of that person be tried and determined in any manner in which any issue or question in an action may be tried and determined.

6. Enforcing judgment or order in actions between partners, etc.

(1) Execution to enforce a judgment or order given or made in—

(a) an action by or against a firm in the name of the firm against or by a member of the firm, or

(b) an action by a firm in the name of the firm against a firm in the name of the firm where those firms have one or more members in common,

shall not issue except with the leave of the Court.

(2) The Court hearing an application under this rule may give such directions, including directions as to the taking of accounts and the making of inquiries, as may be just.

INDEX